Practical Fairness
Achieving Fair and Secure Data Models

Aileen Nielsen

T0256856

Beijing · Boston · Farnham · Sebastopol · Tokyo

Practical Fairness

by Aileen Nielsen

Published by O'Reilly Media, Inc., 1005 Gravenstein Highway North, Sebastopol, CA 95472.

O'Reilly books may be purchased for educational, business, or sales promotional use. Online editions are also available for most titles (*http://oreilly.com*). For more information, contact our corporate/institutional sales department: 800-998-9938 or *corporate@oreilly.com*.

Acquisitions Editor: Jonathan Hassell	**Indexer:** WordCo Indexing Services, Inc.
Development Editor: Corbin Collins	**Interior Designer:** David Futato
Production Editor: Katherine Tozer	**Cover Designer:** Karen Montgomery
Copyeditor: JM Olejarz	**Illustrator:** Kate Dullea
Proofreader: Sharon Wilkey	

December 2020:   First Edition

Revision History for the First Edition

2020-12-01:   First Release

See *http://oreilly.com/catalog/errata.csp?isbn=9781492075738* for release details.

978-1-492-07573-8

[LSI]

Table of Contents

Preface

Welcome to *Practical Fairness*. I wrote this book because data scientists and machine learning engineers are increasingly aware of the fairness implications of their work but are not adequately empowered to do anything about their concerns. Academic research on mathematical solutions to fairness concerns is flourishing, and myriad open source options are available thanks to both academic researchers and technology companies sharing resources. However, delving into the topic in a practical and concrete way remains difficult for the beginner, and best practices have not yet emerged in most industries to address even the most basic concerns. This book's aim is to be an accessible overview for beginners in this field with actionable fairness advice.

Goals of This Book

This book will help practicing data scientists and technologists get their feet wet in the world of fairness. The goal is that after reading this book, you can actively pursue fairness in your own work. Fairness doesn't have a one-size-fits-all solution, but you should be able to:

- Identify potential fairness problems in your organization's workflow and data practices
- Break fairness concerns into conceptually distinct categories and target appropriate areas of research literature accordingly
- Offer accessible guidance to nontechnical colleagues on potential fairness problems and solutions in whatever machine learning products you are developing

In this book I exclusively use Python examples and focus on the easiest interfaces available via open source options for implementing relevant fairness methods. I chose this approach because Python benefits from a large degree of open source work in the fairness domain. However, a good deal of work in other languages unfortunately had to be ignored, including in Java, R, and MATLAB code. Also, code bases with organizational sponsors and with a larger breadth of tools were favored over smaller code bases or code bases maintained by just a few individuals. This also meant that some very interesting and high-quality work was omitted. You should be aware that the goal of this book is far more to help you get conceptually organized and that the packages highlighted here are just one set of tools, not necessarily the best or only tools. The fairness toolbox continues to grow rapidly, and there is every reason to expect more tools and code bases to develop over time. The selections in this book represent just one snapshot of convenient APIs.

Fairness in machine learning and in the technology sector remains an active struggle, an ongoing social concern, and an interesting engineering problem. We need legal, economic, and social solutions as well as technical ones. Toward that end, 50% of the royalties earned on this book will be donated to the American Civil Liberties Union, an organization that has relentlessly pursued fairness for a hundred years. The ACLU is actively working to secure fundamental rights to privacy and fairness in the era of algorithms. Readers should be aware that the ACLU played no part in the writing of this book, has not reviewed it, and has not endorsed it. Nevertheless my hope is that this book will reinforce and support the ACLU's important work in more ways than one.

The other 50% of royalties earned on this book will be donated to Mercy for Animals, an organization dedicated to radically expanding our definitions of fairness to include the well-being of animals and Earth. Mercy for Animals takes a practical approach to addressing devastating cruelty and unfairness practiced in the fundamental industries that bring food to our table. Thus, my hope is that this book's royalties can contribute to our society's ongoing development of a fairer and more inclusive outlook.

Practical Notes on the Book

This book is partly about concepts and partly about coding. With respect to the coding, I found that some of the APIs I used were quite verbose. To cut down on the volume of code presented, I did not always include full running code examples in the text, but the full examples are available in the associated GitHub repository (*https://github.com/PracticalFairness/BookRepo*).

The topic of fairness is necessarily tinged with a political or ideological flavor, but I have tried to avoid politics and ideology. Also, I have written this book as a practical manual, not an academic treatise on the topic of fairness in machine learning. For this reason, many notions are taken for granted or defined at the level relevant for action rather than for philosophical discussion. So if I said anything controversial here, it was unintentional. For those interested in more academic or combative debates, you can find many places for that.

I want focus on the pragmatic task of increasing fairness in cases of obvious injustice, a simple and hopefully uncontroversial task. This book starts with a few premises—namely, that we would all like a world where everyone has equal opportunities and receives fair treatment. We would all like a world where machines and digital interfaces do not undermine our autonomy or our privacy. We would all like a world where our increasing use of digital products and algorithmic decision-making tools results in better, more robust, and more secure outcomes rather than the opposite. This book provides key concepts to get you on your way to building the fairer digital products that will bring us closer to this desirable world.

Conventions Used in This Book

The following typographical conventions are used in this book:

Italic
> Indicates new terms, URLs, email addresses, filenames, and file extensions.

`Constant width`
> Used for program listings, as well as within paragraphs to refer to program elements such as variable or function names, databases, data types, environment variables, statements, and keywords.

`Constant width bold`
> Shows commands or other text that should be typed literally by the user.

`Constant width italic`
> Shows text that should be replaced with user-supplied values or by values determined by context.

> This element signifies a tip or suggestion.

> This element signifies a general note.

Using Code Examples

If you have a technical question or a problem using the code examples, please email *bookquestions@oreilly.com*.

This book is here to help you get your job done. In general, if example code is offered with this book, you may use it in your programs and documentation. You do not need to contact us for permission unless you're reproducing a significant portion of the code. For example, writing a program that uses several chunks of code from this book does not require permission. Selling or distributing examples from O'Reilly books does require permission. Answering a question by citing this book and quoting example code does not require permission. Incorporating a significant amount of example code from this book into your product's documentation does require permission.

We appreciate, but generally do not require, attribution. An attribution usually includes the title, author, publisher, and ISBN. For example: "*Practical Fairness* by Aileen Nielsen (O'Reilly). Copyright 2021 Aileen Nielsen, 978-1-492-07573-8."

If you feel your use of code examples falls outside fair use or the permission given above, feel free to contact us at *permissions@oreilly.com*.

O'Reilly Online Learning

 For more than 40 years, *O'Reilly Media* has provided technology and business training, knowledge, and insight to help companies succeed.

Our unique network of experts and innovators share their knowledge and expertise through books, articles, and our online learning platform. O'Reilly's online learning platform gives you on-demand access to live training courses, in-depth learning paths, interactive coding environments, and a vast collection of text and video from O'Reilly and 200+ other publishers. For more information, visit *http://oreilly.com*.

How to Contact Us

Please address comments and questions concerning this book to the publisher:

O'Reilly Media, Inc.
1005 Gravenstein Highway North
Sebastopol, CA 95472
800-998-9938 (in the United States or Canada)
707-829-0515 (international or local)
707-829-0104 (fax)

We have a web page for this book where we list errata, examples, and additional information. You can access it at *https://oreil.ly/practical_fairness*.

Email *bookquestions@oreilly.com* to comment or ask technical questions about this book.

For news and information about our books and courses, visit *http://oreilly.com*.

Find us on Facebook: *http://facebook.com/oreilly*

Follow us on Twitter: *http://twitter.com/oreillymedia*

Watch us on YouTube: *http://www.youtube.com/oreillymedia*

Acknowledgments

A wide variety of individuals helped make this book project happen. I wish to thank my editors at O'Reilly: Jon Hassell, who green-lighted this book despite it being a novel and difficult topic, and Corbin Collins, who read everything carefully, gave great feedback, and worked tirelessly with me through the complications of writing during the coronavirus pandemic and resulting work-from-home madness. I also wish to thank my production editor, Katherine Tozer, for her relentless and reliable attention to detail and commitment to coordinating a careful review of the book. I wish to thank the copyeditor, proofreader, and sensitivity reader of the book, Josh Olejarz, Sharon Wilkey, and Abby Wheeler, as well as the illustrator, Kate Dullea, who converted all the snippings I had from various sources into beautiful and precise graphics. Thanks to my technical reviewers, Sray Agarwal, Shashin Mishra, and Niall Murphy, for reading the manuscript carefully and providing both detail-oriented and high-level feedback.

Many members of the technical research fairness community also offered help and feedback, as well as generous permission to cite their work and reproduce or repurpose some of their graphics, which are attributed where used. The technical fairness community has been extremely generous in providing guidance to me as I developed this content. I do not include specific names here to avoid implying that they reviewed or endorsed this work.

My work also benefited greatly from time I have spent as a member of ETH Zurich's Center for Law and Economics. I connected with researchers from a wide variety of disciplines who think about the ramifications of algorithmic decision making and the options for alternative design and deployment for all things algorithmic. I also benefited tremendously from the students in my Law and Tech course, who provided a variety of helpful questions and robust feedback on lectures on AI Fairness from a legal and technical perspective.

Finally, I wish to thank my family, as always, for their support in giving me the time I needed to write this book and periodic boosts to morale to make sure I got the job done, particularly my son, Eddie and my husband, Ivan.

All mistakes are mine. If you spot any, please report them in O'Reilly's errata portal or to me personally at *aileen.a.nielsen@gmail.com*. I also welcome feedback regarding how to make the book more useful to you in your real-world fairness tasks. Toward that end, I hope to hear from you. This first stab at a practical guide is just a start, and feedback from the community will enable me (and other authors) to develop better resources as the field matures.

## CHAPTER 1

Fairness, Technology, and the Real World

What is fairness? Everyone has a slightly different definition. Many of the great divides in society result from differing ideas about fairness. It's an age-old debate.

In this book, I won't delve into the philosophy or social histories of how fairness has been defined over time and geography. Rather, I'll take a practical perspective on the matter. Practical considerations most often come up in the form of three fundamental questions a society needs to answer in order to function:

- Who gets what? (Rules of allocation)
- How do we decide who gets what? (Rules of decision)
- Who decides who decides? (Rules of political authority)[1]

Some of the social and philosophical divides in the world originate from these basic questions. Now there's a new and interesting wrinkle in the age of algorithms—one that is not sufficiently acknowledged. We are still asking and answering these same questions, but now algorithms are part of that process.

Software engineers and UX designers don't usually ask these questions at team meetings. And yet they make such determinations every day in their work. The downstream effects of their products have social ramifications that affect who gets what and why.

This book provides both conceptual tools and coding examples to address fairness questions from the point of view of writing computer code and designing digital products. Much of the content emphasizes machine learning, but I also discuss digital products more widely. As I address ML and other digital products throughout this

---

[1] This phrasing is from Shoshana Zuboff's work *The Age of Surveillance Capitalism* (PublicAffairs, 2019).

book, I'll try to emphasize the following fundamental, pragmatic, and unavoidable questions you will need to answer if you work on digital products, even if you don't recognize the choices you are making:

- Is it fairer for everyone to have the same opportunities or to have the same outcomes? *Equality of opportunity* or *equality of outcome*?

- Is it fairer for decisions to be uniform or to embody an element of human empathy? *Impartial justice* or *individual allowances*?

- Is it fairer to let people know how decisions are made or to have an opaque system to prevent cheating? *Transparency* or *security*?

Such questions are about trade-offs, some necessary and inevitable, and others possibly solvable. We also have more specific questions about implementations, details, and human response:

- Is it a problem when a machine learning model has different average predictions for different genders? Does it matter how different the average predictions are? Does it matter whether the model is used in high-stakes or low-stakes decisions?

- What kind of metadata about user behavior is it ethical to collect from apps? When is metadata collection justified for customization, and when is it a form of spying?

- Will people praise a credit-rating algorithm for providing uniformity or resent it for failing to see their individual circumstances? Does any online application for credit need a free-form box for the applicant to supply necessary information or context?

Technological, procedural, and institutional tools are all needed to pose these questions and develop appropriate mechanisms to answer the questions and implement the chosen policies moving forward. For example, from a *technological* perspective, you need a data science or ML pipeline with sufficient documentation and accessibility of relevant attributes, such as the internal specs of a model and information about membership in protected categories for individuals included in your data set. From a *procedural* standpoint, you need training or careful consultation regarding the process for making these decisions in a way that reflects appropriate fairness norms, logic, and ethical consistency with your organization and your society's background laws and cultural codes of ethics. From an *institutional* standpoint, you need leaders and managers of an organization who set the right tone to keep fairness issues on the radar.

My goal is to point out how fairness questions come into play when building digital systems, particularly systems powered by contemporary machine learning methodologies and other data-science-driven insights. I'll call all of these *ML* for shorthand;

that is, I don't distinguish deep learning from analytics from machine learning from statistical analysis, etc.

I take a broad view of how interfaces and code written by interface designers, data scientists, machine learning engineers, and others can violate important fairness norms. With this goal, I discuss best practices and technical tests that can be used in pursuit of a more just digital world by people designing digital products and writing data-driven code.

We'll think about the interfaces that wrap our products in terms of how people see them rather than just the code that powers them. We'll think about how the *human readable* aspects of our products have ramifications for the humans that read and use our products, and also the humans who don't.

Fairness is a hot topic. However, concerns about fairness in technology are far from new. What's more, the concerns raised recently in popular discourse about machine learning, automation, and all things digital are not as new as the media hype implies.

Fairness in Engineering Is an Old Problem

> Technology is neither good nor bad; nor is it neutral.
>
> —Melvin Kranzberg

New technologies and their downstream social impacts have always had fairness implications, and many of these effects center on the same questions that vex us now. Earlier technologies need not look much like the information technologies driving the last several decades of innovation to be relevant. What matters is the social element and the embedding of the technology in a *sociotechnical system*. This fundamental connection between the social and the technical is a constant across time and technologies. It could be a wheel, a railroad engine, a vacuum cleaner, or a computer. Any of these could affect social ordering and organization, and all of them did.

Our societies like to tell a story of "technological progress = better life = fairer and better human experience." However, just about every era of invention, and every individual invention, has easily identifiable victims.

For example, you could make the argument that the current unequal distribution of global wealth is very much connected to Western Europe's Renaissance and the associated advances in science and engineering. Guns! Advances in shipbuilding! Advances in navigation! All enabled colonialism. The inventors of these technologies could have avoided much of the resulting unfairness at the time (for example, de facto slavery in colonies), although whether they wanted to avoid such consequences is another question.[2]

Let's consider another historical example. The next great technological period of Western culture, the Industrial Revolution, had fairness implications both within Western nations and internationally. This period, like the Renaissance, is often taught to Western schoolchildren as quite a good thing, with some pro forma nods to the resulting social chaos, dehumanization of work tasks, and increasing inequality that resulted.

What were some of the foreseeable unfair outcomes of the Industrial Revolution? Consider the way factory machinery was dependent on small bodies and fingers; children made the ideal factory employees for many dangerous tasks. The jump in society's productivity was accomplished in part by the labor of children rather than by better opportunities for children.

Or consider that the style of human work most appropriate to factory tasks was monotonous and tedious, turning artisans and craftspeople into organic repetitive-motion machines. Was that good for these workers? Circumstances varied, but there were clearly distributional- and autonomy-related fairness considerations for people who lost discretion in their work and became machine-like factory workers. These outcomes were foreseeable, so the real question is whether the downsides were worth the upsides at the time, and to whom.

Similarly, when we write code or design technology interfaces now, we can sometimes foresee potential bad outcomes for certain identifiable stakeholders or third parties, and the question becomes whether the downsides are worth the potential upsides, and *for whom?*

I use the child labor example in part because that practice continued into the Gilded Age, a period of vast wealth and power disparity in the Western world organized around the control of new technologies and the downstream demands created by those technologies (railroads, manufacturing, fuel). The design of manufacturing technologies and the sociotechnical complex that complemented the technologies made for a very unfair situation. Children in lower-class families who found themselves working as human cogs in factory machines had little chance to escape this grind; being in it had nothing to do with merit or hard work and everything to do with being born at the wrong place and in the wrong time. Meanwhile, as the children suffered a lack of education and even basic safety, their labor generated enormous amounts of wealth that were concentrated in the hands of very few. Importantly, market pressures were not enough to stop child labor. Rather, it took decades of political crusading before strong new laws were passed to end factory use of child labor in

---

2 Of course, this is quite a simplified presentation of a very complicated history.

Western countries. We learn a historical lesson here because, likewise, many people likewise believe that something beyond market pressures will be necessary to make ML fair.

These are just a few examples to show that technology does not necessarily self-regulate, via either market or social pressures. We should keep this in mind when considering novel legal proposals to address the new generation of concerns about unfairness, such as algorithmic discrimination, invasion of privacy, and the rise of surveillance capitalism. Indeed, many large tech companies have even gone on record indicating that private solutions are either unlikely to materialize[3] or not enough without government assistance in coordination and enforcement.[4] Fairness problems arising from technology are an old problem, and they are not always solved by the market or by social norms. As of this writing in late 2020, popular and industry opinion alike seem strongly in support of fairness interventions from lawmakers.

Our Fairness Problems Now

Many say we are now in a second Gilded Age, as wealth and income disparity are again on the rise worldwide. While we face increasing wealth disparities, we live in a hypertechnological era, and centers of tech reflect a dramatic trend toward income inequality. This is not to argue that tech *causes* inequality but to point out that our current advances in technology seem correlated with increasing inequality. In some ways, we see the old ills reproduced with a newer technology center. But we also have problems associated with qualitatively new ways of doing business or making money thanks to the big data revolution.

Does it have to be this way? Could we have a version of sharing-economy apps that would *distribute* wealth more equally? Could we have a version of social media that wouldn't make people so polarized? And is there anything the coders at technology companies can do, or is this dependent on the structure of our economy? These questions are getting a bit beyond the practical and hands-on applications I address in this book, but we should remember that the outcomes of these profound questions are built out of many small design choices.

Data-driven technologies have created new opportunities for harm or help. Many new uses of data-driven and information technologies have made the world a better place, such as moves toward open data in government and assistive automation and

---

3 Khosrowshahi, Dara. "I Am the C.E.O. of Uber. Gig Workers Deserve Better." *The New York Times*, August 10, 2020. *https://www.nytimes.com/2020/08/10/opinion/uber-ceo-dara-khosrowshahi-gig-workers-deserve-better.html*.

4 Smith, Brad. "Facial recognition: It's time for action." Microsoft.com, December 6, 2018. *https://blogs.micro soft.com/on-the-issues/2018/12/06/facial-recognition-its-time-for-action*.

diagnostics in medical technologies. However, we are not yet doing a good job of minimizing the many avoidable harms caused by these technologies, such as replications of racially biased reasoning in algorithms trained on data that reflects human bias.

As technologists, data scientists, and computer programmers, we should be thinking about many other examples of unfairness. What do we think about stealing someone's time and subverting their autonomy? Social media platforms are addictive by design (*https://perma.cc/RF27-KG3U*). Such platforms consume hours of the average American's day, adults and children alike, every single day, and usually without bringing much (or any) joy or knowledge into our lives. Or what do we think of releasing products into the wild that can be repurposed to abuse vulnerable groups? Apps written for smart homes or smart cars have been repurposed into tools of relationship abuse (*https://oreil.ly/eG9L9*). These are fairness problems too.

These problems of code creating bad behavior aren't limited to vices in our personal lives and in small private companies. Intensely public moral concerns also exist. Rich nations increasingly fight wars with robotic (and soon algorithmically powered) proxies (*https://perma.cc/D5BH-9L8Z*) that seem to endanger mostly those living in poor countries, while those in rich countries tend to reap the economic benefits of these activities as they innovate and sell their inventions for use abroad, often to totalitarian governments that deploy them against their own people. While robotically and algorithmically powered warfare may have some upsides, such as limiting civilian casualties and removing elements of human unpredictability, there are also massive opportunities for abuse.

Clearly, code has to be carefully constructed in such life-or-death situations. We don't have any assurances from our governments that such code passes muster on normative concerns related to fairness. In fact, journalists even suspect that some countries are exporting these sorts of weapons, not only using them in their own militaries but also selling them to other countries (*https://perma.cc/62KK-NSXA*), including aggressive nations known for deploying force.

Likewise, the owners of large data sets and social media empires are finding ways to monetize general observations about humans—observations they don't have to pay for—and turn them into profitable products or services that may harm the very people about whom the data sets were compiled. Consider two common examples. First, fake news has gone from a tool of government propaganda to an actual business strategy, because the code behind social media financially rewards fake news (*https://perma.cc/56MJ-W5TB*). Fake news has become particularly pernicious in part because data-driven news and social media algorithms foster content and ideological echo chambers and social bubbles that tend to exacerbate the spread of misinformation. Data helps this happen, and it makes companies rich in the process. This makes it difficult for consumers to really understand what's going on in the market and what that market is doing to their personal data and their very autonomy.

Second, a common business strategy, resulting from how the internet and all its code are built on top of advertising, is that many applications purporting to do one thing make their money off quite another. Consider the case of an app that advertises itself as a period tracker but then sells information about customers (*https://perma.cc/ ZRX2-PUWY*) based on its estimation of whether they might be pregnant. These use cases for computer code don't comport with usual ideas of what's fair; even if we can very well imagine arguments in favor of the technologies, lawmakers and ordinary people alike seem to agree that something needs to be done. For technical people, the question is, what?

This book will give us tools to talk about these concerns both from a normative perspective (what kind of values do they implicate?) and a technical perspective (what kind of tools can be used to identify and correct problems?). The goal is to write better code in the ethical sense. We want to write code that produces more equitable, secure, transparent, and accurate outcomes.

With just this brief discussion, we can already list general categories for the impacts of technology on fairness. Note that I'll take a broad view in thinking about fairness right now: equality, safety, and privacy, but also distributional considerations—that is, how do wealth and access get parceled out, and who decides how the allocation happens? Also to demonstrate my argument that the interaction between social and technical factors is an age-old pattern, I highlight both contemporary and past examples of fairness patterns with respect to technology in these proposed categories:

- Technical products or design choices that create foreseeable victims in vulnerable populations
  - Historical example: factory machinery that required the small hands of children, ultimately creating economic pressures that brought children out of home and school and into the workplace at young ages.
  - Contemporary example: smart home devices that can be repurposed for domestic abuse, creating new vulnerabilities (*https://oreil.ly/WFA9P*). For example, abusers have used smart home devices to lock victims out of their homes or manipulate the lighting. This isn't the device's fault, but it introduces a vector for abuse, an extreme form of unfairness.
- Technical products that create new victims by devaluing old rights
  - Historical example: the rights of way for railroad infrastructure were rapidly devalued with the invention of affordable automobiles and the shift in United States government spending toward increasing the construction of federal roads. This change made cars increasingly useful and valuable over time and railroads and their associated property rights decreasingly valuable. It also

shifted wealth geographically as well as between different sets of property holders.

— Contemporary example: ride-share apps taking over markets that previously required expensive licenses to operate, leading to outcomes such as New York taxi medallions losing 80% of their value in four years.

- Business structures and organization in technology-driven organizations

— Historical example: the rise of the oil trusts and associated business structures to control the railroads, aiming to reduce or eliminate competition as a result of full control of transportation infrastructure.

— Contemporary example: building and maintaining proprietary data sets as a large company, which may, intentionally or unintentionally, make it far more difficult for new entrants into the market.

- Using technology to avoid accountability

— Historical example: building and running high-pollution factories in poor places that don't have enough resources to enforce environmental laws.

— Contemporary example: storing your data or choosing your customers to avoid the European Union's General Data Protection Regulation (GDPR).

We'll focus mostly on algorithmic fairness, with some discussion that more generally applies to digital products. But it's also worth taking a step back to think about our current enterprise and how it can be situated in the larger history of technology studies.

Let's start by considering a few important aspects of how we judge fairness and why new code-driven technologies require that we expand our technical toolkit to include fairness-enhancing techniques. We'll use these considerations to come up with basic rules and goals that will drive the rest of the discussion in this book. Subsequent chapters will aim to operationalize these goals with concrete engineering guidance, in the form of rules of thumb, principles with which to reason, and code examples for achieving specific goals or ensuring the respecting of specific norms.

Community Norms

One of the most obvious ways fairness touches on technology is the way that technology can interrupt, recalibrate, or violate community norms. Sometimes technology makes it a lot easier for someone to be inconsiderate or impose externalities. An *externality* is an effect imposed on a third party by an action or a decision made by someone who does not experience the effect. A *negative externality* is a cost imposed on a third party, such as the pollution produced by a car and breathed in not by the driver but by the people in the area through which the car is driven.[5]

Consider a loud piece of gardening equipment, such as a leaf blower. This technology makes it easier for people to clean up their yards, but the ease comes at the expense of imposing quite a bit of noise and air pollution on their neighbors (*https://perma.cc/ DF3D-MN3J*). No one would consider it acceptable for someone to be screaming in their neighborhood, yet most people have no hesitation about using a leaf blower or other loud piece of equipment.

Likewise, a drone may help someone take aerial pictures in a beautiful natural location, but it also creates noise and a visual distraction (*https://perma.cc/V554-N8UQ*) for people who are seeking out peace and quiet. There's a good chance the person piloting a drone around a national park would not feel comfortable shouting or playing a radio at the same volume, but this does not factor in when operating the drone.

In these examples we see two ways in which technology can subvert community norms. First, it provides a new channel to transgress old rules, which exposes a lack of social norms or full community consensus regarding the transgression.

Second, a *scaling effect* occurs in that technology can take one person's actions and impose their costs on many other people in the community with no additional effort from that person. Consider a recent incident in which a drone shut down Heathrow Airport (*https://oreil.ly/8uqSV*), a bit of mischief carried out by just one person that inconvenienced thousands and cost airlines and passengers huge sums of money via *knock-on effects* (secondary or indirect effects). Scaling effects can also apply even without intentional harm, such as when the viral success of Pokemon Go caused significant disruption to and trespassing on private properties (*https://oreil.ly/6mkxZ*) where the digital system happened to place game features of importance—despite the lack of any malice on the part of the game's creators (who likely could not have expected the game's uptake to be as extraordinarily fast as it was).

These observations aren't true only for mechanical technologies, such as leaf blowers. They are also true for code. For example, online dating apps offer opportunities for one individual to impose externalities on many others, both one's potential dates and competitors in the dating pool.

Imagine a coder who boosts their odds of matches by deploying a bot to indicate interest in any and all potential partners, simulating a human rather than investing their time in reviewing possible connections. They enlarge their own dating opportunities, but do so at the expense of everyone. Their potential love interests may devote their own time to connecting with a bot (who may eventually be replaced by the real

---

5 Externalities can also be positive, such as when a person practices her piano playing and a neighbor benefits by enjoying the practice session.

coder, or not), unbeknownst to them. Also, competitors for the same partners now need to compete with a bot flooding the dating market with low-quality communication. This in turn might lower the quality of the dating app, harming anyone who is giving their time and attention to a dating market where they hope others are playing fair—namely, putting in the same level of effort and attention as they are. In fact, this seems to be one of the gripes of some dating app users: that they cannot get the high-quality interactions they are looking for. This all comes from the coder violating community norms (e.g., be a real person) and possibly also the website's terms of service.

Technology offers low-cost violations of community norms in many ways. Such opportunities circumvent the usual implied social contract, amounting to low-cost, low-responsibility cheating, given the wrong conditions for technological deployment (such as unduly cheap leaf blowers or poorly designed dating app APIs). Technology isn't the only reason norm violations occur, of course, but it is an important enabler of such misbehavior. We should recognize all technologies as not merely inventions but also potential incursions into the established social order. Whether this is good or bad should be debated, rather than allowing a social change to be steamrolled into existence through sheer force of code.

Equity and Equality

In the US, we are taught from an early age that "all [people] are created equal," but what this means to different people can be wildly different. Usually most of us support *equity* rather than *equality*, but it depends on the circumstances.

Equity implies that individuals get what they deserve (by some metric of deserving), while *equality* implies that individuals all get the same thing. While equality is an appealing concept that is quite appropriate in some use cases, it has not proven very practical when used to structure an economy or society. People are unequal in ability even if they remain equal when it comes to deserving the protection of fundamental rights. For this reason, most of the time equality doesn't survive much intellectual interrogation for practical use cases.

That's why we write ML algorithms not so we can treat people equally but rather so we can treat them equitably—that is, according to their merit on a metric specific to a given task or purpose. For example, most people like that we earn different incomes for different kinds of jobs. Likewise, we don't even want all children to be treated equally. If a child has special needs, such as the need for a speech therapist or additional medical treatment, we'd like to give that child extra resources rather than merely resources equal to those of other children.

Equity itself, however, is not a simple one-size-fits-all solution. Equity involves discerning merit—who might deserve more or less depending on the features we think are relevant.

In mainstream US culture, we tend to assume that hard work, talent, and a good attitude are the virtues to be rewarded by meritocracy. But how did we decide these were the values that should be rewarded? Who made the decision, and how did they reach it? These are important questions for at least two reasons. First, these virtues may seem neutral, logical, and intuitive on first inspection, but we have reason to question them. Prioritizing these virtues has tended to favor those with financial resources over those without such resources. It has favored white Americans over others, men over women, etc. So it might be interesting to consider who elevated these qualities, and whether, in doing so, an overly narrow view of the world was employed (one that does not factor in challenges some groups face). Second, we should remember that our current definitions of virtue might ultimately prove outmoded, sociologically naive, or downright illogical when evaluated by other societies. For example, in history we see societies that valued quite different virtues for meritocracies, such as ability to memorize ancient texts, skill in warfare, religiosity, and ability to have children. So we should have some humility, recognizing that our own ideas of meritocracy might not age well. This is not always obvious, and people can disagree even when motivated by the best of intentions.

One powerful example of why society needs to grapple with different notions of merit, and relatedly fairness, comes from the increasing use of algorithms at various decision points in the American criminal justice system—to indicate, for instance, whether an accused criminal can be released on bail or how long of a sentence to impose on a convicted defendant. In 2016 a widely shared news story (*https://perma.cc/2BST-RQG8*) revealed potential problems with the COMPAS algorithm, which is used to assess recidivism risk when convicted criminals are sentenced for punishment or assessed for early release from prison.

The ProPublica story found that false-positive and false-negative errors for someone labeled high risk to commit a violent crime after release from prison were different for black people and white people. To make this more concrete, imagine a particular black defendant was sentenced with input from the COMPAS algorithm. The ProPublica review found that they would be more likely to be falsely labeled as a high risk for recidivism than if they were white. On the other hand, if a white defendant was sentenced with input from the COMPAS algorithm, ProPublica found that the defendant would be more likely to be falsely labeled a low risk for recidivism. So the algorithm tended to favor white defendants and point in the direction of mistakenly releasing them from prison early—meaning mistakes about white defendants were more likely to result in more leniency, as compared to mistakes about black defendants.[6]

This finding was controversial and garnered a lot of news coverage. Many academics and criminologists admitted the truth of the news story while defending COMPAS as an important instrument for advancing antidiscrimination priorities (*https:// perma.cc/32HL-C6NE*) in criminal justice. These academics pointed out that by other metrics, focusing on individual-level fairness rather than group-level fairness, the COMPAS tool was indeed fair. In particular, the metrics used when originally assessing COMPAS sought to ensure that similar individuals would receive similar treatment regardless of their race.

However, baseline rates of reoffense are different in the white and black defendant populations. Such a difference in baseline rates is itself a result and symptom of racism, but it also means that different models of fairness—either at the group level, as discussed in the ProPublica article, or at the individual level, as measured by the academics—could not both be satisfied. It was not possible to be fair both to individuals and to groups at the same time.

Equity versus equality (in this case, embodied in a debate about individual equity or group parity) has always been contentious, and particularly so with the rise of ML tools applied to a wide range of human experiences and outcomes. The increasing importance of the equity-versus-equality debate results from the increasing potential for transparency and quantization in areas of society traditionally free from such quantitative analysis. As more kinds of important decisions are automated or at least recorded digitally, more decisions can be analyzed, just as happened with the news coverage of the widely used COMPAS algorithm.

Importantly, algorithms in criminal justice are not necessarily bad news; they might lead to greater fairness at the systemic level. While some bemoan the move to *algorithmic justice*, in fact such a move means that the decisions made can be better monitored for quality and fairness. This is because individual judicial decisions or parole decisions have not historically been recorded in an accessible format subject to systematic inspection and review, whereas automated systems offer the potential for better data compilation practices. This means that we can better describe systems in terms of their performance and then debate what kind of performance we want, hence the equity-versus-equality debate.

---

6 Of course "mistake" itself is a problematic word if we recognize the inherently probabilistic and uncertain nature of these predictions. After all, for most convicted criminals, whether they will reoffend reflects quite a complex mixture of individual characteristics and environmental influences, so that it's unclear that a label that turned out to be wrong means there was a "mistake" when it really could just reflect the probabilistic nature of the guess. Still, it remains problematic that these guesses point toward different outcomes depending on a defendant's race.

Our notions of fairness will be tested and further developed over time. This can be a good thing as technology allows us to better and more precisely articulate how we define fairness and what the standards should be for its implementation. We should hope that the coming decades bring a much better definition of equity and equality to society than we have previously had.

Security

New technologies sometimes make us safer and sometimes make us less safe. Often, whether a technology has a security-enhancing or security-reducing effect is debatable, and can depend on the moment we make the assessment. What's more, sometimes the net effect is debatable. Like other information technologies, ML applications can result in either more or less safety, depending on their purpose, the quality of their execution, and whether sufficient emphasis was placed on fairness during their development. In some cases the dangers are related to privacy, but in other cases the concerns are related to protecting digital or physical assets from hostile incursions.

Consider *physical security*. Does a given technology and the accompanying code make us physically safer? That depends. It is predicted that autonomous vehicles (AVs) will be safer than human-driven cars, but that's little comfort for victims of current deficiencies in ML algorithms, such as an Arizona woman who was killed (*https://perma.cc/G59P-LN87*) when an AV's ML algorithms failed to recognize her as a person or to predict her movement in a situation that seemed a human driver would have handled without trouble.

Property security is another vital element of fairness. A fair world is one in which what we own remains in our control in a way that reflects reasonable *ex ante* expectations about the nature of a particular kind of property.[7] In some cases, the property in question is our personal information, in which case it's a privacy concern. In other cases it's not about privacy but about keeping what's ours, be it the financial funds in our bank accounts or the physical electronics we own and the electricity they are consuming. For example, in the case of invasive viruses (*https://perma.cc/EZ79-LDV5*) that co-opt our computers to cryptomine on behalf of someone else, a security failing results in a fairness violation, as victims are paying for resources used by someone else, effectively having their property allocated unfairly and secretly away from their own use.

---

7 *Ex ante* expectations refer to what we can expect before an event, using background knowledge and probability. In contrast, *ex post* knowledge and expectations reflect our judgments given information about what did in fact happen. *Hindsight bias* is the human tendency to judge *ex ante* expectations harshly and not fairly, relating to a point of view that was reasonable before events rolled out in a certain way.

In both physical and property security, one major concern of technological tools is to prevent their misuse. For example, the COMPAS algorithm discussed earlier was developed to assist with parole decisions (whether to let someone out of prison before they serve their maximum sentence), but has since been used for sentencing decisions (setting the punishment prison term). Some might say that this tool was begging to be used in other applications from the start, as we can imagine administrators of the criminal justice system were keen to find quantitative tools that can reduce the workload of judges, even by deploying a tool in a situation for which it wasn't designed.

Sometimes tools violate security even when they are used as designed. Consider the case of a "gaydar" tool (*https://perma.cc/8UJ5-J3PT*) that was designed to identify sexual orientation from a photograph. While the tool was built as a warning regarding ML algorithms, its very existence may serve as a security threat to anyone whose image might be passed through the algorithm. It could be a security threat both to someone's physical safety and to their interests in the world, be it their reputation, their employment, or their right to keep private information private.

Privacy

Privacy is deeply linked to security, but it is also a separate value. Here's a simple example to illustrate. Imagine a company is storing personal data about you. It's a security problem if that data is found by hackers or is insecurely stored such that it's publicly available. But it's a privacy problem if the data is being used in ways you do not expect and have not consented to. In fact, depending on how that data was collected and used, many kinds of privacy infractions could exist.

This should matter to every data scientist, as they should ask themselves whether the analyses they are performing with the data are fair and sensible, given the original purpose for which the data was provided. This should be a particular concern when analyzing metadata, since those providing it are often not even aware that observations of their decisions and actions goes beyond the content they consciously and voluntarily provide.

I do not devote extensive time to taxonomizing privacy, but it's important to recognize the complexity of the topic and different categories of privacy invasion. Here I follow Daniel Solove's "A Taxonomy of Privacy" (*https://oreil.ly/DqDq0*) in delineating four broad categories of privacy violations.

Information collection

Information collection is likely one of the main forms of privacy violation that come to mind when this topic comes up. Here are Solove's general categories of privacy infringements and some ways in which these infringements commonly occur:

Surveillance

Surveillance involves the routine collection of observational data, usually surreptitiously, and characterizes what can fairly be called metadata. In most Western countries, the revelation of surveillance either by the government or by private entities has been met by strong objections from ordinary people and activists alike. However, with the increasing use of digital worlds for much of our waking hours, surveillance has become far less costly and obtrusive. Yet when issues of surveillance emerge in tech, they meet the same widespread criticism and objections. It is far from clear that data subjects are happy about the level of surveillance they experience in ordinary use of digital products, and it's probably not fair anyway, particularly given the structure of the digital markets, which make it nearly impossible (*https://oreil.ly/5ljFK*) to escape the reach of Big Tech.

Interrogation

Privacy violations can fall into the category of interrogation when they involve directly asking for information. While providing information in response to a query may seem to meet typical expectations of notice and consent, this fails to recognize the realpolitik of many situations in which data is solicited directly. Imagine you are running a company that uses puzzles or surveys on job candidates—do they really have a choice as to whether to answer your questions? Likewise, if you are running an ed-tech company that is adopted by a public school district, do students really have a choice about opting out of any onboarding your product specifies?

Information collection is particularly important when thinking about digital products because so much customization and monetization of digital products is currently driven by data collection that can fairly be characterized as surveillance. This is a pervasive element of designing digital products and building machine learning pipelines, but it's not clear that these practices are fair or desirable for future technology development.

Information processing

Another category of privacy violations results from the practice of information processing. Separate from the question of how data is gathered is what is done with that data once it is gathered.

The fundamental legal regime worldwide tends to be *notice and consent*. The idea is that you should use data you collect only in a way that is consistent with the notice you provided and consent you thereafter obtained regarding the data. This is a very lax standard. In practice, it tends to mean that as long as companies honor their own convoluted privacy policies as posted on their websites and the like, they are in the clear legally. So, your legal obligations will often be limited to letting people know what you will do with the data, and you can usually do this with quite broad language.

There are, of course, exceptions to notice and consent. For example, in the US, financial and health data benefits from special protections that set minimum standards for how such data can be collected and what it can be used for. Also, in the EU the GDPR adds enhanced standards to protect *data subjects*—that is, the people about whom data is collected. Similar measures are in place in other jurisdictions, although they're notably lacking in the US, home of Big Tech.

The legal protections, however, hardly establish the best definition of fairness. Ordinary people are quite unhappy about the degree of data collected and processed about them, even as they feel they have no choice in the matter. What's more, even when data is collected under this regime, myriad privacy violations still result from information processing. Some of them are described here, but this is not an exhaustive list:

Aggregation
One problem with information processing is that it generally involves compiling data sets that are not transparent to the data subject even when they have gone through some form of notice and consent. Various data sets may be combined to provide a more complete picture from the data scientist's perspective or more inputs for a deep learning model, but these create new privacy violations. An individual is then seen in a deeper or more revealing way than was consented to, and the individual's data is now in a more threatening and powerful format.

Insecurity
A privacy violation results even where a concrete violation has not been identified if data processing results in insecurity of the data itself—for example, lax cybersecurity standards or even the careless handling of data during exploratory analysis by analysts. This kind of insecurity is a privacy violation regardless of whether any information is disseminated, as the data processing has created an enhanced probability of a successful attack, such as identity theft, and therefore heightened risk to the data subjects.

Labeling and discovery
Often the purpose of processing data is to uncover hidden connections and correlations. This is why so many people from different areas of society, from laypeople to technologists, love machine learning and tend to believe it can do far more than it actually can. Many of us are fascinated by the idea of valuable information being out there in the world if only we could unearth it from the data we have recorded. Apart from the problem of identifying spurious correlations in data sets, leading to bad models that can generate bad outcomes, there is also the problem that ML does indeed uncover true facts and correlations that were previously unknown. These facts then tend to undermine previously private information and lessen its privacy. For example, imagine I built an ML model that can

use facial recognition to determine personality type.[8] Now people have lost privacy they used to have, by virtue of such a model existing. Their personality used to be private from mere visual inspection, but now it is not.

Secondary and downstream use

Another privacy violation results when information was originally collected for one purpose but is then deployed for another purpose. Formally, this is likely a violation of notice and consent, but even if the notice given was worded to allow this, it is not clear that the data subject could have consented if the terms are fairly vague. Such secondary use can result in a variety of harms, such as dignitary harms in commoditizing personal data about someone and harms based on violation of the consent originally obtained for such data. It can also mean that data is being used in a way that the data subject might even find offensive, such as if it is processed to make predictions to assist a political candidate a data subject despises.

Information dissemination

Privacy violations also result from various forms, intentional or otherwise, of information dissemination.

Breach of confidentiality

A privacy problem arises if models are being built that unintentionally "leak" your data, as has been shown to be technically possible (*https://perma.cc/DL7B-ZJFP*) with a variety of natural language models. Researchers have known about this problem for a long time but have yet to discover a solution. A variety of metrics may be able to indicate the likelihood that this happened—but whenever a model is released, the problem remains that it might be possible to back out actual information about a person whose data was used in the original training set. This area of research is ongoing and one in which industry practitioners need to learn to balance the risk and make reasoned assessments.

Exposure

Exposure results when someone's information can be identified as the result of the ML work done. For example, it's a privacy problem if data sets that include your information are released in an insufficiently de-identified form. Given current ML technologies and many opportunities to correlate big data troves, some people question whether data can ever be sufficiently de-identified (*https://perma.cc/P4ET-PP3K*). This is worrying because as data stores increase, what constitutes sufficient de-identification is a moving target. In many cases—even as

---

8 I do not mean to suggest such a model could be built, and believe those interested in fairness should be especially skeptical of the new digital physiognomy (*https://oreil.ly/1H5FC*).

personal as someone's genome (*https://perma.cc/57HN-3ZTQ*)—sensitive data has turned out to be insufficiently de-identified.

The human gaze

In some cases, data subjects may be comfortable with data collection and processing if it is done in a purely automated fashion in a large data set, where they imagine enjoying the effective anonymity of not being seen by the human gaze. It's a privacy problem if humans are observing you or your data when you thought such data would be processed only by computers, as has proven the case with many "home assistant" devices (*https://perma.cc/G82F-E72E*). In such cases, consumers have not realized the extent to which information collected about them was not merely fed into an algorithmic training process but was also inspected by humans who listened to and transcribed various audio recordings, some containing quite sensitive and private information.

Invasion

A privacy invasion occurs not only when you take information from someone or divulge information about someone. It also occurs when you disturb their private moments or private spaces, such as their homes or their very thoughts, attention, and experiences.

Intrusion

It is a privacy violation when your product intrudes into what should be a private space in a way that lessens its intimacy, safety, or security, be it a physical or figurative space. For example, a robotic vacuum cleaner that turns itself on and wanders into a bedroom uninvited is a privacy intrusion. But so is a pop-up notification on someone's phone that does not have permission or justification for the interruption.

Decisional interference

When data is used against someone's interest, such as to convince someone to buy more food than they want or to watch more television than they think wise, this may not be a good modeling. This could be a privacy invasion, as well as a separate harm of invading privacy to work against someone's interests. Incidentally, a legal idea is making the rounds that *information fiduciaries (https:// perma.cc/4Z2U-NQNK)* should not be allowed to work against the interests of those about whom they have information.

Data and Fiduciary Relationships

A *fiduciary* is a person who is in a position of trust with respect to another person and is therefore expected to put that other person's interests ahead of their own. So, for example, fiduciary obligations are imposed on lawyers and doctors when advising their clients and patients. For large tech companies with troves of personal data, the idea of an *information fiduciary* has arisen: since these companies have so much data and so much intimate access to and potential knowledge about their data subjects fiduciary duties of loyalty should apply. Note that this is not the current state of the law but rather a proposal by Balkin (2016)[9] as one means to recognize and respond to the growing discontent with the power and reach of many companies that have made their mark on the market through personal data.

A way of thinking about privacy: contextual integrity

One theme we can see in all of these categories of privacy violation is that they tend to upend norms and normal conceptual understandings of how to classify behavior and whether that behavior is acceptable. One theory that has been advanced to unify thinking about privacy norms and privacy violations is *contextual integrity*, a theory developed by Helen Nissenbaum in her seminal work, *Privacy In Context* (Stanford Law Books, 2010).

Contextual integrity is a useful benchmark as well because it can offer practical guidance appropriate to practicing technologists. Contextual integrity comprises four essential claims:

- A privacy-protecting environment permits information flows in appropriate channels.
- Appropriate channels and directions of information flow conform to informational norms, which are highly context-specific.
- Context-specific norms are assessed by looking at five situational parameters:
  — Identity of the *data subject*, the person about whom data is collected
  — Identity of the sender of that information
  — Identity of the recipient of that information
  — Content of that information

---

9 J.M. Balkin, "Information Fiduciaries and the First Amendment," *UC Davis Law Review*, 2016, *https://lawre view.law.ucdavis.edu/issues/49/4/Lecture/49-4_Balkin.pdf*.

— The *transmission principle*, which reflects the rules of operation for a specific chain of information transition, such as the directionality of information flow and the expected ability to propagate the information forward, or not, as specified by, for example, expectations of confidentiality

- Evolution over time as to ethical concerns and contextual norms for information sharing as culture changes or expected practices evolve, as can happen due to technical or nontechnical factors.

Contextual integrity was fashioned to provide a practical approach to considerations of data collection and analysis policies. Contextual integrity thus takes a pragmatic view, recognizing that fully explicit notice and consent is not only unworkable, given the volume of data stored and analyzed in our digital lives, but also undesirable, given that people will not always find it normal to ask them about basic data collection practices that are widely accepted and judged reasonable or even desirable. So contextual integrity offers a path for privacy analysis that can reduce the friction of notice and consent but also enhance privacy and feelings of appropriateness relative to the notice-and-consent scheme currently governing most electronic data collection policies around the world.

I discuss specific mathematical privacy metrics in Chapter 2. However, the conceptual tools offered by a taxonomy of privacy violations, and one proposed method (among several others) for making assessments as to assessing whether appropriate uses of data, are also important for understanding this very broad and important topic.

Legal Responses to Fairness in Technology

Concerns about technology and fairness go back a long way, even from a legal perspective. For example, as early as the 1970s it was illegal under French law (*https://perma.cc/4QXJ-LC9Y*) to make any decisions affecting human beings in a purely algorithmic manner—that is, without any human supervision. Such concerns about machines regulating humans without any human oversight are also reflected in more recent laws, such as the GDPR, which likewise introduces protections against automated decisions (*https://perma.cc/VEP4-UUXS*).

Similar legislative proposals are also appearing in the US. For example, Washington State has drafted legislation that would issue strict guidelines regarding the appropriate use of, and in some cases prohibit, state governmental agencies from using automated decision-making algorithms in important decision contexts (*https://perma.cc/SX6W-RGG4*).[10] At the federal level, recent legislation has been proposed to address

---

10 The Washington State legislation was referred to a subcommittee and never reached the floor of the main legislative body for debate in the state senate.

both potential bias and a lack of accountability and transparency in ML systems. One example of such legislation is the Algorithmic Accountability Act of 2019; see Figure 1-1.[11] (These are examples of proposed legislation. However, such legislation has, so far, mostly not made it past the stage of a proposal in the US federal and state governments, with some notable exceptions that I will discuss in Chapter 12.)

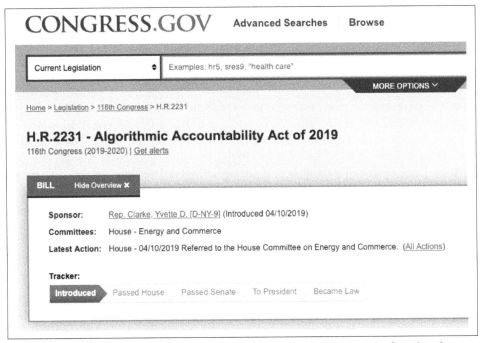

Figure 1-1. In recent years lawmakers around the world have begun drafting legislation to address a host of concerns related to the rise of algorithmic decision making as an increasingly common technology in business and government alike

Unlike the EU, the US does not have any national law in force with respect to algorithmic decision making or data privacy, both of which are covered by the GDPR. In contrast, many Asian jurisdictions are more similar to Europe, such as China (*https://perma.cc/CW68-VW7V*) and Singapore (*https://perma.cc/EB9N-LKXD*), which are both actively developing targeted national legislation and regulations on privacy and ethical uses of ML (and artificial intelligence more generally).

On the other hand, traditional security concerns are more systematically and widely addressed in the US, perhaps because they constitute a longer-standing formalized

---

11 The Algorithmic Accountability Act of 2019 was referred to the Senate's Subcommittee on Consumer Protection and Commerce, and no further action has been taken. This is often the case with legislative proposals generally, and has so far proven to be the case for all algorithm-specific bills proposed at the federal level.

technological concern than do privacy, discrimination, and fairness. The US has national information security laws going back at least to the 1990s, and the US military plays an active role in setting cybersecurity standards that have an international impact, such as for the Internet of Things (IoT).[12] Similarly, governments in other high-tech jurisdictions are keen to assist with setting security standards in technological industries.

As technological fields mature, we see more concrete laws being made about these technologies. We also see technical consensus emerging about best practices and definitions of standards. However, security protocols will continue to evolve because new technologies create new security concerns.

Over time, we can hope to see more consensus from a technical perspective as to what constitutes "fair" technology, particularly with respect to data analysis, machine learning, and more generally the field of data-driven AI. We can expect that as technical standards emerge from community agreement, these standards will allow more consistent and reasonable social and legal expectations. For those in technical positions, you will find yourself having power over the products you design but not necessarily a perfect way to ensure fairness. Indeed, fairness questions remain an area of active discussion and debate within both the legal and the technical communities that think about these problems. However, even if a consensus about best practices has not yet been reached—and may never be—this book will take you through a variety of options, all of which are better than continuing to ignore the problem.

We will discuss rules and standards more toward the end of the book. Many ML-related efforts are underway in this domain, and it's a rapidly changing field, so my goal will only be to make you aware of some interesting examples. It will not be possible to offer a full rundown of what might apply to your own ML practices depending on where you work and where your data subjects and product users are located.

The Assumptions and Approaches in This Book

This book will no doubt meet with many criticisms of inaccuracy, oversimplification, understatement, overstatement, and so on. I am attempting perhaps a fool's errand in reducing "fairness" to a coding book of only a few hundred pages. So I'd like you to have the same understanding regarding the goals of this book and my perspective in writing it.

---

12 The *Internet of Things* is a term used to describe the many devices deployed in our physical world, in either private or public spaces, that connect to the internet and provide information based on physical measurements, be these auditory recordings, image feeds, or other sources of information. These devices can also interact with humans or provide outputs for information or actions having effects at their location.

My perspective on fairness is as a US-trained lawyer who has also worked as a coder and data scientist. Most, but not all, of the anecdotal examples and historical motivations I use to guide this book are grounded in US history. That is not because I believe the US is the center of the world, but because this background is the foundation *and* because the US is one large and important center for the tech industry.

The US is also reasonably representative in the nature of problems that arise everywhere, even if the situational details have different names or different histories. The problems we have here in the US are the problems societies all around the world have in one form or another. The US has problems with gender discrimination, racial discrimination, and discrimination on the basis of other important categories such as religion, disability status, and sexual orientation. We in the US, as in other parts of the world, also recognize other elements of fairness, such as a social environment that respects individual rights to privacy and individual and community needs for security. The concepts explored in this book are of universal interest; all societies ask the same fundamental questions about fairness, even if the dominant or preferred answer in a specific situation varies with culture or geography.

The particular groups affected by fairness concerns in different societies will be different, no doubt, but the senselessness, cruelty, and unfairness of, for example, discrimination will surely be a unifying theme. So wherever you are reading this, please be understanding when I refer to certain historical trials in the US. I would invite you to either substitute in your knowledge of your local context or, if you don't have that knowledge, educate yourself (and me) on your local context. I welcome feedback from readers and look forward to making revisions and additions to this text to provide a more global perspective on fairness (see the Preface for contact information).

Relatedly, I assume my readers have many commonalities with me, even if we don't come from the same country. I assume that all groups of people should be treated equally and that we should come into any problem affecting humans with the assumption that ability is spread evenly throughout the human population.[13]

When I have given talks or taught on topics related to fairness, a question inevitably arises: "What if, for some reason, ability for a given trait is not spread evenly throughout the population?" After all, certain regions of the world seem to dominate certain activities, be it chess playing or marathon running. Perhaps, some like to suggest, there is some genetic component. Shouldn't we account for these sorts of inherent ability issues somewhere in a topic of fairness—that people who actually are better should be recognized as such?

---

13 This does not mean that it is distributed uniformly and identically in each person, but rather that you will find talented and hard-working individuals in any part of the world and occupying any body type and shape, and not-so-talented, not-so-hard-working people in any part of the world, occupying all manners of body types and shapes.

I'd like to point out that for my purposes this is neither an interesting nor an important question. I'll quote Neil deGrasse Tyson's response to a question on a panel about whether women might be less present in the sciences because of ability or genetics. His response got the to meat of the issue:

> I've never been female, but I have been black my whole life. So let me perhaps offer some insight from that perspective, because there are many similar social issues related to access to equal opportunity that we find in the black community as well as in the community of women in a white-male-dominated society…
>
> [T]hroughout my life, I've known that I wanted to do astrophysics, since I was nine years old on a first visit to the Hayden Planetarium…I got to see how the world around me reacted to my expression of these ambitions. And all I can say is, the fact that I wanted to be a scientist, an astrophysicist, was, hands down, the path of most resistance through…the forces of society. Anytime I expressed this interest, teachers would say, "Don't you want to be an athlete?" I wanted to become something that was outside of the paradigms of expectation of the people in power…
>
> So, my life experience tells me that when you don't find blacks in the sciences and you don't find women in the sciences, I know that these forces are real and I had to survive them in order to get where I am today. *So before we start talking about genetic differences, you've got to come up with a system where there's equal opportunity. Then we can have that conversation.* (Emphasis mine.)

If your interest in this book lies in disentangling questions such as, "To what extent are men better than women at science and to what extent is it unfairness that stops women from being better represented in the ranks of Nobel-Prize-winning scientists?" this isn't the book for you.[14] On the other hand, if your question is, "To what extent can I design and build digital products and data analysis processes that ensure people get equal opportunities, thus contributing to a world that looks more equal to everyone?" then this book might be a good starting point.

What If I'm Skeptical of All This Fairness Talk?

My audience always includes fairness skeptics when I give industry talks about fairness practices for ML and digital products. The questions they raise tend to be of two flavors. One flavor is, "But what about treating people according to their merits?" The other is, "But isn't fairness a sideshow in innovation?"

With respect to the first question, yes, fairness is all about treating people according to their merits (alongside other core principles discussed in Chapters 1 and 2). I

---

14 Note, plenty of work attempts to answer this question, despite complaints that some topics are forbidden because of political correctness. I simply don't think these are important questions for our time, or possibly ever. Ultimately, don't we all want a world where each person is judged on their own merits? If we can achieve this, what would be the use of such questions?

addressed this concern in "Equity and Equality" on page 10. So now I turn to the second question.

Won't Fairness Slow Down Innovation?

Short answer: no. In fact, fairness itself is in the midst of a revolution in law, computer science, mathematics, and behavioral sciences. Concerns about fairness are generating new mathematics, new programming, and new legal discussions. If anything, not thinking about fairness for much of the beginning of our current information revolution arguably held up an area ripe for the innovation we are seeing now.

My other rebuttal to this concern is the following:

> The best minds of my generation are thinking about how to make people click ads. That sucks.
>
> —Jeff Hammerbacher

While I don't fully subscribe to the idea that all the "best minds" have gone to the dark side, I share more than a little of Hammerbacher's concerns that the outsize profits that have been generated by uninspiring technical or behavioral science progress in ad clicks may hardly be the kind of "innovation" our society should be allocating resources to. I am not trying to make a political statement about how we should allocate resources, but surely we can agree that much of what passes for "innovation" in digital products is really just aggressive direct-to-consumer marketing. So let's keep our high horse about innovation in check—if we're going to say that basic fairness measures put a damper on tech profits, it's not necessarily a damper on *socially beneficial innovation*.

Are There Any Real-World Consequences for Not Developing Fairness-Aware Practices?

Short answer: yes. In Chapter 12, I discuss some of the laws that regulate data-driven digital products. While I don't like to emphasize the negative aspects of such rules, you should be aware that violating these laws carries real-world monetary consequences. Most notably, the GDPR's penalties can rise to as high as *4% of the annual global revenues* of a firm for severe infringements, and as high as *2% of annual global revenues* for less severe infringements. The penalties can scale with the revenues of a firm precisely to make sure that the penalty will be felt regardless of the size of the organization.

In 2018, over €400,000,000 of fines were assessed, and in 2019 over €440,000,000 were assessed. One notable fine was €50,000,000 against Google for having opaque and inaccessible consent policies, which pertains to the fairness principle of transparency and consent. Another notable fine was €18,500,000 against the Austrian national postal service for processing information related to political affiliation, package receipt frequency, and frequency of relocation for the purpose of direct marketing, a violation of the lawful basis of data processing under the GDPR. We can expect to see many more fines in the future due to intentional and unintentional violations of this wide-ranging law, which establishes some rules governing the fair use of personal data and algorithmic decision making.

In the US, lawmakers have been notably inactive in this area, but companies can still face legal penalties for recklessly disregarding basic fairness ethics and best practices. For example, in 2019 the Federal Trade Commission fined Facebook $5,000,000,000 (that's $5 *billion*) for a variety of improper data practices and misleading statements in its privacy policy that were found to constitute unfair and deceptive practices. These were related to how the code that powered the social media website differed from representations in its privacy policy.

Separately, the US Department of Housing and Urban Development sued Facebook in 2019 for housing discrimination in violation of the Fair Housing Act. Specifically, Facebook was allowing advertisers, even for housing, to target audiences according to a variety of factors that could relate to protected categories, such as race, religion, gender, and family status. In this case, Facebook escaped financial penalties but reached an extensive settlement agreement that detailed the ways in which it had to immediately reform its advertising services to conform to federal law and basic fairness principles.[15]

In yet another recent defeat for Facebook, in 2020 it elected to settle a class-action lawsuit, *Patel v. Facebook*, that came about as a result of violations of the Illinois Biometric Information Privacy Act,[16] a law had been passed years earlier but that had remained underused until recently. The law gives a private right of action for nonconsensual storage of biometric information, which may include information related to facial recognition, a very commonly applied use case in social media as well as in other domains. Facebook will pay out $550,000,000 (that is, more than half a billion dollars) to settle this claim.

I don't cite all these actions against Facebook to scapegoat one company but to point out that years of violating laws can come home to roost, as appears to be the case for Facebook. Realistically, it's possible that these amounts haven't been especially damaging to Facebook (for example, it readily paid the $5 billion FTC fine in cash, without

---

15 Given that such targeted advertising practices were available for years before the lawsuit, some might say Facebook already got away with quite a lot of unfairness and reaped the financial rewards. Unfortunately, the legal system does not always move as quickly as would be desirable to ensure basic fairness. Also, to be clear, in many of these cases Facebook (or other entities) does not necessarily admit wrongdoing, so some of what I write should perhaps be qualified in terms of allegations rather than facts, but I try to keep the language simple here.

16 Note that this is a state law and does not apply across the US to all US citizens.

raising the funds with loans and such), but such large amounts might at the least be noticeable even to a hugely profitable company such as Facebook, and they certainly would be for smaller companies.

What's more, in both the EU and the US we are seeing a "techlash": a populist rising up against these companies that demonstrates pent-up resentment with both their policies and their financial success, which seems to come about in part from violating consumer consent and fairness principles. Many *antitrust* (in EU, *competition law*) investigations are ongoing against Big Tech companies, partly motivated by a sense that these companies may be violating basic notions of fair play against both consumers and competitors.

So the short answer is yes, real-world penalties exist even if you don't find fairness a particularly compelling ethical consideration when you build digital products. And given the political climate of late 2020, we can expect to see ramped-up penalties in future years. So even if you play by the rules of realpolitik, it's a good time to get some basic fairness hygiene into your digital products.

What Is Fairness?

Fairness can mean many different things to many different people, as to both what concerns are fairness concerns and which way the balance of fairness tilts. I don't seek to conclusively and extensively define *fairness*, nor do I seek to debate each nuance. However, fairness has many operational concerns, particularly with respect to fairness in ML systems, which are important to recognize and are discussed in various ways throughout the book. I describe these next and highlight which areas of the book most address this issue.

In the next section, I narrow down the elements that will be most extensively discussed in this book to the following:

- Antidiscrimination (which I also treat as the most important concern of *equality* or *equity*)
- Security
- Privacy

I focus on these three topics for a few reasons. First, these topics have extensive backgrounds of both legal and technical guidance, suggesting that they are particularly ripe for discussion and for the emergence of basic knowledge and good practices expected of every software engineer, data scientist, and ML engineer. In these mature fields, unfortunately, it has been acceptable for far too long to ignore these three issues despite their well-established legal and technical basis for identifying and resolving fundamental concerns.

Second, these concerns cover what appears to affect ordinary people most right now, particularly if we use newspaper coverage as guidance. This is not to say that these are the only concerns, but for the moment they remain the main talking points in the popular media.

Also, as I detail next, the book covers other topics, so I make clear here which chapters address topics in various domains of fairness:

Antidiscrimination

Antidiscrimination seems to receive the most attention in the press and in political discourse when it comes to fairness in ML systems. Antidiscrimination is also extremely concerning with respect to any system because unlike some fairness concerns, which would implicate everyone subjected to a system, discriminatory outcomes often affect only a small group, and usually a disfavored group. Similar to both press coverage and popular discourse, this book therefore gives quite a bit of attention to antidiscrimination. Particular attention is found in Chapters 2 through 6.

Privacy

Privacy has long received attention both in the law and in the technology sector as a salient fairness feature for many consumers. It also seems to form a large component of the techlash, which continues at the time of writing and shows that consumers are particularly resentful of incursions into their private spaces by technology and ML modeling. Particular attention to privacy is found in Chapters 2 and 9.

Safety

Safety is often taken for granted in digital systems but is, in fact, woefully lacking in most of them, particularly those powered by ML models. Cybersecurity will continue to be a key issue because of the very nature of the beast, one in which continued evolution and an arms race will be a routine part of digital security. However, the importance of security related to ML modeling is underappreciated, even by those who develop and release ML models for industry. Such lapses have particular importance now as ML models increasingly have physical real-world implications.

While security and safety are generally treated as distinct from other fairness attributes, this book makes the case that safety is part of fairness and very much part of what an individual should be able to reasonably expect as we think about introducing digital products into the human environment. It would be terribly unfair to make the world less fair all in the name of digital progress. Particular attention to safety is found in Chapters 2, 10, and 11.

Transparency

Transparency is a key value in the rule of law but not necessarily an acceptable practice in all areas of business. For this reason, as ML models and algorithmic decision making become more widespread, we see that calls for transparency have made their way even into areas traditionally occupied only by the private sector. As digital venues and products dominate important markets, sometimes providing the only venues in which speakers or writers can hope to reach sizable audiences, and as businesses enjoy an outsize role in cultural and political life, we can expect to see more calls for transparency regarding many elements of digital product design and the inspection of ML pipelines. Particular attention to transparency is found in Chapters 7, 8, 11, and 12.

Legitimacy

Legitimacy, derived through democratic process, conformance to fairness norms, or other procedural- or outcome-based metrics, is important to the justification for any rollout of a digital system, and particularly one that could have high-stakes ramifications. The techlash of recent years suggests that in many cases the business models and the data practices surrounding data-driven models have suffered from a lack of legitimacy, as such products are perceived as rolled out to the benefit of elites and to the detriment of and against the explicit objections of vulnerable populations. Particular attention to legitimacy is found in this chapter and Chapters 11 and 12.

Accountability

Accountability relates to the need for feedback and consequences from downstream uses of digital products and ML models to make their way back upstream to their developers and designers. In the current digital marketplace it is too often the case that those responsible for digital harms suffer few consequences as a result of their actions. This in turn can mean, first, that too little care is taken to anticipate and avoid harms and that, second, too little is done to remediate harms even when they become known. Particular attention to accountability is found in Chapters 7, 10, 11, and 12.

Autonomy

Digital products can appear to or actually take away autonomy from humans. This can happen in a number of ways. In some cases, computers stand in where humans used to make decisions, removing human cognition and discretion from a system. In other cases, digital products are used to cabin the options open to humans either as decision makers or as data subjects facing an ML model. Finally, digital environments themselves add new possibilities to the lived human experience while simultaneously removing others. These practices can all potentially undermine aggregate human autonomy and individual human autonomy if done carelessly or unfairly. Particular attention to autonomy is found in Chapters 2 and 11, with respect to the design of digital systems.

Minority rights

By simple definition, ML can look like the tyranny of a data set's majority over its minority. More explicitly, minority rights are discussed here with respect to anti-discrimination in Chapters 4 through 6, and then more generally as a concept in Chapter 11.

Distributional concerns

One area of concern discussed earlier in this chapter is that technology can unbalance the distribution of wealth among elements of society. This must be an area of fairness concern, but it is one that can at times be difficult to account for by an individual entity or ML engineer. Nonetheless, these distributional concerns can factor into product design, and for that reason particular attention to them is found in Chapters 11 and 12. Distributional concerns are particularly difficult to study, and we can expect to see more developments on this topic in years to come (and in any subsequent editions of this book!).

Rules to Code By

Here I formulate rules that are generally applicable and widely supported, and these will motivate the aims I pursue in the book's conceptual and coding discussions.

Equality and Equity

- People should be treated equally when doing so makes sense.
  - Equality should be defined in a way that is reasonable and meaningful, given reality.
  - Equality is not always equitable. Providing equal resources when need is unequal will often be unfair rather than fair.
- People should be treated equitably whenever equal treatment would be unfair or unjustified.
  - Only meaningful distinctions should be made between people, and these distinctions should be clearly documented and limited in scope.
  - When we determine a merit metric for the purpose of treating people *equitably*, we should clearly define the metric and make sure we are accurately measuring that metric.
  - All relevant and reasonably available factors should be considered when sorting people.
  - When we write code separating people into categories, it should serve their interests and the interests of the whole community.
- Equity and equality should be evaluated over time, with room to evolve.

— Systems should not be deterministic, and should recognize that individuals can change, and make room for that.

— Systems should recognize that correlations and causes can evolve over time.

— Systems should be quality checked over time and should not create self-perpetuating models of reality.

Security

- If our code can affect the physical world, it should make people more safe rather than less so.

  — Are we sure of our ability to fully test our software before we allow it into the wild?

  — Are we sure our software outperforms the older or nondigital system we are replacing, and can we prove it?

- If our code affects digital assets, it should match the reasonable expectations of the users. Builders of such systems have an affirmative duty to identify these reasonable expectations and act on them.

  — Do our product interfaces fully convey their function?

  — Do our products explicitly or implicitly overpromise the benefit to the user?

- We should not build tools that can be easily misused to threaten either the security of individuals or their rightfully owned assets.

  — Are we building a product that has potentially abusive use cases? If so, what if anything can we do to limit these potential use cases? Should we build this product before we know how to control it?

- Threats to autonomy, freedom of movement, freedom of expression, and other values supported by long-standing cultural norms are threats to security.

  — Are we building products that an abusive entity would love to have? If so, do the potential benefits outweigh the costs of bringing this technology into the world? Are we simply building this product because we assume our competitors will do the same?

Privacy

- It is reasonable for people using systems to determine what is private, not for us to determine what we can find out.

  — If we don't know our users' expectations, can we find out? How are we educating them about our understanding of their expectations?

- The potentially superhuman capacities of ML products should not be used to technologically overrule social norms about what is private.

  — Are we respecting known social norms and taking actions to discover latent social norms?

  — Are we rolling out a product across too many national or cultural boundaries without adapting it locally? Can we justify a uniform design?

- If a product undermines autonomy, sense of identity, or sense of confidence in oneself or one's environment, it is privacy invading.

- Invasion of privacy is a harm even if the person about whom information is deduced is not aware of the observation or could not deduce what is deduced by a technological system.

  — Are we taking on a role that would mostly be appropriate for a trained professional covered by codes of professional ethics (especially physician or mental health provider)? Or the role of an intimate friend?

  — Would our product be acceptable if replaced by a human doing exactly the same thing? If not, is this the explicit value of the program or an unintended and manipulative side effect?

## CHAPTER 2

Understanding Fairness and the Data Science Pipeline

Now that you've read a little background on the history and social context of technology and fairness, let's dig into the engineering aspects of defining fairness. In this chapter, I discuss how to set engineering goals and use fairness metrics. Of course, using metrics can be a dangerous exercise; after all, it's a well-known problem that one gets what one measures. So let's explore these metrics but also remember that no single metric can fully encompass or guarantee fairness.

What do we want our work to accomplish from a fairness perspective? What are our targets with respect to equity, privacy, and security? Should these targets be numerical quotas, or should we leave them deliberately underspecified so that we're always striving to do better? To begin answering these questions, let's start with some brief definitions of what we're after, building on the observations in the previous chapter:

Equality

One version of a perfect world is one in which everyone has about the same and also deserves about the same. Houses would all be about the same size, and everyone would have the same amount of leisure. Everyone would have access to equally good health care and equally good education. Of course, this also supposes that individuals would be equally careful of their health, make equally good use of their educational opportunities, and take equally good care of their homes, which in the real world is not very likely.

This differential use of opportunity is one of the motivations that will often push toward *equity* rather than *equality*. Indeed, *equality* is arguably not all that relevant for algorithmic decision making as it hardly takes an algorithm to allocate resources equally. To be clear, in many cases equality should be the driver of allocation—it's just that you are unlikely to be using machine learning for such use cases. The default assumption should be that everyone receives the same and that you have specific reasons for equitable rather than equal distributions. However, for the rest of the book, the discussion will focus on problems of equitable rather than equal distributions.

Equity

An equitable system treats individuals according to merit; however, merit may be defined in a particular domain and for a particular problem, and hopefully with plentiful domain knowledge and qualitative study to back up the metric used to determine it. Equitable systems distinguish between individuals and the treatment of those individuals—be it rate of pay, extent of medical treatment received, or grade on a final exam—according to what is deserved, where *deserved* should be carefully and explicitly defined.

In striving for an equitable system, we want to make sure that the way a system functions and its ultimate outcomes are tailored to the stated goal served by making distinctions among individuals in the first place. That is, we want to measure and use *merit* correctly. Finally, we also want to leave room for our notions of equity to evolve over time.

Privacy

Privacy is an ever-evolving standard, but it includes at least two important and uncontroversial points. First, with respect to information that is traditionally disclosed only in very specific, protected relationships and at the option of an individual, that information should not be stored or transmitted without the knowledge *and* consent of that individual. Second, if a behavior, decision, or other form of information is public in the sense of being observable by a second or third party outside of a traditionally confidentially relationship, this does not ethically make that information fair game and free of notice and consent requirements or similar measures to protect individual information and autonomy. A privacy-respecting system will also protect individuals from incursions not only from the controller of the system but from third parties too.

For all these reasons, a privacy-respecting system will not seek out information about an individual that traditionally has not been part of what people could deduce about that person based on publicly available information and observations, even if the existence of machine learning algorithms makes it possible to do so. These descriptions tend to reflect what ordinary people want but largely *do not* reflect typical data and modeling practices in most organizations.

Security

In ML applications, *security* most broadly means faithfulness to our intentions and promises in developing a product and holding it out to potential customers or users as available for use.[1] If a product promises that information is held in secret, that information should remain secret. If certain information could make a user vulnerable, such as information that someone with a particular set of observable features is an easy target for predatory lending tactics, that information should probably remain secret regardless of whether it explicitly promises to do so.[2]

Security can be the most onerous burden a data scientist will bear because it requires them to cover more possibilities than they can possibly know. They must aim to keep the user safe from threats of all kinds, from malicious actors who will have varied and highly sophisticated methods. A competent data scientist must assume that their models will be explored for potential attacks, assuming that either a counterparty or a third party has an incentive to do so. No one can offer a perfect security guarantee, but a data scientist or ML engineer should at least take common-sense precautions, be they thinking about potential downstream use cases or direct attacks to fool the system.

This chapter addresses these goals for our technological systems and data pipelines via a multipart examination of measuring and engineering fairness. The structure of the chapter is as follows. First, it introduces metrics related to fairness concerns. Then we examine relationships between different aspects of fairness—for example the relationship between equity and privacy. Finally, the chapter concludes with a concrete checklist of points of entry for fairness concerns and related action items in the data science pipeline. Most chapters include a checklist at the end, and they partly fill in the details of the broader outline posed here. However, given the fast-moving, state-of-the-art, and inherently open-ended nature of fairness in ML, you should take these checklists only as a point of departure for your own context-specific analyses as you develop ML models and digital products.

Before jumping into our discussion, we should also consider what a metric is. In a mathematical sense, *metrics* are measures of distance. They should satisfy the following properties: triangle inequality (*https://perma.cc/6FMM-5XQY*), symmetry,

---

1 While already discussed in the previous chapter, it bears emphasizing that we examine security specifically from the perspective of those who develop and deploy ML models. We do not broadly address cybersecurity issues.

2 Law professor Jack Balkin has argued (*https://oreil.ly/yC6MI*) that companies with large amounts of information about individuals should be "information fiduciaries" because they should owe a fiduciary relationship to their users. They would have to put their users' interests before their own with respect to this information and act in the best interests of their users even if it went against their organizational best interests.

non-negativity, and identity of indiscernibles (*https://perma.cc/356R-FSUZ*). We are going to be more inclusive and generous in our definitions of what constitutes a metric. Sometimes they may be distance measures, but sometimes they may be binary or relative indicators. Also, our interest will be in making sure that the quantities we call metrics of fairness, privacy, and security are well defined but also meaningful to the human consumers of these numbers. Those humans may be those designing technical products or may be the humans who find their data being processed or their outcomes being determined by such products.

We should also be wary from a sociological perspective when considering metrics. An old business management expression warns that you get what you measure (*https://perma.cc/K5YU-EKBU*). Consider common problems such as "teaching to the test," in the case of teachers wary of having their professional performance evaluated according to their students' grades on standardized tests. This phenomenon has been recognized in a wide variety of domains and disciplines, and we want to avoid falling into this trap when developing ML models—the trap of merely maximizing a fairness metric without a more holistic viewpoint.

This chapter covers some potential metrics that can be used in assessing to what extent certain values are respected in data science pipelines. However, we should never make the mistake of thinking that morals can be simplified to a handful of key performance indicators, or KPIs (*https://perma.cc/C6FV-PEXQ*).

Metrics for Fairness

A task becomes an engineering task rather than merely a fuzzy discussion when we have a metric we can optimize or use as an input constraint when designing a system. Anyone who works on technology products will be comfortable with this assertion, but most probably won't have experience developing such metrics, as they relate to normative fairness values rather than more traditional engineering tasks such as assessing whether a certain required functionality has been fulfilled or quantifying measures of user experience. As we will see throughout this chapter, quantifying fairness has its own unique challenges, and many of the relevant challenges are only recently being addressed by academics or industry.

> ## Gender and Other Labels
>
> Throughout this book I have tried to focus on gender rather than sex and to recognize that gender is not binary. Likewise, I recognize that race and ethnic identity are not necessarily categorical variables where individuals check just one box out of the options offered on a survey. Yet you will find me reducing these categories to binaries in example code and cases.

I wanted to present the simplest examples of fairness interventions that can make real inroads toward supporting the ideals described in this book, even if these interventions aren't perfect. For this reason, I focused on categories that treat categorical variables, and specifically binary variables. I note when the methods could be extended to multiple categories or applied in series to one form of binary division and then another. Thus the use of binary categories need not exclude fairness treatments that can accommodate data that hews closer to the complex lived realities we recognize with respect to gender, race, ethnic identity, and other elements of personhood.

Another data science constraint to consider, even as we recognize the diversity and nonbinary nature of many aspects of identity, is that data science remains data-driven and reliant on data size to generate performance and accuracy. For that reason, a data-oriented intervention might not be an effective way to address concerns of groups that are rarely represented in data. Domain knowledge might be a better tool than data-driven model fitting for determining modifications to a data science pipeline or ML model when accounting for the experience of minority groups that are too small in number to be properly modeled in a given situation. Such groups should not be suppressed or go unrecognized with respect to data labels, but a fairness solution might not be as simple as breaking them into a category for interventions if their numbers are too small to generate an accurate and informative model.

Unfortunately, research into ML fairness is still young enough that we don't have much research or best practices regarding how to deal with overlapping identities, nonbinary identities, and traits that might seem more like continua than binary indicators. In the future, we can expect these issues to garner more attention, and hopefully this will eventually result in the formation of best practices when dealing with such considerations.

Traditionally, the domain of fairness concerns was likely to be left to lawyers, ethicists, and politicians. In such professions, notions of fairness have been important and powerful for a long time, even if society didn't always live up to what it espoused. In Western politics, notions of fairness have motivated legal developments for centuries, yet such developments have rolled out almost universally without numbers or explicit quantification of competing values or interests. For example, when President Lincoln issued the Emancipation Proclamation calling for an end to slavery, he didn't say "on balance, a human life is worth X and so our legal regime needs to change." Rather, he cited fundamental principles.

The closest thing to quantifying fairness was perhaps reflected in legal analysis that provided some recognition of conflicting fairness concerns. For example, legal standards have indicated that the imposition on someone's rights had to be *proportional* to the motivating need. Or, in explaining a decision that might have harmed an individual, the government might have to show that it had made a reasonable decision as assessed by some form of a *cost-benefit analysis*. But these analyses were rarely quantified, as a cost-benefit analysis implies they should be.

Such decision-making tools implied measurable values but did not explicitly label the measure of conflicting considerations. Society has gotten along for a long time without quantifying values we'd prefer to pretend are unquantifiable.[3]

Yet resistance to quantification is diminishing in recent years, as more and more human behavior is tracked and measured. Much more is observable than just a decade ago. Economists, public health officials, and others can reasonably estimate such astonishing quantities as how changing auto emissions standards will raise or lower highway fatalities (*https://perma.cc/NM7B-MQDT*) or how much value each person's information contributes to Facebook's total valuation (*https://perma.cc/HE4P-CZ9U*).

Sometimes people see metrics like these and find them intrinsically offensive. How can we put a price on a life, or on someone's personality? It's normal to feel uncomfortable with these calculations when first introduced to them.[4]

While such valuations may seem disrespectful of human life or other human attributes, policymakers and business people alike do this every day, unavoidably. Allocations will be made where resources are limited, which reflects just about every situation in the real world. So ignoring the problem and pretending that sacred values can't be quantified or negotiated tends to lead to shortages and chaotic or random distribution, which is far less humane than recognizing the reality that even a human life needs a number on it for systematic decision making. Metrics about the relative merits of human life and qualities as compared to other property considerations might make us uncomfortable, but such thinking is one of the best tools for fairly and efficiently allocating the limited resources a society has.

As fairness moves increasingly into the domain of quantitative metrics, another aspect of traditional fairness discussions is becoming increasingly apparent. In the past, all sorts of quantities were mixed together as legal or ethical thinkers purported to consider a cost-benefit analysis of conflicting rights and fairness concerns. For example, in tort litigation, liability will often hinge on "reasonable care," which is a legal test determining whether a person was negligent for not exercising the degree of caution that an ordinarily prudent person would. The degree of caution will have taken into account a variety of factors, including weighing the cost to make an object or situation safer against the likelihood of harm and the imputed cost of that harm.

---

3 In contrast, some ancient peoples evinced a more businesslike attitude toward these inestimable values, such as the Code of Hammurabi indicating monetary "prices" to be paid by someone who committed a crime, even crimes as serious as murder and rape.

4 This discomfort even has a name: taboo trade-off. This is well-documented and studied in psychology; see *Scientific American* (*https://oreil.ly/Udq1m*).

No ordinarily prudent person is expected to guard 100% against any possibility of danger, so life and injury are implicitly weighed against the economic cost of design or manual labor needed to make a product safer. Companies do this all the time, and when injury results, juries of ordinary people are convened to determine what reasonable care would have been, where this standard implicates a variety of qualitatively different considerations.

In the past, judges, politicians, and even businesspeople have used pseudo quantitative language, often couched in some kind of cost-benefit analysis, even as the quantities of an equation were a mix of quantifiable factors (such as economic or effort costs to doing something) and intangibles (such as the value of living in a safe community or the value of one person's right to free speech). While economists, data scientists, and policymakers may put dollar values on items and ideas for analysis, no one can fully and objectively measure the value of an intangible in that way. So what does it mean when we want to compare different intangibles?

An intangible for which we can't measure the value is something like freedom of speech, but this isn't the only way metrics might apply to such an intangible. In addition to wanting to value it for some kind of balancing equation, we can also treat it not as a binary, as in freedom of speech or no freedom of speech, but as some kind of continuous variable. How much freedom of speech do we have, we might ask. 50? 50%? 50 units of what, exactly?

Given the quantitative nature of most ML, engineers need to input numbers to quantitatively describe intangible factors or for a metric, to measure it against the performance of a model. Having everyone agree will likely be an impossible task. In some ways, fairness is a matter of ethics, and as we know, ethics varies to some degree both from one individual to another and also from one worldview to another, be it worldview defined by religion, culture, or nation.

The important thing to appreciate is that the choice of a metric is not a foregone conclusion, and so for this reason we will discuss a variety of metrics and how and where they are deployed, while trying to emphasize that the choice of metric is normally a value-laden one. Perhaps you as an engineer will make the decision, perhaps it will be made in a group, or perhaps the law will even offer some guidance eventually. Regardless of who makes the decision, such metrics will inevitably be more like a technical input than a technical conclusion.

The next section discusses metrics as applied to three key components of developing a fair data pipeline: equity, privacy, and security. The primary emphasis of this book is equity, but every data analyst should also give some thought and attention to learning fundamental metrics in privacy and security as well.

Measures of Equity

Usually we emphasize equality rather than equity in common slogans and discussions about fairness, but what most people favor in most situations is equity rather than equality. For example, we don't want everyone to have equal access to becoming a brain surgeon, but we want everyone who is equally hardworking, intelligent, and cool under pressure to have that opportunity. Likewise, in general we don't want equality of hiring in any position, but rather we want some form of meritocracy. So when discussing algorithmic decision making, the goal is to ensure that data points are treated in proportion to their merit; however, that is defined in a given context and when solving a particular task. Notably, membership in a protected category is both *logically* (by our governing assumption that human talent is equally distributed among populations) and *legally* irrelevant to evaluations of merit. Therefore, if outcomes are different because of such attributes, the ML pipeline has a problem.

Operationalizing equity in an ML pipeline is tricky for a number of reasons. Most importantly, how do we define *merit*? If we assign merit as the target variable Y, we will try to predict Y based on input variables in a vector X. Usually, in terms of predicting Y based on X, this would indicate that we need to correctly define our Y, so that the Y we are defining is either identical to or a sufficient statistic for what we ultimately want to know. We can also imagine that the predictors for Y contained in X might have information specifically related to membership in a protected category, such as race, age, gender, national origin, and so on. To promote equity, we want to avoid discrimination, so we want to avoid using the information in X or Y that is purely related to membership in a protected category rather than getting at our underlying idea of merit.

Equity promotion has another angle, however. We can avoid discrimination altogether and still produce inequitable results. While antidiscrimination measures have been stressed in the literature to date, and are also emphasized in this book, equity has at least one other angle. Another way of emphasizing that decisions should be in proportion to merit is to measure the sensibleness of the decision. We will address the sensibility of decisions in our discussion of auditing in Chapter 7 and explainability and model interpretation in Chapter 8.

Antidiscrimination measures of equity

When determining how fair our model is, we can consider two antidiscrimination categories: disparate treatment and disparate impact. In the first, a model should seemingly be neutral with respect to unfair categories. That is, it shouldn't categorize things based on irrelevant information or make rules differently based on protected attributes. Doing so would be known as *disparate treatment* and this notion roughly corresponds to considering what kinds of inputs should even go into a fair model (*direct discrimination* in European law).

In the second, *disparate impact* refers to the situation in which people from different groups on average receive markedly different outcomes from a process that is seemingly neutral (*indirect discrimination* in European law). Disparate impact cases, both in litigation and in ML use cases, are far more common than disparate treatment cases and are the most likely way for discrimination to result unintentionally. Most of this book is about identifying and rectifying disparate impact as well as assessing what extent of correction is appropriate and when disparate impact rises to a level that is justifiable to intervene in what otherwise appears to be a neutral data set.

This book emphasizes antidiscrimination later on, so these measures will be more fully discussed. If you delve into the scholarship on fairness, you'll see that this discipline has not yet coalesced along a specific definition of *fairness*, and such a consensus may never emerge. Technical scholars have made a very good case that we have numerous ways to measure fairness, and that many metrics have validity and utility, depending on the legal and historical concerns at play in a particular situation.

Vocabulary Choices

Throughout this book I use "positive" to refer not to the binary indicator "1" but to the sense of "desired outcome," which in other cases may be the 0-labeled outcome and in some cases may be the 1-labeled outcome. Fairness doesn't come into play when a truly neutral assessment is made (if such a thing even exists). Fairness comes into play when desirable resources are being allocated such that there are clearly better and worse outcomes. We'll use "desired" and "positive" interchangeably and in a way that emphasizes the value of a label rather than its technical definition. This way, we can talk about a variety of models interchangeably with regard to positive outcomes, be it the COMPAS algorithm assessing whether someone is high risk for recidivism (a negative, not a positive outcome) or some other tool assessing whether someone should be offered a job (a positive outcome). In both cases we can imagine the label could come back as "1" in a binary prediction problem, but the "1" is not positive in both cases.

Another vocabulary choice to be aware of is that we'll use "privileged group," "favored group," and "majority group" mostly interchangeably. These labels are not meant to convey any judgment by the author or the readers regarding actual merit but are only meant to be descriptive and to recognize that historically a group has been favored, meaning that it has historically received some kind of privileged status that the disfavored group has not received. Note that the privileged group need not always be the majority group (history is rich with examples of numerically small groups amassing privileges), but if we do speak of a majority group, you can infer that the designation is also as a privileged group. This will simplify our language in coming chapters but is not meant to build in assumptions about actual merit, future merit, or (absent the designation of "majority") numerical representativeness.

Following is a laundry list of fairness metrics. These were chosen as a subset of what is offered through *AIF360*, an open source package on machine learning fairness that was recently released by IBM. At the time of writing, this is one of the most visible and comprehensive fairness packages, and for this reason we will focus heavily on this package in the next few chapters. We will also include other open source and DIY options, but it's good to recognize where the potential for a canon to emerge will come from, and AIF360 seems to offer one possibility.

Do Data Sets Contain Unbiased Correct Answers?

Interestingly, one way fairness definitions and metrics for fairness of data sets or algorithms differ is the extent to which we privilege the "right answer," indicated as an actual outcome in a data set. Some fairness metrics and interventions ensure that more accuracy does not reduce the degree of fairness indicated by a fairness metric, with the defense being that reflecting "true" outcomes should not be seen as antidiscriminatory. However, this justification holds only to the extent that we think such outcomes were not, in turn, influenced by discriminatory factors that should be accounted for when building fair ML models.

These metrics presuppose a label of some kind; that is, these are not metrics divorced from the labels we put on the data. These are not metrics in which I give you only individual characteristics that are all considered inputs. Rather, they assume that some characteristics are inputs and some are outputs. Then discrimination is indicated by the extent to which certain inputs—namely, the ones regarding a protected category—are related to outputs and the relative degree of "success" in different groups, as assessed by the label. The label, in turn, can refer to the predicted label output by an ML algorithm or to the real-world outcome, and we can look for bias in both cases. Such labels can come either from natural ones in the data or labels emitted from a model.

The following is a sample of popular antidiscrimination metrics. They are different mathematical measures of the disparity in outcomes that exists between two groups. In many cases these measures use the same information, but how they process that information has a different emphasis:

Balanced error rate for the disfavored group
    An overall decreasing error rate for an entire data set (or test set) can sometimes look quite satisfying but mask poor performance for minority groups. For this reason, the balanced error rate looks to weigh all groups equally, motivated by the idea that minorities should not be subject to higher error rates in whatever labels they receive from ML models simply because of their minority status. Since most loss metrics measuring accuracy weigh all data points equally, they will

automatically weigh the overall error rate for a minority group less than for the majority group. An error-focused metric will help flag this issue and offer a path to correction.

Disparate impact

This is a term taken from the legal literature that is also endowed with a technical definition. Disparate impact refers to the ratio of the rate of a positive outcome for the disfavored group to the rate of a positive outcome for the favored group. In the legal literature, discussed in more detail in Chapter 3, several US government departments have supported the 80% rule, which means that this ratio should be no lower than 0.8.

Difference in mean outcomes

Difference in mean outcomes is quite similar to disparate impact and uses the same metrics. Difference in mean outcomes looks at success rates (i.e., outcomes) for different groups, and computes the difference rather than the ratio. By this metric, a fairer outcome occurs when the difference in mean outcomes is close to 0, which is the equivalent to the disparate impact being close to 1. The difference in mean outcomes can also be applied directly to non-binary classifications, such as looking at the difference in mean credit score ratings or the difference in mean test scores per group within a protected class.

Equality of odds (and equality of opportunity)

Equality of odds and equality of opportunity are not so much a metric of fairness as one potential definition of fairness. Formally, equalized odds are achieved when the predicted target variable of a model and the label of a protected category are statistically independent of one another conditional on the true value of the target variable. In a binary classification task, this can be simplified to requiring that the true-positive rates and false-positive rates are equal across groups, where groups are determined by the protected category. A slightly less demanding fairness criterion is equality of opportunity, in which only the probability of the true positive is equalized across the various groupings of a protected category.

Statistical parity

For an accessible example of how two fairness metrics/definitions can both be compelling and intuitive but impossible to simultaneously satisfy, see Alexandra Chouldechova's famous paper,[5] in which she shows how a consistency metric emphasizing the importance for a score to mean the same thing for all the

---

5 Chouldechova, Alexandra. "Fair prediction with disparate impact: A study of bias in recidivism prediction instruments," *Big Data* 5, no. 2 (June 2017): 153–163. *https://www.andrew.cmu.edu/user/achoulde/files/dispa rate_impact.pdf.*

individuals with that score regardless of their protected membership status conflicts algebraically with the desire to equalize error rates across groups.

Delta between accuracy and a discrimination measure

This is not formally a fairness metric but can be used as a metric both to optimize for training and to indicate the relative fairness of a model. A strength of this metric is that it recognizes the tension between fairness and accuracy and to some extent leaves a model free to find a solution that is strong in terms of both. This recognizes that we want to maximize accuracy and minimize unfairness at the same time and effectively makes this a single metric. As discussed in earlier chapters, accuracy does have some claim on fairness considerations. After all, a model that is not accurate can easily become arbitrary and capricious as it is untethered to reality. Also, a model that is not accurate lacks a rationale for its very existence, even as it may be subjecting people to decisions that would be better made in a nonautomated fashion, again raising fairness concerns.

Differential fairness

This recently proposed metric for fairness is grounded in the differential privacy literature and recognizes the connection between the mathematics of privacy and of discrimination. Differential fairness takes a lead from differential privacy, which we will discuss later in this chapter. An epsilon term is used to put an upper bound on the probability differences for the favored and disfavored groups; these probabilities are in a ratio form, and the epsilon term describes how far from 1 the ratio is permitted to depart. The advantage of this definition is that it can apply to widely specified groups or narrowly specified groups.

Infra-Marginality and Intersectionality

In a widely cited paper, Foulds et al. explore another fairness assumption that can be different from "all groups are or should be equal."[6] They recognize that the sociologically naive way of looking at the world assumes that the world can be modeled as a level playing field so that differences in "merit" or scoring predictions between groups are considered legitimate and actionable. This is designated as the *infra-marginality principle*.

In contrast, *intersectional theory*, first formalized by third-wave feminism, now redeployed as a proposal for the technical fairness literature, recognizes that the distribution of merit itself is likely to be influenced by unfair social processes. What's more, intersectionality theory recognizes that the degree of unfairness is likely differential for different groups, and that combinations of group memberships can elicit more

---

6 Foulds, James R., et al. "An Intersectional Definition of Fairness." arXiv.org. September 10, 2019. *https://arxiv.org/abs/1807.08362.*

disparities in treatment than a simple addition of different discrimination penalties accounts for. That is, a combination of different discriminated-against identities may have some kind of supra-linear discriminatory effect on an individual (e.g., considering race with gender to notice particular harms to, say, black women).

Rationality measures of equity

To promote equity, however, we don't merely want to think about the potential for discrimination and the prevention thereof. We want more generally to measure whether a decision was sensible, or more formally whether it had a rational basis or was proportional. We can think about this in different ways. Here are some potential categories:

Accuracy

Most of the time it's safe to assume that ML models are developed with a view in mind to maximize accuracy. In reading this book, you have probably already recognized that accuracy need not and should not be the only measure of successfully training an ML model. Nonetheless, it's also worth noting that good accuracy should be regarded as an indicator of fairness—after all, we would not want to see the introduction of ML decision making that created poorer performance than that achieved with traditional systems, which usually entails human decision makers. Introducing a strictly worse system for everyone would represent its own form of unfairness—why should things get arbitrarily worse for everyone?

Consistency

Consistency is one measure of fairness that is not oriented toward group outcomes or equality. Rather, consistency is a check for arbitrariness, and recognizes that in any individual group we can imagine that the members of a favored and a disfavored group within a data set are not necessarily equal. For example, it could be that one group has features that make it highly correlated with desirable attributes. A common example is comparing women in New York City, who are unlikely to have a commercial truck driver's license, with white men in a Midwestern state, where the base rate of having a commercial truck driving license is much higher. If we were to ignore these underlying correlations, we could very well end up with a model too strongly favoring statistical parity. One way we could likely identify this would be a consistency check. Consistency is commonly established by an individually driven methodology, such as a nearest-neighbors metric. The logic here is that individuals who are near one another in the input space should have consistent outcomes, which seems fair in the sense that individuals should be treated as individuals, not merely members of a group. It also enhances fairness in the sense of producing outcomes that are not arbitrary.

Explainability

Explainability is a term used to indicate to what extent a human can understand the internal workings or outcomes from an algorithm. The term has no standard definition, and one of the struggles for researchers who aim to study explainability and to develop explanation techniques for models is that what constitutes a good explanation can heavily depend on context. Chapter 8 is devoted to explainability and discusses some potential metrics. Here, the important features are as follows. Many explainability metrics focus on the human recipients of the explanation, and these can then vary along several axes, including subjective assessments such as how satisfied humans report themselves being with the explanation provided, as well as objective assessments such as how well humans can predict future outputs of an algorithm based on having read an explanation.

Measures of Privacy

Measures of privacy have a longer quantitative history than do measures of fairness, because it has been clear to both industry and academia for quite a while that data analytics and scientific research alike required the development of techniques to enable research while protecting individuals. Toward this end, both legal and technical guidance are long-standing although not absolute when it comes to measures of privacy.

It is interesting to see how privacy concerns have emerged in a wide variety of industry and research areas. A few such areas that are relevant to the modern data scientist are listed next, but there are no limits to where privacy can be implicated, given the ubiquity of technology and sensors in modern life.

Location data

Determining an individual's location or moves as indicated by anything from web browsing to sensors on automobiles to communications from smartphones. Such information could be of high value to police or advertisers, particularly when it may even reveal precise home and work locations.

Social connection data

Determining an individual's identity in an anonymized set of social data or determining an individual's likely social connections, considered private, from publicly available information. Such information could be of high value to police, advertisers, or potential employers.

Medical data

Determining information related to an individual's health or wellness habits through a variety of sources, including anything from lists of prescription information sold by pharmacies to mobile analytics related to healthcare apps to information about someone's shopping and eating habits. Such information can be sought out by life insurance companies or even by potential employers.

Recent laws have recognized two ways of dealing with privacy in data sets: anonymization and pseudonymization. Anonymization is the process of removing personally identifiable information from a data set, either through encryption, removing, or obscuring the data. However, the technical and legal bar for true anonymization is incredibly high and also a moving target (*https://perma.cc/Y9FP-HUJR*). For example, as big data has emerged in recent decades, it has become but even common knowledge that relatively few identifiers are needed to pinpoint a specific individual in seemingly anonymized data sets (*https://perma.cc/V5TA-QZN5*). We will discuss anonymization more extensively in the following section.

Pseudonymization modifies data by replacing values or labels by artificial, that is, pseudonymous, replacements. For example, in a data set including hometown, I might replace "New York City" with "City12," in a way that should not be too transparent (e.g., "BigApple" would not be acceptable). The data that is targeted for pseudonymization in order to comply with legal requirements is the data most likely to be available in public data sets that could be used to identify someone. The choice is subject to uncertainty and different opinions, but some common examples of personally identifiable information that would be likely pseudonymized would include postal codes, birth dates, and names.

There are many advantages of pseudonymization from the perspective of researchers and data engineers alike. First, it is a simpler process than anonymization, boiling down to many FIND→REPLACE operations. Second, it preserves all the links within the data, so there aren't concerns about information loss. However, this second point also highlights one of the major weaknesses of pseudonymization, which is that as all information and connections are preserved, there is more of a chance than with anonymization that an individual's record could be identified. For this reason, pseudonymized data is still considered personal data for legal purposes, most notably under the General Data Protection Regulation (GDPR) of the European Union, as described in this blog post (*https://perma.cc/Y9FP-HUJR*). However, it can be used more liberally than untreated personal information.

As with fairness, there are many measures of privacy, and we will not cover them all. But now we will cover some of the more popular options as represented in recent literature, research, and industry practice. A recent review has offered a helpful taxonomy based on four features of a privacy metric:[7]

Adversary models
> Assumed capabilities of the adversary (that is, the one seeking to extract private information)

---

7 Wagner, Isabel and David Eckhoff, "Technical Privacy Metrics: A Systematic Survey," *ACM Computing Surveys* 51, no. 3, 2018, *https://perma.cc/9NR6-L83G*.

Data sources
> Postulated method for an adversary to obtain outside information that would assist in obtaining the private information

Inputs
> Information used by the private metric to make a quantitative assessment

Class of output measure
> Describes how the *loss* or infringement of privacy is assessed

It can be helpful to keep these in mind while reading to orient our discussion in the much larger landscape we cannot cover here. It is also interesting to consider the class of output measures, to understand the many ways of describing privacy. These are listed in the survey as follows:

- Uncertainty
- Information gain/loss
- Indistinguishability
- Adversary's probability of success
- Accuracy/precision
- Time
- Error
- Data similarity

When thinking about what should constitute a privacy metric, there is not a uniform consensus yet. However, the academic literature points us to a few important considerations. Over time, some of the ideas put forward for a useful privacy metric have included the following:

- Privacy metrics should be understandable by mathematically adept laypeople.
- Privacy metrics should be independent of cost-based or utility-based measures of data or modeling pipelines.
- Privacy metrics should provide bounding information about worst-case scenarios of what an adversary could achieve.
- Privacy metrics should give an indication of how hard an adversary would have to work to achieve the worst-case/maximal possible privacy invasion.
- Privacy metrics should offer probability-like assessments regarding the probability that specific attributes can be compromised.

As with fairness, there is no easy or guaranteed best privacy metric. For this reason, our selection of a privacy metric, as with our selection of a fairness metric, is as much a normative question as it is a technical one.

Technical measures of privacy protection

There are quite a few measures of privacy protection. For example, the review mentioned previously (*https://perma.cc/9NR6-L83G*) identified more than 80 different published metrics for privacy, breaking them down into distinct groups based on their assumptions regarding privacy and domains of application:

Data similarity

Data similarity metrics derive a privacy metric purely from the features and structure of a data set and so are independent of how data is used or what kind of adversary might attack. These metrics are only applied in the case of data sets, such as in data sanitization or preparations for publication of a data set. One of the methods discussed in some detail later, *k-anonymity*, belongs to this class of privacy metric.

Indistinguishability

Indistinguishability metrics measure whether an adversary can distinguish between two entities, be they entities in a communication or sensitive labels in a data set. One of the methods discussed in some detail later, *differential privacy*, belongs to this class of privacy metric. These methods are often the ones associated with formal privacy guarantees.

Adversary's success probability

In general, the idea of this metric is to recognize that a hostile party of some kind would be the concerning entity with respect to potential privacy failings. For this reason, the idea of an *adversary* is a general technical one in which a hostile party with specific capabilities, knowledge, and access to related tools or resources is assumed. Metrics based on an adversary's success probability are considered very general forms of privacy metric, but also ones that clearly depend strongly on the assumptions made regarding an adversary. They also depend on how success is defined, which can make this category of privacy metric overlap with the others discussed. So long as an adversary can be defined, this metric can apply, be it to a communications system or a database.

Uncertainty

Uncertainty metrics operate on the basis that uncertainty serves as an obstacle to breaching privacy. The assumption motivating this form of privacy metric is that privacy is greater when an adversary has greater uncertainty. If an adversary is uncertain in their estimate, they are limited in their violation of privacy. For example, in the case of location tracking, an uncertainty metric would indicate the degree of error in an adversary's estimate of someone's location or the degree of error in an adversary separating out individuals from one another based on location. Entropic measures, that is, measures of a lack of predictability or order in a system, are also associated with uncertainty as a privacy measure. Uncertainty measures have primarily been applied in communications systems and location-tracking applications.

Information gain

Information gain (or loss) metrics measure how much information an adversary can gain (or lose). The assumption is that privacy is higher when an adversary gains less information. Information gain metrics are different from uncertainty metrics in that information gain metrics can explicitly consider the amount of prior information available to an adversary rather than looking at the adversary's posterior estimates. Information gain metrics are useful among a wide variety of contexts, ranging from databases and communications systems to social networks, smart metering, and genome privacy.

Time

Time-oriented privacy metrics define time as the currency most important in assessing the success of an adversary. In these metrics, the working assumption can sometimes be that privacy-enhancing techniques will inevitably fail, so the important metric is how much time an adversary would have to invest for privacy protections to fail. These metrics have largely been used in communications and location domains.

Accuracy/precision

Accuracy-oriented privacy metrics are grounded in the assumption that, the greater the accuracy of an adversary's estimate, the greater the privacy infraction that has resulted. Inaccurate estimations clearly lead to greater privacy than accurate estimations, although the accuracy of an adversary's estimate should not be conflated with the certainty or correctness of that estimate (hence the separate class of uncertainty-oriented metrics already discussed). These metrics have primarily been deployed so far in location tracking but are also applicable to data sets and communications systems.

Next we discuss two widely used privacy measures, k-anonymity and ε-differential privacy. *k-anonymity* describes data sets, while *ε-differential privacy* describes algorithms that operate on data.

k-anonymity.   One of the most well-known measures of privacy is *k-anonymity* (*https://perma.cc/Y6LE-3YCL*), which falls under the rubric of similarity-based privacy measures. A data set has k-anonymity if the information about any given individual in the data set cannot be distinguished from at least $k - 1$ other individuals present in the set.

Imagine a researcher is studying how patterns emerge in the geography of a region, as related to sexual orientation. The researcher wants to look for evidence that people relocate depending on their sexual orientation (let's hope there are ethical reasons for doing this research—another concern I'll discuss later). The researcher wants to publish a paper based on their findings, and the prestigious journal in which the research has been accepted requires that they disclose the underlying data set so others can verify the analysis. The journal also requires that the researcher do so in a way that protects research subjects.

A subsample of the researcher's data, including all subjects who were in Smallville and Biggerville within the region studied, appears in Table 2-1.

Table 2-1. Study data

ID #	Age	Town	Heterosexual?
132	33	Smallville	Yes
244	33	Biggerville	No
112	35	Smallville	Yes
983	27	Biggerville	Yes

Let's imagine I knew that a particular person, Joe Smith, aged 33 and living in Smallville, had participated in the study. If the data set were released as it is—even without names—I would have information about Joe Smith's sexual orientation, information that most agree should be private and disclosed only by Joe himself.

The researchers releasing this data set want to have at least 2-anonymity with respect to Age and Town precisely to give some measure of protection to research participants, because such situations actually do arise in the real world. That means that for any given age and town combination, any individual should be indistinguishable from at least $2 - 1 = 1$ other individual in the data set.

How can we achieve this? We have two means to obtain k-anonymity from data that lacks this feature: suppression and generalization. *Suppression* modifies data sets to produce k-anonymity by taking away some data in a column so that it's not available. If we wanted to use suppression to work toward 2-anonymity for the subset of data, we might consider suppressing the town information for the two 33-year-olds in the data to make their information indistinguishable by Age and Town, as shown in Table 2-2.

Table 2-2. Modified study data

ID #	Age	Town	Heterosexual?
132	33	*	Yes
244	33	*	No
112	35	Smallville	Yes
983	27	Biggerville	Yes

Note that this produces some measure of anonymity to those two individuals, but we have not protected the 35-year-old and 27-year-old with this modification. We would have to continue inspecting the data set to ensure 2-anonymity for all individuals in the data set.

Also, this suppression of location data is not very satisfying, given the described purpose of the study. Suppressing this information reduces the informativeness of the data set in a way core to its original purpose.

Let's consider the other option, generalization. One way to generalize the data set would be to bin the age information because it is part of what is so revealing. We could consider modifying the data set so that only the leading digit of the age was available, as shown in Table 2-3.

Table 2-3. Modified study data

ID #	Age (by decade)	Town	Heterosexual?
132	30s	Smallville	Yes
244	30s	Biggerville	No
112	30s	Smallville	Yes
983	20s	Biggerville	Yes

Notice that now the two individuals living in Smallville have indistinguishable ages, so individual 132 is indistinguishable from individual 112 when we generalize information. In contrast, when we used suppression of information, it was individual 244 who was indistinguishable from individual 132.

Let's continue our focus on the two individuals indistinguishable from one another in this modification, 132 and 112. Remember, the purpose of this anonymization is to protect information about the sexual orientation of individual research participants. Have we accomplished this in the generalization modification scenario?

No, we have not. Look at the sexual orientation column. Both individuals are marked as Yes for whether they are heterosexual. This means that if an individual was known to live in Smallville and to have participated in this study (again, assuming that Table 2-3 is the totality of information in the data set related to Smallville and Biggerville), that individual's sexual orientation has been revealed.

Even this simple example has probably shown you just how difficult it can be to ensure that a data set is k-anonymous, even for a small value of k. In fact, it has been shown that finding the optimal k-anonymization of a data set is NP hard (*https://perma.cc/76NA-8BV3*). Nonetheless, achieving some k-anonymization of a data set can be done even as quickly as O(log k) (*https://perma.cc/YJ3U-KETU*).

Python Modules for k-Anonymization

Unfortunately, k-anonymization has not come into the mainstream enough for a typical Python module solution to exist, but here are some potential solutions:

- k-anonymity (*https://oreil.ly/UBq0z*)
- Mondrian (*https://oreil.ly/YvQOb*)
- Clustering-based k-anonymity (*https://oreil.ly/PEtX7*)
- Python Datafly (*https://oreil.ly/rcjEO*)

NP Hard Problems and Optimization

NP hard is a computer science term that denotes those problems that are at least as hard as any problem that is *NP*. *NP* problems, in turn, are those for which a solution is not found in polynomial time but for which a provided solution can be verified in polynomial time.

This is relevant in the fairness literature only to the extent that you see problems designed as *NP* or *NP hard*, in which case you need to understand that likely proposed solutions will be heuristics that are usually not guaranteed to produce an optimal outcome. In such cases, you will likely see studies that a particular heuristic produces a reasonable outcome in reasonable time.

Unfortunately, many cutting-edge solutions freely posted are written in MATLAB or Java,[8] whereas this book aims to give more-accessible resources via Python. Hopefully in the near future we will see a privacy package similar in scope, documentation, and user base to popular data analysis packages. I fully expect this to be the case, as good privacy practices are fundamental to ethical data analysis.

k-anonymity is only one of many privacy metrics. It is a widely used metric, in part because it is easy to understand and because it is reasonably efficient to generate a k-anonymous data set. Likely for this reason, k-anonymity is also routinely applied as new privacy domains emerge, as a standard, if simple, workhorse. Many variations of

---

8 See, for example, this post on Twitter (*https://oreil.ly/b-Jb1*).

k-anonymity improve on the computational performance and privacy protections of the base definition.

However, some criticisms can include very serious concerns about the application of k-anonymity, which is generally applied when a data set is intended for release. Because k-anonymity does not provide property hiding, it can be insufficient as a privacy protection, especially when a data set can be correlated with other public information. Also, k-anonymity does not offer any privacy protection in the case of multiple releases of the same data set, as different k-anonymous treatments of the same data set, released separately, may offer opportunities to identify private information because the groups of indistinguishable individuals can be different in different releases.

Differential privacy. Another widely used and accessible privacy metric is *differential privacy*, which falls under the rubric of indistinguishability-oriented privacy metrics. The intuition behind differential privacy is that a differential private algorithm applied to a data set (for example, some kind of aggregating SQL query), should look the same regardless of whether a specific data point is included in the data set.

Importantly, differential privacy is a definition that applies to actions undertaken with data rather than to a data set itself. So while a data release might be subject to k-anonymity as a privacy requirement, differential privacy could not be a requirement for a data set release. Rather, differential privacy could be a requirement for computing an average value on a given data set or even something as complex as training a neural network on that data set. An algorithm is differentially private if it is not possible to tell whether a specific data point was used in the computation of the output.

In mathematical notation, ε-differential privacy is described like this:

$$priv_{DP} \equiv \forall S \subseteq Range(K) : p(K(D1) \in S) \leq exp(\epsilon) \cdot p(K(D2) \in S)$$

This equation was first introduced in Dwork et al.'s widely cited paper,[9] and this concept has become important in the privacy literature. Regarding the ϵ value to use, the values are variable and range in a sample of publications from 0.01 to 100.

Usually, differential privacy is engineered by adding noise to outputs of algorithms. In particular, the Laplace mechanism is a common way of doing this, and while the details are beyond the scope of this discussion, they can easily be found in the previously referenced paper and with a broader internet search.

---

9 Dwork, Cynthia, et al. "Calibrating Noise to Sensitivity in Private Data Analysis." In Theory of Cryptography: Third Theory of Cryptography Conference, TCC 2006, edited by Shai Halevi and Tal Rabin. Berlin: Springer, 2006. *https://perma.cc/2TLX-GTJU.*

The availability of differential privacy tools is excellent both in Python and in other languages and use cases.[10] For example, many libraries are specialized for a particular domain, such as differential privacy for SQL queries or differential privacy for training neural networks. In some but not all cases, these tools add minimal computational burden as compared to not using the tools, while in other cases, particularly deep learning, the design of differentially private training mechanisms that do not place a heavy additional computational burden remains challenging.

The benefits of differential privacy are substantial. One important factor is that differential privacy is composable in both sequential and parallel use cases, which means that if an algorithm has a differential privacy guarantee, it can be put in sequence or in parallel to other algorithms with a differential privacy guarantee, and these algorithms can also guarantee differential privacy. The overall number of algorithms in serial or parallel must be finite; that is, the differentially private algorithms cannot be run in an open-ended and unlimited fashion.

Differential privacy is not perfect. For example, the guarantees of differential privacy do not hold in the case of correlated data, such as that coming from social networks. Differential privacy is a topic under active research and use in theoretical academia, industry, and even legal issues related to privacy.

As with every other fairness intervention and technical description, differential privacy provides a way to improve or even guarantee certain forms of fairness properties. However, again, nothing is a panacea that will produce perfect results. Your use of differential privacy and the appropriate settings for a use case will need to depend on domain knowledge and a case study of your product.

Human measures of privacy protection

In addition to the technical metrics described previously, organizational metrics are also relevant to privacy. These should interest you even if they are not within your job's domain, because you should contribute to a culture of privacy awareness at your organization. Some examples of privacy metrics relating to human resources and organization that are relevant include the following:

- Length of time between onboarding new technical employees and their completion of organization-specific privacy training
- Length of time delay in responding to reports of potential privacy infringements in a data repository or analysis pipeline

---

10 See IBM's differential privacy library (*https://oreil.ly/md8Qi*), this independent Python package with multiple differential privacy algorithm implementations (*https://oreil.ly/MJ8bB*), and TensorFlow's differential privacy functionality (*https://oreil.ly/TRMCF*).

- Percentage of technical staff with access to private data
- Percentage of data repositories or analysis pipelines with enhanced privacy measures, such as encryption or anonymization capabilities built into the technical solutions
- Number and frequency of privacy audits

More information can be found in and ideas gleaned from security professional compliance guides.

Measures of Security

Security is linked to but distinct from privacy. For our purposes here, we can think of security as being more concerned with the content of information rather than identification tasks accomplished with that information.

Security is the oldest and most well-documented and well-regulated aspect of fairness concerns implicated by big data, machine learning, and all the other accoutrements of modern data ecosystems. Information security is also probably the most well-developed commercially. For example, there are even cybersecurity policies to protect organizations from the economic consequences of security breaches.

As with equity and privacy, the practice of security is very much an ongoing battle and one with normative components as well as engineering prescriptions.

When determining the kinds of metrics to apply to monitor security practices, one summary of desirable attributes is SMART (*https://perma.cc/6XFY-ZCMJ*):

- Specific
- Measurable
- Attainable
- Repeatable
- Time-dependent

These attributes and their desirability seem largely self-explanatory, although it's worth taking a moment to consider the last one, time-dependent. This attribute stresses that metrics should not simply be descriptions of an overall system but rather opportunities to gauge the quality of a system at a particular moment in time. Measuring the quality of a system is important in order to evaluate performance over time, detect faults, and drive improvements and progress rather than permitting stasis.

As with privacy, many measures of security are highly contextual and organizationally dependent. This is especially important for security because it is a sociotechnical problem, not merely an engineering problem. As is well-known, the greatest security threat to technical systems tends to be humans, at either the level of the user (*https://perma.cc/53GS-H37R*) or the designer (*https://perma.cc/ELR2-V7LJ*) of technology. For this reason, social engineering remains the largest threat and most common tactic for would-be adversaries.

Connected Concepts

So far, the only definition I've given you of fairness globally is to say that, for the purposes of this book, we'll treat it as representing three specific values: equity, privacy, and security. One of the ways we can see that these topics all should come under an umbrella term, such as fairness, is that they are all inextricably linked to one another, sometimes even mathematically and in terms of ML model performance.

For this reason, I'll briefly highlight important ways in which these concepts are connected. In many cases, the connections can be expressed as a trade-off—namely, that given two fairness values A and B, the action of enhancing A tends to reduce B, and vice versa. Such trade-offs should not be taken as a mathematical inevitability, as often we have no mathematical proof as such. Rather, these are rules of thumb gleaned from experience and often insurmountable. However, we can hope that future fairness research will find ways to simultaneously enhance values that sometimes appear to be at odds with one another.

Privacy and Security

Anyone reading this book is likely familiar with the mass surveillance that the US undertook in the years after the 9/11 attacks. At the time, such surveillance (once it was discovered…because the government did not willingly disclose the extent of the program) was argued to be justified on the basis that "only" metadata (*https://perma.cc/6TE9-CWSK*), rather than content data, was collected. What's more, the program's defenders argued, computers rather than people were monitoring this electronc metadata, so the data collection was not an incursion into privacy at all (*https://perma.cc/L726-TFZ4*).

The public was underwhelmed with these justifications, and over time any public support for such programs that might have existed has tended to erode. This debate, however, does make clear a connection between privacy and security. At the limit of no privacy, we would almost surely have greater safety, as our government could observe in real time plans by bad actors. (Of course, a host of other problems would arise, such as the fundamental harm to human dignity and autonomy done by constant surveillance and the opportunities for abuse offered to the government. I am not endorsing this as a security regime, but pointing out the trade-off between privacy and security that sometimes exists in the real world. However, this trade-off doesn't tend to be nearly as extreme or important as some totalitarian governments like to argue is the case.) On the other hand, at the limit of complete privacy and no surveillance, there might be very little security. For example, imagine if any individual could board an airplane, buy a weapon, or travel across international boundaries no matter how many strong indicators they had already given of evil intentions and ability to do harm. Neither of these extremes is appealing to most people. This is a commonly recognized trade-off in balancing two fundamental values, privacy and security. Almost every human society has chosen an approach that is not at one of the extreme ends of the spectrum.

Privacy and Equity

Very early in the short history of concerns about fair ML, researchers noted that privacy, a long-standing concern for engineers, could be repurposed for thinking about discrimination. In particular, researchers noted that if protected attributes could be discovered through the behavior of a model that wasn't supposed to be discriminatory, that tended to suggest that the model was nonetheless ferreting out prohibited information.

Just as privacy attacks try to discover information that is not supposed to be discoverable or accessible by an adversary, people could similarly ask whether they could discover information about, say, race or gender from the output of a model that wasn't supposed to factor either attribute into an outcome. If such information was discoverable, that strongly suggested some kind of discriminatory behavior in the same way that private information being discoverable showed a privacy failure in a model. For this reason, academic research has repurposed privacy methods to be used in fairness and antidiscrimination research (*https://perma.cc/LN76-W4PF*).

Another interesting connection between the two is that they may sometimes be at odds. For example, recent research has noted that models trained with privacy protections may exacerbate undesirable discriminatory behavior relative to baseline models produced without privacy protections (*https://perma.cc/6HNG-C54Z*). This is a relatively new and not-well-understood phenomenon, but keep it in mind as an example of fairness values that may be in tension and require executive decision making and transparency regarding how different values have been prioritized depending on a use case.

Equality and Security

Equality has a strong connection to security, despite a lack of emphasis on this connection. Recent events with the Black Lives Matter movement and investigations into racial or gender bias of AI products used by security forces has begun to bring this connection into greater relief. Notably, as will not have escaped anyone's attention who has been watching the news, certain groups of people, especially black men, are far more at risk of violence at the hands of the police than are other groups of Americans. Hence, audits and metrics that have to date looked mostly at population-level numbers are missing a key indicator: highly variable effects depending on subgroup membership. Likewise, data scientists and machine learning engineers should be asking about differential effects on minority populations with respect to security in ML products. When assessing whether a product is safe, that assessment should factor in the underlying heterogeneity of the user base and of those who could come into contact with a product.

Consider another example: the use of smart home devices in the emerging world of IoT products. They may sound like neutral devices that should generally serve to enhance security. However, the reality on the ground is different. Such IoT devices have been found to be deployed to enable domestic abuse, and unfortunately, because such a use case was largely unanticipated, often the device makers and software suppliers are not able to offer a ready fix or protection. Again, this is an example of a product that when initially offered seemed to enhance security but for some important minority group (namely, victims of domestic abuse) has been quite the opposite.

In 2020 and beyond, as movements to raise awareness about inequality in security continue, it is likely, and I very much hope, that these issues will gain more attention from technologists. Keep this connection in mind, particularly when you are thinking of security as measured by impact on downstream users.

Accuracy and Fairness

Sometimes greater accuracy in a model can lead to greater unfairness. This is why sometimes unfair practices creep in, even unintentionally, because they improve accuracy. For example, adding race to a model can often make it more accurate, in the sense of being more predictive. Whether this is fair, however, is another question altogether and a controversial one, depending on the domain.

This accuracy-fairness trade-off also complicates reasoning about how and when you should take different technical measures to ensure fairness. For example, in the US we as a society feel comfortable saying that banks should not be allowed to use race or gender to make decisions and extend credit to individuals, even if this information may be predictive. For this reason, we have laws such as the Equal Credit Opportunity Act (*https://perma.cc/VTY9-D26B*), which explicitly forbids discrimination in lending. In fact, the decisions about credit are interesting because, in reality, when a bank officer meets with an applicant in person (or merely sees an applicant's name), the officer may infer the applicant's race and discriminate (whether the inference matches the applicant's identity or not). That information, inferred or not, shouldn't influence bank decisions. Therefore it might seem cleaner to keep forbidden outputs out of algorithms. Note that this itself isn't enough to prevent algorithmic discrimination, as we will see in the next chapter.

We can, however, also imagine that sometimes a racial input into an algorithm isn't just acceptable but even desirable. For example, different racial groups in the US show very different incidences of a variety of illnesses, such as cancer (*https://perma.cc/77LG-AJHU*) or heart disease (*https://perma.cc/B9HN-DN8Z*). Gender differences are also quite common on health indicators (*https://perma.cc/8ZSJ-GFR4*). So we could even regard *omitting* race and gender variables as unfair.[11]

One consideration from a technical perspective is to study the extent to which a trade-off is at all necessary between accuracy and fairness values. For example, some have posited a tension between antibias measures and accuracy, as reducing bias tends to reduce accuracy. While there is a variance-accuracy trade-off (*https://perma.cc/AS7C-M8HJ*) (one way of seeing a bias-accuracy trade-off), the trade-off doesn't need to be a statistically inevitable exchange. Rather, researchers have found that smart ways of removing bias from a data science pipeline can have minimal effects on accuracy, although what balance to strike will likely be application specific. Figure 2-1 is an example.

classifier	No pre-processing		0.10-correction	
	accuracy	0.10-discr.	accuracy	0.10-discr.
C4.5	85.60%	4.24%	84.94%	1.07%
Naïve Bayes	82.46%	4.06%	82.33%	2.23%
Logistic	85.28%	6.61%	84.70%	0.61%
RIPPER	84.42%	5.24%	83.98%	3.94%
PART	85.20%	12.62%	84.00%	2.3%

Only the training set changes, the testing set is fixed

Accuracy shows a small decrease

0.10-discrimination reduces substantially

Figure 2-1. Reducing discrimination without a large accuracy cost[12]

These statistics are four years old, and in some cases have been improved upon, but performance will inevitably depend on the techniques under investigation and the particularities of a data set. These statistics show, however, that any costs to accuracy or other KPIs traditionally measured for ML products need not suffer strong performance decreases as fairness is introduced more prominently into ML design and training.

---

11 The medical community is not shy about using race and gender in almost all research precisely because these indicators are so important to accuracy in the biomedical context.

12 Source: Sara Hajian, Francesco Bonchi, and Carlos Castillo, "Algorithmic Bias: From Discrimination Discovery to Fairness-Aware Data Mining," KDD Tutorial, 2016.

Automated Fairness?

A fundamental question that should be asked when considering fairness in ML is whether an algorithmic solution makes sense *at all* in a given context, and if so, what is the current reality as compared to what we might aspire to long-term.

We can also ask whether we'll ever find a catchall solution for fairness, something like an "autofair" package we could just deploy automatically.

Unfortunately the answer is no. Per the "no free lunch" theorem popularly cited in model-selection discussions, no particular algorithm will suit all fairness concerns and applications simultaneously. What's more, understanding what constitutes unfairness and where it is likely to creep into a particular modeling problem is quite domain driven. This enhances the difficulties already known from the no free lunch theorem.[13]

What's more, the current best practices in fairness have known downsides. Most fairness-enhancing algorithms satisfy one specific or a few specific fairness definitions, and never simultaneously because as has been discussed and will be discussed again, many fairness definitions are at odds with one another. Most fairness algorithms target a binary label, and there is insufficient work available for problems of regression or natural language processing, to name just two other important areas of supervised learning. Most fairness algorithms are not especially scalable and are not specialized to cases of high-dimensional data. Most fairness algorithms are not constructed to respond to particular fairness problems associated with data generation or labeling, and they cannot distinguish between different mechanisms that generated unfairness in the first place. Algorithmic interventions into bias are not able to effectively correct unfairness that occurs upstream, and can at most serve as a Band-Aid unless integrated into a feedback loop, which for the moment is quite rare.

Checklist of Points of Entry for Fairness in the Data Science Pipeline

We will be filling in the details of this checklist as we move through the book. For now, this chapter has established some normative goals and related technical and organizational metrics to consider incorporating into ML pipelines and R&D processes.

Here is a beginning list of how fairness goals and metrics can interact with a data science pipeline concretely. The list is compiled in the form of questions you can ask

---

13 Special thanks to IBM staff member Kush Varshney, who has often provided helpful commentary on the AIF360 open source project's associated Slack channel regarding overviews of algorithmic fairness efforts.

yourself for each stage of the pipeline with which you are involved or offering feedback. You should consider this list just a start that you can build on with other chapters of this book but also with wider reading and considerations of your organization's specific workflow and organizational structure:

Assembling a Data Set

- Data collection

  — If you obtain data via your own measurements, how will you avoid data practices that can lead to collecting unfair data or collecting data in an unfair manner? Think about bias but also about privacy and normal expectations of those about whom you are collecting data.

  — If you obtain data from another organization, how will you ensure that their data collection practices respect equity, privacy, and security norms?

  — If you are translating analog data to digital values, how can you do this without introducing unfair artifacts?

- Data input

  — When you prepare data for input into an analysis or modeling pipeline, you will usually do some form of pre-processing. How will you ensure that pre-processing does not erase information needed for fairness awareness and assessments?

  — How will you make the data sources selected and not selected transparent to downstream users so they understand any fairness implications of data selection?

- Access permissioning

  — Who will have access to the data, and is this consistent with the legal and ethical requirements, given the source of a data set and the nature of the information in that data set?

  — How should you balance the privacy and security costs of wider data access against the greater utility gained by expanding access to a data set?

  — Can reasonable pre-processing be done on data to enhance fairness in the case of wide distribution and access of data sets within your organization?

- Storage and retention

  — Given privacy considerations, should diverse data sets be stored together? Could fairness implications arise from keeping data together, particularly with respect to privacy?

  — Is some data publicly available and hence subject to lower consideration regarding privacy and security? Even in this case, does the proposed form of storage create enhanced risks of data distribution or linking of diverse data sets?

— What are the legal and ethical requirements regarding how long you should retain your data?

- Documentation and training

— How can data documentation prevent misuse downstream in the analysis or ML pipeline?

— How can data documentation prevent subsequent misuse over time, accounting for turnover in staff, forgetfulness, and mislaying of original intentions?

— How can data documentation highlight fairness considerations that should guide future permissioning and data storage issues to ensure a uniformly implemented and respected data policy?

Modeling

- The analytical goal

— Does the goal make sense from a fairness standpoint? If you succeed at your modeling task, is that a good thing?

— Is the data you have sufficient to achieve your real goal, or do you run the risk of choosing an *easy* goal that doesn't map onto the problem that actually needs solving?

- Exploratory analysis

— Do you run the risk of browsing data in too individualized a form during the course of your data exploration?

— How will you ensure you don't go fishing? That is, how do you perform a principled investigation rather than opportunistic data mining for any correlations and relationships your data set may offer? This latter is a problem because in many real-world data sets you are just as likely to find a proxy for membership in a protected category as you are a real causal input that logically and empirically is a justified predictor for the outcome of interest on its own merits.

- Choosing a model

— Does your model represent the right level of complexity and explainability for the use case you would like to make?

- Training a model

— Does your model use an appropriate loss function that represents not just the accuracy of what you would like to determine but also other important values?

- Appropriate inputs

— Was the current use case one that could have been reasonably anticipated when people gave consent to the use of that data?

- Evaluating a model
  - Is your model discriminatory?
  - Does your model leak information?
  - Does your model's output make sense?
  - Is your model sufficiently robust to withstand potential security threats?
- Deploying to production
  - How will you describe your model and incorporate it into use cases?
  - What is the appropriate level of consent to obtain from anyone subject to this model?
- Maintenance
  - How long before your model gets stale?
  - What kind of ongoing metrics do you need in order to ensure your model continues to be fair?

Interface

- Design
  - Have you minimized the opportunity for misuse of the product, given a set of diverse and informed perspectives regarding the likely state of the market and potential bad actors who could acquire your product?
  - Have you designed a product that will enhance the well-being of downstream customers but also those who may be analyzed or affected by the product, possibly without their knowledge or consent?
  - Does your product have a fair end goal? Should your product be built?
- The sales pitch and responsible disclosures
  - Are you pitching your product in a way that promotes fair use of the product?
  - Are you pitching your product in a way that minimizes the possibility for misunderstanding the limitations of the product?
- Disclosures
  - Are your data and modeling practices described in a manner that makes the fairness-related elements clear to a layperson?
  - Are your disclosures at various points along your development line, from data collection onward, consistent as well as transparent?

- Use
  - Do you have a system to understand how your product is used over time so you can identify unanticipated fairness problems that may surface in the market?
  - Do you provide a clear and direct way for downstream users or third parties to contact you about fairness concerns or clarify questions regarding your product?

Concluding Remarks

This chapter introduced key concepts and measures in three aspects of fairness: equity, privacy, and security. In some cases these measures reflected technical indicators of quality or performance, while in other cases the measures are organizational level and can provide indicators for a particular organization to improve on over time. The goal was to formalize notions of fairness so that they can be operationalized in subsequent chapters. Finally, the chapter concluded with a preliminary checklist to recognize how broad fairness concerns affect all aspects of the ML pipeline and more generally all aspects of product development.

The next chapter transitions to a focus on one specific portion of the ML pipeline: the identification and gathering of data. This will be done with an awareness of the metrics and concepts already presented in this chapter.

## CHAPTER 3

Fair Data

The choice of what data to use in developing algorithmic and machine learning code is important and will likely continue to be important long into the future. This chapter considers what it means for a data set to be fair and how to identify aspects of a data set that can be problematic for fairness.

In our discussion we will stick to two main themes throughout. First is the concern about *garbage in, garbage out*, which I'll call the *fidelity concern*. An example is building an algorithm for college admissions decisions that is based on students' grades and names that had been mixed up in the data set, creating false information and likely leading to an unrealistic and faulty algorithm. Second is the concern about whether data was obtained in a way consistent with fair play, which I'll call the *provenance concern*. An example is a psychiatrist selling the names of depressed patients to a marketing agency after obtaining these names through their own practice of medicine. If you were a data scientist working in a marketing firm, you probably wouldn't (and shouldn't) feel comfortable using such data once you knew where it had come from.

The fidelity concern is what most people think about when terms like *data integrity* are thrown around. The concern need not have anything to do with fairness. For reasons related to the bottom line, most businesses care about data quality because they want accurate algorithmic products, and accurate algorithms generally require high-quality data. Fidelity is important for fairness concerns too. It's not fair to release products into the wild if those products have been trained on shabby and likely inaccurate data. More specifically, such algorithmic products are unlikely to reflect equity and security concerns.

However, our fidelity concerns go even further than this. We also want to know whether the data set represents a situation we would want our model to reproduce. This is not always the case with data sets measured in the real world, so we want to see how our data set might deviate from desirable outcomes and be aware of these limitations. For this reason, addressing the fidelity concerns requires us to identify aspects of the data set true to the world but inconsistent with our fairness ideals.

The provenance concern relates to consent and the appropriateness of having access to particular data, given how the data was collected. The collection of metadata regarding use patterns of digital products and the concomitant experimentation on human users of products through practices such as A/B testing represent an unparalleled incursion into the world of research by amateurs, most of whom have never sat through a research ethics course or otherwise considered the nuances of notice and consent as applied to ordinary people going about their lives.

It's worth noting that the sorts of A/B testing that junior data scientists assist with used to be the province of a much smaller group of people, who were either market research professionals or social scientists. These professionals tended to have ethics and research protocol training in addition to statistical training and disciplinary training. This was important because well-respected and agreed-upon protocols outlined what constituted consent to be in a research pool and to have data collected about oneself.

With the ease of metadata collection and surveillance, these research ethics have seemingly gone out the window; far more social science is now happening outside academia than inside it, and often without institutional ethics reviews. Not only is ethical oversight lacking, but also far more data used to draw conclusions about human behavior is now collected surreptitiously through digital metadata, such that "research participants" have no way of knowing about or limiting their participation. It is clear that we are in a new world, but we haven't developed new ethics rules to reflect that world.[1] Being thoughtful about provenance of data sets will help us start to reestablish the role of ethics in data analysis.

This chapter considers various aspects of fair data. First, the chapter discusses data integrity concerns as they relate to fairness. Fairness requires that we responsibly handle data so that it reflects the truth, which can't happen with sloppy data collection or storage practices.

Second, the chapter examines qualitatively which aspects of a data set make its use consistent or inconsistent with fairness. We focus on the three aspects of fairness discussed in Chapter 2: equity, privacy, and security, with an emphasis on equity because that is what will most likely influence our initial considerations of which data set to

---

1 On the other hand, it is clear that people don't like being uninformed and unsuspecting guinea pigs for experimentation or social engineering. Consider the backlash several years ago when Facebook published its research onto how user emotions responded to the news in their newsfeeds. Facebook ultimately admitted failure (*https://oreil.ly/85mZq*) in properly considering whether the experiment was appropriate.

choose. These concerns should be handled at the infrastructure level previous to embarking on any data selection for any modeling task.

Finally, the chapter concludes with a practical example of how we might explore a data set for signs of discrimination. This will prepare us for the next two chapters, where we discuss ways of either preprocessing data to enhance fairness or generating synthetic data for the same purpose.

Ensuring Data Integrity

Data integrity is a technical topic, and sufficient writing on this topic is already available for the interested reader to pursue at the general level. Here I cover the topic only from the perspective of how shoddy data practices can have fairness implications. The most basic fairness consideration in machine learning and data-driven computing is whether the training data for a model reflects *true measurements* proportional to the reported sampling technique. What are some ways that this can go wrong? Thinking about this statement, we can see that two considerations are involved. First, how do we label the data we have? What do we think it is versus what is it really? Second, how do our data points relate to the real world, given their *sampling*? How were they collected, and what does that process tell us about how we should use our data to make inferences about the larger world?

True Measurements

The process of collecting and storing measurements can introduce untruths in all sorts of ways. This section summarizes the main ways untruths enter into data sets during collection and storage of data.

Proxies

The undocumented or misremembered use of proxy information presents a serious threat to data integrity that implicates fairness. For example, perhaps a data set column is labeled "wealth" although income was measured, or perhaps the column actually contains a wealth estimation from a machine learning model's output rather than true measured wealth. In such cases, downstream users could understandably misuse this information because it has not been handled with sufficient care.

Unfortunately, proxies are often labeled without a recognition that they are proxies, even when it's abundantly clear that they can't possibly be what they claim. For example, a column might be labeled "friendliness" even though there's no mathematically true and unique way to quantify friendliness. Perhaps "friendliness" resulted from a question asked directly of someone, such as, "Would you describe yourself as a friendly person?" Perhaps it was assessed by that person's peers. Perhaps it was assessed via workplace videos that show some coworkers lunching together and others being loners. Any of these explanations would signal a proxy. While it is far more convenient to have short column/field names in our file storage for data sets, we should try to be mindful when using proxies. We might even name them as such (e.g., "friendliness_proxy"). Even better would be to name them for what they truly are, such as "friendliness_rating_by_peers" or "percent_days_eat_lunch_w_coworkers."

A column name itself can be a powerful force. Once we call something "friendliness" we may start thinking of it that way, making us less likely to recognize or question assumptions built into how we think a proxy should relate to what we want to study. This is a problem for two reasons. First, the data scientist working with the data may over time slide into sloppy thinking; they stop questioning the assumptions built into the proxy and simply take it as a given. Second, imagine downstream users or even subjects of the model are seeking to understand how decisions were made about them. Even if they can see released data, an item such as "friendliness" is not going to let them know how this judgment was made. If they are not aware of the proxy, it reduces their ability to understand algorithmic decisions or to challenge incorrect decision making.

As a concrete example, imagine that part of an employee's performance rating is linked to the "friendliness" proxy. A particular employee wants to know why they did not receive a promotion to a managerial post, and you point to the low "friendliness" indicator. Perhaps you monitored how often employees lunched together and used this as a proxy (note that provenance issues are also implicit in whether it was appropriate to use such data), but perhaps this particular employee has family-related responsibilities at lunchtime that are unaccounted for by the proxy. Without more-detailed knowledge about the proxy, the employee cannot hope to challenge the assessment and show that they are actually a star.

You may wonder whether this is a rare occurrence in industry, but that is far from the case. For example, in 2019 it was found that a major healthcare company had used medical spending as a proxy for seriousness of medical condition. That particular use of a proxy resulted in a racially discriminatory algorithm because the proxy used for training is itself racially discriminatory. While sickness may not racially discriminate, the reality in the US is that healthcare spending does. So this particular proxy resulted in a racially discriminatory outcome, unintentionally, by a large and sophisticated industry player in health insurance.

This is far from the only example. Consider that survey companies routinely use proxies for what they are trying to measure, often without recognizing it. For example, political polling companies use stated voting intention as a proxy for actual voting, even though there are many reasons that survey respondents might not be truthful about who they intend to vote for or who they already voted for. Likewise, the success of commercial artistic endeavors, such as moviemaking, is measured via the proxy of ticket sales, even though the cultural impact or novel contributions of a film may not be reflected in its ticket sales. In some cases, the use of a proxy is known, and the limits of the proxy are intuitive and easily understood, such as in the film example, but in other cases it is corrosive in the culture itself. Losing sight of the nuanced differences between a proxy and a related value is easy, as in the polling case.

Failures of external validity

Failures of external validity are failures to define measures that correlate to a sufficiently general attribute for our inputs or our resulting models to be useful. Consider the "friendliness" proxy. Apart from the fact that such a value is a proxy and might have been used carelessly, we can ask whether it is a measure that translates across a variety of situations and use cases and reflects what we think of as the general attribute of friendliness. This is also related to the concept of *robustness*, which refers to whether consistent results are achieved under a variety of related measures and across a variety of related populations. If a result can be replicated under only very narrow circumstances, that result is not robust and will certainly lack external validity.

Regardless of how we frame it, the key question is whether our analyses or models are expressing a general truth. Can we show that a measure works and means something outside of whatever small situation or data set we have used to *prove* or develop the measure in the first place?

Note that this problem is distinct from the careless use of a proxy described previously. Even if we had our friendliness proxy properly labeled and accounted for, we would separately have to ask whether it represented a concept as general as we asserted. For example, imagine we used having lunch with one's coworkers a high percentage of days as a measure of friendliness. We could imagine that in reality this attribute correlated with ambition rather than friendliness and that someone scoring high on this proxy might not demonstrate much friendliness at all outside of mandatory workplace networking. This would show a lack of robustness in our measure or in the conclusions we had drawn from such a measure if stated in general terms of friendliness.

Undescribed variation

Sometimes values measured and placed into one column, implying a single source of data, actually have a variety of sources. For example, maybe you are recording an employee's subjective performance ratings but aren't recording from whom those performance ratings were provided. If there is a systematic difference from one reviewer to another, as there often is, you leave later modelers or even later human reviewers of an employee unable to provide some adjustment to reflect this important fact related to measuring.

Your data has undescribed sources of variation in the measures, even if you could easily have recorded these sources of variation. You should avoid this whenever possible, in this case by providing all the information known about how the ratings were taken, including who performed individual ratings. Providing such information is important for two reasons. First, it more fully describes important facts known about how the measurement was made. Second, it gives downstream data users the possibility of accounting for some of the variation explained by the identity of the person providing a rating.

One way to think of this is that you are mixing the measurements you put into a particular column. Measurements can be mixed for a variety of common reasons that could easily factor into fairness considerations. Here are some examples of what to look for or ask about:

- Different measuring devices feeding data into the same column (inter-rate reliability), such as different bosses providing different performance reviews
- Measuring devices with poor precision, such as a rating process that is so subjective it doesn't even duplicate its own earlier judgments in response to the same stimulus

It is not only mixed measurements that cause this problem. We also run into the problem of undescribed variation when we do not include all important variables in an analysis, usually because we are not even aware that a variable is important or is an attribute worth mentioning. This can have fairness implications for a variety of reasons. Unaccounted-for variation may make a data set look like it reflects a discriminatory process when, in fact, undescribed variation could also account for the apparent discrimination. Consider, for example, the hiring of personnel at a trucking company. Perhaps we would start by looking at a data set showing that a much lower percentage of women succeeded in obtaining an interview than men. However, if we expanded our data set to include information about who had a commercial driver's license, the variation explaining the women's lack of success could be in this data column. So fairness concerns that motivate us to collect as much data to account for variation as possible can even assuage discrimination concerns.

The problem of undescribed or unaccounted-for variation is one that social science cannot escape. However, the less variation is accounted for, the less fair the data set is and the less accurate the results it will produce. Seeking out additional covariates and labels should always be high on the to-do list when compiling a fair data set. This is quite important because one major finding of statisticians and computer scientists is that the idea of, for example, a race-blind algorithm is actually one that will usually result in *more*, not less, discrimination. Accounting for variation is more desirable than turning a blind eye.

Proportionality and Sampling Technique

Proportionality refers to the need for data to be representative of the system it is measuring with respect to the probability of different kinds of data to be measured. Proportionality encompasses all sorts of expectations for frequency of data collection. For example, here are some ways someone might describe the collection of different data sets that would give us varying understandings of how much data we had relative to the situation being measured:

- The system takes a picture of every car that goes down the block.
- The system takes a picture of every car that goes down the block while over the speed limit.
- The system takes a picture of every car that goes down the block speeding during daytime hours when children are outside playing.
- The system takes a picture of every car going near or over the speed limit, but sometimes technical glitches occur, and we don't know whether these glitches are random.
- The system takes a picture of any car exhibiting suspicious behavior as judged by a proprietary algorithm we bought from a company that did not disclose its methodologies.

We can imagine many other scenarios. The point is that the proportionality relates to how often data collection happens relative to how often qualifying events or data could be collected. Sometimes we will have reasonably good assurances about how proportional and representative our sampling is, such as if we record every car, but other times we will have only a spotty notion, such as if our sampling is passed through logic that itself is opaque regarding how and when to sample. A data set can maintain its integrity only if its sampling technique (that is, the method for obtaining data) is clearly documented, preferably with lots of redundancies, in both metadata and in formal documentation of a data set. Sampling can be imperfect or nonrepresentative so long as we are aware of these deficiencies.

Let's discuss a few specific aspects of sampling with important fairness implications.

Biased sampling

The most-cited example of sampling problems affecting fairness is *biased sampling*. One example of biased sampling that is worth touching on is the possibility that race affects how likely a police officer is to stop a driver and find a reason to search the vehicle. Traffic stops happen disproportionately in the US to people with dark skin.

This then leads to biased sampling for other crimes. For example, while black Americans are convicted at much higher rates for drug-related crimes than are white

Americans, we can ask whether some of this difference is explained by the biased sampling of vehicles, in that white drivers are far less likely to be subject to a traffic stop and resulting vehicle search than are black drivers.[2] Clearly, this has far-reaching fairness implications when basic sampling may be drastically different across groups.

Unfortunately, biased sampling cannot be detected in a data set absent knowledge about or assumptions about baseline rates. This is one of the reasons differences in race in statistics are so hotly debated—because baseline rates as measured are always subject to the question of biased sampling. This is not an issue you will be able to solve on your own, but it is an issue you should be aware of and consider running simulations about, using a variety of baseline assumptions to see how such assumptions would fit your data.

Data duplication

Duplicate data points find their way into the same data set surprisingly often. Perhaps someone's name was misspelled in one round of inputs so that a person becomes more than one person, thereby having greater weight than they ought to in subsequent analyses. Worse is when this happens because of problems with a data pipeline, and particularly if such problems introduce bias into estimates or projects obtained from subsequently applied methods.

For example, imagine a mobile app designed to collect information about people's behavior (hopefully, with their informed consent and for a purpose that serves the interests of the research subjects). Imagine the app engineer wrote code that uploads data to servers, which store the raw data that is later input into a long data science pipeline. Perhaps through a programming error the app itself is not particularly careful about which data has already been uploaded and which hasn't. We can imagine cases in which all the same data is uploaded repeatedly. If deduplication checks do not occur later in the pipeline, older data will always be overweighted relative to newer data.

In addition to lowering accuracy overall, this could lead to all sorts of bad outcomes. For example, if the app is judging whether a person has "reformed," perhaps by judging the ability of a recovering alcoholic to stay away from bars or the ability of a former stalker to stay away from their victim's house, the person's improvement in behavior might not be reflected in the data fairly because the old data would continue to get too much weight. This would then have created a technology that, through bad or duplicated data, was imposing an unduly high or even impossible standard on someone seeking to demonstrate a change in behavior.

---

2 Some experts argue that illegal drug use is the same in black and white populations and that *all* the variation in drug-related offense convictions is due to uneven policing, such as differing probabilities of vehicular searches depending on race.

Choosing Appropriate Data

Separate from the question of true data is the question of appropriate data. When we get to the point of asking, "Should I use this data set?" we'll assume it has already passed muster on the first question of "Do I trust this data?" In this case we move on to the second question, which we can also frame as "Is it fair to use this data, now that I trust it?" This section covers the second question as it relates to our three fairness prongs: equity, privacy, and security.

Equity

Choosing appropriate data for a model has several distinct equity concerns to address. These are defined, and then different aspects of choosing data are broken down according to which branch of equity concerns they most clearly affect:

Bias and improper discrimination
> Bias and discrimination concerns relate to whether ML systems could be using improper considerations, such as membership in a protected category, when measuring merit within a system operating on equity. These are the most common kind of concerns currently addressed by both journalists and academics in the quest for fairer automation and machine learning. Note that discrimination—in the basic sense of sorting or segmenting people—is not necessarily wrong, as arguably all equity-oriented systems discriminate among individuals. The important consideration is the basis for discrimination—that is, the quality that is being used to sort and segment people. When the *basis* of discrimination is wrong, because it is immoral, prohibited by law, or unrelated to the ultimate goal of a system, such discrimination is improper.

Fair play
> Fair play concerns relate to notions that we want a society that promotes individuals from all sectors of society and helps people who need help. We want to make sure everyone has a chance of success. This may sometimes mean we don't want a system that is as accurate as possible. Systems should account for disadvantage, but not always in favor of accuracy. Rather, systems should try to change the dynamics rather than feed into those same dynamics.

Reasonable expectations
> Even apart from fair play concerns are concerns about reasonable expectations. These concerns may evolve over time. Someone might have given you permission to store a particular kind of data, but perhaps they gave that permission before it became clear that such data could make them highly vulnerable to certain privacy, security, or discrimination attacks. You could ask whether your use of data is then in keeping with reasonable expectations from when consent was given and data collected. Even if consent couldn't fully explain everything, what

would a reasonable person at the time have expected? What does a reasonable person expect now? If your pipeline doesn't match reasonable expectations, do you have a compelling reason to ignore this? (Probably not.)

Biased systems

Concerns that ML systems will replicate existing illegal and immoral biases have a basis partly in the fact that real-world systems producing data with which to build ML systems can sometimes quite reasonably be suspected of racial bias. Some common examples are data sets related to policing and data sets related to employment outcomes. Both these domains have had formal and informal divisions based on protected categories, such as race, gender, or religion, for centuries. More concretely, such formal bases for discrimination, particularly in the employment context, have only recently been addressed with formal prohibitions. For example, just a few decades ago it was still legal to fire a woman for being pregnant, and it is an active crisis in US policing that unarmed black people are much more likely to be shot by the police than unarmed people of other races.

Biased sampling

A subsidiary concern about biased systems is that while the functioning of a system and real outcomes may not be biased, reporting *about the system* could nonetheless be biased.[3] This is a subsidiary concern because, from a data science perspective, it hardly matters which is the case—the system is biased either way.

However, it's good to earmark this for yourself as a separate consideration. Perhaps you have received a data set for which you believe you can be entirely sure that the system is not biased. Maybe it is something entirely natural and free from social influence or very likely so. For example, imagine that men and women drivers, as modeled for a car insurance company, were equally likely to be the victim of a DUI.[4] But imagine that for some reason men are less likely to report being the victim of such an accident—perhaps they are more inclined to drive away rather than report the accident to their insurer. In such cases, women may unfairly be charged much higher prices by their insurer on the belief that they are somehow more likely to be the victim of a DUI, even though the underlying facts do not support such a concern.

---

3 For example, marijuana use is thought to be about the same among black and white Americans, even though there is biased reporting if we take drug convictions for marijuana possession as a proxy for the underlying base rate. Of course, this example is a poor one because ample empirical evidence shows that the system itself is biased.

4 Note that this isn't true, despite seeming intuitive and plausible. All sorts of gender variation are related to traffic accidents, even among the victims. For example, because of a bias emphasizing white men in setting safety standards, women are more likely to be injured in traffic accidents than are men (*https://oreil.ly/I0DoK*).

Fair play

In this group of issues related to fair play, we consider whether we are putting data subjects in a position that undermines their autonomy or authority about how their personal information is used. These concerns relate to disclosure, consent, and whether the appropriate conditions are in place for a meaningful exchange of information and assent.

Data collected without notice of its purpose

In regimes where data collection is regulated, it is consistently true that consent is defined to require complete and accurate notice regarding the purpose of data collection. In medical studies, research subjects must know what will happen with the tissues or medical information they provide. Likewise, when participating in psychology experiments, research subjects must be told before, or in some cases after (during a debriefing), about the purpose of the experiment that they participated in. Humans must be given truthful and informative facts about where their information is going.

This is beginning to be true in the realm of personal data more generally, particularly personal data collected on the internet. With the advent of the GDPR, those companies to whom the law applies must provide meaningful notice about not only what kinds of information they collect but what they intend to do with the information. Even in the US, where such consent is not strictly required, most companies have privacy policies and terms of service that explain, in dense and arguably intentionally obscured language, what they do with the data they collect.

If you happen to be using a data set where it is not clear that the people included in the data set provided information knowing how it would be used, you should carefully evaluate the ethics of the situation. In many cases moving forward with such a data set would not be appropriate.

Nonconsensual data collection

Consent is meaningful only if there is a real opportunity not to give consent. This is why the law regulates all sorts of bargains, such as how door-to-door salespeople can behave, what questions an employer can ask, and so on. In some situations the unfair distribution of knowledge, power, or vulnerability makes consent meaningless, or meaningful only within a very narrow limit.

A general example is the case of whether a consumer can give meaningful consent in a monopoly market. One ongoing debate is whether consent to the terms of service of very large companies, such as Facebook, Google, or Apple, can be meaningful when many of the services provided have no meaningful competition. For example, some people would argue that they could not possibly opt out of Facebook, at least not without very sad consequences for their social lives. Under such circumstances, where the metaphor of a market doesn't seem appropriate for an essential and monopolizing service, we can ask whether it is ethical for research work to go on at Facebook or even at third-party organizations buying data from Facebook, given that many people may be on the platform merely as the result of social compulsion in their respective social circles.

Supporting positive change

Another concern could be that data collected could be accurate in the sense of being predictive but without being predictive enough relative to the social harm it imposes by taking away hope or opportunities from those predicted not to succeed or predicted to do worse overall than others. Let's imagine that the school someone attends, usually strongly influenced by race and class, is somewhat predictive of their national exam results.[5] That may not seem like an example that could happen in the real world, but it did in the UK. Students who came from disadvantaged schools were further disadvantaged by an algorithm recognizing that connection and cementing it into code.

Such an example raises clear equity concerns because most of us believe that individuals should not be deprived of the opportunity to transcend their circumstances if they are individually exceptional. But what if all our analysis shows that the system does indeed make individualized decisions premised on relevant factors and without confounding inputs that give information about a protected status? Even in a case when a decision seems unbiased and most predictive based on everything we know, we may decide we won't accept the downstream consequences of embracing predictions and the built-in system of determinism they can entail. Perhaps we don't want a system that is so deterministic there is no room for surprise or second chances. Perhaps we think that even if some individuals are less likely to succeed than others, they still deserve a chance. Even here we should have strong fairness concerns with a system that permanently puts someone into a specific bin or rating simply based on past behavior or past performance. For example, consider the widespread discrimination in hiring against the unemployed. This tends to be a vicious cycle: bad luck or bad outcomes generate more bad luck or bad outcomes. As we build algorithmic systems, in addition to selecting data that truly reflects personal merit, we should leave room for reform, or even just good luck. We should not use predictors that tend to stuff people into vicious and inescapable cycles; that's not a world we want to live in and so it is not a world we should build into algorithmic systems.

---

5 Consider the controversy of the Ofqual algorithm deployed for grading end of school exams for students in the UK in the wake of COVID-19 and the associated lockdowns in 2020. The algorithm explicitly factored in which school a student attended when computing that student's grade. Unsurprisingly, and consistent with warnings that domain experts had given the government prior to use of the algorithm, disadvantaged students were disproportionately impacted (*https://oreil.ly/uvT77*).

Reasonable expectations

Another side of consent is determining what was consented to. Practices can be consented to only if they were meaningfully described and there was a meaningful opportunity to opt out, as explained previously. However, this is not the end of the story, because agreements rarely are absolutely complete or specify absolutely everything. So we need to fill in the gaps by inferring what the parties would have agreed to when a particular situation arises that does not appear to be covered by a past agreement.

Because technological capacity tends to increase over time, we should ask what someone reasonably expected at the time that they agreed to share their data. For example, posting photographs on social media websites was popular long before the advent of modern convolutional neural networks and their powers of facial recognition. For this reason, we can imagine that many people posting photographs before such technologies became commonplace in no way expected the rise of such technologies. We can imagine that while people recognized that putting photographs on the web was somewhat giving up their privacy, they did not know that someday computers would be able to find photographs of them effortlessly in a way that would enable scalable surveillance or predictions of their personality or sexual orientation. One could make the argument that even if consent were given to store and analyze photographs, that consent did not extend to these new technologies and should not be considered as allowing this.

Alternately, we could consider the donation of medical tissue. Perhaps patients in the past donated their brains to scientific study and signed fairly generous waivers as to what could be done with those brains. However, imagine that such waivers were signed before the discovery of DNA. In such a case—and particularly given the implications for descendants of the donor, such as that donor's DNA being readily available through brain tissue or perhaps the identification of genetically transmitted neural ailments—we can imagine the donor might not have signed away their rights to their brains if it might someday compromise the genetic privacy of their descendants.

When you are looking at data, particularly data that may provide new levels of detail or new information because of advancements in technology, you should carefully consider whether the data compromises the subject or makes them substantially more vulnerable than they could have anticipated at the time they gave consent. Consider a recent example: a medical study recently found that facial recognition algorithms, applied to MRI scans rather than to photographs, could identify people based on their scans. So research participants who might have agreed to provide MRI scans to researchers on an anonymous basis in fact gave away a form of data that turns out to be intrinsically identifiable even if their name is removed. If a bad actor gained access to the brain scans and perhaps some wide-ranging facial recognition product, such as Clearview AI,[6] that bad actor could potentially map brain structure—a quite private bit of information—to social media accounts and the like. This is the stuff of reality, not science fiction.

Another example is the very new use of *voice skins* for criminal purposes. With some amount of voice data, someone's voice can be replicated quite reliably. Given this new and unanticipated risk, we can ask whether we really have our friends' permission to record their voices (for example, by video), and post these in unprotected locations.

Privacy

Our discussion of equity was quite wide-ranging and went far beyond the matter of treating similarly meritorious individuals similarly and into the domain of also treating all individuals with a baseline level of respect and autonomy. Some of the data choice matters we've seen have already touched on privacy, but this section discusses cases in which privacy is the main issue with data collection or use.

Personal data

One way of thinking about privacy in a data-driven ML context is through the lens of *personal data*. We can look to two important legal sources to define personal data for us: the GDPR and the California Consumer Privacy Act (CCPA). Each piece of legislation affects a huge portion of technology companies doing business in the US or Europe. Hence, if you have European or US-based users, you are likely already under a legal obligation to comply with these provisions. In complying, you will bring your ML pipelines into good shape with respect to fairness, particularly with respect to privacy issues.

Some specific obligations with respect to data collection and storage that will apply in these cases include the following:

- Complying with an individual's request to know what data is stored about them and the purpose of storing such data

- Respecting an individual's request for data to be deleted

- Respecting an individual's request that their data not be sold to third parties

There are many critiques of both GDPR and CCPA, including the critique that they may not go far enough. And the laws don't touch on every topic related to privacy (let alone topics related to fairness and security). So you may want to think of compliance

---

6 ClearviewAI claims to have scraped billions of photos of Americans from social media and to have built a facial recognition product that can recognize most any American based on a photograph, regardless of whether that American's photograph has ever been put into a criminal database.

with these and other early algorithmic-oriented laws as a starting place rather than a good measure of fairness practices.

Metadata collection

In collecting and using metadata, we should think long and hard about what constitutes an intrusion in domains where an individual reasonably did not expect to be observed, even if something was technically observable. For example, a decade ago it seemed creepy even to web developers to record things such as where someone clicked on a web page and how long they spent on different areas of the page. Now such recordings are standard, but just because they are standard in industry does not mean that they reflect people's expectations or desires with respect to their privacy level when browsing.

When you see data sets in your organization, it's worth asking whether their collection was in accordance with what people would have expected and, more importantly, what they would have wanted. This is particularly true for metadata—that is, data that results from observing someone and for which someone could not possibly avoid observation other than, for example, by not using the internet at all, which hardly seems like a reasonable balance.

Metadata is particularly important from a privacy standpoint for two reasons. First, it's difficult to specify consent when one wants to collect metadata, which comes merely from watching. Intruding with a pop-up that says "we will watch your every movement" seems like an instant nonstarter even though it's true, because people would almost certainly decline if given such an opportunity for notice and consent. Short of this, it's difficult to imagine what could reasonably constitute consent, because most human beings do not consent to total surveillance, and yet the way people are tracked on many internet sites these days could arguably come quite close to total surveillance.

Secondly, metadata even without a name attached is surprisingly invasive of privacy. The behavior of each individual correlates quite tightly to identity, and often individuals can be identified from their online behavior even if traditional personally identifying information is not attached to such metadata. Internet researchers have often been able to re-identify internet browsers merely with information collected as routine metadata during the course of browsing.

Importantly, it's not clear to what extent laws such as GDPR and CCPA protect metadata, particularly if organizations are clever about how they store it. For this reason, your organization may be in full compliance with data privacy laws but nonetheless collecting and exploiting quite intimate and personal information. However, you should be asking whether this is really fair to do, and whether design choices or notices could make data collection and use policies more explicit for the unsuspecting users who are being surveilled.

In fact, my use of "surveillance" in the sense that it sounds like a condemnation probably goes too far. While news coverage does support a sense of outrage about the tracking that goes on inside many digital products, people do tend to expect a level of service from their digital products that presupposes some degree of metadata collection and retention. So metadata collection is not considered all bad; many users favor such practices where necessary to support the use of a product and to enhance the service. For example, when people stream movies and television online, they like to receive recommendations based on their past viewing. Likewise, people appreciate when ordering a meal from a delivery service that their likely choices are anticipated. So determining the fair balance of metadata collection will be context dependent. The key principles should remain (1) serving the user base and (2) giving that user base sufficient information about what kind of data, including metadata, is collected and what happens downstream with such data.

What Is Metadata?

You may not have worked with the term "metadata" before, but nonetheless you have likely worked with metadata in one form or another. Most succinctly, metadata is data about data. But even in the barest form of data storage, you will usually have data about data. For example, even in a simple text file, your operating system will usually provide you with a timestamp indicating when a file was created and when it was most recently updated. That's metadata.

Metadata is the largest source of data for online applications, and arguably drives important ML use cases such as targeted advertising far more than what is regarded as personal data. Consider, for example, articles written by journalists seeing all the data stored about them by Google or Facebook.[7] Quite a large chunk of what they collect is more fairly described as metadata, such as where you were when logging into a website or how long you spent watching a particular video.

Proxies for private information

The more sophisticated techniques grow, the more we might ask whether certain kinds of information that originally seemed not to touch on privacy concerns might eventually do so. For example, if sexual orientation can be determined from someone's photo alone,[8] should even the storage of basic photographs invoke privacy concerns? Should such photographs ever be stored in a way that might connect someone's photo to personal data, such as name, age, or address, such as could be used by someone seeking to hurt people of particular sexual orientations?

---

7 See CNBC (*https://oreil.ly/zqSU7*) and *Fortune* (*https://oreil.ly/ScaLm*).

8 This claim has in fact been made, but there are good reasons to be skeptical about it.

Thus when you collect information that you feed into a model to try to deduce private information, there are good reasons to believe this is inconsistent with fair privacy practices. This is not only because you are trying to discover information that the people being profiled would vigorously object to, but also because you're likely risking disclosing your private deductions to third parties. Consider the well-known case of a teenage girl's father discovering her pregnancy because Target began mailing her pregnancy-oriented marketing.[9] This was an ethical lapse on Target's side not only for trying to discover personal health information about a completely unsuspecting and nonconsenting individual (and a minor at that), but also for disclosing this information in a rather public and flawed way. If you are building a model where a similar violation could occur, chances are you are violating fair privacy practices in a number of ways.

Security

This section considers security-oriented concerns related to holding data and training data-driven models. I highlight cases in which possessing the data could be problematic and holding the data and the risks entailed in the data being found are likely not worth the risk. I also highlight how insecurity can creep into an ML model through data-driven training cases when use of a data set to train a critical model could be problematic.

Data collected from the wild is dangerous

Much of the data driving state-of-the-art models for both natural language processing and image processing has been freely collected from the wild of the internet. As has been increasingly recognized, this leads to inherently unsafe data in a number of ways. First, it is possible for bad actors to build into data various traps when they anticipate that data may be scraped for use in an ML model. So insecurity can be imported into your ML models when you train those models off the internet.

Second, when your ML model learns from the internet, it learns the bad behaviors that occur on the internet, including discriminatory treatment and language. Even in the newest and most cutting-edge models this has proven to be the case.[10] This book focuses on categorization techniques, but methods have also been developed to detect and reduce bias in language models. After reading this book, you should be well prepared to seek out these more advanced topics and implement solutions.

Data is thus weaponized both on purpose and inadvertently. In both cases, you should factor in these security concerns when you collect data from the wild and

---

9 An internet search will return much discussion on the topic. See *Forbes*, for example (*https://oreil.ly/wX-QL*).

10 See findings related to OpenAI's release of its 2020 open source natural language processing model, GPT-3 (*https://oreil.ly/xwn8N*).

ensure you have risk minimization and auditing plans in place to identify bad outcomes.

Inherently dangerous data

In an era of greatly increased cyberattacks, one good question to ask is what your moral and legal liabilities are in storing and analyzing a given data set. The current state of the law is unclear as to whether a party holding sensitive personal information is liable to people about whom data is held when that data is not financial or medical information. In the past such potential liability was usually rejected, but courts are beginning to evolve their positions. This is important because it may change your organization's economic balancing as to whether the risk of holding particular forms of data and the temptation such data offers to malicious third parties is worth the presumed benefit of holding such data.

You might think your organization steers clear of this because you don't handle health or financial data. However, in an era in which increasing portions of our lives are lived online and recorded, more and more organizations hold sensitive and identifying data. Also, there are increasing arrays of bad actors, as online vigilante groups seek to target those whose political or ideological affiliations are viewed as hostile to their interests. You should contemplate whether *any* data you hold—not just data traditionally in sensitive categories—is really worthwhile, given the security risks you may impose on people.

It's important to recognize that keeping routine data can hurt others. Imagine, for example, you keep a carefully compiled list of women who have been abused by their partners, and it includes some form of personally identifiable information. Or remember that during World War II, the percentage of Dutch Jewish citizens who survived was low compared to Jewish citizens of other nationalities because the Dutch government kept excellent records on its citizens, including religion. Apparently no one thought to destroy those records or make them inaccessible when Nazi forces invaded.

In a case closer to modern times, consider a defunct white nationalist organization that was hacked (*https://oreil.ly/wKnRS*) by a private group that opposed white nationalism.

Although many people expressed interest in downloading the newly available data to create visualizations, we might ask about the moral implications if a visualization led to violence. It is possible to find the aims of white nationalists abhorrent and still recognize an ethical obligation toward members of such groups by not engaging in activities that could put someone in physical danger. Data can be weaponized. Even if you don't plan to weaponize it, make sure you work with potentially sensitive data only if you really have to. Make sure any data you are storing is being stored for a purpose that justifies any dangers created by holding it. Keep a forward-looking and expansive definition of what constitutes sensitive data so you don't get caught out by failing to reflect the cultural conversation.

Naively chosen data

Recently, Android phones manifested a serious security breach when it was realized that a new feature, allowing people to unlock their phones via facial recognition, was fundamentally flawed. The facial recognition feature worked even while people were sleeping (*https://oreil.ly/OEOMD*) and presumably even if they had been knocked unconscious. This flaw would allow malicious actors to open a phone without the consent of the phone's owner in ways that should have been anticipated and planned for before such a feature was introduced.

While clear details aren't available as to how the feature was originally trained, the training data likely did not include sufficient photos relating to people clearly not being awake or not willingly participating in the facial recognition. Or if such photos were included, they were possibly labeled the wrong way or incompletely, as a face of a person rather than as a face of a person clearly not in a conscious state.

When choosing an appropriate data set, we need to use domain knowledge, a diverse perspective, and a proving investigation to make sure the data set is complete in as many ways as possible with respect to potential security abuses. Preparation for such abuses should be built into the training data itself. If data is naively chosen only to specify a task without reference to security threats, it's likely that too small and too naively labeled a data set will be used, as appears to be the case with the Android unlocking feature.

Incomplete data

The problem of naively chosen data runs headlong into the related problem of incomplete data, in which certain use cases do not even have all the information necessary to solve a problem. The use of incomplete data could easily pose a security risk, particularly in the case of physical safety depending on the outcome of a technological system. For example, imagine a self-driving car that was trained only in the San Francisco Bay Area but then was deployed across the US, despite quite different road architectures and driving patterns in different regions of the country. This would be a security problem created by releasing a product with incomplete data.

Any machine learning algorithm may prove unsafe if the full space of possible scenarios is not covered. Also, keep in mind that the potential event space includes not only the upstream inputs that can arrive but also the combinations of downstream use cases with potential outputs. Have all potentials been covered? If not, a responsible ML engineer needs to think very carefully about issues such as the explainability of a model that may be used to compensate or determine the full possible event space. How can we be sufficiently confident of its performance?

Fundamental Limits on Data for Complex Systems

The prior list is intended to cover many routine fairness problems shown even in highly sophisticated products coming out of the leaders in machine learning techniques and solutions. However, other fundamental problems plague fairness when we think about data gathering and selection for analysis and ML purposes. These are less discussed in the literature, and sometimes they can't be solved. However, you should keep these in mind when considering the fundamental limits to the kinds of data currently collected:

Higher-order systems

A first-order system simply functions, without impacting its environment. A second-order system reacts to its own functioning. A third-order system reacts to its own functioning but also to its reactions to its own functioning. Or to put it another way, second-order and higher systems will experience reactions from their environments and react accordingly. Most ML systems are built with an implicit assumption of a first-order system.[11]

For example, if you are building a system to sentence people, and in that system you build an assessment of how likely someone is to reoffend, your system itself is going to affect the production of future data. Imagine your system recommends a long sentence for a particular convicted criminal. That criminal will now be spending more time in jail, where they are exposed to more criminal culture and where they lose contacts with their families and communities as a result of the algorithmic recommendation. If that person, when released, goes on to commit more crimes, the assessors of the algorithm may think they got it right, but in fact the algorithm may have caused this result through the assignment of the long sentence. Nonetheless, the algorithm may learn from this training data point that has been formed through its own decisions, and react to it by suggesting even longer sentences the next time around, leading to a runaway self-affirming system, as Cathy O'Neil writes about in *Weapons of Math Destruction* (Penguin Random House). The dangers of systems that do not check themselves, recognize the complexity of systems that react to themselves, or build on their own actions is covered extensively in this book, which makes for excellent and compelling reading.

---

11 There are some exceptions. For example, large financial institutions must build in a way of accounting for their own large presence in small markets when they build trading models.

Low-incidence events

Many kinds of interesting ML use cases are tempting precisely because they purport to forecast low-incidence use cases, such as fire, catastrophic hurricanes, unusual diseases, and so on. If you are seeking to model low-incidence events, you should be very careful about the kinds of data you select. The recent past has shown us that people building ML pipelines are not good at admitting when they cannot predict something because there isn't enough data. They would rather find a proxy.

Unfortunately, using data to identify a proxy rather than the real thing can create all sorts of problems, as we'll discuss in a subsequent case study. Most importantly, some proxies used to predict low-incidence events can lead to extreme unfairness. For example, one fear regarding the commercial instruments used by some governments to predict criminal recidivism is that these algorithms purport to predict future *violent* crimes but are often built from data sets in which the vast majority of crimes are *nonviolent*, resulting in a strongly unbalanced data set, a weak point of most ML techniques.

Likewise, in other cases where ML engineers want to predict outlier or other low-incidence events, the statistical properties that define such events may not be well defined simply because so few data points identifying these events have been sampled. In such cases, building a model with such a great degree of uncertainty may be worse than no model at all.

Case Study: Choosing the Right Question for a Data Set and the Right Data Set for a Question

In a recent *Science* article,[12] researchers identified evidence of racial bias in an ML system that had been constructed by a health insurance company to identify patients who were most likely to need more healthcare in the future and to target those patients for additional interventions. The researchers found that black patients receiving a similar sickness severity score to white patients were actually sicker than the white patients with the same score. The researchers further estimated that about half of black patients who should have been receiving additional interventions were missed by the algorithm. The reason? Healthcare costs had been used as a proxy for sickness, so the algorithm was *predicting healthcare costs, not illness.*

The problem with this is that substantial evidence shows that historically and currently large disparities exist in the amount of care and the amount of money spent on

---

12 Obermeyer, Ziad et al. "Dissecting Racial Bias in an Algorithm Used to Manage the Health of Populations." *Science*, October 25, 2019, *https://science.sciencemag.org/content/366/6464/447.*

that care when comparing white Americans to black Americans. Using such a proxy as a way to identify sickness systematically but *unintentionally* reproduces a long-standing injustice with new technology, even when the goal of the system was to help the most vulnerable.

Researchers believe that inappropriate proxies are one of the biggest culprits in reproducing or creating new sources of bias. So, when you are choosing a data set to answer a specific question, you will likely need to determine whether you are in fact using a proxy rather than the real measure. In the example given here, it's fairly apparent, with hindsight, but clearly some competent professionals at a sophisticated health insurance company did not find this problem apparent as they built the system.

American health records are incredibly complicated. Those in medical billing can tell you that any given practice area uses thousands of codes. What's more, because different insurance companies may have different reimbursement practices or coding policies, physicians and billing professionals alike have to tailor their coding to a given patient's health insurance. Even for a single ailment, both different insurance companies and different healthcare institutions vary their coding practices, so that the same labels don't necessarily mean the same thing in different records.

Under such circumstances, coming up with a rating of healthcare severity is incredibly difficult. Following are a few ways you might be tempted to measure sickness as well as explanations for why these proxies could be just as problematic as the cost proxy discovered in the *Science* article as the source of racial discrimination:

Number of times nursing staff checked on a patient while patient was in the hospital
    This might seem like a good way of gauging how much care professionals thought a particular patient needed, which might be a good proxy for sickness, at least on a short time scale. However, this could also correlate strongly with race, or a patient's wealth, or their family's assertiveness.

Number of specialists seen by a patient
    Same problems as before.

Patient's weight and blood pressure
    This would privilege certain kinds of illnesses without necessarily achieving the global target of identifying all sick patients. It could easily turn out that the kind of illnesses focused on in this way also correlated in some way that produced a discriminatory impact. For example, if women systematically had these health problems but men did not, the algorithm would systematically discriminate against men in the targeting of extra helpful interventions.

This discussion might be incredibly disempowering. After all, if proxies are out and the ground truth isn't available or possibly even knowable, what can be done? Here are a few suggestions:

Proxies aren't out entirely

They should be used carefully. They should also be disclosed openly. The health insurance company targeting people should have made clear that their product was built to target high-cost patients. In such a case, professionals out in the field might have more quickly spotted the built-in bias to the proxy and warned those who had rolled out the product.

Products should be only as ambitious as reality dictates

If something isn't knowable, we're better served recognizing that rather than pretending otherwise.

A mix of proxy variables might better get at a broad concept than a single variable

Some concerns about proxy variables, such as discrimination embedded in a proxy, can be reduced by using several indicators.

Including data that covers racial information can lead to less discrimination

We will see this more fully in the coming chapters, but including racial information and its interaction with a proxy can reduce the unintended harms of proxy variables.

For important applications, get more data instead of using an inadequate proxy

For high-stakes decisions, this is the best way to correct bias. In low-stakes decisions, it can be possible to shape or resample data or to sacrifice some accuracy, but in high-stakes decisions, such as healthcare, organizations need to put more money into data collection and processing.

Quality Assurance for a Data Set: Identifying Potential Discrimination

Assuming we have tried to respect the principles and procedures described in the preceding sections of this chapter, let's now look to how we can code to examine the quality of data with respect to the antidiscrimination concerns of equity and equality.

As you select data for an ML application, you are best situated if you can identify any discriminatory problems with your data as early as possible, such as when first exploring that data. In the following code samples, you will work through data checks that can identify simple problems between groups. Then in the next three chapters, you will learn ways to address any discrimination you may identify in this process.

In this section, I'll focus on some measures of discrimination that are commonly applied, sometimes in legal settings and sometimes in social science research and other indicators. As I have mentioned in previous chapters, definitions of discrimination, equality, and equity vary because of fundamentally different philosophical priorities but also because different definitions are explored for ways they can be implemented to repair data sets or models. For this reason, I do not purport to cover all definitions of fairness.

These measures of fairness don't come close to representing all notions of fairness. Note also that measuring discrimination is not the same as measuring equity. Ideally, when emphasizing equity rather than equality, which will usually be the case, the focus will be on individual outcomes. However, such a problem is unlikely to be one you run into early on, at the stage of determining the extent of discrimination in a data set. At this point we will focus on looking for group-level effects, with an emphasis on group parity. Also, the assumption throughout this book is that group parity will also further individual fairness (i.e., equity), given the standard baseline assumption that everyone is equal until proven otherwise.

Many decisions of interest will ultimately result from some kind of binary decision. An applicant either gets a loan or does not. A defendant gets convicted or does not. Someone gets a job or does not. In such cases, we can imagine success and failure as the binary outcomes. Let us also consider for the moment that we have two groups, the majority group (favored_group) and the minority group (disfavored_group). We will then have success and failure rates that appear in Table 3-1.

Table 3-1. Outcomes by group

Group	Bad outcome	Good outcome	Total
favored_group	$r1$	$r2$	$N1$
disfavored_group	$r3$	$r4$	$N2$
total	$M1$	$M2$	N

If the percentage of the favored group getting a good outcome, $r2/N1$, is much larger than the percentage of the disfavored group getting a good outcome, $r4/N2$, this fact would itself give rise to suspicions of discrimination. Such fairly simple ratios are used in legal settings as one measure of potential discrimination, and US courts notably focus on these *selection rates* when evaluating claims of discrimination.

European courts take a slightly different approach, focusing on measures that stem from the failure rate rather than the success rate. We denote these as $p1 = r1 / N1 =$ failure rate of favored group and $p2 = r3 / N2 =$ failure fate of disfavored group. UK courts tend to look at the difference in failure rates, $p2 - p1$, which is known as the *risk difference*. The European Court of Justice, in contrast, has discussed $p2 / p1$, which is known as the *risk ratio*.

We know that the selection rates of the favored group and disfavored group are unlikely to be identical, even absent discrimination, because of numerical fluctuations. We also know that reasons related to the correlates of group membership could account for differences in selection rates even if there was no group-membership-related discrimination. So what kind of thresholds should we set for the measures of discrimination?

When Will We Reach Equality?

In many real-world data sets, you will find that the success rates or base rates for various behaviors are drastically different from equality. How, you might ask, can you possibly get to equality?

Distinct groups can have vastly different success rates for many reasons. Unfortunately, many of these reasons relate to ongoing social problems as well as to past realities of injustice that continue to have repercussions many generations on. US Supreme Court justices themselves have disagreed quite stridently regarding appropriate timelines to expect equality.[13]

This is all to recognize that you are very likely to encounter extremely different rates of success among different groups in many real-world outcomes. While some corrections can be had through techniques described in these chapters, to train models on fairer data in the hopes of not perpetuating discrimination, such stark disparities also point to the need for institutional reform and policy actions guided toward addressing the root causes of inequality. Unfortunately, ML cannot alone do this.

There is no clear answer from a mathematical or sociological point of view, but the US legal system has provided one rule of thumb that has been in use for decades. This is the *adverse impact rule*, put forth in 1978, which defines the statistical threshold to establish adverse impact in an employment situation. The rule is formalized in some areas of law and in some parts of the world (namely, the US and the UK) as the *80% rule*, or *four-fifths rule*. When the rate for a positive outcome—hiring, promotion, etc.—for the disfavored group is less than 80% the selection rate for the favored group, a prima facie case of disparate impact has arisen.

This case can be rebutted by a defendant showing a business purpose for a selection procedure and also showing that the defendant has chosen an option tailored to the business purpose and minimizing the disparate impact. Note also that the denominator is selected as the most successful group, which need not necessarily be a dominant gender or racial group in a given setting. So the rule was not written to favor a particular traditionally disfavored group, but rather to check that outcomes are similar for all groups, and if not, to establish the means for a legal presumption or regulatory investigation when appropriate. Note that a finding of adverse impact alone is not usually enough to win a lawsuit, as intent to discriminate must also be shown. However, a showing of adverse impact is nonetheless serious and can trigger government

---

13 See *Grutter v. Bollinger* (*https://oreil.ly/3Zs9v*).

investigations and the need for such a disparity to be explained by those in charge of the process producing the disparate results.

The 80% rule can be a good starting point for a discrimination audit, absent domain knowledge or reasons for setting a different rule. Hence, when you are looking for discrimination when first getting familiar with that data set, you should be using these basic measures of discrimination and applying them to potentially vulnerable groups within the data set.

Let's use an example. We consider the German credit data set (*https://oreil.ly/wmpF1*), a heavily used data set when illustrating techniques and metrics associated with discrimination. We then look at the success rates for applying for credit for a variety of gender/marital status combinations, which are described in the accompanying documentation as follows:[14]

```
Personal status and sex
A91 : male    : divorced/separated
A92 : female  : divorced/separated/married
A93 : male    : single
A94 : male    : married/widowed
A95 : female  : single
```

Let's consider the impact of gender and marital status on the success rate for obtaining credit:

```
## read in data
data = pd.read_csv("german.data", delim_whitespace=True, header=None)

## calculate the number of successes and total numbers
success_data = data.groupby(8).agg([lambda x: sum(x == 1),
  lambda x: len(x)]).iloc[:, -2:]
success_data.columns = ["num_success", "num_total"]
A91    0.817910
A92    0.883871
A93    1.000000
A94    0.992754
## determine the rate of the most successful group and compare all other groups
most_successful = np.max(success_data.num_success / success_data.num_total)
print(success_data.num_success / success_data.num_total / most_successful)
```

That yields the following output:

```
A91    0.817910
A92    0.883871
A93    1.000000
A94    0.992754
```

---

14 In this example, I use "male" and "female" because that is how the data is presented internally.

If this were a hiring process, the Equal Employment Opportunity Commission would probably not launch an investigation but might keep an eye on why divorced males in particular (A91) seemed to be doing so much worse than other groups in their applications. However, the 80% rule applies a bright line rule—a clear demarcation where behavior worse than that indicated by the rule is suspicious. But passing this rule doesn't mean that all is necessarily well—as I have said before, and per the no free lunch theorem, no rule or question will automatically ensure fairness, and the same goes for the 80% rule in the case of antidiscrimination. So generally, we will not stop our inquiry or fairness interventions merely because we "pass" the 80% rule. We want to do better than that. If we want to do so with this original data set, we can explore ways to preprocess the data, even before training an algorithm, to make the data set fairer. We will review preprocessing in Chapter 4.

You might be somewhat dissatisfied with the very simplified measure of discrimination in this discussion. Perhaps you also want to think about how to handle cases of explanatory variables. For example, perhaps much of the potential discrimination discussed so far can be explained by other correlated variables. Perhaps the divorced men also have poor financial behavior.

In this case we can use thinking that comes from association rule mining. In particular, we look at Pedreschi et al.'s definition of *α-discriminatory* as a way to study decision rules suggested by associations in a data set.[15] Before studying it, however, we need a few pieces of vocabulary associated with association rule mining.

First, the basics. *Association rule mining* looks for rules in a tabular data set such as A → B and the like, where the probabilities occur at rates that are higher than chance. We call such a rule an *association rule*. The confidence of the association rule A → B is P(A & B) / P(A). This gives us a measure of how often B really occurs when A is a given. How is this helpful?

Say that some kind of protected attribute, X, is legally prohibited from affecting a decision. The entity studied in a data set insists that X is not taken into account, but we do notice some discrepancy in the success rate of individuals in group X compared to individuals in other groups. We can look at the conference of two decision rules, A → B and (A + X) → B, and compare the confidence of these two rules.

In this way, Pedreschi et al. define a decision rule as *α*-discriminatory if

$$\text{conf}((A + X) \rightarrow B) / \text{conf}(A \rightarrow B) > \alpha$$

where alpha is a quantity we would specify before looking at the data. This is a way of quantifying how much stronger an association rule becomes when provided with

15 Pedreschi, Dino, et al. "Integrating induction and deduction for finding evidence of discrimination." Paper presented at the Proceedings of the 12th International Conference on Artificial Intelligence and Law, Barcelona, Spain, June 2009. *https://perma.cc/9VY7-68Z6*.

information about the prohibited class. For our purposes, we set an α value of 2 as our cutoff.

Let's consider that we were concerned about the divorced males in our example. Let's now see whether, given an uncertain savings state, there is still reason to think that divorced males are additionally discriminated against. We do this by computing the confidence of the proposed association rules:

Unknown credit → Bad outcome
Unknown credit *and* Divorced male → Bad outcome

We do this with the following code:

```
## looking at whether a rule is alpha discriminatory
cond1                       = data.ix[:, 8]  == "A91"
num_div_males               = data[cond1].shape[0]

cond2                       = data.ix[:, 5]  == "A65"
num_unknown_credit          = data[cond2 ].shape[0]

cond3                       = data.ix[:, 5]  == "A65"
cond4                       = data.ix[:, 8]  == "A91"
num_unknown_credit_div_male = data[cond3][cond4].shape[0]

cond5                           = data.ix[:, 20] == 2
num_bad_outcome                 = data[cond5].shape[0]

cond6                           = data.ix[:, 5]  == "A65"
cond7                           = data.ix[:, 20] == 2
num_bad_outcome_unknown_credit  = data[cond6][cond7].shape[0]

cond8                                   = data.ix[:, 8]  == "A91"
cond9                                   = data.ix[:, 5]  == "A65"
cond10                                  = data.ix[:, 5]  == "A65"
num_bad_outcome_unknown_credit_div_male = data[cond8][cond9][cond10].shape[0]

### test association rule 1: unknown credit -> bad outcome
rule1_conf = num_bad_outcome_unknown_credit / num_unknown_credit
rule2_conf = num_bad_outcome_unknown_credit_div_male / num_unknown_credit_div_male

## compute elift (ratio of confidence rules)
print(rule2_conf / rule1_conf)
```

This yields

```
0.953
```

This is not only below our threshold, but also below 1, which suggests that, if anything, favorable treatment rather than unfavorable treatment is given to divorced males in the context of unknown credit history. On the other hand, we can compare this to the treatment for divorced females, given these two ratios. The code to do so is essentially identical except that we select for group A92 rather than group A91 in the marital column. The code to do so is in the repository but not reproduced here.

If we do this, the result is

```
1.5172
```

Here we see some evidence whereby inputting the sex rather than just the unknown credit history actually worsens the treatment for females rather than for males. However, the confidence ratio of 1.51 is still below our preset threshold of 2, so we will not treat this as discrimination. Incidentally, note that this ratio of confidence values is also known as *extended lift*.

It is important that we set the threshold in advance so that we can have a uniform metric, preferably across institutions, and also so that we don't "cheat" and find ourselves adjusting our standards for discrimination based on what we find in the data. While you might think of these as additional opportunities to protect discriminated-against groups, someone else might use this same option to let discrimination slide by adjusting the tolerance in the other direction based on what they find. We must not let the data drive the standards.

A Timeline for Fairness Interventions

Broadly speaking, researchers in fairness-aware machine learning divide fairness interventions into three stages: pre-processing, in-processing, and post-processing. These are briefly described here:

Pre-processing
These methodologies refer to attempts to adjust data before training of a model has begun. Such attempts can relate to any aspects of data or its labels that can be adjusted independently of and prior to training a model. For example, one very simple way of pre-processing for fairness that we discuss in Chapter 4 is reweighting the data. This is a way of addressing unfairness by adjusting upward the weight of data points judged to represent cases where an otherwise biased system made the right decision. Likewise, those data points judged to represent instances of potential bias are given lower weightings.

In addition to adjusting the relative weights of data points, pre-processing can relate to different representations of the input data, such as reducing the dimensionality of the data in a way that removes information about a protected category or finding a transformation of the data, including its labels, that preserves as much of the original information as possible while reducing unfairness. Pre-processing methods may be particularly attractive when contemplating the release of a data set in situations where the releaser of the data set wants to take proactive steps to ensure fair outcomes from models trained on the data set. Of course, in such cases, it should be clearly indicated that a data set has been through some processing.

In-processing

These methodologies refer to attempts to ensure fairer outcomes in machine learning by training models in a fair-aware manner. In such cases, the original data is not adjusted, but instead the way in which a model is optimized reflects fairness concerns rather than merely accuracy concerns. For some normative reasons, organizations may prefer to use in-processing rather than pre-processing even though many of the techniques for in-processing have much in common with those of pre-processing. For example, it may give the wrong impression from a publicity standpoint to hear that data has been "massaged," as one might characterized pre-processing, whereas indicating that a model was trained in a fair-aware way might be more acceptable. Use of an in-processing methodology could also be quite attractive when someone wants to maintain maximum control over potential downstream use cases because the fairness is already baked into the model and requires no interventions from downstream users who may not be aware that a model requires additional fitting or modifications.

Post-processing

These methodologies refer to attempts to ensure fairer outcomes using models that have not had data massaged prior to training and that have not been developed through fairness-aware training. These methodologies generally rely on choosing a fairness metric, generally one that is group-oriented rather than individual-oriented, and selecting a fairness metric to equalize between groups. Even in the case of a black-box model, such models can be retrofitted for fairness in post-processing by choosing different thresholds and scoring criteria, or different probabilities of label swapping or categorizations, according to different groups. The methodologies generally work by identifying individuals near classification thresholds and changing or randomizing their labels slightly within some confidence band around the threshold. These methods can be useful in making a black-box model fairer when it has not been trained in a way that emphasizes fairness.

These options are the trickiest for a number of reasons, and they are unlikely to pass legal muster given current US law on discrimination, in that post-processing can amount to disparate treatment, which is a form of behavior clearly prohibited under US law in all circumstances.

You may wonder which of these options you should choose. To some extent, I've tried to address that in the descriptions. The further upstream in the data science pipeline you implement antidiscrimination measures, the more opportunities you have globally to implement antidiscrimination measures. For example, there is nothing to prevent you from implementing both pre-processing and in-processing. However, as you implement multiple antidiscrimination measures, you will necessarily have a more complex fairness pipeline, and your process itself and results will therefore be more opaque and less amenable to straightforward explanations, especially at the level of individual results.

Binary Categories Are Not the Whole Picture

Fairness and discrimination metrics are generally defined for one binary relationship at a time to represent the divide between a privileged or historically favored group and an unprivileged or historically disfavored group. This is how the term has generally been applied in legal case law and scholarship to date. For example, a wrongfully terminated employee might make the case that they were discriminated against for their race or their gender, but usually the employee would not make the case that it was their race and gender combined that created the discrimination. So such an employee would likely make the claim that there was both race and gender discrimination.

However, this might not be completely accurate or fairly reflect realities on the ground. For example, research shows that black women in the US seem to face discrimination that is not accounted for merely by aggregating the effects of their race and gender in a linear fashion. Rather, an *interaction* seems to occur between race and gender that means black women face even more discrimination than we would expect if we simply modeled race and gender as independent terms. From a social science perspective, this is described as *intersectionality*, a term that was coined 30 years ago by Columbia Law School professor Kimberlé Crenshaw. While substantial social science research backs up the theory of intersectionality, most fairness-aware ML methods do not handle these more complicated shades of discrimination as perpetuated in the real-world. Likewise, antidiscrimination law itself still has yet to fully recognize and legally cognize these effects.

As with many decisions relating to fairness, awareness of your technical possibilities is not the same as a clear answer as to which technical option you should use. For example, for greatest transparency and the ability to determine which individual's scores were changed due to a fairness intervention, you should likely opt for post-processing. On the other hand, if you see the discrimination as a fundamental problem with the data set itself, you would be better justified in choosing pre-processing, all else equal.

Comprehensive Data-Acquisition Checklist

- Data integrity issues
  - Do the labels on the data mean what they say, or could they be misleading?

— Was the data collection method sufficiently documented?

— Have potential issues of nonrandom data collection been sufficiently highlighted in data documentation and naming?

- Consent issues

  — Was informed consent appropriate to the sensitivity of the data obtained for a data set?

  — Was that consent solicited in a reasonable way, with opting out as a possibility?

  — Does the current use of the data reflect the originally obtained consent?

- Reasonable expectations

  — What were the reasonable expectations of the data subject at the time of data collection?

  — What were the reasonable expectations of the data collector at the time of data collection?

- Appropriateness of data for modeling goal

  — Can the question being asked be answered with the available data?

  — If a data set has bias, is it possible to collect more data to lessen the bias and answer a critical question?

Concluding Remarks

This chapter has offered an overview of fairness issues as they impact data acquisition and selection for subsequent analysis and ML tasks. The most important fairness impacts are those that can happen earliest in the pipeline. These can be most influential in preventing downstream misuse and can also avoid the most pervasive fairness problems. Proper fairness-aware data acquisition and selection should therefore be at the forefront of any organization's development of fairness-aware methods for future use in improved pipelines or for rehabilitating existing pipelines to improve fairness qualities.

Thus this chapter offers the highest-stage, earliest form of fairness awareness and interventions possible in the ML development process. The next few chapters will take you through more opportunities to intervene, which have been briefly described here—namely, pre-processing, in-processing, and post-processing. However, you should recall that the earliest opportunities for intervention are always the best, so you should always return to first principles no matter how effective or accessible downstream methods become.

## CHAPTER 4

Fairness Pre-Processing

As discussed in the previous chapter, fairness can affect three stages of the data modeling pipeline. This chapter focuses on the earliest stage, adjusting the way that data is translated into inputs for a machine learning training process, also called *pre-processing* the data.

The advantages of pre-processing a data set are numerous. For starters, many regard this as the most flexible fairness intervention, because if done well, it can prevent downstream misuse or carelessness leading to discrimination. If the discrimination is removed from the data, there is less of a concern that naive or careless downstream users could go wrong. Additionally, some methods for pre-processing a data set are more intuitive and inspectable than are methods that act during model training (i.e., *in-processing*).

Because pre-processing is the earliest opportunity for intervening in the data modeling process,[1] pre-processing offers the most opportunities for downstream metrics. When pre-processing is the fairness intervention used in the data modeling pipeline,[2] fairness metrics can be applied at different stages along the pipeline. For example, we can separately measure both how the pre-processing reduces discrimination in the data *and* how the pre-processing affects potentially discriminatory outputs of the model trained on the data set.

Because fairness in machine learning remains a relatively young field without a clearly established canon, and because fairness itself is a slippery subject that will always have different definitions in different contexts, there is no single way to pre-process data. What's more, there is no single way to pre-process data that has been

---

1 Apart from ensuring that data itself is selected and collected as fairly as possible, as discussed in Chapter 3.

2 We will discuss the option of multiple interventions in subsequent chapters.

found to be the "best" even with a particular fairness metric in mind. Different interventions perform differently depending on the data set. I'll start by covering a few pre-processing methods that have gained a following, as indicated by citations to academic papers and by inclusion in a popular AI fairness module, AIF360 (*https://aif360.mybluemix.net*). In the next three chapters, we will maintain our ties to the AIF360 selection while also sometimes covering methods not included in that module. This module is a good way to start working on issues related to machine learning fairness, so it's worth your while to gain familiarity with this open source code base. You might even consider contributing to it, as it's a young project with room to grow.

Simple Pre-Processing Methods

You would likely come up with two simple pre-processing methods on your own if asked to devise a method for pre-processing data to reduce discrimination. One possibility, you might suggest, is to delete any data associated with a sensitive or protected attribute. Don't want to discriminate by gender? Fine, delete the gender information. Another possibility could be to "right the wrongs" in the data set by relabeling data. Can you identify a specific job candidate who seems to have suffered from racial discrimination in not being hired? Change their label—that is, change their outcome to what it would fairly be if consistent with their merit. I briefly discuss these options before proceeding to a discussion of more-sophisticated methods for pre-processing data to reduce discrimination.

Suppression: The Baseline

In some academic work, suppressing not only sensitive attributes but also attributes that are highly correlated with these sensitive attributes has been suggested as a baseline model for removing bias. This can assist with some cases drawn from recent legal history, such as the use of geography as a proxy for race (e.g., redlining) or the use of a high school diploma as an attribute that was highly indicative of race but was a genuine work requirement.[3] We'll give an example of suppression in the following code demonstrations to show one example of suppression and its performance relative to other techniques on a specific data set.

---

3 *Griggs v. Duke Power Co.*, 401 U.S. 424 (1971).

Geography as a Proxy for Socioeconomic Information

Decades after the US civil rights era, the country remains profoundly segregated, even in terms of geography. Geographic information at high levels (e.g., state) and granular levels (e.g., zip code) offers surprisingly informative priors regarding the ethnic identity of individuals who live in a certain geographic region.

This has allowed discrimination without explicit use of prohibited categories in some cases. For example, until the 1980s, banking institutions circumvented antidiscrimination requirements with resulting extreme disparate impacts. This was called *redlining* (*https://oreil.ly/P4gaX*): banks deemed certain zip codes too risky to lend to, so individuals in those communities simply could not get mortgages. The formal reason was that they lived in a high-risk zip code, but descriptively, it was because their zip code was associated with a racial minority. Redlining successfully circumvented requirements of the Fair Housing Act of 1968. It was addressed by the US Congress in alternative legislation in 1977, the Community Reinvestment Act, which required banks to apply the same lending standards to individuals in all communities.

This one example highlights a larger problem with proxies: often in real-world data sets, one variable not formally related to membership in a protected category will nonetheless offer information about membership in a protected category. For redlining, it was zip code as a proxy for race. Now zip code can indicate race, but also other correlates with race, such as religion, socioeconomic status, or political leanings.[4]

This is one reason that suppression is often not a good strategy for building a model that is fair. Simply ignoring the direct information about membership in a protected category will not succeed in removing correlations with other variables.

In fact, such strong correlations are one reason you should be quite suspicious when you find an unexpected "connection" or predictive variable. You should be concerned that you have simply found a proxy for a forbidden category. This may be part of the motivation, for example, in one UK police force taking steps to remove postcode information from its predictive policing tool. Zip code was originally included as a measure of "community depravity," but this is questionable logic to begin with, looking more like guilt by association than guilt of an individual. What's more, postcode could have served as a proxy for sensitive group membership attributes that legally cannot be considered. To learn more about the potentially discriminatory outputs of the HART policing model deployed in parts of the UK, check out this story from *Wired* (*https://oreil.ly/elXlb*).

---

4 Much political campaign work is based on inferring the political beliefs and behaviors of individuals from little more than gender, ethnic identity, and age, and many of these variables are highly correlated with geography. The week of the 2020 US presidential election prompted discussion of this implicitly; votes from different geographic regions were expected to favor one candidate or the other given their demography.

Massaging the Data Set: Relabeling

Two distinct propositions are available for relabeling the data. One way to relabel the data is to identify likely unfair/discriminatory decisions and correct these by changing the outcome to what ought to have happened. The other way is to change the labeled sensitive class rather than the outcome, and this can be done either randomly or in a systematic way to correct discrimination. I don't pursue this second option because such sensitive information is not usually fed into a training algorithm directly, so relabeling it is unlikely to change the outcome. This is because in most cases of importance, considering such protected categories is illegal. Even when inclusion of sensitive variables isn't illegal, it would often appear motivated by unethical considerations. When considering labels is neither illegal nor unethical (such as medical algorithms that recognize difference incidences of disease in different racial categories), you also wouldn't want to relabel the sensitive categories, since in such cases they provide critical information that would help those affected by the algorithm, particularly medical patients.

Relabeling outcome data, where we could imagine that data adjustments could attempt to remove some of the unfairness of the real world to teach an algorithm fairer outcomes, could be done in a number of ways. But it's important to recognize that the judgments as to which points deserve to be relabeled could easily be incomplete or themselves reflect different forms of bias. For example, imagine a society in which racial group A had been historically favored and racial group B had been historically disfavored. Let's further imagine that some kind of racial segregation had just ended, finally permitting students from racial group B to attend a university from which they had previously been barred. When we look at historical data for that university, we might find that students from racial group A historically succeeded in college if they had a certain set of attributes. One way of trying to make a fair data set could be to take past examples of students from racial group B, all of whom had previously been denied entry, and instead find their nearest neighbor from racial group A, and mark them to have the same outcome.

No doubt, this would result in a substantially fairer data set than the one reflecting true history. After all, it would at least include the possibility that students from group B could be admitted to the university. However, it's not clear that this data set would be especially fair. For example, the attributes that marked successful students from group A might not be present in any students from group B because of other associated disadvantages. Imagine that in a privileged group of students, organized sports are readily available in terms of financial and social resources to enable participation. Perhaps for this population, participation in such sports can be good proof of opportunities to develop self-discipline. Perhaps it is also the case that those privileged students who have such an opportunity and fail to take it tend to be less self-disciplined than the others, although this itself would still need to reflect many of the other reasons not to participate in an organized sport, such as health problems, or the pursuit of other interests that require self-discipline. In broad strokes, for such a population, participation in an organized sport could be a useful indicator of self-discipline, and failure to participate might call for inquiry into whether the student could give some other proof of having developed good self-discipline. A model built for such a population could consider participation in such sports as a positive factor and, hopefully, leave open the options for other positive factors to allow for cases where such participation was not possible or desirable.

On the other hand, we can imagine that for an unprivileged group—because of financial or social or structural reasons—organized sports are not readily available. This does not mean that students in this pool lack self-discipline, but instead that they are unlikely to have had the opportunity to develop self-discipline via organized sports. For this population, it might not even make sense to include such a variable if participation is a rare opportunity, rather than a common and accessible proxy. So deploying the model built for the privileged group on this unprivileged group would be unfair and inaccurate.

We could go through a variety of situations to show ways this could be unfair. It points to the possibility that human discretion and constant learning about the specific domain would continue to be important, even if we worried that humans were the ultimate source of racial bias. After all, humans could at least reason about things such as the lack of opportunity to join a sports team, whereas existing algorithms cannot. No doubt, coming up with a fair admissions standard would be a work in progress and would also be subject to different ideas about what constituted fair. As has been stated time and again, the technical literature provides no clear answer because this is ultimately a philosophical question that has more than one reasonable answer. This example is chosen to show that even after we discussed fairness metrics in the previous chapter, the appropriateness of which one to deploy and when, and what would be acceptable in making data meet a fairness criterion, remains very much a complicated philosophical question. This is particularly true in the face of a history of unfairness rather than a single unfair decision that needs to be fixed in a single data set.

I won't demonstrate the example of relabeling the data because this is described elsewhere and because it seems unlikely to be a successful way to move forward with data fairness in realistic scenarios. In general, it will be difficult to generate organizational willingness to relabel data.

AIF360 Pipeline

The AIF360 pipeline is one convenient option for learning and experimenting with fairness metrics and interventions. AIF360 is a convenient package for trying different fairness metrics and interventions. This is because it includes multiple pre-coded fairness interventions for pre-processing data based on widely cited, recent scholarship. It's also because AIF360 comes with the most widely used data sets in the technical fairness literature. Here are two we will be working with:

COMPAS data set (https://oreil.ly/79nox)
> This is the data set built by ProPublica and associated with its 2016 story on racial bias in the COMPAS program's recidivism scoring algorithm as assessed by a statistical parity metric on false positives or false negatives. This data set includes around 6,000 data points, with such sensitive attributes as race and sex.

German credit data set (https://oreil.ly/Hv4tv)
> This widely cited data set contains one thousand decisions regarding whether to extend credit to an applicant. It became public in 1994 and includes around 20 inputs and sensitive attributes including sex, age, and citizenship status.

AIF360 is useful because it provides an easy and accessible interface for loading data and running discrimination metrics on that data.

Loading the Data

You can see how easy it is to load the data with a simple example:

```
gd = GermanDataset()
```

If you then print the data set, you can see it's in a nice, digestible format:

```
               instance weights features

                            month credit_amount
instance names
0                     1.0      6.0        1169.0
1                     1.0     48.0        5951.0
2                     1.0     12.0        2096.0
3                     1.0     42.0        7882.0
4                     1.0     24.0        4870.0
...                   ...      ...          ...


               investment_as_income_percentage residence_since
instance names
0                                          4.0             4.0
1                                          2.0             2.0
2                                          2.0             3.0
3                                          2.0             4.0
4                                          3.0             4.0
...                                        ...             ...
```

```
            protected attribute
                   age number_of_credits people_liable_for
instance names
0                  1.0              2.0              1.0
1                  0.0              1.0              1.0
2                  1.0              1.0              2.0
3                  1.0              1.0              2.0
4                  1.0              2.0              2.0
...                ...              ...              ...
                                    ...
            protected attribute     ...
                   sex status=A11   ...   housing=A153
instance names                      ...
0                  1.0        1.0   ...            0.0
1                  0.0        0.0   ...            0.0
2                  1.0        0.0   ...            0.0
3                  1.0        1.0   ...            1.0
4                  1.0        1.0   ...            1.0
...                ...        ...   ...            ...

            skill_level=A171 skill_level=A172 skill_level=A173
instance names
0                      0.0              0.0              1.0
1                      0.0              0.0              1.0
2                      0.0              1.0              0.0
3                      0.0              0.0              1.0
4                      0.0              0.0              1.0
...                    ...              ...              ...

            skill_level=A174 telephone=A191 telephone=A192
instance names
0                      0.0            0.0            1.0
1                      0.0            1.0            0.0
2                      0.0            1.0            0.0
3                      0.0            1.0            0.0
4                      0.0            1.0            0.0
...                    ...            ...            ...

                                                 labels

            foreign_worker=A201 foreign_worker=A202
instance names
0                      1.0              0.0   1.0
1                      1.0              0.0   2.0
2                      1.0              0.0   1.0
3                      1.0              0.0   1.0
4                      1.0              0.0   2.0
...                    ...              ...   ...
[1000 rows x 60 columns]
```

Because all the categorical variables have been converted to binary columns, we have quite a wide data set. The protected attributes of age and sex in the data set are conveniently labeled as such. If you haven't noticed that, backtrack and look at the labeling just above the column name at the top of the output. This won't be the case when you create AIF360 data sets with your own data, but it will be the case when you use one of the existing data sets.

The fact that this data comes with the AIF360 package is useful not only because it saves you the trouble of having to download it, but also because it saves you some trouble relating to pre-processing the data. For example, the German credit data set comes with its own idiosyncratic labeling, such as "A201" for foreign worker status, whereas AIF360 provides some utility methods to convert these sorts of values into typical numerical labels. Here's how to access these utility functions:

```
from aif360.algorithms.preprocessing.optim_preproc_helpers.data_preproc_functions
        import load_preproc_data_german
priv_group   = [{'sex': 1}]
unpriv_group = [{'sex': 0}]
              ## utility function to collapse categories
              ## according to details of dataset
preproc_gd   = load_preproc_data_german(['sex'])
preproc_gd
```

This prints out a simplified data set that can be more useful to work with and that has been used throughout the AIF360 tutorials:

	instance weights	features	
		protected attribute	
		age	sex
instance names			
0	1.0	1.0	1.0
1	1.0	0.0	0.0
2	1.0	1.0	1.0
3	1.0	1.0	1.0
4	1.0	1.0	1.0
...	...	...	...

	credit_history=Delay	credit_history=None/Paid
instance names		
0	0.0	0.0
1	0.0	1.0
2	0.0	0.0
3	0.0	1.0
4	1.0	0.0
...	...	...

```
                    credit_history=Other savings=500+ savings=<500
instance names
0                              1.0            0.0          0.0
1                              0.0            0.0          1.0
2                              1.0            0.0          1.0
3                              0.0            0.0          1.0
4                              0.0            0.0          1.0
...                            ...            ...          ...


                    savings=Unknown/None employment=1-4 years employment=4+ years
instance names
0                              1.0                     0.0                 1.0
1                              0.0                     1.0                 0.0
2                              0.0                     0.0                 1.0
3                              0.0                     0.0                 1.0
4                              0.0                     1.0                 0.0
...                            ...                     ...                 ...

                                       labels

                    employment=Unemployed
instance names
0                              0.0    1.0
1                              0.0    2.0
2                              0.0    1.0
3                              0.0    1.0
4                              0.0    2.0
...                            ...    ...

[1000 rows x 13 columns]
```

This need not be a canonical data set, but it can be a way to start with a cleaner and well-sized and shaped set of inputs. You can see the decisions made in pre-processing by looking at the source code for this utility function:

```
def load_preproc_data_german(protected_attributes=None):
    """
    Load and pre-process german credit dataset.
    Args:
        protected_attributes(list or None): If None use all possible protected
            attributes, else subset the protected attributes to the list.
    Returns:
        GermanDataset: An instance of GermanDataset with required pre-processing.
    """
    def custom_preprocessing(df):
        """ Custom pre-processing for German Credit Data
        """

        def group_credit_hist(x):
            if x in ['A30', 'A31', 'A32']:
                return 'None/Paid'
```

```python
        elif x == 'A33':
            return 'Delay'
        elif x == 'A34':
            return 'Other'
        else:
            return 'NA'

    def group_employ(x):
        if x == 'A71':
            return 'Unemployed'
        elif x in ['A72', 'A73']:
            return '1-4 years'
        elif x in ['A74', 'A75']:
            return '4+ years'
        else:
            return 'NA'

    def group_savings(x):
        if x in ['A61', 'A62']:
            return '<500'
        elif x in ['A63', 'A64']:
            return '500+'
        elif x == 'A65':
            return 'Unknown/None'
        else:
            return 'NA'

    def group_status(x):
        if x in ['A11', 'A12']:
            return '<200'
        elif x in ['A13']:
            return '200+'
        elif x == 'A14':
            return 'None'
        else:
            return 'NA'

    status_map = {'A91': 1.0, 'A93': 1.0, 'A94': 1.0,
                  'A92': 0.0, 'A95': 0.0}
    df['sex'] = df['personal_status'].replace(status_map)


    # group credit history, savings, and employment
    df['credit_history'] = df['credit_history'].apply(lambda x:
      group_credit_hist(x))
    df['savings'] = df['savings'].apply(lambda x: group_savings(x))
    df['employment'] = df['employment'].apply(lambda x: group_employ(x))
    df['age'] = df['age'].apply(lambda x: np.float(x >= 25))
    df['status'] = df['status'].apply(lambda x: group_status(x))

    return df
```

```
# Feature partitions
XD_features = ['credit_history', 'savings', 'employment', 'sex', 'age']
D_features = ['sex', 'age'] if protected_attributes is
  None else protected_attributes
Y_features = ['credit']
X_features = list(set(XD_features)-set(D_features))
categorical_features = ['credit_history', 'savings', 'employment']

# privileged classes
all_privileged_classes = {"sex": [1.0],
                          "age": [1.0]}

# protected attribute maps
all_protected_attribute_maps = {"sex": {1.0: 'Male', 0.0: 'Female'},
                                "age": {1.0: 'Old', 0.0: 'Young'}}

return GermanDataset(
    label_name=Y_features[0],
    favorable_classes=[1],
    protected_attribute_names=D_features,
    privileged_classes=[all_privileged_classes[x] for x in D_features],
    instance_weights_name=None,
    categorical_features=categorical_features,
    features_to_keep=X_features+Y_features+D_features,
    metadata={ 'label_maps': [{1.0: 'Good Credit', 2.0: 'Bad Credit'}],
               'protected_attribute_maps': [all_protected_attribute_maps[x]
                             for x in D_features]},
    custom_preprocessing=custom_preprocessing)
```

This utility function makes use of the standard `GermanDataset` initializer but provides inputs beyond the defaults for the many arguments the initializer takes. You can use this as a baseline from which to write your own utility function if you would like to add more input features or perhaps change the labels on some of the inputs. Utility functions are provided for all the standard data sets. Also, helpfully, several of these loading functions are tied directly to recent NeurIPS fairness research papers,[5] so that this can be a good source of code if you are looking to replicate or extend existing state-of-the-art results and techniques.

Fairness Metrics

Once we have loaded a data set, we can also assess the data itself even before training models, to determine the extent of unfairness we think is represented in the data set.

---

5 NeurIPS is one of the most prominent international conferences on machine learning, along with other large conferences such as KDD and ICML. Increasingly, such conferences include important submissions on fairness research, and even tutorials and workshops fully devoted to the topic of fairness. I strongly recommend looking at the video presentations and publications of such conferences to stay current on emerging topics in algorithmic fairness.

As described in Chapter 3, the technical fairness literature discusses and optimizes multiple fairness metrics, and it's unlikely that a metric can ever cover every situation. AIF360 recognizes this and provides numerous options. A few of them are demonstrated in this section, showing how easy it is to get a quick report on a data set, either a standard data set that comes with AIF360 or a novel one you are loading to preprocess. I start by creating a `BinaryLabelDatasetMetric` object, which then includes a number of convenience methods, as shown here:

```
# Metric for the original dataset
gd_metrics  = BinaryLabelDatasetMetric(preproc_gd,
                                      unprivileged_groups = unpriv_group,
                                      privileged_groups   = priv_group)
```

We can then compute a variety of metrics as shown here:

```
>>> gd_metrics.consistency()
array([0.645])
>>> gd_metrics.disparate_impact()
0.8965673282047968
>>> gd_metrics.statistical_parity_difference()
-0.07480130902290782
```

These metrics are defined in the Chapter 3. They are also defined with mathematical notation in the AIF360 documentation (*https://oreil.ly/Hs04U*). Note that for reading this and similar documentation, you should have taken a basic probability course that would expose you to the notation generally used in probability and statistical definitions.

The US Census Data Set

For the pre-processing examples that follow, we will use a US Census data set often also known as the Adult data set. It is available via the UCI Machine Learning Repository (*https://oreil.ly/WR-UX*) as well as through the AIF360 module. This data set is used extensively in the fairness literature. We will be pre-processing it to make it fairer with respect to sex (male or female) when the outcome measured is income as a binary variable of ≤ \$50,000 or > \$500,000. We can load the data set and see its initial fairness indicators with the following code:

```
priv_group   = [{'sex': 1}]
unpriv_group = [{'sex': 0}]
census_data  = load_preproc_data_adult(['sex'])

dset_raw_trn, dset_raw_vld,
            dset_raw_tst = split_data_trn_vld_tst(census_data,
                                               priv_group,
                                               unpriv_group)

## calculate the metric of interest
metric_raw_trn = BinaryLabelDatasetMetric(dset_raw_trn,
```

```
                                        unprivileged_groups = unpriv_group,
                                        privileged_groups   = priv_group)
    print("Difference in mean outcomes = %f" %
          metric_raw_trn.mean_difference())
    print("Disparate impact = %f" %
          metric_raw_trn.disparate_impact())
```

This leads to the following output:

```
Difference in mean outcomes = -0.19
Disparate impact = 0.36
```

In case you have forgotten from Chapter 3, the *difference in mean outcomes* represents the difference between the mean outcome for the favored group and the mean outcome for the disfavored group. Ideally, this number should be as close to 0 as possible. *Disparate impact* refers to the ratio of the success rate for the disfavored or unprivileged group to the success rate of the favored or privileged group. Ideally, this number too should be as close to 1 as possible, and as discussed in Chapter 3, values below 0.8 would be, in the domain of employment law, grounds for an investigation into hiring practices by the Equal Employment Opportunity Commission.

Note that the split was calculated using a class method convenience function for dividing up AIF360 data set classes for training, validation, and testing of models:

```
def split_data_trn_vld_tst(data_raw, privileged_groups, unprivileged_groups):
    dset_raw_trn, dset_raw_vt = data_raw.split([0.7], shuffle=True)
    dset_raw_vld, dset_raw_tst = dset_raw_vt.split([0.5], shuffle=True)

    return dset_raw_trn, dset_raw_vld, dset_raw_tst
```

Let's also examine what this data set looks like so we have an idea of what we're working with through the rest of this chapter:

```
                instance weights features
                                     protected attribute
                             race                sex Age (decade)=10
    instance names
    0                   1.0          1.0          1.0          0.0
    1                   1.0          1.0          1.0          0.0
    2                   1.0          1.0          1.0          0.0
    3                   1.0          0.0          1.0          0.0
    4                   1.0          0.0          0.0          0.0
    ...                 ...          ...          ...          ...

                    Age (decade)=20 Age (decade)=30 Age (decade)=40
    instance names
    0                   0.0          1.0          0.0
    1                   0.0          0.0          0.0
    2                   0.0          1.0          0.0
    3                   0.0          0.0          0.0
    4                   1.0          0.0          0.0
    ...                 ...          ...          ...
```

```
                 Age (decade)=50 Age (decade)=60 Age (decade)=>=70
instance names
0                            0.0            0.0            0.0
1                            1.0            0.0            0.0
2                            0.0            0.0            0.0
3                            1.0            0.0            0.0
4                            0.0            0.0            0.0
...                          ...            ...            ...

                 Education Years=6 Education Years=7 Education Years=8
instance names
0                            0.0            0.0            0.0
1                            0.0            0.0            0.0
2                            0.0            0.0            0.0
3                            0.0            1.0            0.0
4                            0.0            0.0            0.0
...                          ...            ...            ...

                 Education Years=9 Education Years=10 Education Years=11
instance names
0                            0.0            0.0            0.0
1                            0.0            0.0            0.0
2                            1.0            0.0            0.0
3                            0.0            0.0            0.0
4                            0.0            0.0            0.0
...                          ...            ...            ...

                 Education Years=12 Education Years=<6 Education Years=>12
instance names
0                            0.0            0.0            1.0
1                            0.0            0.0            1.0
2                            0.0            0.0            0.0
3                            0.0            0.0            0.0
4                            0.0            0.0            1.0
...                          ...            ...            ...

                 labels
instance names
0                    0.0
1                    0.0
2                    0.0
3                    0.0
4                    0.0
...                  ...

[48842 rows x 20 columns]
```

You can see that protected attributes of race and age are listed first and that age and education are broken into broad categorical variables, such as whether someone's age puts them in their thirties, or whether someone has more than 12 years of education.

You can also see that a model we could build with this data set would operate on the theory that income should be predicted by education and age, and that if we were to apply fairness metrics to this model, we would have the operating assumption that race and age should not be predictive of income, given education and age, even though we know this would likely not be the case, at least in the 21st-century US context (or any previous century in US history, tragically).

Suppression

Previously, I briefly mentioned *suppression*—that is, removing the explicit information about membership in a protected category and building a model that ignores this input. As described previously, this is problematic because, in real-world data sets, membership in a protected category is invariably highly correlated with other covariates. For this reason, your default expectation should often be that removal of information about a protected category without other fairness interventions is unlikely to yield less-discriminatory results and may even yield more-discriminatory results than other fairness interventions that do incorporate information about membership in a protected group.

Fairness Performance Metrics

There is no generally accepted way of comparing methods, be it with respect to metrics or data sets. There are some canonical data sets on which fairness algorithms are generally demonstrated, but no theoretical or empirical research indicates that these are necessarily the best or most representative samples. So the observations made in one set of examples may not carry over to other data sets with respect to performance of a particular fairness intervention.

In the following code, the information about the protected category is dropped, and then a model is fitted. Finally, I calculate the same discrimination metrics as used in the previous example to compare the performance of a model where suppression is the only fairness intervention used:

```
def build_logit_model_suppression(dset_trn,
                                  dset_tst,
                                  privileged_groups,
                                  unprivileged_groups):

    scaler = StandardScaler()
    X_trn  = scaler.fit_transform(dset_trn.features[:, 2:]) ❶
    y_trn  = dset_trn.labels.ravel()
    w_trn  = dset_trn.instance_weights.ravel()

    lmod = LogisticRegression()
    lmod.fit(X_trn, y_trn,
```

```
                sample_weight = w_trn) ❷

        dset_tst_pred = dset_tst.copy(deepcopy=True)
        X_tst = scaler.transform(dset_tst_pred.features[:, 2:]) ❸
        dset_tst_pred.labels = lmod.predict(X_tst)

        metric_tst = BinaryLabelDatasetMetric(dset_tst_pred, ❹
                                    unprivileged_groups,
                                    privileged_groups)
        print("Disparate impact is %0.2f (closer to 1 is better)" %
                metric_tst.disparate_impact())
        print("Mean difference  is %0.2f (closer to 0 is better)" %
                metric_tst.mean_difference())

        return lmod, dset_tst_pred, metric_tst

    # reproducibility
    np.random.seed(316)

    sup_lmod, sup_pred,
            sup_metric = build_logit_model_suppression(dset_raw_trn,
                                            dset_raw_tst,
                                            priv_group,
                                            unpriv_group)
```

❶ The columns containing information about sensitive attributes are dropped from the training data.

❷ The model is fitted to the training data.

❸ The columns containing information about sensitive attributes are dropped from the testing data to produce labels.

❹ The original testing data, containing the sensitive labels, is used to measure metrics of fairness, specifically metrics related to discrimination.

The preceding code produces the following output:

```
Disparate impact is 0.60 (closer to 1 is better)
Mean difference  is -0.06 (closer to 0 is better)
```

In this case, this is an improvement compared to the raw data; that is, building a model that suppresses information about the protected category, for this data set and this chosen model, does not exacerbate the disparity in outcomes between groups. This result goes against the warning I have given previously. I have previously mentioned that machine learning researchers, and their predecessors in low-tech HR, admissions, and many other sorts of organizational offices, have found that ignoring protected attributes is not effective at enhancing fairness of outcomes, particularly when fairness is assessed on a group-oriented basis, such as statistical parity.

However, this shows that there are exceptions, as with many rules of thumb that apply to data about humans.

If you have free time, you might consider giving some thought to why the advice doesn't bear out here. For example, what does that imply about the structure of the data? Try generating synthetic data to see if you can prove out any theories you develop.

Reweighting

Reweighting the data set has a number of positive aspects to recommend it as compared to the suppression and relabeling techniques discussed earlier. Suppression is not guaranteed to move a model toward any notion of fairness. Moreover, throwing out data is rarely a good idea, and removing labels can even lead to more-discriminatory models. Also, to determine which labels you ought to change via relabeling, you need to have some underlying model of merit, but of course that is a difficult question. So, a method that enables you to avoid having to directly determine merit can be somewhat more automatic and helpful if you want to have justification for a fairness intervention that doesn't require you to debate the way you define or measure merit. In such a case, reweighting the data is attractive because you are not defining merit, but merely ensuring that success and failure are equally weighted within all subgroups of the population, further lessening the risk that an ML product will find membership in a protected category, or variables proxying for such information as strong in the decision-making process. In particular, the risk that a model will develop a logic of [input indicating membership in a protected category] → merit will be diminished, and this will happen through a transparent process.

Relabeling involves taking an active state in the construction of the data set, and this can look quite a bit like social engineering. We are changing reality by acting as if things happened differently from the way they actually did. We can imagine in many scenarios that people would find this ideologically objectionable, a literal rewriting of history.

Reweighting the data set, on the other hand, does not entail such drastic acts of removing data or rewriting history. Instead, it takes aim at correcting past wrongs by weighting *correct* cases more heavily and weighting *incorrect* (that is, discriminatory) cases less. What's more, reweighting can be much more principled in aiming at an ultimate fairness outcome, most particularly some predefined mathematical notion.

Note that adjusting sampling can be viewed as just another way to adjust weights, and can be appropriate for methods that do not directly take in a weighting vector.

How It Works

Reweighting works by postulating that a fair data set would show no conditional dependence of the outcome on a protected attribute. Hence, it postulates that P(group) membership in group G *and* an outcome (T) should be equal to P(group membership G) × P(outcome T); that is, group membership and outcome should be statistically independent. Reweighting adjusts the data point weights to make this so.

Note that this is such a simple procedure that it could be handcoded. The advantage of AIF360, however, is multifold:

- Integration with a larger API, including the data sources and metrics covered in the preceding section.
- Code from an open source project will have had many eyes on it and more opportunities for error correction than a DIY option.
- It's preferable to work within a code base where different processing options can be swapped in and out, rather than pre-committing all code to a particular solution simply because you can code it yourself.

Code Demonstration

The code for reweighting is relatively simple and can be found within the `fit` and `transform` methods available on the `Reweighing` class, which inherits from the more general `Transformer` class. The API is similar to that of `sklearn`, so those familiar with the popular `sklearn` library should adapt quickly to AIF360's interface.

Let's consider the `fit` code:

```
def fit(self, dataset):
    """Compute the weights for reweighing the dataset.
    Args:
        dataset (BinaryLabelDataset): Dataset containing true labels.
    Returns:
        Reweighing: Returns self.
    """

    (priv_cond, unpriv_cond, fav_cond, unfav_cond,
    cond_p_fav, cond_p_unfav, cond_up_fav, cond_up_unfav) =
            self._obtain_conditionings(dataset) ❶

    n = np.sum(dataset.instance_weights, dtype=np.float64) ❷
    n_p = np.sum(dataset.instance_weights[priv_cond], dtype=np.float64)
    n_up = np.sum(dataset.instance_weights[unpriv_cond], dtype=np.float64)
    n_fav = np.sum(dataset.instance_weights[fav_cond], dtype=np.float64)
    n_unfav = np.sum(dataset.instance_weights[unfav_cond], dtype=np.float64)

    n_p_fav = np.sum(dataset.instance_weights[cond_p_fav], dtype=np.float64) ❸
    n_p_unfav = np.sum(dataset.instance_weights[cond_p_unfav],
```

```
                   dtype=np.float64)
        n_up_fav = np.sum(dataset.instance_weights[cond_up_fav],
                         dtype=np.float64)
        n_up_unfav = np.sum(dataset.instance_weights[cond_up_unfav],
                           dtype=np.float64)

        # reweighing weights
        self.w_p_fav = n_fav*n_p / (n*n_p_fav)     ❹
        self.w_p_unfav = n_unfav*n_p / (n*n_p_unfav)
        self.w_up_fav = n_fav*n_up / (n*n_up_fav)
        self.w_up_unfav = n_unfav*n_up / (n*n_up_unfav)

        return self
```

❶ `self._obtain_conditionings` refers to a private class method used to prepare logic vectors indicating which data points fall within which kind of condition. This includes both simple conditions (are they in the privileged set?) and combination conditions (are they in the privileged set *and* did they receive a favorable outcome?).

❷ These lines of `np.sum` count the data points, adjusted by any custom nonuniform weights that have been supplied, correspond to the simple binary conditions of privileged or unprivileged and favorable outcome or unfavorable outcome.

❸ These lines of `np.sum` count the data points, adjusted by any custom nonuniform weights that have been supplied, correspond to the combination conditions that include both group membership and outcome.

❹ This is where the reweightings are calculated. In each case, dividing the numerator by n represents the rate of a particular combination of group membership and outcome that should occur if group membership and outcome were statistically independent. The other portion of the denominators represents dividing by the actual rate, which presumably represents some form of bias. So these weights act to replace the empirical but nonindependent rate with a rate that would be consistent with statistical independence of outcome and group membership.

Once these weights have been calculated, the `transform` method simply applies these weights to each individual data point. We do not reproduce that code for simplicity, but you can easily read it in the project's GitHub repository (*https://oreil.ly/3WDex*).

Thanks to the handy packaging of the AIF360 module, we can then perform the reweighting with a few lines of code:

```
## transform the data set
RW = Reweighing(unprivileged_groups = unpriv_group,
                privileged_groups   = priv_group)
RW.fit(dset_raw_trn)
```

```
dset_rewgt_trn = RW.transform(dset_raw_trn)

## calculate the metric of interest
metric_rewgt_trn = BinaryLabelDatasetMetric(dset_rewgt_trn,
                                    unprivileged_groups = unpriv_group,
                                    privileged_groups   = priv_group)
print("Difference in mean outcomes = %f" %
      metric_rewgt_trn.mean_difference())
print("Disparate impact = %f" %
      metric_rewgt_trn.disparate_impact())
```

This yields an output that looks perfect, in the sense that any statistical measure of fairness will now show perfect fairness:

```
Difference in mean outcomes = -0.0 ## 0 is desirable to minimize
difference between groups
Disparate impact = 1.0 ## 1 is desirable as this is a ratio of the
groups rather than a difference
```

Now we have a data set in which we have reweighted points to make group-oriented fairness metrics come out even. We have pre-processed the data not by changing labels or changing the vector space in which we represent inputs, but merely by adjusting the weighting of data points. The weightings can be one of four values, one for each combination of group membership (favored group or disfavored group) and outcome (favorable or unfavorable). We can verify that we have only four weightings as follows:

```
>>> set(dset_rewgt_trn.instance_weights)
{0.7868545496506331, 0.853796632203106, 1.0923452329973244, 2.2157900832376507}
```

Not surprisingly, two of the instance weights are < 1 (likely those with unfavorable outcomes for the unprivileged group and favorable outcomes for the privileged group) and two of the instance weights are > 1 (likely those with favorable outcomes for the unprivileged group and unfavorable outcomes for the privileged group).

The test of the method, however, is not whether it gives sensible weightings but whether the pre-processed data, when passed through a model training process, leads to an end product that is fairer than a model trained on unprocessed data. In this chapter we will train a logistic regression model and compare the model trained on the unprocessed data to the model trained on the reweighted data. As a reminder, I emphasized in preceding chapters that no single metric would establish a model as fair or not fair. Here we will use two metrics to assess models, consistency (a measure of individual fairness) and disparate impact (a measure of group fairness). These were defined in Chapter 3's list of fairness metrics.

We will train our model on the raw data only once, and record its metrics. Keep these in mind when we look at other examples. First, let's introduce a convenience function that wraps all our training and reporting functionality:

```
def build_logit_model(dset_trn,
                      dset_tst,
                      privileged_groups,
                      unprivileged_groups):

    scaler = StandardScaler()
    X_trn  = scaler.fit_transform(dset_trn.features)
    y_trn  = dset_trn.labels.ravel()
    w_trn  = dset_trn.instance_weights.ravel()

    lmod = LogisticRegression()
    lmod.fit(X_trn, y_trn,
             sample_weight = w_trn)

    dset_tst_pred = dset_tst.copy(deepcopy=True)
    X_tst = scaler.transform(dset_tst_pred.features)
    y_tst = dset_tst_pred.labels
    dset_tst_pred.scores = lmod.predict_proba(X_tst)[:, 0].reshape(-1,1)  ❶

    fav_inds = np.where(lmod.predict(X_tst) == dset_trn.favorable_label)[0]  ❷
    dset_tst_pred.labels[fav_inds] = dset_tst_pred.favorable_label
    dset_tst_pred.labels[~fav_inds] = dset_tst_pred.unfavorable_label

    metric_tst = ClassificationMetric(dset_tst, dset_tst_pred,
                                      unprivileged_groups, privileged_groups)  ❸
    print("Consistency is     %f (closer to 1 is better)"
          % metric_tst.consistency())
    print("Disparate impact is %f (closer to 1 is better)" %
          metric_tst.disparate_impact())


    return lmod, dset_tst_pred, metric_tst
```

❶ Use the logistic regression model fit on either the raw or pre-processed training data to generate predictions for our raw training data.

❷ Determine which indices in the predictions correspond to the favorable and unfavorable label and add these to the prediction data set accordingly.

❸ Feed the data to a handy metric class built to compare data and predicted labels for that data and output two useful fairness metrics.

Applying this first to train a model on raw data, we see the following metrics:

```
>>> ## raw training data
>>> raw_lmod, raw_pred, raw_metric = build_logit_model(dset_raw_trn,
                                                       dset_raw_tst,
                                                       priv_group,
                                                       unpriv_group)
Disparate impact is 0.00 (closer to 1 is better)
Mean difference  is -0.22 (closer to 0 is better)
```

Wow, this looks pretty bad. In fact, this shows how a situation that is already unfair as reflected in the underlying data can become even worse when a model is trained on this data.

Modeling Can Exacerbate Bias

If we recorded the same figures for the raw data set itself, rather than a model, we need not have the same figures for fairness measures. In fact, some papers even study what additional unfairness the act of modeling may introduce to worsen a biased data set. This has been studied, for example, in models that label images or produce images based on labels, whereby a disparity (say, in gender representation in the real world), is worsened in the compilation of a data set and then worsened still more in the training of an image recognition model. So even if at the end of your studies in fairness you were to conclude that you'd rather use minimal or no intervention (unlikely to lead to anything like a fair outcome in many situations), you might introduce bias or additional bias merely by the act of training a model in a non-fairness-aware manner.

If you come away with nothing more from this book, remember that models can exacerbate the disparities represented in unfair data sets.

We can also evaluate a model trained on the data that has been pre-processed using reweighting. We apply the same convenience method to the reweighted data and see the following output:

```
>>> ## fairness pre-processed data
rewgt_lmod, rewgt_pred,
        rewgt_metric = build_logit_model(dset_rewgt_trn,
                                         dset_raw_tst,
                                         priv_group,
                                         unpriv_group)
Disparate impact is 0.66 (closer to 1 is better)
Mean difference  is -0.07 (closer to 0 is better)
```

Interestingly, this is quite a bit better! But this is still far from fair if we are defining fairness in terms of statistical parity, since the groups are far from equal. Note, however, that we do better this way than with mere suppression as assessed by the disparate impact metric.

Learning Fair Representations

Let's now turn to a technique that involves a fundamentally different way of pre-processing data to be fair. We examine a method proposed in a paper called "Learning Fair Representations."[6] The techniques described in the preceding section largely focus on enhancing group fairness by enforcing statistical parity. However, the two more sophisticated techniques described in this section and the next recognize the tension between group fairness and individual fairness, and so aim to develop techniques that recognize the importance of both kinds.

How It Works

Learned fair representations aim for a middle ground between group fairness and individual fairness by turning fairness pre-processing into an optimization problem, where different terms in the optimization relate to group fairness and individual fairness. A third term represents a typical loss function and so relates to accuracy.[7]

So far I've described the goals of the optimization, but I have not discussed what is being optimized—namely, mathematical representations of the data. The idea behind transforming the data from the original inputs into an alternative representation is to minimize the amount of information regarding membership in a protected category that is present in the transformed representation, while maximizing all other information present in the original data. In the words of Zemel et al., they sought to *obfuscate* the protected category while *encoding* the other information.

There are many imaginable ways to do this. Learned fair representations do this in a way that maintains the data in the original vector space but collapses it down to a set of "prototypes" of the input v_k and parameters that defined the mapping from the original input space to the representation space w_k.

The optimization's goal is then to learn the appropriate locations for the prototypes and the appropriate mappings from the inputs to the prototypes. Here I describe the overall expression to be optimized in broad strokes in order to avoid getting into the notational weeds. The authors of the paper seek to optimize an equation with hyperparameters for the relative weightings for expressions corresponding to group fairness, individual fairness, and accuracy. The authors point out that these

---

6 Zemel, Rich, et al. "Learning Fair Representations." Paper presented at the Proceedings of the 30th International Conference on Machine Learning, Atlanta, Georgia, June 2013. *https://oreil.ly/V3Js4*.

7 Yes, there can be accuracy even when a model has not been built and we are pre-processing, and this will be explained later.

hyperparameters can be tweaked either according to domain knowledge or according to an overall performance metric, and they optimize to two fairness-aware performance metrics: (1) minimizing discrimination and (2) maximizing the difference between accuracy (desired to be higher) and discrimination (desired to be lower).

As with the choice of what fairness metric to choose, the balance of decisions made in an optimization problem still involves fairness norms and ultimately still relies on you, the operator, to determine the appropriate hyperparameters to build a fair pre-processed data set. These decisions will likely vary depending on your domain knowledge relating to the societal and personal costs paid for different kinds of wrong decisions and how that might impact how you balance accuracy and antidiscrimination efforts.

Let's consider two real-world use cases in which we might need to balance accuracy and antidiscrimination. First, consider building a medical treatment tool for brain cancer. I am completely fabricating this example and don't imagine it is true, but imagine that for some reason the probability of successful treatment for men differed strongly from that probability for women, with the solution found after extensive ML modeling and training. We might be concerned about this from an antidiscrimination perspective (if we could find no biological explanation) and so insert an antidiscrimination penalty. However, given the life-or-death stakes, we would probably not want to put in a very strong antidiscrimination penalty. Most people would not find it fair to reduce discriminatory outcomes if it meant that more people died of brain cancer overall. In fact, how such a decision would be made and who would make that decision itself is a complicated ethical question that other entities, such as a hospital ethics review board, would be better positioned to make than would an ML engineer. However, the bottom line is that in this example most decision makers would likely include a small antidiscrimination penalty and put more weight on accuracy and obtaining good outcomes.

Consider as a second example university admissions. My 17-year-old self thought of this as a defining moment in life, where the "accuracy" in determining the "best" and "most deserving" student (obviously me, I would now say with irony) should override any concerns about group parity. Luckily, the society in which I live had already come to a wiser conclusion and at the time already recognized the need both to promote diversity in elite universities and to recognize the wider difficulties faced by some groups, and so had enacted affirmative action that promoted health and equality and equity. It's also worth noting that "accuracy" is a misleading idea for purposes of university admissions because there are many competing visions of who the ideal university student is and what their most important attributes are, something 17 year olds and their parents can easily lose sight of.

Some might see this as a penalty to accuracy. (I would argue that even this notion is far from obviously true.)[8] In this case, we could frame a calibration of an ML university admissions product as choosing a relatively large antidiscrimination penalty in our weighting of accuracy versus antidiscrimination prerogatives. This could partly result from recognizing that the benefits of equality in this case far outweigh whatever downsides there could be to slightly reduced "accuracy." Increasing diversity and equality at these institutions has a tremendous effect in sending a clear pro-equality message to the world.

Learned fair representations demonstrate impressive results particularly with respect to minimizing discrimination. This was interesting when assessed on the performance of a model, while showing only a fairly small diminishment in accuracy as compared to models trained on the raw data. What's more, Zemel et al. also showed that attempts to predict membership in a protected group from the pre-processed data showed relatively low accuracy, suggesting that much of the information regarding protected attributes had indeed been removed, as was desired. Choice of hyperparameters could even lead to greater suppression of the information, depending on the algorithm operator's priorities.

Advantages of learned fair representations are numerous. First, they can serve to develop a tool that can be deployed for a data release, even supposing that downstream users will not be interested in enhancing fairness. Second, they result from a relatively simple optimization problem that can be run on a standard laptop for small or medium data sets. Third, they can be used for transfer learning; that is, even if the optimization was developed to protect a particular category with respect to a particular outcome, models can be built on the same representations to predict other outcomes in a way that also enhances downstream fairness of those models.

Code Demonstration

Since you have already seen an example of how the AIF360 pre-processing pipeline works, the following code should be relatively readable. Note, however, that now test data has to be transformed as well as training data. This is because the model is now trained on a different representation of the data to which the original inputs were mapped. That is, now all data has to be pre-processed, not just the training data, because the representation itself has changed.

---

8 This book is not a disquisition on affirmative action. I simply note that good arguments exist in favor of the idea that affirmative action could *increase* accuracy by better accounting for the real challenges that members of historically disfavored groups encounter for a variety of reasons, including but not limited to structural inequalities and implicit but unacknowledged biases that can, in turn, affect all other inputs to admissions decisions, such as subjective grading decisions, availability of extracurricular activities, etc.

An additional wrinkle is that, unlike reweighting, learned fair representations provide a way not to go all in. In particular, a threshold hyperparameter can be set to indicate how strongly the operator wants to remove all information that could be related to discrimination. This is important because, as the authors acknowledge, unfortunately membership in a protected group can sometimes be informative in predicting an outcome.[9] For this reason, the algorithm does provide a way for the operator to tune the data transformation when there is a concern that learned fair representations may remove too much useful information while pursuing the nondiscrimination goal.

First, we fit the LFR object, as is standard with the AIF360 pipeline:

```
TR = LFR(unprivileged_groups = unpriv_group,
                        privileged_groups = priv_group)
TR = TR.fit(dset_raw_trn)

dset_lfr_trn = TR.transform(dset_raw_trn, thresh = 0.5)
dset_lfr_trn = dset_raw_trn.align_data sets(dset_lfr_trn)

dset_lfr_tst = TR.transform(dset_raw_tst, thresh = 0.5)
dset_lfr_tst = dset_raw_trn.align_data sets(dset_lfr_tst)

metric_op = BinaryLabelDatasetMetric(dset_lfr_trn,
                        unprivileged_groups = unpriv_group,
                        privileged_groups   = priv_group)
print("Mean difference:  %0.2f" % metric_op.mean_difference())
print("Disparate impact: %0.2f" % metric_op.disparate_impact())
```

This produces the following output:

```
Mean difference:   -0.21
Disparate impact: 0.00
```

This doesn't seem to do especially well if we look at the transformed data, but what if we use it to train a model and then apply that model to the raw data?

```
>>> lfr_lmod1, lfr_pred, lfr_metric = build_logit_model(dset_lfr_trn,
                                                        dset_raw_tst,
                                                        priv_group,
                                                        unpriv_group)
Disparate impact is 0.95 (closer to 1 is better)
Mean difference  is -0.02 (closer to 0 is better)
```

This gives outstanding performance!

Note, however, that we're not really done with what has been presented. Normally, we would also want to tune the hyperparameters of the various weight settings of the three expressions that contribute to the objection function we seek to minimize: L_x, L_y, and L_z. For example, in the paper describing LFR, the authors indicated that they

---

9 As discussed in Chapter 3, even when this is true, it is still illegal to use this information.

---

performed a grid search over potential hyperparameters for these terms and even included grid terms that would allow the weights to go to 0. So, in a real-world application you should not accept the default values of these (as we did by not setting them in our function call) but should instead plan for hyperparameter tuning. You should do the hyperparameter tuning in accord with a metric that can reflect your organization's decisions as to how to balance fairness and accuracy. For example, in the paper, the authors trained both to minimize discrimination but also, separately, to maximize the difference between accuracy (which we want to maximize) and discrimination (which we want to minimize). Interestingly, both of these methods yielded similar performance metrics among a variety of data sets.

Optimized Data Transformations

Optimized pre-processing is a name for a specific technique to transform the data again in the same vector space as the original data but in a way that makes the data set fairer while also preserving as much nondiscriminatory information about the data as possible. This section describes it in detail and then demonstrates it by means of the AIF360 Python module.

How It Works

Our next method was proposed by Calmon et al. in a paper titled "Optimized Pre-Processing for Discrimination Prevention".[10] This paper defines a probabilistic remapping of the original inputs, information about protected attributes, and labels (X, D, Y) respective to a remapped set of inputs and labels $(\hat{x}, \hat{y})$. The remapping occurs in the original vector space of the inputs, meaning that the pre-processed data can still be read in the same form and with the same column labels. The goal of the remapping is to keep the processed data's distribution (in the sense of probability density function) as close to the original data's distribution as possible, subject to the following two constraints:

- The dependence of the transformed outcome, $\hat{y}$, on group membership D, is below a preset threshold (pushing the data to model a fairer world where group membership in a protected class does not predict outcomes).
- The difference in the distribution of (X, Y) and the transformed distribution $(\hat{x}, \hat{y})$ is not above some threshold for a given specific group D.

These conditions are enforced for all possible groups, not just for the disfavored group. This leads to a model in which data is adjusted by small amounts but in a way

---

10 Calmon, Flavio, et al. "Optimized Pre-Processing for Discrimination Prevention." Paper presented at Neutral Information Processing Systems 2017, Long Beach, California, 2017. *https://perma.cc/4U8H-PBFD*.

to ensure that data is mostly adjusted for just one group beyond a certain threshold and also to lead to a fairer outcome by removing dependencies between group membership and outcome.

How are these values to be set? Earlier I mentioned "some threshold" a number of times. This threshold is to be set by the person doing the data transformation. How you set the threshold will depend on your organization's priorities, the quality of the original data, and the importance of the outcome. Perhaps for some data sets one set of fairness thresholds is appropriate even though it would not be appropriate for another data set. You might even consider using cross-validation to set the thresholds depending on the ultimate outcome you are seeking. In such a case, this would be a multistep process: (1) vary the hyperparameters of the data pre-processing, (2) train a model on the pre-processed data, (3) vary the hyperparameters and compare.

As with earlier discussions, I avoid getting into the weeds of notation, but the paper is quite accessible if you want more details.

Code Demonstration

The input parameters as needed are embodied in the following code, used to run the AIF360 implementation of Calmon et al.'s optimized pre-processing algorithm. These parameters indicate, among other things, a way of measuring distortion (`distor tion_fun`)—that is, the way of calculating how different a data point is from a proposed perturbation to that data point, in a way that allows the data analyst to indicate which sort of perturbations would be acceptable and their relative merits. The parameters also indicate the various distortion categories (`clist`) as indicated by the return value of the distortion function and acceptable probability maximums for each of these categories occurring (`dlist`). Finally, a parameter defines the permitted upper level of deviation from a form of statistical parity (`epsilon`).

While the setup requires more work and settings from us compared to earlier methods described, the pipeline otherwise looks quite similar, as shown here:

```
optim_options = {
    "distortion_fun": get_distortion_adult,
    "epsilon": 0.05,
    "clist": [0.99, 1.99, 2.99],
    "dlist": [.1, 0.05, 0]
}

OP = OptimPreproc(OptTools, optim_options)

OP = OP.fit(dset_raw_trn)

# Transform training data and align features
dset_op_trn = OP.transform(dset_raw_trn, transform_Y=True)
dset_op_trn = dset_raw_trn.align_data sets(dset_op_trn)
```

The distortion function refers to how we will measure the distance between the original probability and the new probability. epsilon refers to the first bullet point condition limiting the dependence of the outcome on group membership. The clist parameters refer to the constraints on the distortion metric, and the distortion metric is provided by the function get_distortion_adult, which is a utility function provided in AIF360.

Let's take a look at that function:

```
def get_distortion_adult(vold, vnew):
    """Distortion function for the adult dataset. We set the distortion
    metric here. See section 4.3 in supplementary material of
    http://papers.nips.cc/paper/
    6988-optimized-pre-processing-for-discrimination-prevention
    for an example
    Note:
        Users can use this as a template to create other distortion functions.
    Args:
        vold (dict) : {attr:value} with old values
        vnew (dict) : dictionary of the form {attr:value} with new values
    Returns:
        d (value) : distortion value
    """

    # Define local functions to adjust education and age
    def adjustEdu(v):
        if v == '>12':
            return 13
        elif v == '<6':
            return 5
        else:
            return int(v)

    def adjustAge(a):
        if a == '>=70':
            return 70.0
        else:
            return float(a)

    def adjustInc(a):
        if a == "<=50K":
            return 0
        elif a == ">50K":
            return 1
        else:
            return int(a)

    # value that will be returned for events that should not occur
    bad_val = 3.0

    # Adjust education years
```

```
eOld = adjustEdu(vold['Education Years'])
eNew = adjustEdu(vnew['Education Years'])

# Education cannot be lowered or increased in more than 1 year
if (eNew < eOld) | (eNew > eOld+1):
    return bad_val

# adjust age
aOld = adjustAge(vold['Age (decade)'])
aNew = adjustAge(vnew['Age (decade)'])

# Age cannot be increased or decreased in more than a decade
if np.abs(aOld-aNew) > 10.0:
    return bad_val

# Penalty of 2 if age is decreased or increased
if np.abs(aOld-aNew) > 0:
    return 2.0

# Adjust income
incOld = adjustInc(vold['Income Binary'])
incNew = adjustInc(vnew['Income Binary'])

# final penalty according to income
if incOld > incNew:
    return 1.0
else:
    return 0.0
```

This convenience function provides an implementation to match published research. This is very helpful for replicating existing research or even for better understanding how a research paper relates to the code that implements the research paper. The preceding code is a great example. Notice also that we can use this distortion metric to implement our own changes if we want to define distortion differently. The *distortion* is used to regulate the preferred or disallowed data transformations, so this is where we would adjust code to reflect how we think changes to education, age, and so on should be viewed, depending on the data set.

Before we run our convenience function to train a model, we also need to transform our test set. Unlike reweighting, which does not require a transformation of the test set, we do need to transform the test set here because the model itself is trained on a remapped version of the data. Luckily, we can consistently remap the data and can still apply this method in an online fashion because the transform is learned only once, for the training data:[11]

---

11 For those who may have statistical qualms regarding the possibility that the test set's distribution is different from the training set's distribution, Zemel et al. provide bounds to show such a potential problem is most likely not a problem.

```
## Transform testing data
dset_op_tst = OP.transform(dset_raw_tst, transform_Y=True)
dset_op_tst = dset_raw_trn.align_data sets(dset_op_tst)
```

Once we have transformed the test data as well, we can assess the performance:

```
>>> ## fairness preprocessed data
>>> op_lmod, op_pred, op_metric = build_logit_model(dset_op_trn,
                                                    dset_op_tst,
                                                    priv_group,
                                                    unpriv_group)
Disparate impact is 0.63 (closer to 1 is better)
Mean difference  is -0.06 (closer to 0 is better)
```

We see very good performance on the group fairness metric (disparate impact) but also good performance on the individual fairness metric (consistency). Note also that to the extent that we were unhappy with the balance of group and individual fairness metrics, we could adjust the impact parameters related to epsilon and clist to adjust how stringent the conditions related to group and individual fairness were during the optimization.

Let's consider one final point in the optimized transform methodology. As mentioned, a convenience method to calculate the distortion of data points is provided. We are, however, free to adjust this when our domain knowledge or priorities are different from those of Calmon et al. This change of the distortion calculation can also impact the group and individual fairness results, so this is another way you might consider tweaking the performance of downstream models. One example to make the distortion metric less stringent and therefore offer a larger space over which to maximize group fairness (likely at the expense of individual fairness or accuracy, or both, since we now allow greater distortion of the data). I cut the code short for space, but the modified portions are included and highlighted in comments:

```
def get_distortion_adult2(vold, vnew):
    ### ... omitted code ... ###

    # value that will be returned for events that should not occur
    bad_val = 3.0

    # Adjust education years
    eOld = adjustEdu(vold['Education Years'])
    eNew = adjustEdu(vnew['Education Years'])

    # Education cannot be lowered or increased in more than 1 year
    ##############################################################
    if (eNew < eOld - 1) | (eNew > eOld + 1): ## LESS STRINGENT
        return bad_val
    ##############################################################
    # adjust age
    aOld = adjustAge(vold['Age (decade)'])
    aNew = adjustAge(vnew['Age (decade)'])
```

```
# Age cannot be increased or decreased in more than a decade
############################################################
if np.abs(aOld-aNew) > 15.0: ## LESS STRINGENT
    return bad_val
############################################################

### ... omitted code ... ###
```

We can see how straightforward modifications to existing code allow us to inject domain knowledge, institutional preferences, or differing norms into the code base. As long as you understand how a methodology works generally, you will, with some careful reading of open source code, discover ways to make the code your own.

Fairness Pre-Processing Checklist

- Pre-processing appropriateness evaluation
  - Are there any legal or reporting requirements that might affect how or whether you can perform pre-processing as a fairness intervention?
    - How does fairness pre-processing interact with GDPR or CCPA requirements to show each data subject the data about them? Do you need to prepare the pre-processed data for inspection as well?
  - How will you document the changes made to the raw data by pre-processing?
  - Will you store the raw data, and how will you determine which use cases continue to use raw data as compared to which will use pre-processed data?
  - You need to plan at the start for incorporating the pre-processing into your live production settings. If not, pre-processing is not appropriate. Is pre-processing in production feasible, and can it be accomplished with a unified team and model to ensure consistency?
- Choosing the form of pre-processing
  - If pre-processing is acceptable and feasible in your use case, you still need to choose the form of pre-processing.
  - Will you simply eliminate sensitive data (this can sometimes make an outcome *less* fair)?
  - Will you relabel data explicitly or simply find a fairer representation of the data?

- Assessing performance of pre-processing
  - Choose important performance metrics *before* assessing your model. Performance metrics will include accuracy and other measures of model performance, including one or more metrics that measure fairness of outcomes.
  - Apply performance metrics to a validation set as you tune hyperparameters available in pre-processing methods.
- Determining good balance of fairness and other performance metrics
  - Use a validation data set to assess potential trade-offs between the fairness metric and accuracy. You can even define the trade-off numerically and plot it across different pre-processing methods or different hyperparameters.
  - Discuss trade-offs with appropriate stakeholders; this should be a transparent and full documented part of the modeling process.
  - Your chosen hyperparameters and pre-processing method should not only reflect pre-processing validation data performance. You should also have qualitative and well-articulated reasons, expressed in human language rather than code, for the choices you are making, and these reasons should be viable ex ante—that is, even before you see that a model produced valid results.
  - Come up with a reasonable impact assessment to determine the downsides as well as the upsides of pre-processing. Will particular individuals or kinds of individuals be hurt by this? If so, are you confident the harm to these individuals is justified in pursuit of a greater total fairness in your data set? Can you balance individual and group fairness?
- Rolling out your pre-processing to production
  - Create a schedule for consistently checking the performance of your fairness metrics over time.
    - Is there a chance pre-processing will be less important over time?
    - Can you do ex post impact assessments to see how your model might have affected individuals?
    - Consider a randomized A/B-test-style rollout of your fairness pre-processing so that you can make stronger assertions about the counterfactual scenario when assessing the impact of your fairness pre-processing interventions.
- Keep an up-to-date list of what models are using pre-processing rather than raw data sets. This should be clearly documented. Dependencies should be strictly accounted for.

Concluding Remarks

If you were careful in working through the code and discussion in this chapter, you might have noticed that we trained the data by including the protected attributes. We did even better when training the data by including the protected attributes, than we did when we suppressed them.

However, one thing I haven't discussed is whether the model makes sense in terms of a fairness intervention. The purpose of our model was to predict the income of people based on their basic demographic information. If we want to predict the real world, including the likely racial and gender biases that are part of that world, it might not make sense to have a fairness intervention. For example, if we are seeking to know candidates for low-income assistance programs, we'd want to know realistically who is hardest hit by the problems of low income.

On the other hand, if we are using income as a proxy for something that equates higher income with higher merit for downstream decision making, we would want an intervention because what we would really be interested in is who would likely have a high income in a fairer world than the one our data set models, and pre-processing is one attempt to answer this. For example, if we (probably wrongly) used high income as a proxy for leadership abilities or investment in one's community or likely success in running for political office, we would certainly want to have a fairness intervention in our model.

## CHAPTER 5

Fairness In-Processing

This chapter focuses on fairness interventions that can be used *during* the process of training a model. While most guidance will encourage a fairness intervention as early in the data pipeline as possible, sometimes the earliest stages of fairness interventions, related to data pre-processing, won't be available. Some potential cases where data pre-processing won't be available could include the following:

- Proprietary or licensed data stores that may come with rules about how they can be stored or modified.

- Organizational guidelines that express disapproval of modifying baseline data sets. We can imagine some people having philosophical objections even if they are otherwise in favor of fairness interventions.

- Data sets that are so large that pre-processing interventions are not computationally feasible given your resources.

- A desire for the simplest pipeline and overall fewer numbers of steps from raw data to results.

If these or any similar use cases describe your constraints, you should consider in-processing as an optimal point in the data modeling pipeline for a fairness intervention. *In-processing* refers to any fairness intervention that modifies the training process for a machine learning model. If we want to think more broadly than machine learning training pipelines, an in-processing intervention would be an intervention in which the decision-making process itself is modified by changing the feedback that is used to assess whether the decision was good.

The Basic Idea

The feedback to assess whether a decision is a good one and how good it is comes through a loss function in traditional machine learning. Without incorporating fairness, a loss function will usually rely most heavily on some metric that assesses how close a model's label or prediction was to the true label or true outcome. Loss functions can be used in all forms of machine learning, and even a novice data analyst will be familiar with the variety of options available, such as mean absolute error or mean squared error in the case of regression problems. Often even the choice of a loss function apart from fairness concerns will reflect the values and expectations for a data modeling problem. For example, mean absolute error as compared to mean squared error puts a different amount of emphasis on outliers, and this can make sense in different contexts.

Outside of fairness interventions, loss functions are also modified to reflect more than just a desire to make a model's outputs match reality as much as possible. *Regularization* is one process to make a model more regular, general, and transferable than it would be if trained with a simpler loss function. The idea of regularization is not to allow any particular inputs to become unduly important, with an underlying theory that if certain inputs were given too much weight, that could likely reflect idiosyncrasies of the data rather than the true situation.

Many in-processing fairness interventions take this idea one step further by doing the same thing as regularization—namely, adding an additional term to the overall loss function. This will be a separate parameter that can be identified as a fairness penalty, itself then only part of a larger loss function reflecting other penalties, be they related to correctness or regularization. The first of the two techniques we discuss in this chapter takes this approach of adding a fairness term to the loss function.

The second technique makes use of a newer idea, *adversarial learning*. Adversarial learning has come to more widespread attention in recent years because of the advance of generative adversarial models, but it is not only for generative models. The second technique I describe uses an adversarial training model as a way to train a machine learning model while reducing the amount of unfair information that leaks through the outcomes in a way that suggests the outcomes are unfairly related to a protected category.

The Medical Data Set

Before we jump into greater detail regarding the methods we'll study, we'll also move on to a new data set. This is a medical data set that is quite complex and that I won't explain in detail. A practicing data scientist would want to understand all inputs and labels for maximum comprehension, but in the interest of brevity we will omit this crucial work. However, we will take a quick peek at the data set. We'll load the data set, divide it into standard training, validation, and testing subsets, and look at our training data. We'll skip some boilerplate code that has already been presented in Chapter 4 regarding training, validation, and testing splits, and just focus on loading the medical data.

Note that at the time of writing this medical data set was available in AIF360 but wasn't described in the documentation. However, some information is available on GitHub (*https://oreil.ly/cpSoV*). We will load this complicated medical data set and then break it into training, validation, and testing sets:

```
med_data = MEPSDataset19()

dset_raw_trn, dset_raw_vld, dset_raw_tst = split_data_trn_vld_tst(med_data)
```

We can see that the protected attribute in this data set comes labeled as RACE:

```
>>> dset_raw_trn.protected_attribute_names
['RACE']
```

Given that we know this, we set some variables we'll use in our in-processing code:

```
priv_group   = [{'RACE': 1}]
unpriv_group = [{'RACE': 0}]
```

We can also take a look at the data set by printing it out:

```
                instance weights features
                                 protected attribute
                                 AGE       RACE  PCS42  MCS42
instance names
12253           1067.939606      32.0      0.0   30.66  67.77
14989           2967.981450       3.0      0.0   -1.00  -1.00
16101           5032.958327      53.0      1.0   57.22  48.98
4757            1997.534112       2.0      0.0   -1.00  -1.00
319             5940.946099      36.0      1.0   -1.00  -1.00
...             ...              ...       ...   ...    ...
7590            6848.927895      57.0      0.0   41.60  60.26
11267          16845.067812      85.0      1.0   35.45  57.97
4928            3387.295774      80.0      0.0   38.84  42.16
7702            2701.148468      41.0      0.0   52.93  61.52
12524          20513.738229      15.0      1.0   -1.00  -1.00
                                                 ...
                                                 ...
         K6SUM42 REGION=1 REGION=2 REGION=3 REGION=4 ... EMPST=4
```

```
instance names                                              . . .
12253            0.0    0.0    1.0    0.0    0.0  ...    0.0
14989           -1.0    0.0    0.0    0.0    1.0  ...    0.0
16101            2.0    0.0    0.0    0.0    1.0  ...    0.0
4757            -1.0    0.0    0.0    0.0    1.0  ...    0.0
319             -1.0    0.0    0.0    1.0    0.0  ...    1.0
...              ...    ...    ...    ...    ...  ...    ...
7590             0.0    0.0    0.0    1.0    0.0  ...    0.0
11267            1.0    0.0    0.0    1.0    0.0  ...    1.0
4928             3.0    0.0    1.0    0.0    0.0  ...    1.0
7702             2.0    0.0    0.0    0.0    1.0  ...    0.0
12524           -1.0    0.0    0.0    1.0    0.0  ...    0.0


                POVCAT=1 POVCAT=2 POVCAT=3 POVCAT=4 POVCAT=5 INSCOV=1 INSCOV=2
instance names
12253             0.0      0.0      1.0      0.0      0.0      1.0      0.0
14989             1.0      0.0      0.0      0.0      0.0      0.0      1.0
16101             0.0      0.0      0.0      1.0      0.0      1.0      0.0
4757              1.0      0.0      0.0      0.0      0.0      0.0      1.0
319               0.0      0.0      0.0      1.0      0.0      1.0      0.0

...               ...      ...      ...      ...      ...      ...      ...
7590              0.0      0.0      0.0      1.0      0.0      1.0      0.0
11267             1.0      0.0      0.0      0.0      0.0      1.0      0.0
4928              1.0      0.0      0.0      0.0      0.0      0.0      1.0
7702              0.0      0.0      1.0      0.0      0.0      0.0      1.0
12524             0.0      0.0      1.0      0.0      0.0      1.0      0.0


                        labels


                INSCOV=3
instance names
12253             0.0    0.0
14989             0.0    0.0
16101             0.0    0.0
4757              0.0    0.0
319               0.0    0.0
...               ...    ...
7590              0.0    0.0
11267             0.0    0.0
4928              0.0    1.0
7702              0.0    0.0
12524             0.0    0.0

[11081 rows x 140 columns]
```

The data has been pre-processed via a function written in AIF360 to simplify the variables and produce a binary label outcome that indicates whether an individual used healthcare services 10 or more times. This is accomplished, along with some variable renaming and removal of rows with missing data, via a function default_pre-processing, as shown in GitHub (*https://oreil.ly/gT5vr*):

```
>>> dset_raw_trn.label_names
['UTILIZATION']
```

It turns out that people in the privileged group are high-utilization patients at a higher rate than are people in the unprivileged group, as we can see either by a measure of disparate impact or by a measure of mean difference:

```
>>> metric = BinaryLabelData setMetric(dset_raw_trn,
                                unprivileged_groups = unpriv_group,
                                privileged_groups=priv_group)
>>> metric.disparate_impact()
0.492
>>> metric.mean_difference()
-0.138
```

If you wanted an optimistic outlook, you might try to argue, "Hey, the unprivileged group gets less sick and has better outcomes. It's some uplifting news." But you'd be wrong. With some domain knowledge, you would know, for example, that nonwhite life expectancy in the US is lower than white life expectancy for both sexes. You would also know that nonwhite communities on average have less income, wealth, and insurance coverage. All this points to an alternative and less satisfying reason why the unprivileged group uses fewer healthcare resources: they have various economic and social impediments to accessing healthcare even when they need it.

This might seem obvious now that you've read it, but as recently as October 2019 just such a flawed oversight was discovered in a healthcare algorithm deployed by a large US health insurance provider. The provider had not applied this basic domain knowledge when developing an algorithm to identify the most at risk patients, where it used healthcare utilization as a proxy for being at-risk (*https://oreil.ly/r8mdV*). The original algorithm built in even more favorable treatment for privileged patients by highlighting them as the ones needing extra attention at a rate higher than what it ought to have if the decision were driven by a patient's medical condition.

As we can see from this anecdote, this data set and possible use cases regarding healthcare utilization offer a compelling example of when we would want to remove prejudice from a data set. For any sort of intervention targeting, we would want to get at the underlying truth of who is likely to be sick rather than at a discriminatory proxy of healthcare utilization. This is in contrast to the income data set we used in our last example, in which we might want to keep the discriminatory elements of a prediction insofar as they would identify who had low income in the prejudiced world if we wanted to identify low-income people for assistance of some kind. So whether and how to remove prejudice, and how much, will very much depend on the ultimate use case. In a case like this, which has an underlying ground truth that is more important for prediction than the proxy, we certainly do want to intervene.

Prejudice Remover

The first technique we'll look at dates back to 2012 and was first discussed in "Fairness Aware Classifier with Prejudice Remover Regularizer" by Kamishima et al.[1] This paper included a discussion of sources of unfairness in data sets as well as a presentation of a prejudice remover regularizer. The authors discussed the existence of three distinct causes for unfairness present in machine learning applications:

Prejudice
> They defined prejudice in a statistical sense as some dependence between the outcome of a process or decision and a protected attribute.

Underestimation
> Underestimation was their description for a machine learning model that should theoretically converge but might not converge because of limited data availability. Importantly, underestimation would be recognized by the fact that the outcomes of a model were less fair than the underlying data set, something earlier chapters have already discussed.

Negative legacy
> The authors used this to refer to either unfair sampling or unfair labeling in the data itself. For example, if members of a protected group are over-policed so that they are sampled more often in police data sets, or if members of a protected group are unfairly denied credit by banks even though they were just as deserving as majority group members who did receive credit, these would be negative legacy problems. The authors indicate that this problem, though a real and troubling one, is difficult to identify in a freestanding data set and therefore is not dealt with via the method. The authors also mention that the best way to deal with suspicions of negative legacy is to find a related data set where such suspicions are not present in order to apply transfer learning.

After reading this list, you might question the distinction between *prejudice* and *negative legacy* and whether it matters. Allow me to highlight a few key differences. First, negative legacy is undetectable, whereas prejudice is measurable. Second, negative legacy would always involve a bad fact in the measurement rather than an unfortunate fact about the ground truth. On the other hand, *prejudice* could occur because of negative but true facts that do distinguish different groups. For example, the poverty rate of women is higher than the poverty rate for men in the US. This is not due to some form of unfair sampling or labeling but rather reflects underlying unfairness. So this would not feature a negative legacy issue but would include a prejudice problem.

---

1 Kamishima, Toshihiro, et al. "Fairness-Aware Classifier with Prejudice Remover Regularizer." Paper presented at the European Conference on Machine Learning and Principles and Practice of Knowledge Discovery in Databases, Bristol, UK, 2012. *https://link.springer.com/chapter/10.1007/978-3-642-33486-3_3*.

The postulate of the authors of this paper, as well as of the work in this book, is that men and women are not different in a way that should fairly account for differences in poverty rates.[2] So our goal for designing a machine learning algorithm would be to remove the prejudice—that is, to look only at the other attributes of men and women that should indicate their likelihood to fall below the poverty level due to individual human attributes rather than individual gendered attributes.

At this point, you should ask yourself whether a fairness intervention in a model even makes sense. Let's continue with the poverty example. Imagine you are running a nongovernmental organization building a model for who is likely to fall below the poverty level, so you can target those people for some kind of beneficial information campaign. In such a case, if your model removes prejudice by becoming less accurate, you might argue that a fairness intervention might not serve the final goal of fairness. After all, if women are more likely to live below the poverty line in the first place because of unfairness, it seems doubly unfair that some of them will miss out on benefiting from the program in the name of building a less prejudiced machine learning model.

On the other hand, let's imagine you are building a model to predict who is not below the poverty line because you are working off of a model of the world where income roughly approximates ambition and drive.[3] Perhaps you will use the model to determine who is most promising as a target for election campaign advertisements[4] or as a target for an invitation to a volunteer event. In such a case it would seem that removing prejudice would be fair because you would be using financial status itself as a proxy, which suggests that you need to think more about the costs of unfairly excluding people from protected groups who otherwise do have the attributes you are seeking via your proxy.

Fairness Is Not a Formula

As discussed earlier in the book, fairness is not a simple mathematical formula. There are many moving parts, and it will always be up to you to determine which way a particular fairness intervention should push the model.

---

2 Can we think of a fundamental difference that might explain this? Sure, one difference is the differential rates of being a single parent as a woman rather than a man. But the point is that this itself highlights a structural unfairness rather than providing an acceptable explanation.

3 I am not saying this is the case, but I am imagining someone is building a model based on such a premise.

4 The obvious reference here is the Cambridge Analytica scandal. Given the strong public reaction against the use of that data, it seems that ordinary Americans find it quite offensive from a fairness perspective to be using personality models to target them for voting advertisements. So you may have other fairness problems to consider when building such a model.

How It Works

Kamishima et al. opted to include both a traditional regularizer, which penalizes coefficients as they grow larger in absolute value, and a separate fairness regularizer. The equation the authors imposed as the loss function for a classification task was as follows:

$$\sum_{(y_i, x_i, s_i)} lnM[y_i | x_i, s_i, \Theta] + \eta R_{PR}(D, \Theta) + \frac{\lambda}{2} \sum_{s \in S} \| w_s \|_2^2$$

The first expression is the traditional logistic regression penalty. The middle expression is the regularizer aimed at removing prejudice. That expression is more explicit here:

$$R_{PR}(D, \Theta) = \sum_{(x_i, y_i) \in D} \sum_{y \in (0, 1)} M[y | x_i, s_i; \Theta] ln \frac{\widehat{(Pr)}[y | s_i]}{\widehat{(Pr)}[y]}$$

With this expression,[5] we are adding a term to minimize over the empirical domain a measurement of the mutual information between the outcome y and the protected category s_i. Note that there is a weight on this term η, which is up to us to choose in calibrating, in comparison to the third term in the expression, which looks more like a typical regularization term. As implemented in AIF360, this other regularization term λ is set to 1, so we set η in relation to this term. This third term has fairness implications as well as regularization implications, because the sensitive category weights are regularized to encourage these weights to be small. Regularization might also compare with another potential attribute of fairness, that it's suspicious if any indicator is strongly influential in an outcome in an otherwise high-dimensional data set.

For example, at least in the US, university admissions decisions purport to be complex and holistic decisions that treat people as more than a number, particularly more than the number represented by a GPA or an SAT score. Many Americans regard this as fairer than systems in other regions, such as in Europe and Asia alike, where sometimes the results of a single exam can determine university or professional school admissions. So, note that the idea of fairness and the importance of a single indicator

---

5 The estimates for the two probabilities (indicated by a hat on top of the probabilities) indicate that these probabilities are themselves estimates. For more on how to do this estimation in a computationally tractable way, see the original paper (*https://oreil.ly/_-hyM*).

as a fair way of making a decision will vary not just by domain context but also culturally and geographically.

Code Demonstration

Again, the nice thing about an open source package that implements cutting-edge fairness algorithms is that we don't need to worry about the sticky bits of implementing an optimization ourselves. While we have developed intuition about how these methods work based on the preceding description, quite a bit remains in the nuts and bolts of the methodology that is provided to us via AIF360. So as we'll see in this section, applying this method is straightforward, thanks to the work of contributors to AIF360.

First we define a function that will run the in-processing `PrejudiceRemover` algorithm with various values of η. (Within the algorithm the value of λ is set so that η is relative to this.)

```
def test_eta_bal_acc(ETA, dset_raw_trn, dset_raw_vld, dset_raw_tst):
    pr = PrejudiceRemover(sensitive_attr = 'RACE', eta = ETA)
    scaler = StandardScaler()

    dset_scaled_trn = dset_raw_trn.copy()
    dset_scaled_trn.features = scaler.fit_transform(dset_scaled_trn.features)

    pr_fitted = pr.fit(dset_scaled_trn)

    accs = []
    thresholds = np.linspace(0.01, 0.50, 10)

    dset_val = dset_raw_vld.copy()
    dset_val.features = scaler.transform(dset_val.features)

    ############# STEP 1 TRAINING WITH IN-PROCESSING ####
    pr_pred_prob = pr_fitted.predict(dset_val).scores

    ############# STEP 2 PICKING THRESHOLD WITH VALIDATION DATA ####
    for threshold in thresholds:
        dset_val_pred = dset_val.copy()
        dset_val_pred.labels = (pr_pred_prob[:, 0] > threshold).astype(np.float64)

        metric = ClassificationMetric(
                    dset_val, dset_val_pred,
                    unprivileged_groups = unpriv_group,
                    privileged_groups=priv_group)
        accs.append((metric.true_positive_rate() + \
                    metric.true_negative_rate()) / 2)

    pr_val_best_idx = np.argmax(accs)
    best_threshold = thresholds[pr_val_best_idx]

    ######### STEP 3 TEST DATA ####
    dset_tst = dset_raw_tst.copy()
```

```
dset_tst.features = scaler.transform(dset_tst.features)

pr_pred_prob = pr_fitted.predict(dset_tst).scores


dset_tst_pred = dset_tst.copy()
dset_tst_pred.labels = (pr_pred_prob[:, 0] > best_threshold).astype(np.float64)

metric = ClassificationMetric(
            dset_tst, dset_tst_pred,
            unprivileged_groups = unpriv_group,
            privileged_groups   = priv_group)
test_acc = (metric.true_positive_rate() + metric.true_negative_rate()) / 2
test_disp_impact = metric.disparate_impact()

print("Testing accuracy with ETA %0.2f = %0.2f\n
        Disparate impact %0.2f" % (ETA, test_acc, test_disp_impact))
return (test_acc, test_disp_impact)
```

This function has three main components, as indicated by the block comments. The easiest and most effortless part from a coding perspective is training `PrejudiceRe mover`. Once `PrejudiceRemover` is trained, we then select a cutoff value based on maximizing balanced accuracy—that is, the average of false-positive and false-negative rates. Note that in doing this, our assumption is that each of these errors is equally bad, although in practice this might not be true, depending on the relative costs and dangers to patients.

Though we won't undertake a comprehensive study here, let's first look at two potential values for η:

```
>>> test_eta_bal_acc(5.0, dset_raw_trn, dset_raw_vld, dset_raw_tst)
Testing accuracy with ETA 5.00 = 0.73
Disparate impact 0.62
>>> test_eta_bal_acc(50.0, dset_raw_trn, dset_raw_vld, dset_raw_tst)
Testing accuracy with ETA 50.00 = 0.64
Disparate impact 1.08
```

Given that testing accuracy goes down and disparate impact correction goes too far (values over 1 imply some unfairness to the privileged group), we check whether an intermediate value of the ETA variable might better optimize both balanced accuracy and our discriminatory measure:

```
>>> test_eta_bal_acc(20.0, dset_raw_trn, dset_raw_vld, dset_raw_tst)
Testing accuracy with ETA 20.00 = 0.71
Disparate impact 0.77
```

Is this a good compromise? We now have accuracy almost as high as we have with a lower η but with better disparate impact (that is, closer to 1). However, we don't know whether this is good enough, as we haven't determined all sorts of basic elements to the puzzle. Some of those are as follows:

- What is the best accuracy we can get without any fairness interventions?

  — Whether a certain accuracy level is acceptable will depend on what is theoretically possible.

  — Whether we even want to use balanced accuracy should also depend on real-world domain knowledge.

- What are the second-order effects of deploying this model? How will end users respond to this model?

  — If it turns out that members of the privileged group are more persistent and aggressive in seeking medical care, maybe we do want a disparate impact value of more than 1 (because we don't think the privileged group will be harmed by underestimating their need).

- Does the individual fairness matter in this case? We have not examined consistency but should also consider incorporating this.

- Healthcare has legal requirements relating to nondiscrimination and even record-keeping requirements. How might fairness interventions fare in the relevant legal analysis?

  — This question is not just for data analysts but others at the organization too.

Adversarial Debiasing

If you have some familiarity with deep learning and the recent advances of generative adversarial networks (GANs), then you will likely find adversarial debiasing a quite intuitive method. And if you don't have familiarity with these methods, (a) you should quickly do a few minutes of web searches and reading for your own information, because this is interesting, *but* (b) it's not required to understand how the GAN method works.

Adversarial debiasing uses the same insight as GANs—namely, that if you can train one model to perform one task, you can train another model to try to outsmart it on some measure related to that task. As each model improves, the other will have to as well.

In the case of adversarial debiasing, the situation is more specific. The original model you train seeks to predict a value or a label of some kind—for example, whether an individual will have high utilization of healthcare services. An adversarial model, on the other hand, will be motivated by a fairness intuition, which is that the outputs from the model should not include or leak information about the protected category. If this holds, it means the output from the original model should not be useful in predicting the protected category.

The process is iterative:

1. Train the target model to predict the variable of interest.

2. Train the adversary model to use outputs from the target model to predict the protected category.

3. Iterate.

We want the target model to do as well as it can to predict the variable of interest while also minimizing the adversary model's success in predicting the protected category. Ideally, the adversary model fails at predicting the protected category because the outcomes and the target model's predictions should not give any information about group membership. Realistically, however, we may need to settle for a less-than-perfect outcome and focus on minimizing the amount of information about protected group status that is conveyed from the outputs of the target model (see Figure 5-1).

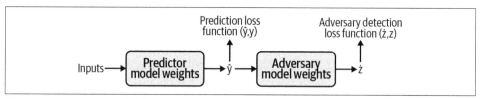

Figure 5-1. Adversarial debiasing architecture: a schematic layout of the two neural network models in sequence to result in adversarial debiasing

If you know how deep learning works and how open source deep learning projects are implemented, you probably realize that the description provided so far is already enough to start working on a model. However, as with other deep learning models, tricks of the trade make this work more effective, and those are described in "Mitigating Unwanted Biases with Adversarial Learning" by Zhang et al.[6] In particular, the authors describe the terms that ought to be in a loss function to ensure that the predictor model and the adversary model are in fact trained in an adversarial way, pursuing conflicting goals, rather than finding a facile but unhelpful solution that is a local minimum that satisfies both without achieving the goal.

---

6 Zhang, Brian Hu, et al. "Mitigating Unwanted Biases with Adversarial Learning." arXiv.org, January 22, 2018. *https://arxiv.org/pdf/1801.07593.pdf.*

Some of the strengths Zhang et al. indicate in the paper are the following:

- The method can be used to enforce a variety of definitions of fairness rather than being designed around one specific definition of fairness. The available definitions of fairness that Zhang et al. mention are demographic parity and the equality of odds. (If you are not familiar with these terms, revisit Chapter 3.)

- The method can be used for either categorical or continuous outputs without modification of the underlying technique.

- The method can be applied regardless of the form or complexity of the predictive model. What's more, a simple adversary works even in the case of a complex predictive model.

- If some simple mathematical assumptions are true in a given case, the authors provide proofs of optimality. However, in any case the fairness intervention won't hurt the model, so this is essential only if you have quite specific mathematical notions of the performance you need or the efficiency in achieving it.

One aspect of this paper that is particularly impressive is that Zhang et al. demonstrate utility for natural language processing and for binary classification for income on the Adult data set we discussed in Chapter 4. No other processing method we will discuss is quite so general out of the box.

How It Works

The mechanics of the method are simple. First, you define whatever model you might choose to work with on a predictive task, be it as simple as a logistic regression or as complicated as a deep learning model. You define a loss function $L_P(y, \hat{y})$ for this model. You then define an adversary that receives "the output layer" of the predictive model. This can be just a single label if you are predicting a binary label or could be of the same dimension as what you are outputting, so that if you are predicting something multidimensional, all the dimensions would be passed on to the adversary.

Zhang et al. provide the following concrete guidance about the outputs from the predictor model to the adversary for a given fairness metric:

- For demographic parity, the adversary receives only the estimated label $\hat{y}$.

- For equality of odds, the adversary sees both the model's estimated label $\hat{y}$ and the truth label y.

- For equality of opportunity, the adversary again sees both the model's estimated label $\hat{y}$ and the truth label y. The difference here is that the cases examined are limited to those in which $y = 1$ (that is, the successful outcome/opportunity).

The loss of the adversary is then set as L_A.

Then the important calculation from the authors to ensure proper training comes as follows:

$$\nabla_W L_P - proj_{\nabla_{L_A}} \nabla_W L_P - \alpha \nabla_W L_A$$

Zhang et al. point out that it is a portion of this loss, $-proj_{\nabla_{L_A}} \nabla_W L_P$, that ensures that the gradient calculations will not push the predictor to move in a direction that could help the adversary, as would otherwise occur. Likewise, the last term in the loss, $-\alpha \nabla_W L_A$, ensures that the predictor tries to hurt the adversary because the sign of the adversary's loss is set to be opposite the sign of the predictor's loss, so that minimizing the predictor's loss and maximizing the adversary's loss take on the same sign and become the same goal.

Once we have a loss function, we can benefit from the accumulated wisdom, expertise, and open source code available from the deep learning community to either implement our own version or take advantage of AIF360's implementation, as we do in the next section.

Code Demonstration

As has been emphasized in this chapter and the last, a helpful aspect of AIF360 is that everything comes in one package and is implemented. Remember that even if you understand in theory how a method works, it is quite another thing to implement it. There are many tricks of the trade to numerical optimization, and running into problems can lead to days of frustration as you try to work out what's wrong and how to fix it.

However, in this case AIF360 is not quite as self-contained as usual. There is a TensorFlow dependency. It is not at all necessary to have a GPU for training, as is typical in deep learning, but you do need to have the `tensorflow` module installed.

Once you do, you can implement adversarial debiasing in a workflow that will look familiar if you have seen some deep learning. Even if you haven't, we will walk through this together, and you will see that it is not so complicated.

First, we set up standard parameters, most of which are related to the deep learning/ optimization setup and others that are related to the desired debiasing:

```
tf.reset_default_graph()
sess = tf.Session()

kwargs = {
    'privileged_groups'       : priv_group,
    'unprivileged_groups'     : unpriv_group,
    'scope_name'              : 'debiased_classifier',
```

```
    'debias'                      : True,
    'sess'                        : sess,
    'adversary_loss_weight'       : 1.0,
    'num_epochs'                  : 25,
    'batch_size'                  : 128,
    'classifier_num_hidden_units': 16,
    'debias'                      : True,
    'seed'                        : 117
    }

# Learn parameters with debias set to True
debiased_model = AdversarialDebiasing(**kwargs)
```

Some of the parameters that should be clear in the preceding code include `privi
leged_groups`, `debias`, and `seed` (this last to ensure reproducibility). On the other
hand, some of the parameters are related to the deep learning paradigm for training:

- `scope_name` uses a TensorFlow option to provide scoping for variable names.
  When you are building a small model, this is unimportant, but it could matter if
  you are doing this debiasing within a larger framework.

- `sess` is a TensorFlow session, which you can think of as being an environment
  isolated from other TensorFlow environments, where all your relevant variables
  exist. For our purposes, as with `scope_name`, it's not important to know more.

- `num_epochs` indicates the number of times you want to iterate through the data as
  you train your model.

- `batch_size` indicates the number of training examples you want to include in a
  given iteration step for calculating the update in gradient.

- `classifier_num_hidden_units` indicates the amount of complexity you want
  your model to have. Note that AIF360's implementation of adversarial debiasing
  is not as flexible as the original model, as it assumes a particular form of a predictor model. However, with a small degree of exposure to TensorFlow, you could
  likely modify the source code to include any model you would like to use.

Now that you have set these standard training parameters, you will want to normalize
your data. Because of the way weights are initialized in deep learning models, you will
want to standardize your data before inputting it for training. In the following code,
we do this and kick off the training process:

```
scaler = StandardScaler()

dset_scaled_trn = dset_raw_trn.copy()
dset_scaled_trn.features = scaler.fit_transform(dset_scaled_trn.features)

debiased_model.fit(dset_scaled_trn)
```

You will notice a lag at this point and see output on your screen as the training process continues, as shown here:

```
epoch 0; batch classifier loss: 0.680142; batch adversarial loss: 0.7514
epoch 1; batch classifier loss: 0.515734; batch adversarial loss: 0.7286
epoch 2; batch classifier loss: 0.551049; batch adversarial loss: 0.7501
epoch 3; batch classifier loss: 0.472371; batch adversarial loss: 0.7119
epoch 4; batch classifier loss: 0.390764; batch adversarial loss: 0.6837
...
epoch 19; batch classifier loss: 0.547377; batch adversarial loss: 0.6222
epoch 20; batch classifier loss: 0.378127; batch adversarial loss: 0.6741
epoch 21; batch classifier loss: 0.354155; batch adversarial loss: 0.6660
epoch 22; batch classifier loss: 0.338008; batch adversarial loss: 0.6153
epoch 23; batch classifier loss: 0.327994; batch adversarial loss: 0.6343
epoch 24; batch classifier loss: 0.279365; batch adversarial loss: 0.6351
[1794  581]
```

If you know something about machine learning, you know that you can look at how the error drops over time to determine whether you are overtraining or undertraining. That is beyond the scope of this book, but many excellent blog posts and resources are available (*https://oreil.ly/ADPr7*).

Once we have trained our model, we look at how a variety of thresholds would perform on our test data. When following best practices, we would want to do this on validation data and then apply only the selected threshold to test data, but we combine the steps for brevity. Remember, our focus is on fairness, so sometimes we do cut corners in the demonstrations. On the other hand, in a real-world scenario, of course the ethical and fair practice of data science necessarily entails following best practices to ensure reproducibility and high performance as well as fairness principles.

```python
dset_tst            = dset_raw_tst.copy()
dset_tst.features   = scaler.transform(dset_tst.features)

thresholds = np.linspace(0.2, 0.60, 5)

for thresh in thresholds:
    dset_tst_pred        = dset_tst.copy()
    dset_tst_pred.labels = debiased_model.predict(dset_tst).scores > thresh
    print(np.bincount(dset_tst_pred.labels[:, 0].astype('int')))

    adv_deb_metric = ClassificationMetric(
                        dset_tst, dset_tst_pred,
                        unprivileged_groups = unpriv_group,
                        privileged_groups   = priv_group)

    test_acc = (adv_deb_metric.true_positive_rate() + \
                adv_deb_metric.true_negative_rate()) / 2
    test_disp_impact = adv_deb_metric.disparate_impact()

    print("\n\nThresh: %0.2f\nTesting balanced accuracy
```

```
                        %0.2f\nDisparate impact %0.2f" % \
                        (thresh, test_acc, test_disp_impact))
```

This leads to the following output, which gives us an idea of the range of trade-offs of accuracy and fairness by one fairness metric:

```
Thresh: 0.20
Testing balanced accuracy 0.74
Disparate impact 0.67

Thresh: 0.30
Testing balanced accuracy 0.71
Disparate impact 0.64

Thresh: 0.40
Testing balanced accuracy 0.69
Disparate impact 0.61

Thresh: 0.50
Testing balanced accuracy 0.66
Disparate impact 0.73

Thresh: 0.60
Testing balanced accuracy 0.59
Disparate impact 1.05
```

We could also contemplate making graphs of balanced accuracy and disparate impact to illustrate the trade-offs.

If you are paying attention, you will have noticed that I did not specify which definition of fairness is used in the fit in the preceding code. In fact, because AIF360 is an open source effort, and a young one at that, most algorithms tend to be implemented with limitations. In the case of AIF360, this limitation is that only one fairness metric, equalized odds, is included, which is why we did not select a fairness metric when we instantiated the AdversarialDebiasing instance. This is similar to the fact that the classifier model that will be used (and the fact that it is a classifier model rather than a regression model) is fixed. As with everything that is fixed, given the simplicity and availability of the source code along with its excellent style and documentation, it would be straightforward to modify any aspect of this that you would seek to customize. If you do so successfully, consider sharing your efforts with this open source project.

In-Processing Beyond Antidiscrimination

Training methods for machine learning models can be modified to pursue antidiscrimination, but they can also be modified in the service of other fairness prerogatives. Some of these are included here, but this is just a small sampling of how machine learning training methods have been modified in service to concerns that fall under the rubric of fairness.

Security

Attacks on machine learning models have existed for as long as machine learning models have existed. Even very simple and seemingly robust methodologies such as logistic regression are vulnerable to various attacks in which a manipulation of training data can lead to predictably wrong outcomes that an adversary can turn to their advantage. In recognition of this, machine learning researchers have developed training methodologies that enhance robustness to such security attacks. This area of inquiry can be identified under "robust training" and related methodologies. This is briefly discussed in Chapter 10. Relatedly, even typical regularization, which tends to lead to more generalizable and hence robust models, already represents a simple form of in-processing that promotes security as well as other values such as transferability and reproducibility and consistency across data sets.

Privacy

A specific form of attack on machine learning models is a privacy attack, in which an adversary seeks to obtain or make inferences about data that was used to train a machine learning model via access to the model. Given that many machine learning models are trained on sensitive data, especially for crucial applications such as those in healthcare, finance, and education, it's important that such models, safeguard the privacy of those data subjects who provided data for the model. In such a case, models must be trained to reduce or prevent attack success. One privacy-aware form of model training is *training with differential privacy*. For example, machine learning packages exist to train neural networks in a differentially private way as well as other more traditional machine learning models. Another model for training machine learning models with a privacy-preserving process is *federated learning*, in which machine learning algorithms are trained across a multientity decentralized network so that data need not be consolidated to a central repository or widely shared. This is briefly discussed in Chapter 9.

Minority rights

By definition, an ordinary loss function that weights all errors and all data points equally will necessarily favor those more *typical* in a data set as compared to those less typical. Any loss function that considers disparity in error rates between different groups represents a step toward ensuring minority rights and keeping the data tyranny of a numerical majority in check. So even simple modifications to a loss function to account for such problems already represent a form of pro-fairness in-processing.

Distributional concerns

Economists have long recognized that different metrics of well-being can give radically different indicators of whether a system is good or bad, and in particular a general measure of distribution of benefits over different populations can be important in assessing social welfare even when it is not critical to determining whether a more narrowly defined task is fulfilled. Likewise, loss functions can consider such distributional concerns in machine learning, even if this has not to date been much appreciated. As a concrete example, consider the case of a hiring algorithm. In one version of the hiring algorithm, the *best* candidate by some criterion is selected, and this would be a typical ML use case where the task and its loss function are narrowly related to one another. In a more expansive version with more open-minded thinking on distribution, we might try to design an ML model that awards jobs on merit but also on individual preference. For example, perhaps the best candidate for job A would actually prefer job B and be qualified for that job as well. In such cases, a loss function that measured both aptitude and preferences could be an example of considering one version of distributional concerns, in which preferences as well as aptitude were taken into account.

While this list may be overwhelming, in any given domain you will likely see the most important fairness concerns either from knowledge of your data set or domain knowledge or from knowledge of the downstream use cases for a product. In some cases it will be mathematically impossible to maximize all fairness criteria at once. This is not a problem created by ML but rather a problem made far more explicit and quantitative than it has been in previous times.

If we do our fairness interventions in a smart and principled manner, we can make improvements even if we cannot reach perfection. It's important to recognize that this is no different from many state-of-the-art ML applications. Most ML applications, and most humans, do not reach 100% accuracy or 100% on any KPI. This doesn't make a product worthless, and we should see our fairness interventions in the same way. Improvements are meaningful and further the cause of fairness even when we cannot guarantee perfection.

Model Selection

In the previous sections, I described two methods of a model-training process that could penalize one element of fairness (namely, discrimination), when computing the loss function of a model and enabling a model-training process to reduce loss. However, another element of model training that can be considered at the in-processing step comes from considering the model training step in a data science pipeline more broadly. In addition to training a particular kind of model given a data set, this process usually involves *model selection*, which is the selection of particular model types or architectures as well as particular final training models, be they specific hyperparameters or actual model values, such as the weights in a neural network.

The model selection step can also be an opportunity to reduce unfairness both in the sense of reducing discrimination and in the sense of choosing pro-fairness elements when selecting among several viable models.

Note that model selection can be applied in addition to other forms of in-processing, as model selection could be performed among models that had been trained with a variety of in-processing methods or hyperparameter selections. Model selection can also be applied in addition to other fairness interventions earlier in the pipeline, as described with pre-processing in Chapter 4.

Model selection can also be an opportunity to introduce a *complementary fairness metric*. So, for example, imagine you used an in-processing methodology that penalized based on a group parity metric to emphasize an antidiscrimination prerogative. You could then introduce an individual parity metric, such as consistency or calibration, to select among models regularized with a group parity term. In this way, both concerns would receive some weighting in the model-training stage of your data science pipeline.

Finally, while we have emphasized antidiscrimination metrics, model selection can also be used in the service of other fairness prerogatives. For example, if you were able to develop a model that is amenable to explanation or even interpretation, you might choose that model if it performs as well or only slightly worse than a model without these characteristics. Likewise, if one model is the result of processes that ensure robustness or privacy, you might weight these against slightly different accuracies. How and when to do so is partly a matter of domain knowledge and organizational priorities, but it should be recognized that fairness, such as lapses in antidiscrimination or lapses in security, can very much have legal and financial consequences as well as being morally problematic. Therefore, even for the most cynical organization, it is imperative to recognize that it is not merely "accuracy" or the targeting of KPIs that should be considered during model selection.

Concluding Remarks

I have covered both cases of the methods in this chapter in less detail than those discussed in Chapter 4. However, the implementation details of these methods are no trickier to understand. I would encourage you to look at the source code after having worked through these methods on a few data sets or if you ever have a sense that they are not working well on your data set. This will give you insight into the methods and possibly give you ideas for small modifications that can help tackle a problem in your data set that might be unique to your organization or modeling problems. In such a case you might even consider making an open source contribution yourself.

## CHAPTER 6

Fairness Post-Processing

Post-processing methods are fairness interventions that come at the last stage of the data modeling pipeline. Data has already been selected and pre-processed. A model has already been trained. You may know nothing about that model. Perhaps it has come to you as a black box, and you are to take that black box and find a way to make it fairer according to some metric before deploying.

If this sounds like an unrealistic limitation, you have likely not worked in the real world for long enough. Proprietary software is deployed even in governmental applications. Consider the COMPAS algorithm used by many states to predict criminal recidivism. This prediction has real consequences, as it may decide whether a defendant can receive bail to be free while awaiting trial, whether a convicted defendant will receive a lighter or harsher sentence, and whether an imprisoned defendant is eligible for parole.

What's more, while proprietary models are often criticized, there are of course many justifications for these models. Though this is not the main point of this chapter, it's important to be aware of some of these justifications, in part so you can determine whether they apply to a model you might receive so that your reasons for objections to the black-box nature of a model would be met with related rebuttals. That doesn't mean the black-box model is always right, but it's good to understand the logic. Here are some of the justifications:

Intellectual property

This is the most common justification used by companies that release only black-box models. They argue that much of their hard work—from collecting data sets to cleaning the data to training, an expensive and time-consuming process—can nonetheless be reduced to a few hundred lines of code or a few files with model weights. In such cases, the product of much work and investment is easy to steal, and such theft may be undetectable if the thieves in turn use the model only privately. Related to the property rights assigned to these models and protected by black-box distribution is the argument that these property rights and the profits they produce create incentives to build and improve such models in the first place.

Enforcement

Another argument sometimes used for black-box models, in the era of machine learning and even before, is that limiting knowledge about how a model works reduces the ability of people to game the system—that is, to tweak themselves, their behavior, or their answers to surveys to get a more favorable result. For example, the IRS consistently refuses to release information about the algorithms it uses to select tax filings for auditing, hence making this algorithm a black-box model to taxpayers, who get only the output of whether they are audited or not. In the case of the IRS this makes sense, since people can tweak their tax returns without tweaking the underlying behavior. On the other hand, with a case like a criminal recidivism assessment tool, where the inputs are major factors in an individual's life, such as number of past criminal convictions, a person cannot easily manipulate this information. To the extent a person did adjust the inputs, it would likely reflect actual changes in behavior, which is a desirable result if those changes reflect someone doing fewer things that are likely to lead to criminal behavior.

Quality control

Organizations that put out models may be interested in quality control and concerned that making a white-box model will lead people to tweak that model but still leave the original developer on the hook for bad publicity or threats of legal liability. Those who want to control their reputations and the quality of their work product may use a black-box release model as a way to control what their model can be used to do and to make sure they know how it is being used. In fact, this is not so different from makers of physical products, who void warranties if products are modified after they are sold.

Post-Processing Versus Black-Box Auditing

You may have noticed that the next chapter, Chapter 7, covers black-box auditing. How, you might wonder, is post-processing different from black-box auditing? Is this a conceptual difference or merely a matter of emphasis? I can give you the frustrating answer *yes*, to both.

Post-processing methods and black-box auditing are related in a number of ways:

- No need to see the source code of the model
- No need to know how the model works

- No need to know all the details of the training data used for the model

- No need for a model of causality regarding what could lead to discrimination

However, there are important differences:

- Black-box auditing does not imply any action other than identifying problems or opportunities for improvement. Such auditing is just as likely to be done by an outside entity as an insider.

  — On the other hand, post-processing will likely be done by the developer of a model or someone who is morally or legally on the hook for the outputs of the model.

- Black-box auditing does require at least some access to run a model, whereas post-processing does not require access to run a model.

  — This can have real-world implications. Sometimes a "proprietary score" is provided without a model, or perhaps a model is provided but is expensive to run—so expensive that a customer would be reluctant to run the model more times than is strictly necessary.

- Post-processing needs real data—namely, information about the protected group status associated with each output. In contrast, black-box auditing can rely on its own data, including synthetic data generated by accessing the model with hypothetical inputs.

- Black-box auditing may discover new biases not well-known by those who originally developed the model and examined only the performance on their data. This is because the degree of bias exhibited in a model very much depends on the data that is used to test the model, and the degree of discrepancy or discrimination can depend on the underlying structure of data. If test data used for auditing is different, new biases or a different degree of bias will be discovered.

  — With post-processing, the known behavior will be corrected but potential new behavior or problems will not be identified or prevented in future uses of the data.

- Black-box auditing is a wider-ranging exercise that has more potential future benefits but will also rely on more action downstream once findings are known, while post-processing takes immediate corrective action.

- Post-processing does not rely on or produce interpretable results, unlike black-box auditing, which relies partly on the same motives as questions about explainability.

Ideally, an organization that is a producer of models would act more affirmatively at upstream points in the data science pipeline, as has been discussed, for example, with respect to data selection, data cleaning, pre-processing, and in-processing fairness interventions. In such a case, where an organization maintained the ability to react to downstream findings, black-box auditing, perhaps by an outside expert organization or independent internal team not connected to the original decisions of developing a model, would be best deployed.

In contrast, post-processing should be viewed as a last resort and not one that should be employed when upstream actions is possible. Additionally, as will be seen in upcoming examples, because post-processing is a black-box method in that it is ignorant of how a model functions, its solutions are largely limited to randomizing decisions that presumably had some reasonable logic beforehand. As Pleiss et al. highlight,[1] by injecting randomness, these methods can incentivize upstream producers of models to collect more data so that they can have higher accuracy because the only way to reduce this randomization is through the development of a fairer and more complete data set. Otherwise the model's owner must allow the lower accuracy induced by randomization in service of antidiscrimination.

However, in the meantime, the unfortunate situation does develop that randomness is explicitly injected into a model's decisions, which can feel like the opposite of a fair outcome. This provides just one of many examples of how pursuing one fairness objective can indeed feel very unfair and shows why different fairness metrics can be at odds functionally, just as earlier chapters discussed findings that different measures of fairness can be at odds theoretically. A mathematical incompatibility of fairness in which *calibration*, a method of assessing individual fairness (whether individuals with different scores behave differently in a way that reflects their scoring), is found to be at odds with statistical parity is clearly highlighted in the second example method we cover.

The Data Set

We have gotten all the way to Chapter 6 before touching on the most famous data set associated with algorithmic fairness—a data set compiled by the journalistic organization ProPublica in order to study the COMPAS recidivism scoring algorithm.

The details and description of compiling the data set can be found on the ProPublica website (*https://oreil.ly/3hrT_*). I will not go into a full description of the data set, but we will see how to access it via the AIF360 library and will take a look at some of its properties. If we had access to the COMPAS scores associated with the data points, we could even treat COMPAS as the black box and then use the post-processing methods we will study in this chapter to test out fairness interventions on the

---

1 Pleiss, Geoff, et al. "On Fairness and Calibration." arXiv.org, November 3, 2017. *https://arxiv.org/pdf/ 1709.02012.pdf*.

black-box model. As it stands, we will build our own black-box model and then apply post-processing to this.

An important fairness complication of the COMPAS data set is that the data collected here reflects people who were scored by the COMPAS system and whose subsequent treatment, such as bail or sentencing decisions, may have been affected by it. This means that ultimately this is a system that reacts to the algorithmic rating. Presumably, the original COMPAS algorithm was not developed in such a system since it would have been developed first before it could be deployed. One hopes that COMPAS continues to monitor the predictive performance of the model so that the shift from a system that does not react to COMPAS scores to one that does has not reduced external validity or consistency, but we do not know that based on information released from COMPAS. So we have to keep in mind that we are, in effect, modeling recidivism in the presence of COMPAS scoring and any effects that scoring itself might have, either on defendants directly or through the treatment they receive from others who have used the COMPAS scoring to determine how to treat them.

However, this consideration may not be very important in the current data set because the authors indicate that for each person rated by the COMPAS algorithm in the data set, they looked for recidivism within two years of the scoring. The mean time not in prison during the two years was more than 620 days, indicating that the people in the data set had ample time (620 out of a putative 730 days) to reoffend even if the system was reactive to the COMPAS value. Of course, there could be more complicated dynamics such as a subset of defendants being most affected by the COMPAS scores. If we wanted to determine whether this might be important, we could consider generating a variety of simulations to reflect different options. That is beyond the scope of this book.

All this being said, let's take the time to get to know the data set a little with AIF360's usual interface to preload such data:

```
from aif360.algorithms.preprocessing.optim_preproc_helpers.data_preproc_functions
            load_preproc_data_compas
compas_data = load_preproc_data_compas()
```

As discussed, someone has been nice enough to put in some utility functions to preprocess the data sets into manageable chunks of labeled data. Some of the things this utility function does for COMPAS data in particular include the following:

- Limit data to Caucasian and African American individuals
- Turn length of stay in prison and number of prior convictions into categorical variables
- Turn COMPAS score into a binary indicator rather than a three-level variable

The full source code can be read on GitHub (*https://oreil.ly/1CG1G*) and indicates that the function was adapted from code adapted from the author's published repository, discussed in Chapter 4. We can see what this yields:

```
                    instance weights   features protected attribute
                                         sex   race    age_cat=25 to 45
instance names
3                           1.0         0.0   0.0           1.0
4                           1.0         0.0   0.0           0.0
8                           1.0         0.0   1.0           1.0
10                          1.0         1.0   1.0           1.0
14                          1.0         0.0   1.0           1.0
...                         ...         ...   ...           ...
10997                       1.0         0.0   0.0           0.0
11000                       1.0         1.0   0.0           1.0

                    age_cat=Greater than 45 age_cat=Less than 25 priors_count=0
instance names
3                              0.0                  0.0                1.0
4                              0.0                  1.0                0.0
8                              0.0                  0.0                0.0
10                             0.0                  0.0                1.0
14                             0.0                  0.0                1.0
...                            ...                  ...                ...
10997                          0.0                  1.0                1.0
11000                          0.0                  0.0                0.0

                    priors_count=1 to 3 priors_count=More than 3 c_charge_degree=F
instance names
3                            0.0                 0.0                  1.0
4                            0.0                 1.0                  1.0
8                            0.0                 1.0                  1.0
10                           0.0                 0.0                  0.0
14                           0.0                 0.0                  1.0
...                          ...                 ...                  ...
10997                        0.0                 0.0                  1.0
11000                        1.0                 0.0                  0.0

                                        labels
                    c_charge_degree=M
instance names
3                          0.0         1.0
4                          0.0         1.0
8                          0.0         1.0
10                         1.0         0.0
14                         0.0         0.0
...                        ...         ...
10997                      0.0         0.0
11000                      1.0         0.0

[5278 rows x 12 columns]
```

We can also briefly look at some fairness measurements related to this data set:

```
>>> metric_orig_test = BinaryLabelData setMetric(dset_raw_tst,
                            unprivileged_groups=unpriv_group,
                            privileged_groups=priv_group)
>>> print("Difference in mean outcomes between unprivileged and
           privileged groups = %f" % metric_orig_test.mean_difference())

Difference in mean outcomes between unprivileged and privileged groups = -0.0794
```

We take this data set and do the same treatment shown in previous chapters of breaking it into training, validation, and testing sets. I do not reproduce that code here in order to save space and prevent repetition, but it is available in the Jupyter notebook for this chapter. Likewise, I do not reproduce the steps to train a standard logistic regression model on this unmodified training data, but the existence of that model is taken for granted in the post-processing code that I show here.

As you will see in the discussion, in fact the logistic regression model that we train on this data substantially exacerbates the disparity between the unprivileged and privileged groups, with an increase in the difference in mean outcomes.

Equality of Opportunity

The first method comes from a much-cited 2016 paper titled, "Equality of Opportunity in Supervised Learning" by Hardt et al.[2] This method, necessarily true as a post-processing method, requires only knowledge about membership in a protected class as well as the predictions of a method. It then imposes a fairness model of equality of opportunity, meaning that for each group, of the individuals who should have a positive label (ground truth), their probability of having a positive label is the same.

The use of this fairness definition and the associated implementation has many upsides:

- It does not rely on the functional form of the model and can be ignorant of the training data and underlying method to produce a label or prediction.
- It can be viewed as "shifting the burden" in the words of Hardt et al. from the protected class to the decision maker or model developer, in that the decision maker pays a substantial enough price for misclassifying members of a small minority to pay attention, whereas without a fairness metric some minority groups may be so small that they can all be misclassified if decision makers simply seek to maximize some group-blind cost function.

---

2 Hardt, Moritz, et al. "Equality of Opportunity in Supervised Learning." arXiv.org, October 7, 2016. *https://arxiv.org/pdf/1610.02413.pdf*.

- Relatedly, this definition of fairness thus incentivizes decision makers to collect or develop better input features to enhance accuracy, as this definition of fairness is not inherently antagonistic to accuracy, and a 100% accurate label will also be fair by this criterion, which is not the case for earlier definitions of fairness we have examined.[3]

As we have seen in other discussions throughout this book, sometimes a seemingly positive attribute or a seemingly reasonable method is dubious once you think about it in context. I would say that's the case with the last bullet point just given, that this fairness definition incentivizes decision makers to achieve higher accuracy and is not in tension with accuracy. While that "sounds good" in the sense that when pitching such an intervention, you don't need to apologize to your boss about taking a business hit, it also has some problems. Consider even the COMPAS data set we are working with. Do we believe that the true outcomes as measured are fair? Perhaps some would argue that they are in this COMPAS data set, insofar as the data set measures who reoffended.

However, as the ProPublica data set creators (and others before them) describe, there is no single definition of recidivism. For example, Northpointe, the commercial developer of the COMPAS product, defines recidivism as "a finger-printable arrest involving a charge and a filing for any uniform crime reporting (UCR) code" (*https://oreil.ly/ThGPB*). However, as ProPublica points out (*https://oreil.ly/3hrT_*), all sorts of record-keeping difficulties challenge a clean definition of recidivism. For example, it may be unclear which arrest a COMPAS score correlated with, and that could make it difficult to determine whether a subsequent arrest occurred.

Also, even in the ProPublica definition, we (and surely its journalists) could see some problems. For example, recidivism is designated relative to an arrest that correlates with certain criminal definitions and also an arrest for a new crime (as compared to an arrest for not showing up for a court appearance). However, perhaps in some cases police stop a putative crime but decide not to arrest anyone. Or perhaps police officers exercise discretion in how to code the arrest. Or perhaps a record of an arrest is simply lost. And ultimately, why should we code recidivism for an arrest if we presume innocence until someone is proven guilty? These definitions perhaps should be updated in light of subsequent outcomes in court. Of course, that assumes the court system is fair, whereas many have provided evidence to doubt this, given quite disparate racial and socioeconomic outcomes. So clearly this is a difficult problem, and far beyond the scope of the book. However, it raises the point of whether an accurate model is the fair one.

---

3 Whether this is appropriate is another question. In some cases, if the labels themselves seem problematic, we probably don't want a 100% accurate method even if we can achieve it.

Another problem with this method, and likely with most fairness methods, is *uniden-tifiability*: the method treats and modifies models the same way, even if the models result from training data with quite different underlying causal patterns. As the authors point out, this is not due to a lack of access to the training data, as even with such access the problem arises. Causality is a tricky beast, but unfortunately this is the crux of why domain knowledge is so important in fairness interventions and why "fair AI" cannot be automated. The underlying causal model and pursuit of truth rely on knowing what is likely happening to produce a seemingly unfair outcome. The difficulty, or even impossibility, of empirically or experimentally determining causality in many social problems leads to the worry that machine learning might unintentionally reproduce historical unfairness.

How It Works

The post-processing solution proposed by the equalized-odds-inspired post-processing methodology is that the domain for solutions lies in the overlapping region of two quadrilaterals—one defined for a privileged group and one defined for an unprivileged group, where these quadrilaterals are defined by points related to false positives and true positives of the developed models as well as extreme perfect and imperfect points. The authors then seek to find a "derived predictor" from the original predictions, and show that such a derived prediction would need to fall within the quadrilateral and also that each quadrilateral (privileged and unprivileged group) will have its own region. This is shown in Figure 6-1.

Hardt et al. show that finding an optimal solution can be reduced to a linear programming problem solvable with standard packages, such as `scipy`. The linear programming problem in particular is reduced to the following:

$$\min_{\tilde{Y}} \mathbb{E} l(\tilde{Y}, Y)$$
$$s.t. \, \forall a \in 0, 1 : \gamma_a(\tilde{Y}) \in P_a(\hat{Y})$$
$$\gamma_0(\tilde{Y}) = \gamma_1(\tilde{Y})$$

I need to explain a few expressions in the preceding equation. First, $P_a(\hat{Y})$ is the quadrilateral discussed in the first paragraph of this section and depicted in Figure 6-1. Second, $\gamma_i(\tilde{Y})$ describes a pair of numbers, calculated for group i—namely (false-positive rate, true-positive rate), where group i can be either 0 or 1, depending on whether it is for the unprivileged or privileged group.

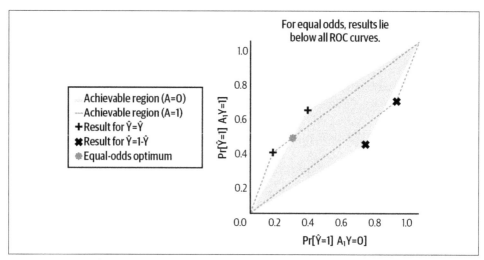

Figure 6-1. Equalized odds: the space of possible solutions and the one chosen by equalized odds post-processing[4]

Note that it's not obvious why this should be a linear programming problem. That depends on reformulating the description of the loss function, as is shown in Hardt et al.'s paper. Here our aim is simply to be able to skim the code implementation and see that it does something consistent with the preceding example.

By the way, what is $\check{Y}$? This is what we are solving for: which labels as output from a model we should "correct" in the sense of flipping them to minimize the loss function while respecting the constraints that make this a *derived predictor* and that enforce *equalized odds*.

We again use AIF360, and our code to post-process is relatively straightforward. Also, although an optimization is involved, a linear programming problem is relatively straightforward from a computational perspective, and the standard implementation from `scipy.optimize.linprog` is used. You can read the scipy documentation (*https://oreil.ly/m4Sam*) or see details of the implementation on GitHub (*https://oreil.ly/mfQ0a*).

---

4 See the full color version posted online (*https://oreil.ly/Practical_Fairness_Figures*) if you're reading in print.

Code Demonstration

The following code, as with other AIF360 interfaces, is standardized and quite short relative to what it does for us:

```
SEED = 94

# Learn parameters to equalize odds and apply to create a new data set
eop = EqOddsPostprocessing(unprivileged_groups = unpriv_group,
                           privileged_groups   = priv_group,
                           seed                = SEED)
eop = eop.fit(dset_raw_vld, data set_orig_valid_pred)

eop_trn_pred = eop.predict(data set_orig_train_pred)

eop_trn_metric = ClassificationMetric(dset_raw_trn, eop_trn_pred,
                           unprivileged_groups=unpriv_group,
                           privileged_groups=priv_group)
```

We set a seed for reproducibility because the optimization might not reach identical results in all cases with different initializations, as with most computational optimization.

Now let's compare the fairness metrics for a logistic regression trained without fairness interventions and the post-processing outputs from the preceding code:

```
>>> logit_classifier_metric = ClassificationMetric(
                           dset_raw_tst, data set_orig_test_pred,
                           unprivileged_groups = unpriv_group,
                           privileged_groups = priv_group)
>>> print("Mean difference in outcomes")
>>> print(logit_classifier_metric.mean_difference())

Mean difference in outcomes
-0.2883
```

Here are the metrics for the post-processed data:

```
>>> eop_test_pred = eop.predict(data set_orig_test_pred)
>>> eop_test_metric = ClassificationMetric(dset_raw_tst, eop_test_pred,
                           unprivileged_groups=unpriv_group,
                           privileged_groups=priv_group)
>>> print("Mean difference in outcomes")
>>> print(eop_test_metric.mean_difference())

Mean difference in outcomes
-0.0008
```

So we can see that the post-processing made quite a difference in the mean outcome, but on the other hand it did not make a difference to the false-positive and false-negative rates.

Calibration-Preserving Equalized Odds

The second method comes from Pleiss et al. In this paper, the authors work from the perspective, very much applicable to something like the COMPAS problem, that a black-box model is available but also that an important property of that model holds: calibration.

What Is Calibration?

Calibration is an important property of tools that are deployed in risk analysis, such as recidivism risk assessments. They are also traditionally used to prevent discrimination by numerical instruments. To quote Pleiss et al., "If we look at the set of people who receive a predicted probability of *p*, we would like a *p* fraction of the members of this set to be positive instances of the classification problem. Moreover, if we are concerned about fairness between two groups…then we would like this calibration to hold simultaneously for the set of people within each of these groups as well."

What does that mean concretely? Let's imagine we build a logistic regression scoring tool. Remember that the score that comes out of such a tool is not the probability of a positive label, but we can back out that probability. Let's imagine we do so for a variety of individuals and bucket those scores into reasonable ranges. We might then look at the group of people who were rated as having approximately 90% probability of a positive instance. If our model were calibrated, we would expect that once we had seen the outcome, 90% of those with a score of around 0.9 would achieve the positive outcome. Likewise, if we looked at the group with scores of around 0.5 and then found out their actual success rate, we would expect about half to be successful.

What's more, to ensure that our calibration was fair, we would want to make sure that these calibrations held within racial groups as well. In fact, this is commonly asked, for example, in the education literature—namely, some assurance that scoring instruments mean the same thing when applied to both genders or to various racial groups. Why? Think about the opposite possibility. Imagine that COMPAS scoring algorithms for black defendants did not mean the same thing as they did for white defendants. If you looked at a group of black defendants with a COMPAS score of 0.5 and found that 75% of them had a successful outcome, and then compared this to a group of white defendants with a COMPAS score of 0.5 and found that 50% of them had a successful outcome, we know the scoring did not mean the same thing.

This would be problematic not just because of the seemingly unjustified racial disparity but also because of the behavior it might prompt from end users. Imagine, for example, the case of judges using an algorithm that they knew did not score black defendants and white defendants the same way. Perhaps the judges might know that black defendants with bad scores were still more likely to do well (that is, not reoffend) than were white defendants with the same scores. That would probably encourage the judges to take the algorithmic score and then add their own knowledge of how this score meant different things for different races. The result would be troubling not only because judges would be using race as a factor but also because the combination of a dodgy algorithm and an unpredictable judge (even a well-motivated one) would make for a noisy or even chaotic system—the opposite of what most seek to achieve when they use algorithms to make decisions.

How It Works

The interesting thing about how the calibrating equalized odds method works is that it doesn't. The insight from Pleiss et al. is specifically that it is the *withholding of predictions* from a model that can ensure both calibration and a measure of fairness. In the words of the authors, you are "withholding predictive information for randomly chosen inputs to achieve parity and preserve calibration." In this case, parity is determined either through the false-positive or false-negative right.

Let's back up and consider a more detailed overview of this method. The authors of this paper offer a fairly intuitive geometric understanding of the problem (Figure 6-2).

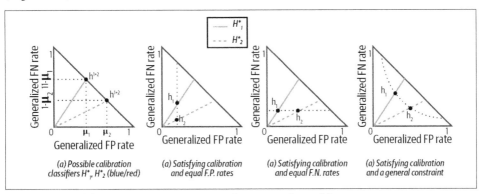

Figure 6-2. Calibration preserving parity: the range of possible outcomes

Pleiss et al. make use of a known result (derived by one of the authors in a prior work) that for a calibrated classifier, the false-positive and false-negative rates of the classifier for a given group have a linear relationship, and what's more, the coefficient of that linear relationship is a function of the underlying base right for that group. So h1 and h2, the calibrated classifier for two groups, will have a linear relationship between the false positives and false negatives, but the slope of that line will be different for two calibrated models because of the different underlying base rates for their respective groups. Therefore, the h1 and h2 will race out different lines in the 2D plane depicted as the generalized FP and generalized FN rate in the planes depicted in Figure 6-2.

So this shows us that the possible range of solutions for reasonable classifiers for these two groups will necessarily lie on different points unless they are both perfect—falling at the origin (0,0).

The authors propose a relaxation of preserving parity given this graphical showing that it is not possible to have all forms of parity as well as calibration. They propose a cost function be defined, such as those shown in the curves in the graph. Then each classifier for each group can be calibrated so that all classifiers lie along the same cost function, enforcing a kind of parity while also preserving calibration.

How are the classifiers adjusted along the line? In fact, the same blunt instrument is used as in the first example of equalized odds: injection of randomization. Pleiss et al. show how the cost function can be used to determine the degree of randomization needed and in which groups to ensure parity. Note that some randomization in both the unprivileged and the privileged groups will be necessary to bring their relevant classifiers into parity in the sense of the cost function. As an exercise for yourself, once you have run through the upcoming code demonstration, consider taking a look at the difference between the original model output and the post-processing to get a sense of how this would have real-world impacts, and whether the randomization could be justified depending on the particular domain.

Why Randomization?

Randomization can have all sorts of instrumental purposes. For example, sometimes social scientists see randomized decisions as opportunities for "natural experiments" to study effects of a policy in the real world. Others study the effects that randomization, apparent randomness, or unpredictability of outcomes can have on behavior, such as making products more addictive by making them somewhat random or unpredictable.[5]

Randomness can be a tool to make products addictive in a way that is far from fair. After all, few would say fairness is best pursued by randomization.

On the other hand, you could argue that injecting some randomness is no different from the real world, where lots of random elements impact all sorts of major life outcomes. Perhaps what we will miss in an increasingly digitized world is some random element of decision making, which can make room for good luck or "mercy" that gives us the opportunity to take advantage of a new chance, even if it's not a chance we deserve.

---

5 See Adam Alter's *Irresistible: The Rise of Addictive Technology and the Business of Keeping Us Hooked* (Penguin Press, 2017) where he identifies some aspect of randomness as part of what makes certain social media and games so addictive.

Whether randomness can be appropriate for the application you are thinking of may depend a lot on context. For example, randomness in medical decision making seems like it would help no one. On the other hand, some element of randomness in hiring might help shake up your company culture or discover someone new.

One recent newsworthy scandal occurred in the summer of 2020. In the wake of the 2020 coronavirus pandemic, the UK decided to use an algorithm, alongside teacher-recommended grades, to produce final grades to substitute for the usual end of high school grades (A-levels and GCSEs). One motivation for the use of an algorithm was the need for an adjustment to keep the distribution of school-leaving grades roughly the same from year to year. This itself is a priority in part to smooth over crises, such as coronavirus, with the well-founded assumption that the overall ability and hard work of high school graduates nationally is unlikely to vary from year to year and that this distribution should therefore remain steady.

With this as a motivation, the UK's education authority introduced an algorithm to adjust the grades recommended for students by their teachers to ensure an overall distribution that would be the same as other years. However, to ensure this distribution, the algorithm also needed to award a certain number of Us, which is the failing grade usually reserved in normal years for students who don't show up for the exam, perhaps because a loved one just died or they got sick. In normal years, where an actual exam took place, a very small percentage of students would randomly miss an exam and get this grade.

In the year of the pandemic and no official exam, of course, no random chance kept students away from the nonoccurring exam. To maintain the same grade distribution, an algorithm had to pick students at random to receive the failing grades normally reserved for students who don't show up for the exam. That certainly didn't feel like a fair outcome to those students, and the effects of the algorithmic adjustments created such an uproar that the UK government ultimately reversed course and allowed students to have the higher of the algorithmic grades and the teacher-estimated grades that had been provided prior to algorithmic adjustment.

Code Demonstration

We can see the training in the following few lines of code. Unlike the previous method, which is nonparametric in the sense that it solves a linear optimization and that the loss function is hardcoded in (it would otherwise be open for us to set), in this case we choose which error rate we want to equalize. The options are shown in the documentation and are false-positive rate, false-negative rate, or a weighted average of the two. This allows us to customize according to which metric is the most important.

For example, in the COMPAS algorithm, which metric is most important could depend on where we think the most harm would occur. If we think greater harm occurs to the person mislabeled when it is a false-negative rate, then that is where we would want to equalize. If we think greater harm occurs to the person mislabeled when it is a false-positive rate, then that is where we would want to equalize. Note that in either case, the way the error rate will be equalized will be to make the group for which the classifier is more accurate worse; that is, we get equality through down-grading the performance of our model. This may not be appropriate in every circumstance, and perhaps the COMPAS algorithm may already be such an example. The decision about how long to sentence someone to prison or whether to grant them early release can have a truly profound influence on their life and the lives of others connected to them. These connections include considerations that concern both a false positive or a false negative.

Risks of Incorrect Labeling

If a person is incorrectly labeled as high risk (false positive), that person as well as their friends and family members, sometimes including young children, miss out on an essential social connection. This toll falls particularly heavily on people of color in America, and has done so for decades. On the other hand, if a person is incorrectly labeled as low risk, someone could end up becoming the victim of a subsequent crime that could have been prevented with the right label.

However, it's harder to think about the false-negative case because a label of "high risk" does not guarantee that someone will reoffend even when it might very well be the right label. After all, these labels ultimately come down to probabilities.

In a real-world example, it's incredibly important to think about exactly what a label means in its own technical specification as well as what the costs are of an incorrect label. It's also important to think about how the labels will be used and understood in a given sociotechnical context.

Some have argued that, in the case of high-stakes decisions, fairness interventions like this might not be appropriate and that the disparity in error rates is better addressed through collection of wider (more columns) or longer (more samples) data sets, rather than accepting even slightly reduced accuracy. This debate is not related to coding but is one that we should recognize.

In the case of the criminal justice system, the flip side, and one rebuttal, is that this is a very "noisy" system in any case, one that may not show as much consistency and uniformity as we would like. Therefore, if a system can improve, but perhaps to a limited degree because of fairness constraints, that is arguably still an improvement.

In any case, here we decide that a false-positive rate—falsely deciding that someone is high risk when they are not—is the most damaging error and the one in which we would like to reduce the disparity in error rates between the unprivileged and privileged groups:

```
# Learn parameters to equalize odds and apply to create a new data set
cpp = CalibratedEqOddsPostprocessing(privileged_groups = priv_group,
                                     unprivileged_groups = unpriv_group,
                                     cost_constraint='fpr',
                                     seed=76)
cpp = cpp.fit(dset_raw_vld, data set_orig_valid_pred)
```

We then use this new object to post-process the data, form a classification metric, and look at the statistics relative to the standard logistic regression we trained:

```
>>> data set_transf_test_pred = cpp.predict(data set_orig_test_pred)
>>> cm_transf_test_metric = ClassificationMetric(dset_raw_tst,
                                                 data set_transf_test_pred,
                                                 unprivileged_groups = unpriv_group,
                                                 privileged_groups = priv_group)
>>> print("CALIBRATING EQUALIZED ODDS PERFORMANCE ON TEST DATA")
>>> print("Difference in GFPR between unprivileged and privileged groups")
>>> print(cm_transf_test_metric.difference(
            cm_transf_test_metric.generalized_false_positive_rate))
>>> print("Difference in GFNR between unprivileged and privileged groups")
>>> print(cm_transf_test_metric.difference(
            cm_transf_test_metric.generalized_false_negative_rate))
>>> print("Mean difference in outcomes")
>>> print(cm_transf_test_metric.mean_difference())

CALIBRATING EQUALIZED ODDS PERFORMANCE ON TEST DATA
Difference in GFPR between unprivileged and privileged groups
-0.0572
Difference in GFNR between unprivileged and privileged groups
0.1727
Mean difference in outcomes
-0.7203
```

As a reminder, here are the numbers for the original logistic regression again:

```
Difference in GFPR between unprivileged and privileged groups
-0.1259
Difference in GFNR between unprivileged and privileged groups
0.1261
Mean difference in outcomes
-0.2883
```

So we have reduced the false-positive rate disparity between the unprivileged and privileged groups. However, this has come with an *increase* in the disparity between the false-negative error rate and an *increase* in the disparity in mean outcomes. This is mathematically inevitable, as Hardt et al. show, and as has been shown in earlier work discussed in this book.

No Free Fairness

If you push for fairness in one direction, as a rule of thumb you can expect to pay for it on another metric. This is not a mathematical certainty in all cases, but it is borne out in many data sets and with many methods. And in some cases it is a mathematical certainty, as was discussed in Chapter 2.

What may very well be preferable about this method, relative to the equalized odds approach, is that this method preserves calibration. Since calibration reflects some measure of individual fairness, this also means that we are choosing a post-processing method that shows some weight for individual fairness as well as some weight for group-level fairness.

Concluding Remarks

Post-processing can feel like the most obscure of the options available for fairness processing. This is not a coincidence. Ultimately, post-processing takes the output from a model, already somewhat obscure without extensive analysis, and then further modifies it. Of course this doesn't feel straightforward.

However, as discussed in this chapter, post-processing can be the best option for numerous common scenarios, given various constraints associated with modeling processing. Also, one important way in which post-processing can feel more transparent than pre-processing and in-processing is that it produces a clear counterfactual for each data point regarding how the fairness intervention made a difference to an individual. In contrast, pre-processing and in-processing do not have this clear connection for individual data points.

This chapter concludes our emphasis on intervening in the machine learning data preparation, model training, and model output processes. In the next few chapters, we will focus on other elements of fairness to be considered once a model has been trained, with a discussion of model auditing (as opposed to model interventions) as well as considerations of other elements of model and data quality, with respect to explainability, privacy, and security.

## CHAPTER 7

Model Auditing for Fairness and Discrimination

An *audit* is a process, system of tools, or expected work product to describe the results of a system complex enough that a certain set of outcomes or qualities cannot be guaranteed by those working in the system. This explains why audits are necessary even when good intentions are assumed by all. The scale or complexity of a system makes it difficult to anticipate potential problems or ensure there are none, so an audit becomes part of assisting regulation of a system to keep it performing according to desired metrics and values.

This chapter takes a different approach to the problem of ensuring fairness. Rather than imagining we are the data scientists or modelers doing data analysis or building out a machine learning system, let's imagine that we have been handed a system and asked to evaluate it. This can happen under two paradigms: white-box auditing and black-box auditing.

If you are not familiar with this terminology, *white-box auditing* implies that we can see the code powering a model and get into the internals of a system, whereas *black-box auditing* means that the internals of the model itself are not available to us but we can still run the model.

White-box auditing might sound easy, but remember that just because a model is available does not mean it is easy to understand. For example, white-box auditing is separate from the issue of interpretability. Remember that even researchers who develop deep learning models may be at pains to explain how the models work. Though feature visualization is an area of interest, even full access to a model may not enable easy use of it.

We should also distinguish white-box auditing from retraining, although they can feel related. When we treat this topic of auditing, we will imagine that for whatever reason we are not in the business of building any alternative models, either because the resources are not available or because organizationally at that point we should kick the problem back to the model's developer.

Black-box auditing refers to a situation in which the model or pipeline to be audited is a black box, meaning we may be able to see what we put in and then what comes out, but we can't see what is going on inside the black box. When academic researchers and activists attempt to figure out what tech companies are doing with their algorithms online, their investigations are one form of black-box auditing. When you might try to reverse engineer some kind of score online, that can also be a form of black-box auditing.

Black-box auditing sounds quite a bit more challenging than white-box auditing, but the level of challenge will depend on the technical constraints. For example, an audit whereby we run real-world data through a model, and can access the model as many times and as rapidly as we want, would be a relatively easy black-box audit. At the limit of very generous usage (no constraints), a highly accessible black-box model might not prove much more challenging to audit than a fully inspectable model that happened to be very complex and therefore relatively difficult to audit despite full availability of its code.

On the other hand, a black-box audit could include as little as an API with limits on how often we can make requests. In such a case we'd have to use each access opportunity wisely and limit our expectations as to what we could accomplish.

In fact, white-box and black-box audits represent two extremes of the same process rather than two definitively different categories. Most of this chapter's discussion focuses on black-box auditing and auditing systems sufficiently complex that they may as well be black boxes, as white-box auditing can partly be thought of as an explainability task, which is covered in Chapter 8.

Chapter 8 covers the topic of explainability and how this can be audited and understood. For our purposes, that will serve as the introduction to white-box auditing as well.

The Parameters of an Audit

An audit can be an extensive dive into a system or a quick check against basic rules or standards. This section briefly touches on the major factors that should be considered when contemplating an individual audit or putting a larger audit infrastructure in place:

Stakeholders

Ideally, an audit of a data science pipeline or a particular algorithmic product should include as many stakeholders as possible in the auditing process, preferably including representatives of those who are affected by the algorithm. In selecting representative stakeholders, you should keep two perspectives in mind. On the one hand, you want the makeup of stakeholders to have a connection to the underlying distribution of stakeholders (a representative sample). On the other hand, you want a diverse perspective that includes minority viewpoints, so you should be sure that even small groups are not left out. As we have seen time and again, enormous harms may be targeted at only a small subpopulation, and we want to make sure we can hear about such potential or actual harms from stakeholders. For example, most statistics indicate that Reddit has a male super-majority, but obviously it would still be good to consider the viewpoints of female users. Some Reddit forums are female-dominated, and what's more, some of the problems on Reddit to which algorithmic solutions could be applied might disproportionately affect females. Among these are deep fakes, which include an array of synthetic nonconsensual porn depicting women.

Technical dependencies

An audit should define the system that it will audit and over which it can make changes. Obviously, such a system can expand indefinitely into whatever opportunity the auditors in question have to make changes. However, with a technical product this range can expand quite a bit beyond the algorithm itself.

Time

There is a recognized mismatch between the culture of tech, emphasizing "move fast and break things," and the culture of government work and corporate responsibility usually associated with audits. Proper audits may take time, particularly if they are going to include the human elements of interacting with stakeholders and collecting points of view rather than simply a technical analysis.

Goals

The goals of an audit should be specified both at a high conceptual level and more concretely at the start. This does not mean that an audit can never extend beyond its original set of directives, but it can help rein in excessive analysis discussion and keep the humans involved in the audit focused on achieving a specific goal. Also, specifying the goals in advance avoids the potential to forget important goals and values if one particular aspect of a system turns out to be very distracting for whatever reason.

High-Profile Tech Audits

A variety of large tech companies have undertaken audits of their products and overall place in society, coming away with insights to guide algorithmic development in the future.

To give an example of an audit that took a very high-level and wide-ranging approach —involving quite a large community of outsiders, and extensive time, which is much more in line with a traditional audit than with the tech industry—consider the civil rights audit Facebook (*https://oreil.ly/QVpog*) undertook for more than a year, beginning in 2018, spearheaded by an outsider, a leading civil rights attorney.

As outsiders, we can't know exactly how the audit was conducted, but we can rely on the descriptions. It seems the lead on the audit began not by looking at Facebook but by speaking with over 70 American civil rights organizations, which highlighted a variety of concerns, including discrimination in advertising for housing, credit, and employment, and the use of Facebook to spread messaging and organize events related to white nationalism.

Indeed, from the materials Facebook has portraying the audit, much of the audit seemed focused on downstream real-world effects rather than specific outputs of Facebook's algorithmic or platform products. In this case we can see the audit would have provided feedback to then guide technical, human resources, and business development initiatives as inappropriate advertising categories were removed, more personnel were taken on to identify inappropriate content, and more machine learning training was devoted to spotting problems of fake news, such as misinformation or news encouraging people not to vote.

We can also look to guidance from experts in deploying complex machine learning systems with real-world consequences. In early 2020, Google researchers released a proposed auditing framework (*https://oreil.ly/NBJVG*).[1]

Google started from the point of recognizing that individual tools can be used for both auditing and proactively pursuing fairness. These include systems to encourage the reporting of standard metrics on the performance of a model (*https://arxiv.org/abs/1810.03993*) and systems to report attributes of data sets that are likely to be used for machine learning models' data sheets (*https://arxiv.org/pdf/1803.09010.pdf*).

An audit offers opportunities to characterize fundamental aspects of all parts of the data science pipeline that might affect fairness, from fundamental attributes of a data

---

1 In addition to our discussion, you should check out Google's presentation at FAT* 2020 (*https://oreil.ly/rv_3G*).

set's content or structure to the public-facing deployment of whatever product is ultimately selected for production use.

However, these discrete tools that treat segmented parts of the pipeline from a fairness perspective do not offer specific guidance for the following important opportunities:

- Recording decisions made along the entire pipeline with respect to design and balancing of risks and benefits
- Enabling and even encouraging interventions along that pipeline
- Maintaining a conversation and visibility regarding fairness and ethics, particularly in large-scale processes

For example, Google looks to more experienced players who have faced both high regulatory and ethical implications for use of complex systems: aerospace, medical devices, and finance. It takes inspiration from all of these industries and lays out the following. In Figure 7-1, the structure of an audit, multifaceted and sequential in the same way as a data science pipeline, is laid out according to one set of guidelines developed and published by Google.

Scoping	Mapping	Artifact collection	Testing	Reflection	Post-audit
Define audit scope	Stakeholder buy-in	Audit checklist	Review documentation	Remedial plan	Go/no-go decision
Product requirements document (PRD)	Conduct interviews	Model cards	Adversarial testing	Design history file (ADHF)	Design mitigations
AI principles	Stakeholder map	Datasheets	Ethical risk analysis chart		Track implementation
Use case ethics review	Interview transcripts			Summary report	
Social impact assessment	Failure modes and effects analysis (FMEA)				

Figure 7-1. An overview of Google's proposed internal audit framework for AI systems[2]

2 Raji, Inioluwa Deborah et al. "Closing the AI Accountability Gap." arXiv.org, January 27–30, 2020. *https://arxiv.org/pdf/2001.00973.pdf*.

You can see that the organization is broken into a sequence of stages. At each of these stages, a variety of tools are available. Not every tool may be helpful or necessary, but they are available and most reasonably used in the stages indicated.

The major stages of the proposed internal audit framework are as follows:

Scoping
> In this stage, the goals and extent of an audit would be discussed, preferably with a diverse group to explore a variety of perspectives. Also, the intended impact and potential for revision of the system should be discussed at this stage. This is particularly important given known findings that commitment mechanisms can be helpful for both individuals and teams to follow through on their intentions. Specifying these intentions formally (for example, in writing), can help groups recall and honor these intentions, even when accomplishing them following difficulties or complexity identified during the audit takes more work or investment than had originally been expected.

Mapping
> In the mapping phase, those participating in the audit understand what systems are already in place, what opportunities exist for testing, what resources are already available and worked on, and the like. This is also a time to identify the internal parties, rather than just external parties, who can serve as informational sources or who should participate in an audit.

Artifact collection
> Collection of artifacts is a way to document the state of the system as it was encountered during the audit. This can also be the time to centralize relevant documentation, which may be relatively spread out, or to enforce the creation of documentation that may have been omitted during the original development process, as can happen because of time or personnel constraints.

Testing
> This is the stage of the auditing process that likely looks like what you'd think of when you think of auditing. Here, technical tests may be run, perhaps to identify quantitative measures of fairness that are not complied with to expectations. Such tests should have been specified in the previous stages, as it is also important to make sure that testing is done in a way that has been specified at least to some minimal degree. For example, we could otherwise imagine a tendency to go "shopping" for the right tests to employ in an audit to ensure maximal "passing," but of course that's not really the goal of the audit. We should also keep in mind that testing need not be merely quantitative and code-based. It could also entail collecting ethnographic study information from downstream users, looking at customer feedback, and considering other elements of data that would be collected from outside the confines of the system or algorithm being audited.

Reflection

This stage is the time that should be formally set aside for examining the results of testing, relating these results to the goals and scope of the audit established in the scoping phase, and enhancing the artifacts already gathered with the results of the testing. This phase is also the time to develop guidelines, action items, and risk assessments that can be handed either up or down the pipeline to make necessary interventions, and optional improvements, and also to allow the ultimate decision makers to have full information regarding the outcome of the audit.

For each of these stages, the Google framework includes some key systems for completing the work associated with a stage. In most cases, this work and the tool will continue through multiple stages. There are too many such tools to discuss them, and more tools can be specified.

I won't detail all the sample components, but here is one: the failure modes and effects analysis (FMEA). This is taken from the aerospace industry, where it is crucially important to think through all the ways that a system may fail and the potential consequences. We follow the layout from Google's Inioluwa Deborah Raji presentation. In this case, let's analyze plans to develop a COVID-19 contact tracing app using a decentralized system that is supposed to be better for protecting privacy (but still imperfect). In this case, we imagine the system will also have some machine learning built in so that app users receive a risk score rather than a simple binary metric. We expect that app users will use this risk score to decide whether to self-quarantine and what other measures they should take when it seems they may have been exposed to coronavirus. Table 7-1 shows some considerations applied to the COVID contact tracing app thought experiment.

Table 7-1. Failure modes and effects analysis for contact tracing apps

Consideration	Assessment
User action and intended response	User installs the app and gives it permission to use low-energy Bluetooth protocols to detect duration and proximity of contacts with other people using the app. User receives a notification upon significant exposure to someone later diagnosed with COVID-19 via an authenticated viral test.
Potential failure mode and mechanism of failure	User's contacts are not detected because the user usually wears phone under a heavy jacket and app fails to account for different clothing and weather patterns; this happens because app was calibrated in sunny California but then deployed everywhere in the US.
Potential harms of failure	App users in colder states are overconfident in the performance of the app based on statistics reported from use in California. For this reason, app users in colder states experience higher rates of false positives, which can result in viral spread.
Severity of harm	If the app receives significant uptake and trust, resulting harm could be substantial to the extent false positives contribute to the spread of the virus. This will very much depend on how the app is viewed and whether governments and institutions rely on it rather than it being merely a consumer product.
Detection likelihood	Depends on outreach; high if users trust the app and believe that their feedback will help improve the app; low if users do not report back the *false negatives* they later discover through testing positive for the virus despite not receiving a notice from the app.

You're probably frustrated with Table 7-1. It has vastly simplified just one possible problem (of many) that could occur with the development of a COVID-19 tracking app.[3] You may also disagree with the assessment. But even if you dislike what I've written, recognize that it's better than nothing, which is what most AI systems have as a systematic failure analysis.

It's worth going through the thought exercise of what other kinds of failure modes we could anticipate for the app. The preceding could be boiled down to the false negative failure mode. You should consider at least a few other broad modes of failure, such as the ones I've listed here (and you can probably identify more):

- False-positive failures
- Privacy and cybersecurity failures with respect to failure to safeguard a user's health or social contact information from bad actors, be they snoopers, hackers, or even governments looking to co-opt this tool for nondisease surveillance
- Notification failures such that a notification is not sent to a user even when someone has sent in a notice of a COVID-19 diagnosis
- Notification failures in product design such that a user's attention is not properly called to an existing notification

The good aspect of this tool, even if it is poorly implemented or cannot be implemented to full complexity, is that it forces certain discussions and documentation. If this is completed before the app is released, it will likely prompt questions at various levels along the pipeline that can then be pushed to the right person. For example, imagine a product manager spots the problem of whether heavier clothing in colder climates might influence the determination of what kind of signals are judged epidemiologically significant for purposes of warning someone about potential exposure.[4] All sorts of actionable concerns for different aspects of an app team could come out of this, only some of which are discussed here:

- Running a variety of Bluetooth hardware experiments to determine what geographic and environmental factors might systematically distort the distance calculations crucial to determining an epidemiologically significant exposure
- Consulting with public health experts regarding questions such as how air temperature, humidity, UV level, and other physical indicators should be factored into the app's calculations for determining exposure

---

3 At the time of writing, the debate about whether such apps will be useful and whether such utility is worthwhile, given potential privacy harms, is ongoing.

4 I am not an authority on the physics or computer science involved in making Bluetooth work, but I am told that damp clothing in cold wet weather might impact its performance. The theory that thickness of clothing might affect performance likely has no basis in reality.

- Working with the marketing team to determine the best way to describe a product to both enhance trust and make clear the performance limits of a contact tracing app with respect to false negatives

- Planning for a calibration process with the machine learning team and determining in consultation with both hardware and public health experts what sort of zones (be they climate zones, urban space zones, or cultural zones), might be appropriate as behavior and climate shift in ways that would cause the app to work worse for certain groups unless calibrated to their needs

So, part of an audit can be about process. Perhaps the audit should itself come at the end of any development process and before a launch, precisely to raise novel questions when it is most meaningful to raise them.

The Rules Versus Standards Debate

Anyone who's been to law school will be familiar with rules and standards; most others may know the concept but perhaps not the language. When thinking about how to offer guidance, the question is, do you give specific actionable advice or commands that remove discretion from the one receiving the advice or commands? The benefit is that you hopefully achieve clarity and it is easy to assess compliance. The downside is that it is rare for a single specific piece of guidance to apply logically to all situations where it might be applied. This is the "rule" approach.

The other option is to offer more general guidance that describes the goal to be achieved and perhaps some analyses as to how costs and benefits should be compared. It leaves the party who needs to comply in the position of best deciding how to comply given a particular set of constraints, which is good. On the other hand, it also leaves the party freer to look for loopholes or look for ways to passively non-comply. This is the "standards" approach.

If you are part of an organization looking to develop guidelines to be used for audits, you will find yourself balancing concerns about rules versus standards if you are thinking about an approach that would apply uniformly. Do you want to say a certain group parity threshold must be met in all cases (sounds more like a rule), or do you want to say that nondiscrimination should be pursued as vigorously as possible, with a preference for maximal removal of sensitive information consistent with achieving business objectives (sounds more like a standard)?

As you set out the parameters for a single audit or a system of audit, remember to keep in mind that both approaches can work in different situations, and it may be good to experiment with the style of guidance applied to your technical products.

Scoping: What Should We Audit?

In addition to setting the parameters for the audit, as mentioned, we must also consider the subject of the audit. When an algorithm or data science pipeline is audited, what should be audited? The answer will partly depend on the goals already discussed, but even then there is the question of where and how the goals should be applied.

One fundamental question is whether the process should be audited, or only the outcome. In the previous chapters on fairness interventions, our metrics tended to depend on outcome in the sense of a group or individual fairness metric—say, group parity of false positives or consistency to gauge individual fairness. However, a process-oriented audit might very well not stop at the satisfactory outputs of a particular algorithm, but instead look at whether the fairness intervention was in keeping with standards applied in a particular company or setting.

Another question to think about is whether you should audit only those aspects of the system that are within your control or whether you will extend your audit to take into account how the system is received beyond your control, be that further down the technical pipeline but away from your mandate or out in the real world. In some cases you may be able to tweak reception downstream even by adjusting only what is within your power. However, whether that is appropriate, particularly where it will affect downstream members within your institution, will depend on context.

In addition to thinking about the institutional extent of what to audit, you need to think about the subjects to audit in a particular study. For example, an audit might implicate antidiscrimination but might also implicate transparency or safety or privacy. Is it appropriate to deal with all these topics at once, or could having an overly broad brief doom the audit to failure, as it will be too wide-ranging to come up with digestible and feasible action plans in a reasonable scope of time?

Black-Box Auditing

Next I'll talk about a few intuitive ways that black-box models can be audited. These are described briefly, as you would be able to implement them yourself depending on the details of your code base and the populations of interest. The point with these is to make you aware of some very simple but useful techniques for auditing.

We then do a deeper dive into a technique to audit for indirect influence of a feature with a black-box model. This covers the important case of a sensitive attribute that may not be included in the inputs of a model but is nonetheless influencing the results in a way that could impact fairness considerations. We examine the mathematics underlying the technique and run through some code examples with an open source module implemented by the creators of the method.

Running a Model Through Different Counterfactuals

We have numerous manual options to run a black-box model through counterfactuals. Assuming you have an unlimited number and rate of data point submissions, you can be quite extensive in your auditing. Of course, with the curse of dimensionality, it could still take a very long time to explore how class membership might work for a large number of inputs that can all be computed.

Let's imagine that we developed a hiring algorithm for new college graduates that takes gender as input. It also takes GPA, class rank, textual inputs regarding extracurricular activities, recommendation letters from faculty, and performance on a timed assessment. Imagine this gives rise to roughly two hundred inputs once the textual inputs are passed through a natural language processing model that attempts to extract information about certain characteristics and provide some kind of summary vector with established embeddings.[5] How would you go about kicking the tires to see whether this algorithm is a good and fair one?

The difficulty in such cases is that many important algorithms are already not susceptible to this form of testing because the inputs are ones that are difficult to quickly vary. For example, with facial recognition data, how do we fairly transform the same face from female to male to do such counterfactual testing? That itself would involve another algorithm, and we'd have to ask whether that algorithm was fair. Is there really such a thing as a female and male version of the same face? This is a question for biology or philosophy but not for algorithmic auditors.

In such cases, it makes more sense to do population-wide testing. We can run an algorithm through what we feel are fair and representative samples of candidates with different qualities and combinations of factors to see how they fare. One study of facial recognition software used faces of elected politicians from around the world as samples. In this way, the auditors of the model did not impose their own notions of what a fair data set would be but rather picked a process that would produce a representative data set for fairness testing.

Another example that may be more digestible is to consider how group-oriented fairness metrics will vary when measuring the same algorithm depending on what data is used to test the algorithm. One example has been provided by a law review article that demonstrates with simple simulations that different samples of financial data will lead to better or worse measured disparities when gauging the fairness of a model.[6]

---

5 It's not important if you don't know what these are; simply take for granted that a letter or a string could be sensibly reduced to some kind of high-dimensional vector that would *make sense* to subsequent algorithmic consumers of this information.

6 Gillis, Talia B. and Jann L. Spiess. "Big Data and Discrimination." University of Chicago Law Review 86, no. 2 (2019). *https://lawreview.uchicago.edu/publication/big-data-and-discrimination*.

One way that this latter idea, of testing sample populations, may be more helpful than directly testing individuals with variations is that directly testing individual counterfactual situations is helpful only in identifying the direct influence of a variable on an outcome. However, the focus on direct influence leaves an important problem. Without extensive domain knowledge, the direct influence of a seemingly nonsensitive attribute may seem reasonable and be ignored when, in fact, it is serving as a proxy for a sensitive attribute. This would not be identified if an auditor is looking only for direct influence of sensitive variables. Hence, we move on to considering a formalized method developed to identify indirect influence of variables.

Model of the Model

Another option to audit a black-box model, which those familiar with the explainability literature or with literature relating to model compression might recognize, is simply training a new model based on the outputs of the black-box model. Within this paradigm, you have at least two options.

First, you can consider using an interpretable model, such as a linear model or a decision tree, which would enable you to detect whether certain features have an influence that seems inappropriate (such as race influencing hiring decisions) or difficult to explain and needing investigation (such as zip code influencing hiring decisions). In this case, you will need to be sure not to build a model that is so large that you cannot work with the results even if they are, in theory, interpretable to the extent of providing a way to rank feature importances.

Second, you can build a model that is meant to use the outputs of the black-box model to predict a sensitive attribute. We have seen this technique before, such as in Chapter 4, in which we saw that we could find a new representation of the data that would minimize the ability to predict. Likewise, a very basic but important audit would be to see whether the output of a black-box model enabled us to directly predict a sensitive attribute, such as someone's gender or race, with high accuracy. This would itself be concerning with no fancier a technique needed.

Auditing Black-Box Models for Indirect Influence

Adler et al.'s paper "Auditing Black-box Models for Indirect Influence" provides a technique for auditing black-box models that focuses on determining the extent of influence of individual features, and the authors also developed and released an open source Python module that implements these techniques and includes easy integration of new data sets and algorithms to be tested with the underlying technique.[7]

---

7 Adler, Philip, et al. "Auditing Black-box Models for Indirect Influence." arXiv.org, November 30, 2016. *https://arxiv.org/abs/1602.07043*.

Adler et al. take a perspective we have already seen in our earlier discussions of fairness interventions. They argue that the extent to which a feature is informative can be estimated by predicting that feature from the remaining features. The authors extend this idea and argue that the influence of a feature, even when only its proxies are included in a model, can be eliminated by modifying the data (as little as possible) so that the feature can no longer be predicted. In this way the information in the data set about a sensitive attribute that is coming even from proxies can be eliminated. Once the data set has been treated in this way, now called the "obscured data set," the drop in accuracy in a black-box model reflects the indirect influence of the variable that was obscured in the processed data set.

Next we will look a little more in detail at the mathematical motivations and implementation of the technique and then run through an example of how to use the available open source code base.

How it works

As described in the previous section, Adler et al. develop a technique designed to remove direct and indirect influence alike of a feature from a data set so as to determine the impact on a black-box model's performance that results from this.

They use the balanced error rate as their metric of interest. We have encountered this error metric before, but as a reminder, the balanced error rate is the average of errors over each class in the data set. The balanced error rate is then used to define two important concepts for the technique:

ϵ-obscure
> A data set is ϵ-obscure with respect to a specific feature x_i if x_i cannot be predicted from the data set with a balanced accuracy greater than ϵ.

Indirect influence
> The indirect influence of a feature x_i is the accuracy when a black-box model is run on the original data set minus the accuracy when a black-box model is run on an ϵ-obscure version of the data set.

We now treat the paradigmatic case in which the feature we wish to obscure is numerical (such as a test score) and the feature we wish to remove is categorical, such as a protected attribute, typically race or gender.[8] Adjusting the distributions of each input variable within each group so as to obscure group membership mathematically minimizes the earthmover distance between the original distribution of the variables and the distribution used to obscure group membership.

---

8 The authors also provide a feature for the alternative possibilities of obscuring a categorical feature or removing a numerical feature. The latter seems quite unlikely, although the need to obscure a categorical feature will commonly occur.

That procedure is the following. For a feature to be obscured with another feature to be removed, we define $O = x$ as the feature to be removed and $W = X_j$ as the feature to be obscured. The cumulative distribution function for the distribution within a specific category of O is $F_x(w) = Pr(W \geq w \mid O = x)$. We then define the *median distribution* as the distribution of the feature to be obscured, X_j, such that the inverse cumulative distribution function is as follows:

$$F_A(w)^{-1} = median_{x \in O} F_x^{-1}(w)$$

It is this new distribution, A, that maximally removes information about O while minimally changing the distribution over W. This procedure can be applied to all input variables to a particular black-box algorithm with respect to a particular feature to be removed, where the feature to be removed is not itself going to be an input into the black-box algorithm.

Earthmover Distance

The *earthmover distance* is just what it sounds like, if you envision measuring how the area of a curve of a function is not changed but rather moved as the shape of that function is changed, as depicted in Figure 7-2.

Figure 7-2. An intuitive view of the earthmover distance

Earthmover distance in our discussion applies specifically to *cumulative density functions*. If you are not familiar with this concept, take a break for a quick internet search and then return to reading this chapter.

Adler et al. realize that completely removing information about a feature could prove unacceptable in terms of performance degradation, and for this reason they also provide an easy means to calibrate how much a distribution is removed with a hyperparameter that varies between 0 and 1, where 0 represents an unchanged data set and 1 represents the maximal removal of information about the feature to be removed. This calibration parameter is available in the black-box auditing library, and we will use this option to see how the relative amount of information removed impacts performance. Techniques like this are useful for enabling an auditor not only to iden-tify problems but also to help find a solution that works for the many motivations of an algorithm developer, as both accuracy and fairness are values that most developers want to pursue, neither to the detriment of the other where possible.

Incidentally, this test also relates to some introductory statistics you likely encoun-tered, perhaps long discarded in a dusty part of your brain if you don't often do popu-lation comparisons. Interestingly, the authors are able to show that this data manipulation to remove the influence of a variable is the same as creating a data set on which the F-test will fail; that is, the null hypothesis of population equivalence will not be rejected.[9]

We will not be running through a full kicking of the tires of this package in the code demonstration because of space limitations. However, I briefly summarize here the published results of Adler et al. with respect to testing their technique on a variety of data sets. The ones they cover that we will focus on are the Adult census data, in which the baseline data set shows quite different income outcomes for men as com-pared to women and whites as compared to nonwhites; the German credit data set, which similarly shows quite different outcomes for men as compared to women; and the COMPAS recidivism data set, which shows quite different outcomes in the error rates for black as compared to white defendants.[10] The results of the method when applied to these data sets are described briefly here:

Adult census data set
> In this model the ranking changed depending on which model had been used. The variable of age had a large impact, while the variable of race had a surpris-ingly small impact.

German credit data set
> The results of the German credit data set showed a very noisy ordering between the models. This suggests that the original training of the model was poor, per-haps indicating overfit.

---

9 Of course, this relies on assumptions of normality regarding the variables, which is a standard type of assumption for many assertions about models and algorithms. Your mileage will vary depending on your data.

10 The interested reader should check out Adler et al's full paper. One very cool aspect of this paper is that they also include synthetic data and a scientific data set to show how problems inspired by socially impacted data sets also include broader concepts about data analysis. They also show that fairness relates to explainability and the need to audit models even when there aren't obvious fairness implications, such as in the dark reac-tions data, which is a data set used to train models to predict the outcome of chemical reactions.

Recidivism data set

This data set showed strong consistency of importance of features regardless of which model was used to train on the original data. The important features were the prior arrests of the prisoner, the age at release, and the time served.

In addition, some general observations could be taken from the authors' results. First, the degree to which a particular feature was ranked as important in the black-box model varied by model. This shows there is no guarantee that a particular feature will be important in all models. Second, in some cases, obscuring a data set improved model performance. This would tend to suggest that the obscuring removed some noise from the data set.

Code demonstration

As with previous examples, we'll take advantage of the built-in data sets with the library of interest. So, we begin by loading the `Black-BoxAuditing` module and an associated data set, which we'll discuss in a moment. We also import the model we'll use to be the black-box model, as we recall that the indirect influence is computed with respect to a specific proposed black-box model:

```
import pandas as pd
import Black-BoxAuditing as BBA

from BBA.model_factories import SVM

ricci_data = BBA.load_data('ricci')
```

The data set. The Ricci data set comes from a recent and famous US Supreme Court case. This case discussed the differences between various forms of discrimination—namely, the differences between disparate treatment (in Europe, *direct discrimination*) and disparate impact (in Europe, *indirect discrimination*). The case also discussed the pitfalls by which an organization could, in taking steps to limit disparate impact, possibly end up guilty of discrimination for disparate treatment. The decision is quite helpful in revealing the current thinking at the highest level of the judiciary on issues related to antidiscrimination and affirmative action.

Ricci v. DeStefano

In the US Supreme Court decision *Ricci v. DeStefano* (557 U.S. 557, 2009), 20 firefighters at the New Haven Fire Department, 19 white and 1 Hispanic, claimed discrimination under the Civil Rights Act of 1964. Their complaint indicated that they had passed a test for promotion to management positions but had been denied promotion. Instead, the City of New Haven invalidated the test results for all test takers because no black firefighter had scored high enough to be considered for a management position.

In a contested 5-4 decision, the Supreme Court held that the city's decision to invalidate the test results violated Title VII of the Civil Rights Act. The city had defended itself by saying that it feared using the test would subject it to disparate impact litigation from black plaintiffs, but the Supreme Court said that the city did not have a good reason to fear such litigation. In particular, the Court said that the City failed to show a "genuine dispute that the examinations were job-related and consistent with business necessity," as would have been required by any plaintiffs seeking to bring a disparate impact lawsuit.

This decision by the Supreme Court was a complex one, and highlighted the tension between a citizen's right to equal protection under the laws regardless of race, as guaranteed by the Constitution, and the Civil Rights Act's provisions to prevent racial discrimination. As we can see with the City of New Haven's decision, some entities, including algorithm developers, may feel that they are damned if they do and damned if they don't with respect to fairness interventions.

Note that an entity's decision not to use a scoring instrument because of extreme racial disparities, like the disparities observed in the New Haven management exam, have some precedent. For example, some colleges have considered or even decided to drop the use of SAT scores because of observed disparities in results according to race and income. Some universities have explained that the disparities themselves seem sufficient to invalidate the claim of such a testing instrument to be a fair and accurate evaluation of abilities. This remains a highly contested area of dispute, particularly for public university systems.

The data set is loaded as a tuple, and the easiest way to see what is in that tuple is to go to the source:

```python
def load_data(data):
  if data not in preloaded:
    raise KeyError("{} is not an available data set".format(data))
  if data == "DRP":
    return load_DRP(data)
  filename = preloaded[data]["filepath"]
  testdata = preloaded[data]["testdata"]
  correct_types = preloaded[data]["correct_types"]
  train_percentage = preloaded[data]["train_percentage"]
  response_header = preloaded[data]["response_header"]
  features_to_ignore = preloaded[data]["features_to_ignore"]
  with open(filename) as f:
    reader = csv.reader(f)
    data = [row for row in reader]
    headers = data.pop(0)

    for i, row in enumerate(data):
      for j, correct_type in enumerate(correct_types):
        data[i][j] = correct_type(row[j])
```

```
    if testdata is None:
      train, test = split_by_percent(data, train_percentage)
    else:
      train = data
      with open(testdata) as f:
        reader = csv.reader(f)
        test = [row for row in reader][1:] # Ignore headers.

      for i, row in enumerate(test):
        for j, correct_type in enumerate(correct_types):
          test[i][j] = correct_type(row[j])
  return headers, train, test, response_header, features_to_ignore, correct_types
```

This function has a few items to note. First, we are loading preloaded data, so we can imagine that the `preloaded` specifications will apply. We also see the data is simply stored in a `csv` file, so we can easily see that our own data could be loaded by this same function.

Looking at the return line, `returnheaders, train, test, response_header, features_to_ignore, correct_types`, we can now make sense of the output when we examine `ricci_data`. Let's look at that output as a way to get to know the Ricci data set. We'll go through the tuple one by one:

```
>>> ricci_data[0]
['Position', 'Oral', 'Written', 'Race', 'Combine', 'Class']
```

Per the `return` line in the preceding function, I can see that these are the column names in the data set. It's not a particularly large data set either, by dimension or by sample size (more on that soon).

We next inspect the training data:

```
>>> ricci_data[1][:10]
[['Captain', 89.52, 95, 'W', 92.808, '1'],
 ['Captain', 88.57, 76, 'W', 81.028, '1'],
 ['Captain', 76.19, 84, 'W', 80.876, '1'],
 ['Captain', 76.19, 82, 'H', 79.676, '1'],
 ['Captain', 70.0, 84, 'H', 78.4, '1'],
 ['Captain', 80.0, 74, 'W', 76.4, '1'],
 ['Captain', 73.33, 74, 'W', 73.732, '1'],
 ['Captain', 70.0, 76, 'W', 73.6, '1'],
 ['Captain', 82.38, 64, 'W', 71.352, '1'],
 ['Captain', 78.57, 64, 'W', 69.828, '0']]
>>> len(ricci_data[1])
59
```

We can also do some quick tabulations on this data, which you can see in Figure 7-3, although we won't thoroughly kick the tires:

```
>>> df.groupby(['Position', 'Race']).count()
```

```
In [68]: df.groupby(['Position', 'Race']).count()
Out[68]:
```

		Oral	Written	Combine	Class
Position	**Race**				
	B	4	4	4	4
Captain	H	4	4	4	4
	W	14	14	14	14
	B	6	6	6	6
Lieutenant	H	8	8	8	8
	W	23	23	23	23

Figure 7-3. A simple groupby operation gives us a sense of the Ricci data

The texting data comes next and is similar. In particular, we see that the training/testing split seems to have been 50%:

```
>>> ricci_data[2][:10]
[['Captain', 80.0, 95, 'W', 89.0, '1'],
 ['Captain', 82.38, 87, 'W', 85.152, '1'],
 ['Captain', 76.19, 82, 'W', 79.676, '1'],
 ['Captain', 73.81, 81, 'W', 78.124, '1'],
 ['Captain', 84.29, 72, 'W', 76.916, '1'],
 ['Captain', 87.62, 69, 'W', 76.448, '1'],
 ['Captain', 79.05, 74, 'H', 76.02, '1'],
 ['Captain', 73.81, 77, 'W', 75.724, '1'],
 ['Captain', 76.67, 74, 'W', 75.068, '1'],
 ['Captain', 82.38, 70, 'B', 74.952, '1']]
>>> len(ricci_data[2])
59
```

If we wanted to verify this, we could look at the `preloaded` variable in the `load_data` function we examined earlier, but we'll try not to digress too much in this text. Rather, if this is a library you will likely use, it will serve you well to poke around on your own and get familiar with the module's structure.

We look at the target that will be used for training and auditing (called `response_header` in the code):

```
>>> ricci_data[3]
'Class'
```

We also look at whether any columns were set to be ignored:

```
>>> ricci_data[4]
[]
```

Finally, we see that the types of the data per column are stored at index 5, but these are not pictured because they're not particularly interesting.

A vanilla audit with default library options. We then train the auditor with a few simple lines of code. In this case, we are learning how the library works and do not have an existing model, but the library works with this possibility by providing a model factory from which we can select some plausible models. In this case we'll select the SVM option, which itself relies on an import from sklearn, which we can see by looking at the course code of *SVM.py* in the model_factories submodule of BBA.

We then train, which entails deciding on an output directory because the results of the audit are saved in a variety of formats:

```
auditor = BBA.Auditor()
auditor.ModelFactory = SVM
auditor(ricci_data, output_dir="ricci-audit-output")
```

This process can take a few minutes and produces the following output in addition to an extensive directory of results:

```
Training initial model. (12:14:12)
Calculating original model statistics on test data:
Training Set:
Conf-Matrix: {'1': {'1': 26, '0': 1}, '0': {'1': 2, '0': 30}}
accuracy: 0.9491525423728814
BCR: 0.9502314814814815
Testing Set:
Conf-Matrix {'1': {'1': 23, '0': 6}, '0': {'0': 25, '1': 5}}
accuracy: 0.8135593220338984
BCR: 0.8132183908045977
Auditing: 'Position' (1/5). (12:14:12)
Auditing: 'Oral' (2/5). (12:14:13)
Auditing: 'Written' (3/5). (12:14:13)
Auditing: 'Race' (4/5). (12:14:14)
Auditing: 'Combine' (5/5). (12:14:14)
Audit file dump set to False: Only minimal audit files have been saved.
Audit files dumped to: ricci-audit-output.

Ranking audit files by accuracy. (12:14:14)
[('Combine', 0.322), ('Oral', 0.220),
  ('Written', 0.169), ('Race', -0.0169),
  ('Position', -0.0677)] (12:14:14)
Ranking audit files by BCR. (12:14:14)
[('Combine', 0.317), ('Oral', 0.221),
  ('Written', 0.170), ('Race', -0.0172),
  ('Position', -0.067)] (12:14:14)
Audit Start Time: 2020-05-20 12:14:12.724933
Audit End Time: 2020-05-20 12:14:14.827193
Retrained Per Repair: False
Model Factory ID: 1589991252.7249682
Model Type: DecisionTree
Non-standard Model Options: {}
Train Size: 59
Test Size: 59
Non-standard Ignored Features: []
Features: ['Position', 'Oral', 'Written', 'Race', 'Combine', 'Class']
```

```
Ranked Features by accuracy: [('Combine', 0.322), ('Oral', 0.220), (
  'Written', 0.169), ('Race', -0.016), ('Position', -0.067)]
Approx. Trend Groups: [['Position'], ['Oral'], ['Written'], ['Race'], ['Combine']]

Ranked Features by BCR: [('Combine', 0.317), ('Oral', 0.221),
  ('Written', 0.170), ('Race', -0.017), ('Position', -0.067)]
Approx. Trend Groups: [['Position'], ['Oral'], ['Written'], ['Race'], ['Combine']]

Summary file written to: ricci-audit-output/summary.txt
  (12:14:15)
```

This already gives us quite a bit of information, most notably the ranked features, which are ranked by both accuracy and the balanced classification rate. In the case of this data set, the two measures are not too different, but they should both be checked because there will likely be greater disparity in even-more-unbalanced data sets. In fact, if you look at the tabulation earlier in the data discussion, we see that the data is surprisingly balanced. While whites are a majority by racial group, they are not a supermajority (unlike in the case of many other data sets that include race information in the US).

We can then inspect the directory in Figure 7-4 and see that quite a bit is prepared, including graphics files, data files, and text log files.

	Name ↓	Last Modified	File size
0 ▾ / Ch07 / ricci-audit-output			
		seconds ago	
accuracy.png		2 hours ago	18 kB
accuracy.png.data		2 hours ago	1.19 kB
BCR.png		2 hours ago	19.8 kB
BCR.png.data		2 hours ago	1.21 kB
Combine.audit		2 hours ago	1.32 kB
Combine.audit.repaired_1.0.predictions		2 hours ago	716 B
Combine.audit.test.repaired_1.0.data		2 hours ago	1.83 kB
Oral.audit		2 hours ago	1.26 kB
Oral.audit.repaired_1.0.predictions		2 hours ago	682 B
Oral.audit.test.repaired_1.0.data		2 hours ago	1.86 kB
Position.audit		2 hours ago	1.33 kB
Position.audit.repaired_1.0.predictions		2 hours ago	920 B
Position.audit.test.repaired_1.0.data		2 hours ago	1.86 kB
Race.audit		2 hours ago	1.28 kB
Race.audit.repaired_1.0.predictions		2 hours ago	455 B
Race.audit.test.repaired_1.0.data		2 hours ago	1.83 kB
summary.txt		2 hours ago	879 B
Written.audit		2 hours ago	1.32 kB
Written.audit.repaired_1.0.predictions		2 hours ago	514 B
Written.audit.test.repaired_1.0.data		2 hours ago	1.86 kB

Figure 7-4. Files created by the BBA.Auditor object as it runs an audit with default settings; image files, data files, and log files are all automatically created

Most interesting, Figure 7-5 shows how accuracy is influenced by the gradual obscuring of a variety of inputs.[11]

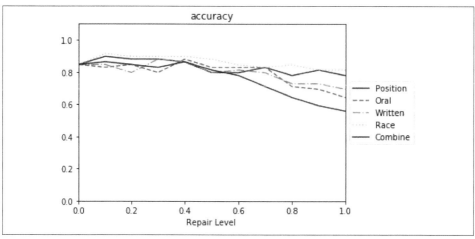

Figure 7-5. The relative change in accuracy as a particular feature is obscured (interestingly, race and position seem to cause the least change in accuracy, while the written exam feature's obscuration seems to most impact the accuracy)

In Figure 7-5, we see the automatic plot generated by the code. We can also load some of the audit data back into our Jupyter notebook to examine it there. For example, we can load in the computed accuracy data for each *repair level* and then use it to compute the influence factor Adler et al. describe by ourselves, manually, if we imagine contrasting no repair and full repair:

```
>>> acc_data = pd.read_csv("ricci-audit-output/accuracy.png.data")
>>> print(acc_data)
    Repair Level  Position      Oral   Written      Race   Combine
0            0.0  0.813559  0.813559  0.813559  0.813559  0.813559
1            0.1  0.830508  0.830508  0.847458  0.864407  0.779661
2            0.2  0.864407  0.847458  0.864407  0.881356  0.779661
3            0.3  0.847458  0.847458  0.813559  0.915254  0.813559
4            0.4  0.864407  0.813559  0.796610  0.898305  0.796610
5            0.5  0.830508  0.728814  0.813559  0.915254  0.796610
6            0.6  0.898305  0.779661  0.813559  0.915254  0.745763
7            0.7  0.864407  0.745763  0.745763  0.915254  0.711864
8            0.8  0.864407  0.745763  0.728814  0.932203  0.711864
9            0.9  0.864407  0.711864  0.627119  0.847458  0.559322
10           1.0  0.881356  0.593220  0.644068  0.830508  0.491525
```

---

11 I have lightly modified the default graphing function of the package to use line types and grayscale rather than solid color lines to accommodate the book's black-and-white printing. You will see a more colorful version when you run the code yourself.

We can then look at *influence*—that is, how much the accuracy changes from not obscuring a feature at all to completely obscuring it:

```
>>> def influence(df):
>>>     return (df.iloc[0][1:] - df.iloc[-1][1:])
>>> influence(acc_data)
Position   -0.067797
Oral        0.220339
Written     0.169492
Race       -0.016949
Combine     0.322034
dtype: float64
```

And we can look at what happens if we want to see the influence if we imagine a repair level of 0.5:

```
>>> def influence_partial_repair(df):
>>>     return (df.iloc[0][1:] - df.iloc[5][1:])
>>> influence_partial_repair(acc_data)
Position   -0.016949
Oral        0.084746
Written     0.000000
Race       -0.101695
Combine     0.016949
dtype: float64
```

In Figure 7-6, you can visualize the difference per feature between a full repair and partial repair. Note this merely contains redundant information compared to the accuracy plot, but may nonetheless be more helpful in processing the information were you in the position of determining what level of repair and intervention you might recommend to those upstream developing the model.

```
>>> deltas = influence(acc_data) - influence_partial_repair(acc_data)
>>> plt.bar(x = deltas.index, height = deltas.values)
```

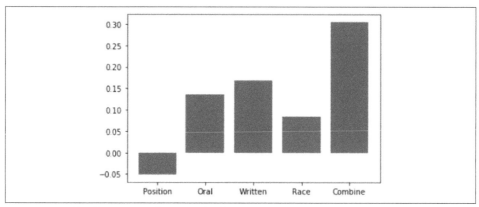

Figure 7-6. The change in influence of a feature when going from a full obscuration of that feature to a partial, where positive values indicate that the feature shows more influence with a full obscuration, which would be the expected result in that it indicates a greater change in accuracy when a feature is fully obscured rather than partially obscured

A black-box model audit.   The preceding example was somewhat synthetic in that we used an existing built-in data set and built-in option for a model. That model was actually trained in the course of auditing even though this is theoretically unimportant. Let's run through something more realistic. Let's say you received a model from someone in a pickle file format as well as a csv file with the data. We'll start at that point.

We can load our own data rather than using one of the provided data sets with a simple utility function that expects us to provide the basic information, such as which column is the target variable, what percentage of the data to use for training, and so on. (Remember the different members of the tuple returned by load_data in our earlier discussion.) Hence, we load our data as follows:[12]

```
synthetic_data = load_from_file("synth_data.csv",
                        correct_types = np.repeat([float],
                                                 [len(col_names)]),
                        response_header = 'hire',
                        train_percentage = 0.5)
```

Now that we have the tuple of our loaded data, we need a way to perform the audit with our own model rather than by building a model from one of the kinds provided by the module. Luckily, the creators of the Black-BoxAuditing module anticipated

---

12 The code to generate the synthetic data is in the repository for this book but isn't shown here to save space.

this scenario and provided two abstract base classes that can be used for this, and we import them here:

```
from Black-BoxAuditing.model_factories.AbstractModelFactory
import AbstractModelFactory
from Black-BoxAuditing.model_factories.AbstractModelVisitor
import AbstractModelVisitor
```

We then use these to load our pretrained and `pickled` model (in this case, a logistic regression object from `sklearn`) and apply it to the data provided in the specific format anticipated with the `Black-BoxAuditing` functionality, a list of lists:

```
class HirePredictorBuilder(AbstractModelFactory):
    def __init__(self, *args, **kwargs):
        AbstractModelFactory.__init__(self, *args, **kwargs)
        self.verbose_factory_name = "HirePredictor"  ❶
    def build(self, train_set):
        return HirePredictor()  ❷

class HirePredictor(AbstractModelVisitor):
    def __init__(self):
        with open( 'lr.pickle', 'rb' ) as f:
            self.lr = pickle.load(f)  ❸

    def test(self, test_set, test_name=""):
        return [[
                v[-1],    ❹
                self.lr.predict(  ❺
                        np.expand_dims(np.array(v[:-1]),  ❻
                        axis = 0))
                ]
                for v in test_set]
```

❶ We provide the name of the model factory so that the name can be printed in the logs.

❷ We provide the class of the model factory so that an instance can be made upon request by the `Auditor` object.

❸ We can load a pretrained file from a `pickle` object, or do anything else at this point we would normally do to build a model of our own or retrieve a pretrained model, independent of what is on offer in the model catalog of the `Black-BoxAuditing` module.

❹ The testing module expects a list to be returned, and within each member of a list the actual and predict values of the target variable are included.

❺ To produce the predicted value, we make use of the `predict` functionality with `sklearn`'s `LogisticRegression` classifier.

❻ Because the `LogisticRegression` classifier expects a two-dimensional array, we must reshape it before passing it to the `predict` method.

Note that there is no built-in limit to how to access your model or how opaque it can be. For example, within `test` we can even imagine making API calls to an inaccessible model, or we could imagine loading a very dense neural network during the `init` phase.

So, we have seen that auditing our own models and associated data sets, or those that others might provide to us, is also relatively straightforward with the `Black-BoxAuditing` module.

We then run the audit as we do with the built-in models, with very little difference in the implementation:

```
auditor = BBA.Auditor()
auditor.ModelFactory = HirePredictorBuilder
auditor(synthetic_data, output_dir="synthetic-audit-output")
```

Again, in addition to an extensive log output in the command line (omitted for reasons of space), this code also produces a directory of images, data files, and log files. We can see the outcome of the audit in Figure 7-7. See if you can make sense of this image once you have looked at the code that generates the synthetic data, available in the GitHub repository (*https://github.com/PracticalFairness/BookRepo*).

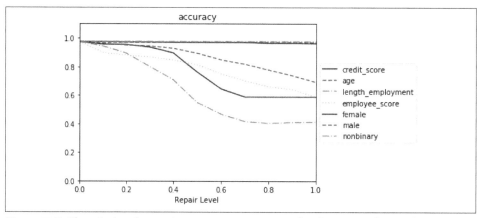

Figure 7-7. The relative change in accuracy as a particular feature is obscured

Concluding Remarks

The chapter discussed audits at two levels, both considering the black-box nature of systems or models.

First, we thought about audits from an institutional and goals perspective. What should they look like? How can we formalize them? Is there a set of best practices? While audits are very much a work in progress that is emerging in Big Tech and the AI community more generally, we can expect best practices to shift and evolve over time. What's more, some component of an audit will always be a matter of judgment, distinct to a particular context and a set of concerns around what a particular AI product is doing, how it's being deployed, and who the end users are. However, certain general guidelines can be expected to last, as we've discussed here.

Second, we got into the more specific problem of auditing a black-box model, in the sense of coming to some judgments about that model without having full or possibly any access to that model beyond being able to inject inputs and observe outputs. A variety of techniques are available to do this, some simple and some more demanding as far as assembling new data sets, thinking about potential deployment scenarios, and the like. We examined one open source library available to use and easy to integrate with custom data sources and models. We can expect more to become available in the coming years.

Interpretable Models and Explainability Algorithms

Up to this point we have focused our coding efforts primarily on fairness as understood from the perspective of parity and antidiscrimination. Another type of fairness sees us all as victims when we consider threats that can result from arbitrary, capricious, or opaque decision making. The protection against such experiences is established in most countries through guarantees of transparency, the rule of law, and due process. This last, due process, in turn can be divided into procedural due process (the right to a good decision-making process) and substantive due process (the right to a reasonable decision).

In recent years we are seeing that the same concerns that have been evinced for centuries or even millennia with respect to human decision making in the role of government are also relevant to machine learning. If computational models will make decisions that affect us, be they important or even relatively unimportant decisions, shouldn't we check them out to make sure these decisions make sense and are reached in a sensible way? This touches on a variety of values that all relate to fundamental needs and expectations of humans that when we design systems, these systems should make sense.

It also reflects security concerns, much like the ones that guided the original desires for transparency and due process in government. If an arbitrary decision can happen at all, then it is a threat to anyone who is subjected to that system. An arbitrary or silly decision coming out of a machine learning model is likewise cause for concern because it highlights the potential for future decisions to also be problematic.

This discussion already points to some of the useful features when examining issues of interpretability and explainability. It provides a way to check the quality of our model overall and also to better predict that model's behavior.

In this chapter we cover a few related topics, including the following on interpretable models:

- The difference between designing interpretable models and explaining existing models
- The trade-offs between interpretability and performance
- Some options for building interpretable models that can match the performance of uninterpretable models

and the following on explainability:

- A taxonomy of explainability
- Some options for explainability analysis with varying emphases on potential use cases
- Some warnings on the potential for bad actors to game explainability techniques
- A brief review of legal requirements that may affect explainability needs for an organization

For the code examples, we will use IBM's open source explainability module, AIX360, a sister project to the AIF360 code base covered in previous chapters on fairness interventions.

Interpretation Versus Explanation

Neither interpretability nor explainability has a single uniform technical definition, so we will rely on intuitive understandings of these terms. Generally, *interpretation* requires that we understand what the model is actually doing. *Explanation* requires that we understand why or how the model came to that decision; our understanding can work by simplification or analogy rather than by direct understanding or interpretation of the model.

Explainability has, in general, been a more popular discussion in legal circles, in industry, and in academic research. Up until recently the working assumption about black-box models, which are far too complicated to be understood by humans, has been that they necessarily outperform models that can be understood and interpreted. The roots of this assumption come from the amazing performance we have seen from extremely complicated neural networks, which can classify images with more accuracy than humans can and can produce near-human levels of sensible language, among other tasks.

However, in recent years, scholars have pointed out the threat of focusing on explainability. Computer scientist Cynthia Rudin (*https://oreil.ly/8PiqR*) has led the way in pointing out that our own cognitive biases and behavioral patterns favor black-box models for a variety of reasons, including perceived advantages both by machine learning practitioners and the public. Some of these assumptions and beliefs about explainability models are listed here, but it is important to note that in most cases they are not well justified:

- Little or no need for feature engineering
- Discovery of knowledge that would otherwise evade humans, who cannot see the big picture
- Believed to be more accurate
- Arguably easier to develop than interpretability models because explainability tends to be about taking derivatives while interpretability requires framing and solving an optimization problem

Rudin points out that the bias in favor of black-box models is so extreme that in many basic machine learning classes interpretable models are no longer even taught. However, she also points out that to greater or lesser extents, the assumptions about the trade-offs between black box and interpretable models are often untrue. In particular she points out that some widely circulated infographics, such as the famous DARPA image showing a complexity versus performance trade-off (Figure 8-1), is in no way a general mathematical fact for all data sets and classes of models.

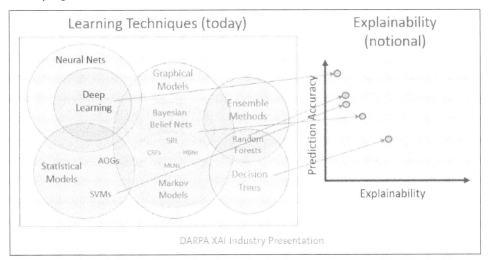

Figure 8-1. Though famously circulated in a DARPA presentation, as Cynthia Rudin highlighted (https://arxiv.org/pdf/1811.10154.pdf), this graphic never included information about the models that were run, the actual accuracy, or the data set used. This is just a schematic with no details and no basis for generalizability.

The accuracy-interpretability trade-off has no mathematical guarantees, and interpretable models have been built to match the accuracy of black-box models across a wide domain. While Figure 8-1 likely does reflect the reality of certain tasks or data sets and specific models trained to those data sets, we should be careful not to overgeneralize.

Even apart from the issue of whether our working assumptions and cognitive biases make us unduly favor explanation over interpretation, some problems with explanation suggest that exploring other avenues would be worthwhile. In her work, Rudin identifies some problems with explainability, including the following:

- You are relying on two models: the original model and the model you built.
- The models will necessarily disagree. More specifically, your explanation model will be wrong some percentage of the time.
- Sometimes explanations won't make sense.

We will divide our focus in this chapter between interpretable models and explainability algorithms suitable for post hoc explanation. Note that the explainability algorithms we examine will expect a white-box approach—that is, they will expect that the original model and data remain open to produce the explanation. If this is not the case, the methods discussed in Chapter 7 are more appropriate, be they to get some sense of explainability or to look for signs of discrimination.

Interpretable Models

Most people with some modeling experience will have encountered at least a few interpretable models. For example, linear regressions, particularly those without many coefficients, are certainly interpretable. By looking at the coefficients of inputs, we can see exactly how the value of a certain input affects the output. Likewise, with logistic regressions we get the same information, although in this case, because of the odds, we have to think a little harder or do a little math to understand exactly what the coefficients mean in terms of the final output.

Another class of models that is interpretable is decision trees. Decision trees can model nonlinearities in the data more automatically than linear regression models, for which we would need to design the nonlinear features. However, decision trees, though interpretable in the sense of being human readable, lack some of the interpretable qualities of a linear regression because it is more difficult for a human to get a sense globally of the logic, and this will be increasingly the case as the depth of the tree increases.

With a renewed focus on interpretable models, researchers have also developed new forms of interpretable models, some of which can match the performance of models traditionally viewed as not interpretable, or black-box. The next section discusses one recent example, generalized linear rule models by Wei et al.,[1] which was designed by IBM researchers and has been implemented in AIX360.

GLRM: How It Works

Generalized linear *rule* models (GLRMs) build on the idea of generalized linear models based on the original inputs from a data set but then deriving rules that can both model nonlinearities and produce interpretable coefficients. Wei et al. build on earlier work of designing rules as a way to develop interpretable models while also providing the opportunity to capture nonlinear regressions.

I won't go into the mathematics of the model explicitly in this case, as the math is beyond the level of this book. However, I will sketch out the general approach.

First, the authors assume that all features are binarized. With categorical features, this is done via one hot encoding. With numerical features, this is done via bidirectional comparisons to thresholds. For example, a numerical input feature might be translated into a series of binary features such as $x < 1, x \geq 1, x < 4.5, x \geq 4.5$, and so on.

These binarized features are then used as potential inputs for the rules. Note that the search space for rules is exponential because a rule can be composed of one feature, or multiple features, up to and including all the features. The authors describe this as the *column generation subproblem* because it is distinct from the optimization problem, determining which inputs to provide to the optimization problem. The column generation problem is solved via *integer programming*, which is an NP hard problem. This means that a brute-force solution would be necessary. The authors instead propose an approximation to limit the search space, but also note that their training process allows rules to be both added and removed from a model.

Inputs being selected in the column generation subproblem is one portion of a larger optimization problem. The optimization problem is then designed as minimizing the negative log likelihood of the model on the training data along with an l_1 regularization term to control the complexity of the model. GLRMs use the idea of generalized linear models but then contribute a separate idea of producing an interpretable model by breaking numeric variables down into binary categories. Once the variables are binary, the coefficients for these variables are easier to interpret and lend themselves to the formulation of rules based on these binary variables.

The authors point out that with this approach both regression and classification problems can be treated, with only slight differences in the numerical forms of the optimization problem.

---

1 Wei, Dennis, et al. "Generalized Linear Rule Models." arXiv.org, June 5, 2019. *https://arxiv.org/pdf/1906.01761.pdf*.

Code Demonstration

We return to the MEPS data set we read about in Chapter 5. Somewhat inconveniently, AIX360 asks users to download the MEPS data set directly from the provider. We already have access to this data via our use of AIF360, so let's use that convenience from our earlier work:

```
from aif360.data sets import MEPSData set19
med_data19 = MEPSData set19()

X_train, X_test, y_train, y_test = train_test_split(
    med_data19.features, med_data19.labels,
    random_state = 0, stratify = med_data19.labels)
```

In this case, AIX360 expects pandas DataFrame inputs, so we convert our arrays accordingly:

```
X_train = pd.DataFrame(X_train)
X_train.columns = med_data19.feature_names
X_train.head()
```

From this code we can get an idea of what the MEPS data set looks like in its raw form (Figure 8-2).

```
In [17]: X_train.head()
Out[17]:
     AGE  RACE  PCS42  MCS42  K6SUM42  REGION=1  REGION=2  REGION=3  REGION=4  SEX=1  ...  EMPST=3  EMPST=4  POVCAT=1  POVCAT=2  POVC.
0   40.0   1.0  48.45  41.88      3.0       0.0       1.0       0.0       0.0    1.0  ...      0.0      0.0       0.0       0.0
1    8.0   0.0  -1.00  -1.00     -1.0       0.0       1.0       0.0       0.0    1.0  ...      0.0      0.0       1.0       0.0
2    0.0   0.0  -1.00  -1.00     -1.0       0.0       0.0       0.0       1.0    1.0  ...      0.0      0.0       1.0       0.0
3   69.0   0.0  39.01  58.39      0.0       0.0       0.0       0.0       1.0    0.0  ...      0.0      1.0       0.0       0.0
4   43.0   1.0  56.15  57.16      1.0       0.0       1.0       0.0       0.0    0.0  ...      0.0      0.0       0.0       0.0

5 rows × 138 columns
```

Figure 8-2. The data in its original format from the MEPS 19 panel

We also do the same for the test data features and for the labels in both training and test sets:

```
X_test = pd.DataFrame(X_test)
X_test.columns = med_data19.feature_names

y_train = y_train[:, 0]
y_test = y_test[:, 0]
```

As discussed in the previous section, the linear rule-based regression model expects features to be binarized for the purposes of forming rules. Though we could do that by hand, AIX360 provides a class that will handle this for us, FeatureBinarizer.

One useful aspect of the FeatureBinarizer is that it gives us the opportunity to control the inputs, such as whether to allow negations (which we want) and whether to also return the numerical data, which we likely want as it provides additional inputs as well as the newly generated rules themselves. We adjust this in the initializer parameters:

```
from aix360.algorithms.rbm import FeatureBinarizer
feat_bin = FeatureBinarizer(negations = True, returnOrd = True)
```

Unfortunately, the `FeatureBinarizer` class is not explicitly included in the AIX360 documentation (*https://aix360.readthedocs.io*), but we can easily find the source code (*https://oreil.ly/LzozX*), which includes this information in the doc string:

```
def __init__(self, colCateg=[], numThresh=9,
             negations=False, threshStr=False,
             returnOrd=False, **kwargs):
    """
    Args:
        colCateg (list): Categorical features ('object' dtype
                         automatically treated as categorical)
        numThresh (int): Number of quantile thresholds used to
                         binarize ordinal variables
        negations (bool): Append negations
        threshStr (bool): Convert thresholds on ordinal features
                          to strings
        returnOrd (bool): Also return standardized ordinal features
    """
```

From this, we see how we can determine whether to return the standardized ordinal features as well as what it means to set `negations` to `True`. We also see that we can set the number of thresholds for numerical values as they are turned into binarized features, but in this case we leave it to the default.

We then `fit_transform` the `FeatureBinarizer` on our data as follows. Note that the API helpfully matches that of AIF360, showing synergies when we are familiar with more than one of IBM's AI and accountability frameworks (Chapter 9 discusses another one).

```
X_train, X_train_std = feat_bin.fit_transform(X_train)
X_test, X_test_std = feat_bin.transform(X_test)
```

Surprisingly, we get back two objects from transforming our data set. Why is that? Again, a peek at the source code (*https://oreil.ly/LzozX*) helps:

```
if self.returnOrd:
    # Standardize ordinal features
    Xstd = self.scaler.transform(data[self.ordinal])
    Xstd = pd.DataFrame(Xstd, index=data.index, columns=self.ordinal)
    # Fill NaN with mean (which is now zero)
    Xstd.fillna(0, inplace=True)
    return A, Xstd
else:
    return A
```

Because we have `returnOrd` set to `True`, we receive both the rule-based version of our input, binarized as needed, and another version that includes standardized ordinal inputs.

We can get an idea of what the output looks like after it has been binarized by looking at one feature. The return form helpfully uses a pandas `MultiIndex` for easy indexing. In Figure 8-3 we thus see the binarized output for the age variable, which has been transformed from one numeric variable to many binary variables:

```
X_train['AGE'].head()
```

```
In [25]: X_train['AGE'].head()
Out[25]:
```

operation	<=									>								
value	6.0	12.0	19.0	26.0	33.0	41.0	49.0	57.0	66.0	6.0	12.0	19.0	26.0	33.0	41.0	49.0	57.0	66.0
0	0	0	0	0	0	1	1	1	1	1	1	1	1	1	0	0	0	0
1	0	1	1	1	1	1	1	1	1	0	0	0	0	0	0	0	0
2	1	1	1	1	1	1	1	1	0	0	0	0	0	0	0	0	0
3	0	0	0	0	0	0	0	0	1	1	1	1	1	1	1	1	1
4	0	0	0	0	0	1	1	1	1	1	1	1	1	1	0	0	0

Figure 8-3. The binarized data for the original AGE input

Notice that we see nine thresholds, corresponding to the default setting we used when we initialized the `FeatureBinarizer`.

Now that we have our data in the required format, we are in a position to train our model. This will take a noticeable period of time (about 15 seconds on my laptop):

```
from aix360.algorithms.rbm import LogisticRuleRegression
lrr = LogisticRuleRegression(lambda0=0.005, lambda1=0.001, useOrd=True)

# Train, print, and evaluate model
lrr.fit(X_train, y_train, X_train_std)
```

We can then check the performance of our classifier, and here you can see that it's quite high and that training and testing accuracy match:

```
>>> print('Train accuracy: %0.2f      Test accuracy: %0.2f' %
>>>          (accuracy_score(y_train, lrr.predict(X_train, X_train_std)),
>>>          accuracy_score(y_test, lrr.predict(X_test, X_test_std))))
Train accuracy: 0.86      Test accuracy: 0.87
```

Now we can look for an explanation via the standard method call:

```
df['rule/numerical feature'][1]
df.style.set_properties(subset=['rule/numerical feature'],
                        **{'width': '300px'})
```

The method is provided as in Figure 8-4. It comes in the form of a pandas Data-Frame, and because of the rule complexity, it's helpful for us to change the default display parameters to make sure we are seeing the full rules involved.

```
In [97]: df['rule/numerical feature'][1]
         df.style.set_properties(subset=['rule/numerical feature'], **{'width': '300px'})
Out[97]:
```

	rule/numerical feature	coefficient
0	(intercept)	-1.13541
1	CANCERDX=1 not AND ADHDADDX=1 not AND PREGNT=1 not	-1.63278
2	ACTLIM=1	0.846972
3	RTHLTH=1 not AND INSCOV=3 not	0.840548
4	WLKLIM=2	-0.726861
5	ARTHDX=1 not AND PREGNT=1 not	-0.69067
6	SEX=1	-0.682084
7	ADSMOK42=2 AND INSCOV=3 not	0.661183
8	PCS42 <= 48.98	0.609904
9	RTHLTH=2 not AND INSCOV=3 not	0.587725
10	RACE	0.519394
11	POVCAT=5	0.447884
12	ADHDADDX=2 not AND INSCOV=3 not	0.425283
13	EMPST=4	0.418738
14	K6SUM42 <= 0.00	-0.416382
15	AGE <= 57.00 AND PREGNT=1 not	-0.351557
16	REGION=3	-0.286482
17	JTPAIN=1	0.279151
18	SEX=2	-0.264088
19	CHOLDX=1	0.236594
20	AGE <= 49.00 AND PREGNT=1 not	-0.143575
21	HIBPDX=1	0.116074
22	AGE	-0.0697709
23	K6SUM42	0.0507793

Figure 8-4. The tabular explanation information provided by the model object

Because the underlying model is a linear model, where the nonlinear complexity is added by creation of rules rather than functional form, we can read off the explanation in terms of the absolute value of a coefficient. This is also why it's important to binarize all inputs and scale any numerical inputs between 0 and 1, so that coefficient magnitudes can be compared. Note that after the intercept, the features are listed in decreasing magnitude of coefficient.

For any columns that are unclear, check the documentation (*https://oreil.ly/jmViR*). We see from this that the first rule seems pretty clear in indicating that, in terms of needing medical services or not, it is certainly relevant that someone does not have cancer, has not had a diagnosis of ADHD, and is not pregnant. Meeting all these criteria makes one quite a bit less likely to use medical services.

On the other hand, this rule does not necessarily seem like a logical one or one that would apply equally to everyone. For example, the ADHD column is indicated as applying to those ages 5 through 17, while the pregnancy column was able to be given a positive indicator for only females ages 16 through 44 (even though the private version of the questionnaire asks females ages 15 through 55). So one problem is that these questions arguably do not even belong in the same rule as a logical matter.

Indeed, it does not seem like the most sensible interpretation that not having cancer and not having an ADHD diagnosis and not being pregnant leads to someone not using healthcare, as this is selecting a fairly narrow range of people. There is probably another way to select this range of people without putting nonsensical values together. To give a more intuitive nonmedical example, imagine someone asked for an interpretable model predicting who is admitted to a prestigious college. Imagine if the first answer were: don't be a criminal and don't be an overly aggressive toddler and don't be a teenaged parent. Whether this was true or not, I likely wouldn't give this version of advice to any person because it wouldn't all be actionable, since it is such a mash-up of various factors that it does not feel like an explanation in any sense of the word. If I were speaking to a toddler who wanted such advice, I'd focus on the toddler element. If I were speaking to a teen, I'd focus on the teen parent element. If I were speaking to a juvenile delinquent, I'd focus on the criminal element.

Note that in this model I just described, elements of the explanation would still be missing—such as, where and why did this guidance emerge? What does the probability distribution look like—are these dealbreakers or just correlates that may influence college admissions but don't have to? Is this a model of how college admissions officers think (probably not since they're unlikely to know about your toddler aggression issues) or how they behave regardless of how they say they make decisions (because often how we make decisions differs from how we believe we make those decisions). All this would be relevant to evaluating the advice and thus relevant to providing an informative explanation to a human.

The point is that just because a rule can be interpreted, that doesn't necessarily mean that it makes sense. So even an interpretable model will need some supervision. Interpretation is not the end in and of itself—especially if we interpret something that is a little bit silly.

For this reason, you might want to give the more complicated rules a more careful look as compared to the simpler rules. You can do this with the following code. I don't show the output to save space, but you'll see for yourself that this simply gives the subset of the previous output that corresponds to higher-degree rules (that is, compound rules):

```
df = lrr.explain(highDegOnly = True)
```

This is not to say that this interpretable model is not useful. The shorter rules in particular seem helpful for a broader sense of interpretation. Consider the next most influential variable, ACTLIM, which indicates whether someone having reported limited activities due to a health issue is also predictive of their use of medical services. This passes a gut check in terms of common sense, as do many of the other rules on the list (I leave it to you to go through them yourself).

I have two final points to make here, given the outputs. First, notice that the linear terms we elected to include by setting returnOrd = True in our FeatureBinarizer also show loadings, but these are mostly lower than our rules. So our rules are, in fact, adding useful features compared to simply running the unaugmented inputs through a logistic regression (you can verify this for yourself by building a simple logistic regression model).

Second, we have an interpretable model, but whether it is a fair model depends on our going through the interpretation, involving domain experts, and considering carefully whether and how variables should be predictive. For example, it is not surprising but it is disappointing to see that RACE and SEX are both in the top half of coefficient magnitudes. Remember, this is a data set that describes reality, which we know is biased, but if we are going to use this data set to make decisions about the future, we'd want to find a way to correct this bias rather than reinforcing it.

We can visualize these features with the following code. Note that the visualization expects a pandas DataFrame of the original data, not the binarized data, and takes this in combination with the FeatureBinarizer:

```
orig_inputs = pd.DataFrame(med_data19.features)
orig_inputs.columns = med_data19.feature_names
lrr.visualize(orig_inputs, feat_bin)
```

This will produce a plot for each feature. Figure 8-5 shows a few samples but not all the plots for lack of room.

One final option in this code base to consider before moving on to explainability is that there isn't just one GLRM per data set. Rather, there are tuning parameters we can use to adjust the complexity of the model, particularly two aspects of that complexity:

- How many rules to include in the model
- How complicated those rules should be

We do not set these parameters directly but rather have two regularization constants we can adjust to reflect the relative weightings of the regularization terms. In this case, we elect to see what happens when we adjust these regularization parameters in favor of fewer rules but also in favor of more complicated rules.[2]

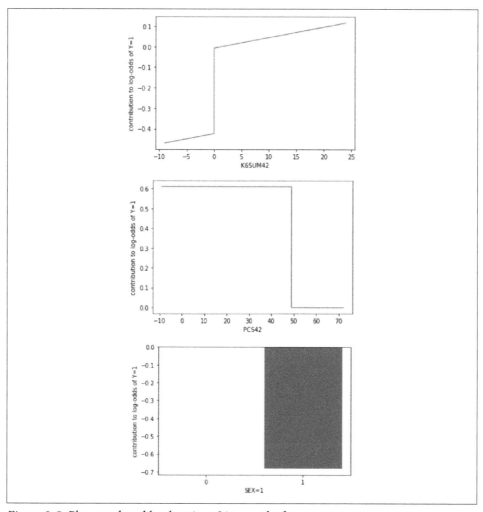

Figure 8-5. Plots produced by the `visualize` *method*

---

2 Despite this, we can imagine there would be informative compound rules, and here we make more of an effort to look for them.

In the following code, we create another `LogisticRuleRegression` object, keeping everything the same except the hyperparameter values for `lambda0` and `lambda1`:

```
## from documentation
## lambda0 (float, optional) - Regularization - fixed cost of each rule
## lambda1 (float, optional) - Regularization - additional cost of
## each literal in rule

### now let's imagine we're willing to allow more complex rules but want
### fewer rules. let's adjust lambda and see what that does to performance
# Instantiate LRR with good complexity penalties and numerical features
lrr_alt = LogisticRuleRegression(lambda0=0.01, lambda1=0.0001, useOrd=True)

# Train, print, and evaluate model
lrr_alt.fit(X_train, y_train, X_train_std)
```

Once we fit, we again check the performance, which is essentially the same as in our first model:

```
>>> print('Train accuracy: %0.2f      Test accuracy: %0.2f' %
>>>           (accuracy_score(y_train, lrr_alt.predict(X_train, X_train_std)),
>>>           accuracy_score(y_test, lrr_alt.predict(X_test, X_test_std))))
Train accuracy: 0.86     Test accuracy: 0.86
```

Let's check whether the rules that drive the model are the same. The following simple code and a few display parameters produce an easy-to-read graphic (Figure 8-6), whereby the rules are listed in decreasing order of importance, with the most important rule coming first. Importance is established by the size of the coefficient, which makes sense given that everything is a binary variable and that we are working with a generalized linear model:

```
lrr_alt.explain()
```

There is a surprising degree of difference here. Now we have 20 rules instead of 23, and the top rules are not the same. We can see here that in training an interpretable model, we would still need to do a hyperparameter search. In this case, though, we might not look only at overall performance in terms of accuracy but also look for a model that had more robust rules, perhaps as assessed with some predetermined logic checks we would apply automatically, or perhaps by some review by human domain experts who could compare models and determine which ones were more likely to generalize and avoid unnecessary mistakes.

```
In [116]: df_alt = lrr_alt.explain()
          df_alt['rule'][1]
          df_alt.style.set_properties(subset=['rule'], **{'width': '300px'})
Out[116]:
```

	rule	coefficient
0	(intercept)	-3.47274
1	MARRY=8 not AND ARTHDX=1	1.74884
2	ARTHTYPE=-1	1.49094
3	CANCERDX=1 not AND ARTHTYPE=2 not AND ADHDADDX=1 not AND PREGNT=1 not AND SOCLIM=1 not AND PHQ242=5 not	-1.03838
4	WLKLIM=2	-0.569916
5	ACTLIM=1	0.540003
6	MARRY=8 not AND RTHLTH=1 not AND INSCOV=3 not	0.530802
7	MARRY=8 not AND ADSMOK42=2 AND INSCOV=3 not	0.502144
8	RACE AND MARRY=8 not AND MARRY=10 not AND ACTDTY=1 not AND INSCOV=3 not	0.492107
9	PCS42 <= 48.98 AND INSCOV=3 not	0.379767
10	K6SUM42 > 0.00 AND INSCOV=3 not	0.349805
11	RTHLTH=2 not AND INSCOV=3 not	0.349318
12	SEX=1 not AND INSCOV=3 not	0.297954
13	EMPST=4 AND INSCOV=3 not	0.276775
14	JTPAIN=1	0.273037
15	AGE <= 57.00 AND PREGNT=1 not	-0.265745
16	AGE <= 49.00 AND PREGNT=1 not	-0.241115
17	CHOLDX=1	0.208726
18	AGE > 33.00 AND MARRY=8 not AND MARRY=9 not AND MARRY=10 not AND ACTDTY=1 not AND HONRDC=4 not AND INSCOV=3 not	-0.119855
19	AGE > 26.00 AND MARRY=8 not AND MARRY=10 not AND INSCOV=3 not	0.0966005
20	MARRY=8 not AND MARRY=9 not AND MARRY=10 not AND ACTDTY=1 not AND HONRDC=4 not AND HIBPDX=1 AND INSCOV=3 not	0.0520947

Figure 8-6. The tabular explanation information provided by the model object

Explainability Methods

A key question for the start of an explainability analysis is, *explainability for whom*? Explainability can be a useful attribute of a system for many parties, including downstream nontechnical users, regulators, and upstream developers seeking to understand how their own product works. Notably, a few aspects of a good explanation will be different depending on the audience:

- Attributes of the explanation offered
  - — End users will likely be more interested in an explanation that affects their circumstances, while government regulators might want an explanation that addresses core concerns, such as systemic risk of a financial product or potential racial discrimination in decisions affecting consumers.
- The level of detail
  - — Developers seeking debugging assistance will want very granular information, while government regulators might seek a more holistic view.
- The technical background assumed in the explanation
  - — End users will likely want nontechnical explanations, while government regulators and developers alike will bring more technical know-how to their ability to evaluate explanations.
- The question that can be answered with that explanation
  - — Developers will be looking for actionable explanations, while consumers will be looking for transparency and logic.

There are many uses for explainability generally, including comparing models and determining which one to run in production, and determining whether additional data added as inputs to a model is useful.

In Figure 8-7, you can see a taxonomy of methods for explainability algorithms, because as with fairness metrics, there are many ways of defining explainability, depending on what kind of metric is used to assess the ultimate performance of an explainability method or what definition of explainability is emphasized.

This taxonomy reflects some fundamental ways in which technical solutions to explainability can work:

- Does the explanation directly explain the model (interpretation) or offer a post hoc analysis?
- Does the model focus on specific data (local) or overall performance (global)?
- Does the model provide a single fixed explanation (static) or the opportunity to investigate and vary parameters of the explanation itself (dynamic)?

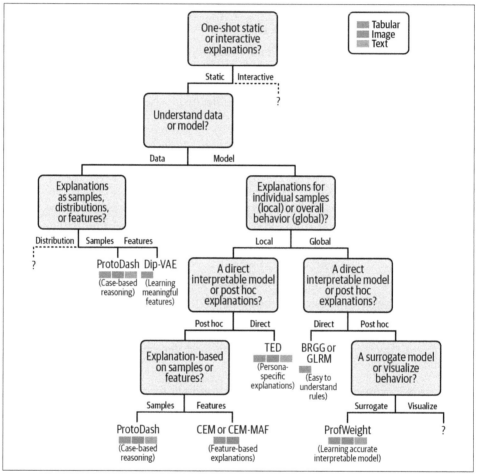

Figure 8-7. A classification system for a variety of explainability algorithms[3]

---

3 This taxonomy was provided by the IBM AIX360 library to represent the options currently included in the module. This figure is borrowed from Vijay Arya and Amit Dhurandhar's presentation on AIX360 at CSIG 2019, presentation recording available on YouTube (*https://oreil.ly/9NgHO*). See the full color version posted online (*https://oreil.ly/Practical_Fairness_Figures*) if you're reading in print.

No doubt there are or soon will be other axes along which explanations can vary, but these are important ones. Earlier in this chapter we looked at developing an interpretable model, and this chapter more widely distinguishes explanation from interpretation even if the end goals of the approaches are different. We now turn to explanation and focus specifically on local post hoc explanations in the form of SHAP and LIME, two long-established and common methods, and a newer offering, ProtoDash. As Figure 8-7 shows, LIME and SHAP emphasize features in explanation while Proto-Dash emphasizes data points, showing another way to divide methods of explanation with regard to whether their currency of explanation is data or feature categories.

SHAP and LIME: The Workhorses for Local Post Hoc Explanations

In this section, we address two long-standing go-to methods for explaining the machine learning algorithms SHAP and LIME. While other explainability methods now receive more attention, it's important to know the basics of these long-standing and widely used methods to know what a baseline explanation looks like and then to think about when a standard and simple method like these can be used as compared to deploying something more specialized.

LIME

The concept of Local Interpretable Model-Agnostic Explanations (LIME) was first proposed in 2016 by Ribeiro et al.[4] They identified the following attributes as especially important for explainability:

- Interpretable
- Local fidelity
- Model-agnostic
- Global perspective

They proposed to offer explanations based on specific data points, or ensembles of data points. For each data point an explanation would be generated in the form of an interpretable model, usually but not necessarily a linear model, hence providing interpretability and local fidelity.[5]

---

4 Ribeiro, Marco Tulio, et al. "'Why Should I Trust You?' Explaining the Predictions of Any Classifier." arXiv.org, August 9, 2016. *https://arxiv.org/pdf/1602.04938.pdf*.

5 In extreme cases, a model might not be approximated linearly even when examined in a very local region. However, in a series of empirical experiments, Ribeiro et al. did not find that this concern about local nonlinearity tended to be a problem.

How it works. The nonlinear decision service represents the actual model, whereas the linear model that would be created by LIME is shown in Figure 8-8. The bolded cross is the actual point selected for the location of the decisions and the smaller points indicate the classification.

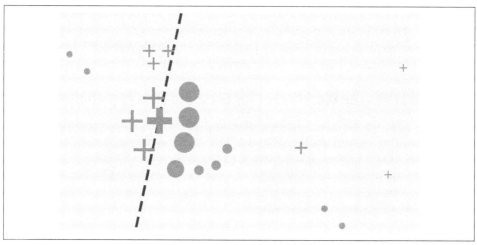

Figure 8-8. A schematic indicating the motivation behind LIME

The authors express their method in terms of the following equation:

$$.\,\xi(x) = \operatorname*{argmin}_{g \in G} L\!\left(f, g, \pi_x\right) + \Omega(g)$$

f is the original function, g is the explanation, and π_x represents a weighting function for points around the local point; this weighting is used when sampling points. $\Omega(g)$ is a complexity penalty term that will vary depending on the kind of model used for g. For a linear model, for example, this could be the number of nonzero coefficients permitted in the model.

Code example. Ribeiro et al. released their code as a Python module available for installation from GitHub (*https://github.com/marcotcr/lime*) or via `pip`, and here we run through a simple example, again with the MEPS data set. We make use of Ribeiro et al.'s code, but we access it via the AIX360 module.

First, we need to train an opaque model we want to explain.[6] We do that with the following code:

```
## we convert the data to the form expected by the model
orig_inputs = pd.DataFrame(med_data19.features)
orig_inputs.columns = med_data19.feature_names
orig_target = med_data19.labels

from sklearn.ensemble import RandomForestClassifier as RFC
rf = RFC(n_estimators=500)
rf.fit(orig_inputs, orig_target.ravel())
```

Normally we'd want to kick the tires, have training and validation sets, and so on, but we omit this for purposes of studying the API. Instead, we instantiate an explainer as follows. We make use of AIX360's wrapper for the lime module's functionality:

```
from aix360.algorithms.lime.lime_wrapper import LimeTabularExplainer
ltf = LimeTabularExplainer(X_train.values,
                           feature_names = X_train.columns,
                           class_names = y_train.ravel(),
                           categorical_features = cat_idxs,
                           discretize_continuous = True
                          )
```

As we instantiate the explainer, we provide information about feature names and class names. We also indicate that we would like to discretize continuous variables for purposes of making the rules more accessible. Finally, we specify which features are categorical. This is all used so that the explainer can identify features in the proper format.

We then produce an explanation for a specific data point:

```
i = 5097
exp = ltf.explain_instance(X_train.values[i], rf.predict_proba, num_features=5,
top_labels=1)
```

Once we have this explanation prepared, we have multiple options for how to visualize it. We can read it as text, as shown here:

```
>>> exp.as_list(y_train.ravel()[i])
[('ACTLIM=1=0', 0.10019862517682016),
 ('SOCLIM=2=1', 0.06853814444363135),
 ('WLKLIM=1=0', 0.06355565006438692),
 ('WLKLIM=2=1', 0.06182287340870138),
 ('ACTLIM=2=1', 0.04114688045097612)]
```

---

6 We could also train an interpretable model and compare it to the explanations generated by these methods. I leave that as an exercise for you.

We can also see a simple visualization in Figure 8-9:

```
fig = exp.as_pyplot_figure(0)
```

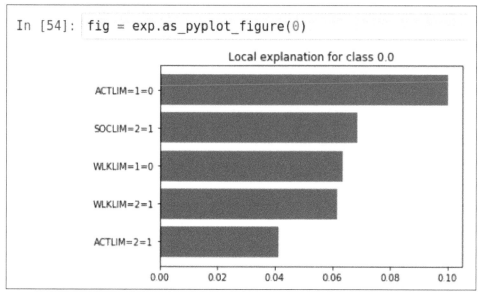

Figure 8-9. A graphical depiction of the relative importance attributed to various features in the decision space near the selected point

While empirical studies show that many of the same features will surface in explanations for different points, we can also expect some variation between points. We can see this by generating an explanation for another data point and observing its visualization, which has some common features with Figure 8-9 but some that are different, specifically *K6SUM42 > 2.00* and *AGE > 53.00* (and notice how these continuous features have been broken into discrete categories for purposes of the explanation):

```
i = 1001
exp2 = ltf.explain_instance(X_train.values[i], rf.predict_proba, num_features=5,
top_labels=1)
exp2.as_list(y_train.ravel()[i])
fig = exp2.as_pyplot_figure(0)
```

This code produces Figure 8-10, which shows that for this point the influential dimensions are similar but not identical to the first point for which we plotted a visualization.

```
In [70]:  fig = exp2.as_pyplot_figure()
```

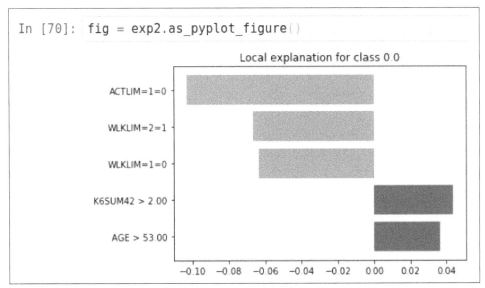

Figure 8-10. An explanation for a second data point. Here some features are new com-pared to the first model[7]

Note that all this is directly available via the lime module. We have used the AIX360 wrapper partly for convenience and partly in the hopes that AIX360 will continue to grow and be a place to centralize explainability, rather than us having to use individual repositories with specific methods spread out over many repos.

SHAP

A year after LIME was introduced, Lundberg and Lee wrote a paper showing that LIME, and a number of other metrics that had been proposed for explainability, all reflected models within an additive feature attribution class of methods.[8] They defined these as models that have an explanation model that is a linear function of binary variables. The binary variables are the indication of whether a specific variable from the original input should be included in the explanation.

This observation is important because Lundberg and Lee show that for the class of models they indicate, the Shapley value is the method that can guarantee three properties:

---

7 See the full color version posted online (*https://oreil.ly/Practical_Fairness_Figures*) if you're reading in print.

8 Lundberg, Scott M. and Su-In Lee. "A Unified Approach to Interpreting Model Predictions." arXiv.org, November 25, 2017. *https://arxiv.org/pdf/1705.07874.pdf*.

Accuracy

The model is guaranteed to match the actual label or value of the original input.

Missingness

This requires that any features missing in the original data input should have no impact on the explanation.[9]

Consistency

If the model to be explained changes so that the influence of an input remains the same or increases, its influence in the explanatory model should not decrease.

How it works. Mathematically, only one possible model follows the definition of an additive feature attribution model and guarantees the three properties just mentioned.

$$\phi_i\!\left(f, x\right) = \sum_{z' \subseteq x'} \frac{|z'|\,!(M - |z'| - 1)!}{M!}\left|f_x\!\left(z'\right) - f_x\!\left(z'\prime\right)\right|$$

This equation is a little confusing, and we won't belabor the point. If you don't usually work with combinatorics, you may have forgotten that this is where factorials tend to appear, and that is what is reflected. This is summing up the ways to fit a model with a particular feature missing from all possible combinations of subsets of the original data. This is easier to understand in graphical form, as shown in Figure 8-11.

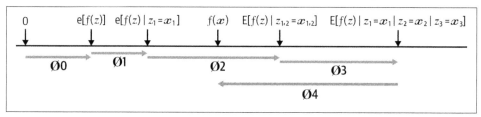

Figure 8-11. A graphical depiction of calculating the Shapley value

The SHAP value "attributes to each feature the change in the expected model prediction when conditioning on that feature," according to Lundberg and Lee. However, in the case of nonlinear models or inputs that are not independent of one another, the ordering in which features are re-added to the model in the process depicted previously will matter. For that reason, the SHAP value reflects an average taken after calculating all possible sequences of adding inputs in. This is why calculation of the

---

9 Note that this assumes that missingness is something that a particular model can handle or that the idea of missingness is otherwise well explained.

exact SHAP value can be quite taxing, and for this reason model-agnostic approximations are also available.

This method uses an approximation that can be applied to any black-box model, which Lundberg and Lee dub the *Kernel SHAP* and describe as Linear LIME + Shapley values. They prove that if the following are set as the parameters and functions of LIME training, the desirable properties will hold and hence the SHAP values will be approximated:

$$\Omega(g) = 0,$$

$$\pi_{x'}(z') = \frac{M-1}{(M choose |z'|)z'(M - |z'|)},$$

$$L(f, g, \pi_{x'}) = \sum_{z' \in Z} \left[f\left(h_x^{-1}(z')\right) - g(z')\right]^2 \pi_{x'}(z'),$$

where $|z'|$ is the number of nonzero elements in z'.

Note that this is very helpful because it provides a less computationally taxing way to approximate the SHAP values without a full calculation and using linear methods.

Code example.   We'll look at the SHAP authors' code next (*https://oreil.ly/m53Rf*). You can install it via `pip` or download it directly.

As before, we first load the data and train some kind of model. Note that we can train any model we want, but of course this exercise makes more sense with a relatively opaque model. In this case we train a random forest classifier:

```
from sklearn.ensemble import RandomForestClassifier as RFC
rf = RFC(n_estimators=200, max_depth = 4)
rf.fit(X_train, y_train.ravel())
```

We also confirm that this is a fairly accurate and not overtrained model:

```
>>> print('Train accuracy: %0.2f      Test accuracy: %0.2f' %
          (accuracy_score(y_train, rf.predict(X_train)),
           accuracy_score(y_test, rf.predict(X_test))))
Train accuracy: 0.86     Test accuracy: 0.85
```

We will now initialize a `KernelExplainer` object that implements the methodology discussed previously. However, to do so we must pass a function that will produce the outputs of the model given the inputs. Shapley values will be calculated for each output of a multioutput model, but experience shows that these mostly mirror one another. For this reason, we cut the output of the random forest object to include only the predicted probability of 1 as output, with the convenience of a lambda function:

```
rf_prob_1 = lambda x: rf.predict_proba(x)[:,1]
```

This is not removing any information but merely cutting down on the number of Shapley values (presumably redundant) that will be calculated to one set rather than two sets per data point (since if we provided two classes/probabilities, a set of Shapley values would be calculated for each). We now provide this prediction function along with the relevant data to the KernelExplainer initializer:

```
ke = shap.KernelExplainer(rf_prob_1, shap.sample(X_train, 100), link = 'logit')
```

The initialization of ke is instantaneous, showing that no processing or fitting has occurred. Why, then, do we already provide data? The explanation is available in the documentation (*https://shap.readthedocs.io/en/latest*), and also, as always from reading the source code directly. As the documentation says (*https://oreil.ly/AtVh-*):

> data : numpy.array or pandas.DataFrame or shap.common.DenseData or any
> scipy.sparse matrix::
>
> The background dataset to use for integrating out features. To determine
> the impact of a feature, that feature is set to "missing" and the change
> in the model output is observed. Since most models aren't designed to han
> dle arbitrary missing data at test time, we simulate "missing" by replac
> ing the feature with the values it takes in the background data set. So
> if the background data set is a simple sample of all zeros, then we would
> approximate a feature being missing by setting it to zero. For small prob
> lems this background data set can be the whole training set, but for
> larger problems consider using a single reference value or using the k-
> means function to summarize the dataset.

Remember that the SHAP values are calculated in part by removing features and seeing how the model performs. However, as is pointed out in the documentation, for a model-agnostic treatment, it can be difficult to know what "removing" a feature means. In this case, removing the feature is defined by substituting in the values from this background data set, one at a time.

Now that we have initialized our object, we calculate the SHAP values as an explanation via this LIME-inspired heuristic:

```
shap_values = ke.shap_values(X_test[:100], nsamples = 100)
```

The first parameter indicates the data points for which we want Shapley values. Each data point will have its own Shapley value for each feature indicating, for that data point, how much each of its features contributed to the output value. The nsamples parameter indicates the number of times the model is reevaluated for each prediction in calculating the SHAP values.

Once we have the SHAP values, we can, of course, look at them individually, as they are returned in a list. The list is the length of the number of output classes, and each element of the list is an array of number of data points by number of inputs. We can then read off the SHAP values for a specific data point. These would constitute a form of explanation that could apply to a specific individual. For example, if an individual wanted to know how our model had estimated whether they were likely to consume healthcare services, we could pull up the SHAP values for their data point and walk them through these values (positive increasing the likelihood of using health services, negative decreasing the likelihood, and magnitude indicating the contribution of the feature to the ultimate value).

We can also achieve population-level explanations, particularly with some helpful plotting visualizations. shap offers quite a few visualizations, and we show only two of these options here. You can try out more by looking at the API and documentation as well as numerous tutorials available on GitHub (*https://oreil.ly/m53Rf*):

```
shap.summary_plot(shap_values, X_test[:100])
```

Figure 8-12 provides one example of the very helpful and descriptive default visualizations that are easily accessible via the SHAP API.

The summary plot has one data point per individual per feature, with each feature pictured separately in its own horizontal slice of the graph. At a glance, this population-wide imaging offers quite a bit of information. We can see the spread in the effect (that is, the SHAP value) of each feature from the horizontal location, and we can get a sense of how uniformly a feature affected the population from the color consistency. Ideally, points in the same part of the spectrum should mostly have the same color, although this not being the case can point to some nonlinearity or some interesting interaction with other features rather than a bad model.[10] In fact, this is arguably part of what we are seeing with the AGE feature, which seems to have a mix of blue and red.

We can use a dependence_plot to get a better visualization of how AGE affects different individuals, as shown in Figure 8-13:

```
shap.dependence_plot('AGE', shap_values,  X_test[:100])
```

---

10 This is where domain knowledge is invaluable.

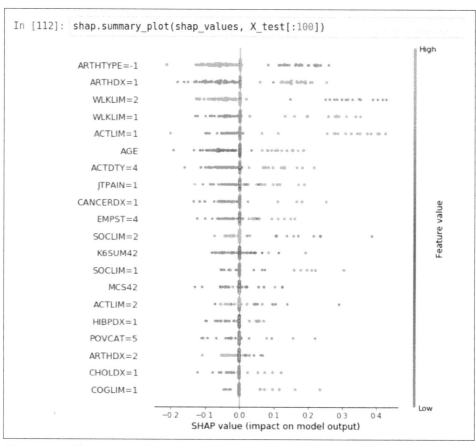

```
In [112]: shap.summary_plot(shap_values, X_test[:100])
```

Figure 8-12. The outputs of a `summary_plot`, which shows the contribution of each feature for each of the sample points[11]

---

11 See the full color version posted online (*https://oreil.ly/Practical_Fairness_Figures*) if you're reading in print.

```
In [116]: shap.dependence_plot('AGE', shap_values, X_test[:100])
```

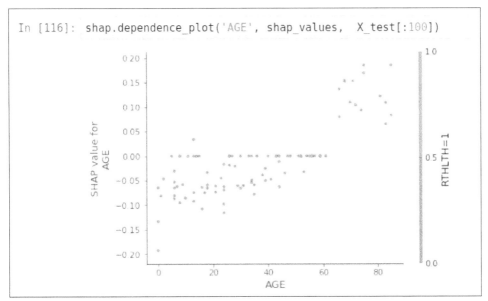

Figure 8-13. The particular complexity penalization, loss function, and sample weighting function we must apply to the LIME procedure to recover the SHAP values and ensure the desirable properties discussed earlier[12]

Data-Driven Explanation

Another way to think about explanation is in terms of concrete examples drawn from the data set. In the previous section we described methods to interpret variable importance, either by building an interpretable model (LIME) or by an intuitive, if complicated, set of calculations to score the importance of a feature and its contributions to a model relative to others in the case of a specific data point.

Now we consider another way to understand the outcome of a particular data point, by looking for data points that are close to the relevant data point by distance and that achieved either the same or the opposite outcome. We can imagine this being useful to less technical audiences seeking an explanation who perhaps do not want to look at variable coefficients but rather want to understand how they stack up against real peers.

---

12 See the full color version posted online (*https://oreil.ly/Practical_Fairness_Figures*) if you're reading in print.

How it works

We use the ProtoDash algorithm, which takes as input a data point or group of data points that we want to explain with respect to the training data. So imagine we have two distributions, p and q. The maximum mean discrepancy (MMD) is a measure of the difference between two distributions that is calculated by looking at the difference in means calculated over a distribution and certain set of kernel functions:

$$MMD(p, q, f) = \sup_{f \in K} E_{x \, p}[f(x)] - E_{y \, q}[f(y)]$$

The ProtoDash algorithm (and a number of similar methods) seeks to *minimize* the MMD—that is, *minimize* this "worst case scenario" of differences in distributions, by selecting specific data points to constitute the set q where the set p has already been provided. This can be used in a few ways:

- p can represent the entire training data set, so that selecting q is a way of summarizing the entire training data set.
- p can represent a specific data instance with a positive outcome, and selecting q can then serve to identify similar instances that also had a positive outcome.
- p can represent a specific data instance with a negative outcome, and selecting q can then serve to identify similar instances that also had a negative outcome

We won't go into the specifics of the algorithm, but on a high level this algorithm goes through the data points and chooses the data point for which the gradient of the change to the MMD would contribute the most to minimizing the MMD. Then for each iteration, optimal weighting of the included data points is also included. This weighting is also reported as a weight of determining the relative importance or relevance of the selected data points.

Code example

This algorithm is directly implemented in AIX360. I demonstrate use of the code in this section and take a look at the results.

As usual, we must start with loading our data and splitting it into testing and training sets, as we have previously done. For that reason, I include only the following last portion of loading the data to remind you of our process:

```
X_train, X_test, y_train, y_test = train_test_split(
    med_data19.features, med_data19.labels,
    random_state = 0, stratify = med_data19.labels)
```

What is different now compared to previous methods is that we need to scale our data, as ProtoDash expects scaled inputs. This makes sense intuitively as, in selecting prototypes, ProtoDash is intrinsically comparing not just between examples but between features, to determine which data samples are good prototypes:

```
X_scale = np.vstack((X_train, X_test))
Xmax = np.max(X_scale, axis = 0)
Xmin = np.min(X_scale, axis = 0)

## scale
X_scale = (X_scale - Xmin)/(Xmax - Xmin)
X_scale = X_scale - 0.5
```

This produces features with guaranteed minima and maxima of –0.5 and +0.5 as required by ProtoDash, although the mean per feature is not guaranteed to be zero. In this case we have *scaled* our data but we haven't *normalized* it.

We can see this with a quick printout of the scaled data:

```
>>> np.mean(X_scale, axis = 1)
array([-0.21634108, -0.23529069, -0.2359727 , ..., -0.22081677,
       -0.22313438, -0.23571694])
>>> np.min(X_scale, axis = 1)
array([-0.5, -0.5, -0.5, ..., -0.5, -0.5, -0.5])
>>> np.max(X_scale, axis = 1)
array([0.5, 0.5, 0.5, ..., 0.5, 0.5, 0.5])
```

We then train a random forest, which ensures we will want some kind of explanation, as these are opaque decision makers:

```
from sklearn.ensemble import RandomForestClassifier as RFC
rf = RFC(n_estimators=200, max_depth = 4)
rf.fit(X_scale_train, y_train.ravel())
```

And we confirm that this model doesn't give nonsense and isn't overtrained:

```
>>> print('Train accuracy: %0.2f     Test accuracy: %0.2f' %
          (accuracy_score(y_train, rf.predict(X_scale_train)),
           accuracy_score(y_test, rf.predict(X_scale_test))))
Train accuracy: 0.86     Test accuracy: 0.85
```

A `ProtodashExplainer` will expect three parameters: a base data set from which to draw explanations, a data set to explain, and the number of prototypes to return. The algorithm does not have specific requirements about how the data set to explain and the data to be explained must be related. For example, the data set to explain and the base data set could be identical, in which case you are using ProtoDash to summarize the data set. It's also possible, at the other end of the spectrum, to have just a single data point to explain, which is what we will do now, as this would offer an example of looking at a data point and trying to understand its outcome by identifying similar data points. Note that in this latter case you should remove that data point from the base data you will use to select prototypes, as otherwise it is quite likely your very same data point will be returned.

You can also have intermediate use cases, such as a group of applicants, perhaps all of whom are seeking to dispute their outcome, and see what the prototypes are to summarize this group. This could be a way of identifying people likely to complain despite a fair outcome, identifying people likely to be misclassified, or something in between.

In our case we will use the test data as our prototypes to explain and take one example out of the test data as the data we wish to explain. We look at cases where the outcome has been 0.0 in the data set—that is, no utilization:

```
## predict values from our model to divide data points
## according to predicted values
predicted_vals = rf.predict(X_scale_test)
results_df = pd.DataFrame(np.hstack([X_scale_test,
                                     predicted_vals.reshape(-1, 1)]))

## looking at those with UTILIZATION == 0.0 (as a binary variable of 0 or 1)
base_data set = results_df[results_df.Class == 0.0].values

## select an example to explain
selected_example_idx = 5
data_to_explain = np.expand_dims(base_data set[selected_example_idx], axis = 1)
data_to_explain = data_to_explain.transpose()

## remove the example of interest from the base data set
base_data set = np.delete(base_data set, selected_example_idx, 0)

## how many prototypes do we want returned?
num_prototypes = 5
```

The ProtoDash heuristic is extremely fast and returns nearly instantly on my laptop:

```
exp = ProtodashExplainer()
(W, S, _) = exp.explain(data_to_explain, base_data set, m = num_prototypes)
```

W holds the weights of the prototypes, and S holds the indices of the prototypes in the base data set. The _ neglected return value relates to the stage of the optimization and is no of interest to us here.[13]

For easy visualization, we can then put the selected prototype values along with their weights into a data frame:

```
dfs = pd.DataFrame.from_records(results_df.iloc[S, 0:-1].astype('double'))
dfs.columns = X_test.columns
dfs[138] = 'Good'
dfs.columns.values[138] = 'Class'
# Calculate normalized importance weights
dfs['Weight'] = np.around(W, 4)/np.sum(np.around(W, 4))
```

---

13 You can better understand the return values by working through the source code (*https://oreil.ly/Wzp8f*).

For ease of reading, I also append the original data point to explain and give it the highest weight so we can distinguish it:

```
x_row = pd.DataFrame(data_to_explain)
x_row[139] = 100 ## the weight column is added after 138 existing features
x_row.columns = dfs.columns
dfs = dfs.append(x_row)
```

We also now sort according to the original weight and transpose for ease of reading:

```
## reorder with Weight
dfs.sort_values('Weight', inplace = True, ascending = False)
```

We can see a subset of the results here. The data point to be explained is in the left-most column with the `Weight` of 100 in Figure 8-14:

```
dfs.transpose()
```

```
In [87]:  dfs.transpose()
Out[87]:
```

	0	0	1	4	3	2
AGE	-0.441176	-0.358824	-0.005882	-0.370588	-0.205882	-0.111765
RACE	-0.500000	-0.500000	-0.500000	-0.500000	-0.500000	-0.500000
PCS42	-0.401320	-0.401320	0.310534	-0.401320	0.140928	0.346429
MCS42	-0.405337	-0.405337	0.344752	-0.405337	0.073897	0.178381
K6SUM42	-0.257576	-0.257576	-0.227273	-0.257576	-0.015152	-0.196970
...	...	...	...	...	...	...
INSCOV=1	-0.500000	-0.500000	0.500000	0.500000	0.500000	0.500000
INSCOV=2	0.500000	0.500000	-0.500000	-0.500000	-0.500000	-0.500000
INSCOV=3	-0.500000	-0.500000	-0.500000	-0.500000	-0.500000	-0.500000
Utilization	0.000000	0.000000	0.000000	0.000000	0.000000	0.000000
Weight	100.000000	0.396837	0.396648	0.101695	0.070448	0.034372

140 rows × 6 columns

Figure 8-14. The results of the ProtoDash selection for data points to explain, with the data point to be explained as the leftmost column

Even once we have an "explanation," it's not easy to process. This data set has 137 features. The human eye cannot take this in so well.

We can take a few routes from here:

- Carefully going over the data but allowing proper time to do so. This would be particularly appropriate for a domain expert who would give meaning to the different features
- Using high-dimensional plotting options, such as t-SNE (*https://oreil.ly/Jd9pB*) or principle components analysis
- Computing feature similarities between each prototype and the data to be explained

Hopefully, these methods are familiar. If not, the IBM tutorial on the HELOC explainability test set (*https://oreil.ly/_wJrw*) provides an example of computing feature importances. PCA and t-SNE are both implemented in `sklearn`. For domain expertise, it will, of course, depend on your data set.

That concludes our exploration of several methods related to explainability. Based on a review of the taxonomy earlier in the chapter, you will realize that we are far from covering the methods offered by AIX360 alone, let alone the methods developed by researchers more generally. Hopefully, this chapter has shown you some notions of explainability and given you the vocabulary to see their limitations. To me, the most important insight is that even when we arrive at "explanations" from these technical methods, they still clearly need elucidation, even for technical people.

Explanation will remain an iterative and human process for the foreseeable future, even with technical solutions.

Explainability Metrics

As with fairness, numerous proposed metrics indicate the performance of an explanation. Some proposed metrics relate to human-measured indicia, such as the following:

- Whether the explanation enables a human to compare models and select a better one or avoid a poor one
- Whether the explanation promotes trust by the human
- Whether the human can predict future outcomes by a machine learning model
- Whether the human can explain why mistakes are made by the algorithm in a specific case

Other metrics that can be seen in the literature seek computationally accessible forms of measuring explanations. Some of these include the following:

Faithfulness

We can think of this more generally as correctness. One way to do this is to establish relative performances of different metrics, by creating synthetic data sets with inputs that should or should not be included in an explanation. Consider the percentage of times that inputs are inappropriately labeled as explanatory or nonexplanatory.

Monotonicity

For a given variable, generally the expectation is that this variable in some way contributes overall in a positive or a negative way to the outcome, such that more or less of the variable is a good thing or a bad thing. While this may not always reflect reality—for example, low blood sugar and high blood sugar both contribute to bad outcomes in diabetes patients—we can imagine rewriting variables in a way that would make this true. For some data sets, monotonicity has been established as a desirable feature in explanations of the performance of attributes, and indeed we may sometimes see a lack of monotonicity in an explanation (say, if we visualize the results of an explainer object) as a reason to dig into a particular variable and its role in a model.

Stability

This reflects the tendency for an explanation to be consistent for similar or neighboring examples. This would seem to match both human expectations and technical expectations implicit in building models to provide explanations. Since the purpose of a model is to systematize decision making, the expectation is that a system should be relatively consistent locally, as indicated by stability.

What Interpretation and Explainability Miss

Interpretable models and explainability algorithms are helpful for a variety of purposes, as shown earlier. However, they also miss quite a lot, and it's clear for the moment that fairness audits generally should not simply focus on a simple explainability test, as is sometimes the case in industry.

Many fundamental questions will not be answered by an explainability audit or even by an interpretable model. Some of these relate to upstream concerns. For starters, these techniques will not tell us whether sampling problems with data or representativeness problems with the data exist such that our model will not translate well in other cases. Likewise, these models will not tell us whether a particular indicator really should appear in an explanation, which is especially important for more technical or complicated systems. If we lack fundamental knowledge about the inputs to a system, we won't even know whether they are appropriately influencing the outcome.

There are also downstream concerns that explainability won't address. For example, an input might be cited in an explanation or used in an interpretable model in a way that seems to make sense, but this will not highlight the correlation structure within a data set. It can still be the case that an input can look sensible on its face but in fact be most instructive as a proxy for a protected attribute. So while a model may seem sensible in how it is explained, it may result in disparate impact because of correlational structures. Also, just because a model is explained as making a decision in a certain way, this can't guarantee that this logic will hold downstream. For example, if a model is applied to only a subset of potential candidates downstream, this would be one way in which only a subset of the logic that had been applied did, in fact, ultimately apply. For example, if a recidivism algorithm was developed on a whole population but rolled out only in the poorest districts of a state, then only a portion of the logic would apply. Would this retain the original explanation and sense of the model? It would be hard to say, and downstream audits would be needed to show that the explanations still served their original purpose.

Mittelstadt et al.[14] have done a particularly good job of identifying ways in which the explainability methods currently fail to reflect the broader expectations of the public. In particular, they point to ways in which explanations expected in other fields, such as law, philosophy, or sociology, differ in fundamental ways from what is generally proposed in technical solutions. The researchers discuss three specific trends in human explanations not well reflected in the machine learning research on explainable machine learning to date, and I summarize their commentary here as a helpful critique of what we've covered in the technical discussion in this chapter.

Human explanations are contrastive

Empirical evidence suggests that humans prefer contrastive explanations, even when other forms of explanation are no more complicated. In particular, humans are motivated to explain outcomes that are perceived as abnormal and to explain why a normal or expected outcome did not result. This is logical; to some extent humans seek out an explanation only when one seems called for one seems called for because something out of the ordinary has occurred. While contrastive explanations have been developed in machine learning, these tend to contrast nearby data points, whereas a human would be looking for a contrastive explanation that indicated the contrast between the atypical happening to be explained and what would have happened in the ordinary course.

Human explanations are selective

People do not tend to expect a full explanation that accounts for all links of causation that led to a particular outcome. Rather, people expect that, with context, the provider of the explanation will select those features that are most relevant, given the situation and the outcome. In this case, in contrast to machine learning

---

14 Mittelstadt, Brent, et al. "Explaining Explanations in AI." arXiv.org, November 4, 2018. *https://arxiv.org/pdf/1811.01439.pdf.*

explanations, which may offer a general weight to indicate significance and prioritize accordingly, a human explainer and recipient of an explanation would likely expect that which features were stressed would depend not only on this absolute measure but also on context that indicated what the audience cared about or why they were seeking an explanation.

Human explanations are social

Human explanations are inherently social, as they involve conveying information from one human to another. This would usually be expected to be an interactive process, as is reflected in approaches to teaching in the field of education and to investigation in the fields of law enforcement and legal practice. Explanations can be viewed as a way to identify and address a knowledge asymmetry. We can in this way imagine explanations as iterative and involving investigation and information exchange rather than a one-way provision of explanation.

Empirical and interdisciplinary investigation into the most effective way to define and provide an explanation continues. What remains clear is that defining an explanation is complicated and no one perfect explanation will ever fit all demands and all models. We can think of this as a broader reflection of the no free lunch theorem.

No Free Lunch Theorem

In the words of the two mathematicians who proved the NFL theorem (*https://oreil.ly/kYEds*), "any two optimization algorithms are equivalent when their performance is averaged across all possible problems." This tells us that there isn't going to be a "free lunch" when it comes to solving problems such as explainability or interpretability. While we may develop methods to determine best solutions in individual cases, no single explainability solution will exist for every ML model.

This lesson applies to machine learning and mathematics more generally. No matter what class of problem you are looking at, there will be no free lunch—that is, no automatic carefree way to know that a specific method will be guaranteed to yield the best results across all use cases.

In the course of writing this chapter, I happened to hit upon a very good example of the difficulties of explanation when chatting with my three-year-old son. I was in the process of closing the windows as I do every evening, and my son asked why the windows were open. I told him it was because his grandfather had been at the house earlier in the day and opened all the windows. He told me, no, the reason the windows were open was that this lets cool air into the hot house. We were both right.

Attacks on Explainable Machine Learning

Interpretation and explainability are not the be-all, end-all solution to fairness in machine learning. They are only one aspect of fairness and security, and even within that aspect they are imperfect.

Recently, researchers have been increasingly looking into attacks on fairness and explainability metrics. For example, Slack et al. show a way to fool LIME and SHAP, demonstrating an adversarial attack on local post hoc explanation methods.[15] This is particularly important because for many in industry who do take steps to address explainability, the steps taken are often limited to LIME and SHAP because these methods are simple and well-known. However, it turns that that elementary attacks can fool them.

In Slack et al.'s model, the researchers assume there is an entity with an incentive to deploy a biased classifier. This classifier will be audited in black-box form, and the entity's goal is for the bias in the classifier not to be detected by post hoc explanation techniques. This model presents a framework that takes the black-box classifier and the training data set as an input and outputs a classifier that will behave exactly like the original classifier except that it will not reveal its underlying biases when probed with LIME or SHAP.

The intuition behind the framework that can be used to cloak behavior is that these methods generate data by perturbing the features of individual data points. However, these perturbations can potentially result in data points that don't reflect the actual distribution and are labeled as *out of distribution*. In fact, they find that it is relatively easy to identify real data points as compared to data points perturbed as part of the standard LIME methodology. Because the data points can be distinguished, a bad actor can build a model that processes real data points in a discriminatory manner but processes perturbed synthetic data points in a manner that would pass muster with post hoc local explanation methods. The researchers find this is the case for the COMPAS data set and the German credit data set, both of which we've seen earlier in this book.

The authors show the same finding when examining the Community and Crime data set, which predicts violent crime rate based on a variety of demographic factors. The Community and Crime data set is another often used data set in the fairness literature. It is available on the UCI Machine Learning Repository (*https://oreil.ly/Cg1YG*). This data set combines socioeconomic information at the community level with measures of crime in those areas.

---

15 Slack, Dylan et al. "Fooling LIME and SHAP: Adversarial Attacks on Post hoc Explanation Methods." arXiv.org, February 3, 2020. *https://arxiv.org/pdf/1911.02508.pdf*.

Slack et al. make their code available (*https://oreil.ly/3l1_j*), should you want to experiment with the technique yourself.

In any case, this should be enough to convince you that no single method can suffice for an explainability audit, let alone an entire fairness audit of any complex machine learning pipeline. This is because detecting and defeating it would be relatively easy if multiple metrics were used in auditing a model. On the other hand, it's unfortunately realistic that many practitioners and organizations will look for a simple explanation and want to choose a single test or metric to use to determine whether their pipeline passes muster. This has a few benefits from their perspective, including simplicity, which means they don't have to do much and also don't have to learn much. Unfortunately, more generally we should heed the no free lunch theorem.

Interpretation and Explanation Checklist

Explanation is a broad category. Here is a checklist of considerations when you are approaching the problem of an explanation:

- What is the purpose of the audit?
  - If the purpose is to ensure certain foreseeable model behaviors, consider an interpretable model.
  - If the purpose is for some degree of local or global understanding, but specific guarantees are not needed, consider explanation.
  - Consider explanation when the model itself is unavailable.
- Who is the audience for an explanation?
  - What is the level of technical sophistication of the audience?
  - Is the audience seeking an explanation for what has already happened or what could happen?
  - Is the audience seeking an actionable explanation or a rationale for general understanding?
- At what level is an explanation to be provided?
  - Is a white paper under preparation?
  - Will the explanation be deployed at scale?
  - Are there opportunities for second-order effects as the result of explanation, such as the decision maker weighing the outputs of the model less or someone subject to the model opting for a different decision route?

Concluding Remarks

The explanation and interpretation domains of algorithmic fairness are young areas of research with respect to technical implementations of explanation as well as the subjective human experience of receiving explanations and interpretations. We expect they will continue to be areas of active technical, behavioral, and legal research and development. What's more, a variety of laws and legal conventions explicitly or implicitly require some measure of logic and inspection with respect to decisions that affect people.

It is incredibly valuable to be able to explain your model's behavior to yourself, internal stakeholders, and to those who are affected by decisions your model makes. Humans distinguish themselves from most other animals through our ability to communicate extensively and logically and to develop complex systems of decision making, coordination, and prediction. We find it frustrating when the outside world does not appear to behave in an orderly way or follow norms regarding fairness. When you release ML models into the wild that are not logical, transparent, and explainable, you contribute to a sense of lawlessness and futility for ML model subjects. On the other hand, when you prepare models that can and are explained to those affected by these models, you uphold norms of fairness and legitimacy regarding the increasing role of ML in decision making for both low-stakes and high-stakes applications. It's best to plan to be part of the solution that enhances logic, transparency, and fairness, rather than part of the problem.

## CHAPTER 9

ML Models and Privacy

Privacy is difficult to define and audit for. In the real world, organizations tend to opt for "good enough," because as technology advances or as new data sets become available, data that was originally thought to be anonymized may no longer be anonymized. But taking reasonable privacy precautions with the technical tools available at a given point in time is clearly better than doing nothing. And in some cases, we already have technical tools that guarantee mathematically ensured degrees of privacy, and that's even better because it provides a measure of future-proofing.

In addition to being a moving target because of evolving technical and mathematical knowledge, privacy is an evolving legal norm. For example, technical experts have pointed to the difficulties in fulfilling the requirements of emerging legal norms, such as the "right to be forgotten" in Europe that has been controlling law for some time and is now formalized in the GDPR. Several researchers have pointed out that technical implementations of the right to be forgotten may be different depending on what definition of that right and underlying motivation for that right are used to guide technical implementations.

Is the motivation for providing a right to be forgotten (more concretely, a right to data deletion), that all statements related to a given data set will be robust to a data point's deletion? This is not entirely feasible, for example, if organizations have published aggregate statistics that have not been calculated with differential privacy.

Alternatively, is the right to deletion related to a right to control the data regardless of past footprints that would be left behind? In that case, perhaps what would be most important in implementing a right to deletion would be some kind of deletion verifiability, such as a database with a public-facing verification method so an individual could verify that their data was truly gone.

The Right to Be Forgotten

The right to be forgotten is a right distinct from but related to a right to privacy. The right to privacy is, among other things, the right for information traditionally regarded as protected or personal not to be revealed. On the other hand, the right to be forgotten can be applied even to information that has been in the public domain.

The right to be forgotten broadly encompasses the right of an individual not to be forever defined by information from a specific point in time. It broadly describes the right of an individual to have even public information about that individual not be readily accessible or permanently publicized.

One motivation for such a right is to allow individuals to move on with their lives and not be defined by a specific event or period in their lives. For example, it has long been recognized in some countries, such as the UK and France, that even past criminal convictions should eventually be "spent" and not continue to affect a person's life.

The strongest legal basis for a right to be forgotten at present is in the European Union. Notably, the GDPR cemented the right to be forgotten in the digital data context via the right to deletion, described in Article 17 (*https://gdpr-info.eu/art-17-gdpr*). However, even before the GDPR was enacted into law, EU law included protections for individuals securing elements of the right to be forgotten, as was most notably highlighted in media coverage (*https://oreil.ly/h8JUy*) regarding individuals seeking to remove certain links from Google search results and citing their right to be forgotten.

The right to deletion, or right to be forgotten, is particularly important from a technology perspective due to the wide applicability of the GDPR and the technical challenges that lie ahead regarding what it means to delete data, particularly when that data may at some time have been used in machine learning training pipelines for public-facing products.

As with other rights, the right to be forgotten can sometimes come into conflict with other rights. In such cases, a right to be forgotten may be limited by other fundamental rights. For example, formal exceptions are sometimes delineated for security or public health reasons. Similarly a right to information is also implicated in contestations of the right to be forgotten. So while a right to be forgotten may sound good in theory, sometimes too strong a right could compromise other social prerogatives or individual rights necessary for a healthy democracy.

The bounds of what is private information also shifts over time, due in part to evolving social norms and advances in technology. For example, machine learning may enable the discovery of new scientific facts, perhaps along the lines of "trait X plus trait Y leads to outcome Z" or more likely probabilistic notions such as "all else equal, trait W is associated with outcome Z." This brings previously unknown information about people to light if traits found to be predictive are also readily observable, either to human observers or to machine observers. So to some extent, the bounds of privacy (when we define it as the reasonable expectation of information that will not be readily known) will change over time. This is one justification for privacy rights that protect information that can be known precisely because we can otherwise expect privacy to diminish over time as human behavioral sciences and digital surveillance technologies advance. But of course we don't want fundamental human needs like privacy to be disregarded or abridged by human technological progress.

Imagine that a machine learning model identified some combination of publicly observable biometrics that together pointed toward the likelihood of a genetic disease. For example, say a long pinky combined with a small forehead and a large chin point to a high probability of having disease A. This would compromise not only the privacy of anyone in the training set but all people. This is one of the reasons we discuss in Chapter 11 whether a particular model is appropriately built and contemplate how likely it is that a model succeeds given that knowledge and techniques cannot be walked back.

My large chin example is entirely made up, but models that purport to diagnose mental illness or sexual orientation from photos may just discover what we already know from social signaling and careful observation of our peers—but in doing so, those models may turn previously private information into public facts.[1]

For this reason, our review of privacy focuses on specific problems, to give you a flavor of what is possible and what needs to be considered when releasing models publicly. In the computer science literature in general, a review of privacy attacks and other attacks on machine learning shows that researchers are careful to define the specific problem addressed. We must recognize that there is no homogeneous, all-inclusive "privacy attack"; rather, privacy can be violated in various ways.

Membership Attacks

In a *membership attack*, the adversary has access to a potential training data point and uses the attack to infer whether that data point was part of the original training data set. We will define this as a per se privacy breach, but to motivate why this could be, consider a few potential examples:

---

1 We should also keep in mind that machine learning models cross borders at nearly the speed of light. While you may feel we live in a society that no longer stigmatizes such facts, you are probably unduly optimistic and should remember that in some countries these facts can have serious consequences, even physical violence or criminal punishment.

- A successful membership attack against a model trained on a data set compiled to study a genetic disease would tend to suggest that the revealed individual was more likely to have that disease than a typical member of the public, probabilistically revealing private health information.

- A successful membership attack against a model trained to identify likely criminal juvenile offenders (court records about them are usually sealed) could lead to publicly identifying an individual with an erased juvenile offender record, undermining the legal protections put in place to keep youthful offenses secret.

- A successful membership attack against a model trained to identify post-traumatic stress disorder could not only reveal someone's mental health status but also reveal information associated with some kind of traumatic attack that an individual might wish to keep private.

- A successful membership attack against any model may violate the terms of consent under which data was obtained in the first place. That is, even if the data is not particularly sensitive, it may have been provided only by consent that the data not be publicly available or publicly revealed.

There are a variety of ways to perform membership attacks. In one form or another, they rely on the general model of supervised machine learning—namely, that there must be patterns to how a model treats the data depending on whether the model has seen that data before, and likely involving the model's relative degree of confidence when classifying a particular example. This requires access to the final layer of a neural network, which indicates the estimated probability of membership in all protected categories. Note that this is more information than merely the final label, where this final label would be the class from the final layer with the highest probability. These estimations of the model targeted for attack become the inputs for an adversarial attack model, with the idea that the distribution of these inputs with respect to the correct value will look systematically different for training data as compared to test data.

For this, training data is needed to train an adversarial model—that is, a model meant to perform the membership attack—by labeling data that either was or was not used in training the original model. You may very well raise your eyebrows here. After all, if access to at least some of the original training data is needed to train for such a membership attack, the risk of a membership attack seems substantially smaller than if such data were not needed for training. *However*, over time researchers have shown that it is not necessary to have access to the original training data—if access to some of the original training data were possible, that would itself constitute a larger and more serious privacy infringement, and the focus should be on protecting the data. As it turns out, there are many ways to train a model for such an attack without having access to the actual training data.

I'm going to talk about an ingeniously simple attack originally published in 2016 by Shokri et al.[2] I'll repurpose the code published along with the paper to port to a PyTorch implementation, so that you can have the experience of a full implementation. However, be aware that Professor Shokri has gone on to package membership attacks for both black-box and white-box models in a convenient Python package that comes with pre-implemented algorithms along with helpful visualizations. It is available as the ML Privacy Meter (*https://oreil.ly/qUuOX*) and can be found at the project's GitHub account. For practical purposes, you are advised to start with this implementation rather than a homespun solution.

How It Works

The previous section talked about the conundrum of how to train a model to infer membership in the training data without some data from the training set on which to train such an adversarial model. In Shokri et al. the authors suggest and validate three approaches:

Model-based synthetic data
> The attacker can use their access to the model itself to generate data points and the labels for such data points, relying on the intuition that records classified with higher confidence are more like data from the training data set than are records classified with lower confidence. Not all potential data points created in this synthetic data generation process are kept. Rather, only the points that can generate a highly confident classification from the model are kept. In this case, no prior knowledge or access is assumed for the attacker, but the attacker has to devote computing resources to developing the data set, and this assumes a degree of access to the targeted model that is relatively high and free of constraints, even if the model is a black-box model. For example, rate limits on use of an API would slow down the process of generating synthetic data. This attack works only if the space is not so high-dimensional as to make the problem of searching the input space computationally intractable.

Statistics-based synthetic data
> When the attacker has a sense of the general distribution of training data, they can use this to generate statistically grounded sample distributions of the training data.

Noisy real data
> The attacker may have access to data that is similar to but not overlapping with the target model's data set. We can consider this a *noisy* version of the real data

---

2 Shokri, Reza, et al. "Membership Inference Attacks Against Machine Learning Models." arXiv.org, March 31, 2017. *https://arxiv.org/pdf/1610.05820.pdf*.

set. For example, perhaps the attacker knows that the target model was trained on certain Reddit posts, but not which ones. The attacker can then in parallel do similar scraping and preparation of a data set.

Shokri et al. found that all these ways of generating a training data set, none of which relied on any access to the original data, could produce viable membership inference attacks.

Once the attacker has a training data set, the next task is to train shadow models. The idea of the *shadow models* is that their training is a logical parallel to the training of the original attack model. What's more, multiple shadow models are trained to generate a wider set of data that should help an attacker generalize more easily. In the original paper, Shokri et al. did their own shadow model training, using a model that reflected the known architecture of the target model, while otherwise treating the target model as a black box. However, they also offered a more realistic paradigm for the attack, using machine learning models as a service provided by mainstream tech companies, showing that if they trained both the black-box models and the shadow models on this service, they were able to replicate the findings.

In Figure 9-1 we see the training processes that occur *before* the training of the adversarial model for the privacy inference attack.

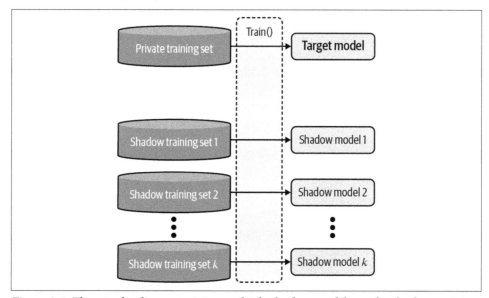

Figure 9-1. The attack relies on training multiple shadow models on the shadow training data set, mirroring the presumed way in which the black-box target model was trained with its private data

Figure 9-2 demonstrates the logical setup and parallel of these shadow models to the target model. The shadow models are not interesting as models for purposes of this attack but rather are the producers of the training data set that will be used by the adversarial attack model that will perform the membership inference. Specifically, for each synthetic data point used to train the shadow model, the following is recorded:

- The outputs of the final layer of the model (presumably the relative probabilities of classification for the potential classes)
- The label of that final layer as either having been used for the shadow model's training set *or* having been in the test set for the shadow model

In this way, the attack generates a training set that indicates how a shadow model classified a data point (inputs to the adversarial membership attack model) and whether that data point was in the relevant shadow model's training set (output label on which to train the adversarial membership attack model).

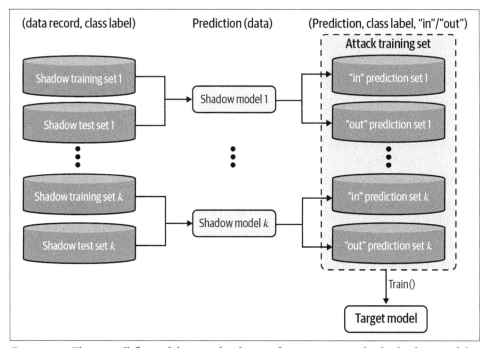

Figure 9-2. The overall flow of the attack relies on first training multiple shadow models, each contributing to the data set that is then compiled to train the membership inference attack model

The flow of this training can be seen in Figure 9-2. The final output is an attack model trained to determine, based on the outputs of the final layer of a model, whether the inputs for the model came from the model's training set or not. The authors found on a variety of data sets that this method can do far better than chance at assessing whether a particular data point was in the training data set for the black-box model, despite having no access to that black-box model's parameters or its original training data.

For simplicity, the demonstration in the next section will cover the CIFAR-10 training set, a data set used for image classification and not directly affecting sensitive information. However, Shokri et al. also showed results on data sets related to shopping behavior and medical treatment, and the attack also worked on such real-world data.

Note that in saying an attack *worked*, I mean that a model performed better than chance at determining whether a data point had been used in training. However, the model did not, and no model could, make a certain determination. As has been discussed, privacy need not be a deterministic compromise of specific information. It can also refer to enhanced probabilities of correctly inferring on a probabilistic basis sensitive information.

Code Demonstration

We will implement the code ourselves in PyTorch, patterning the code on the GitHub repository (*https://oreil.ly/eBCIn*) released by the researchers. We will implement our attack on the CIFAR-10 data set as such attacks work best and are a more realistic threat on high-dimensional data sets.[3]

Note that this code directly implements a deep learning model and training. If you are not familiar with deep learning, I recommend that you take a short detour to familiarize yourself with the basic concepts. One good source of a conceptual review is a video tutorial (*https://oreil.ly/T6q2q*) from 3Blue1Brown's series on deep learning.

First, I'll describe the main components of the program. We distribute the code over three files:

cnn_model.py
    This specifies the model architecture.

classifier_methods.py
    This provides the training infrastructure for the model.

run_attack.py
    This runs the attack from the command line and provides the overall structure of the experiment. You will recognize the structure from the flowchart in this file.

---

3 The attack has been demonstrated on data sets that directly implicate fairness and privacy, such as a hospital data set, but these data sets have strict data handling provisions and also require extensive pre-processing, and for both reasons are not presented here.

We will take a top-down approach to the code. The overall structure is most important to understand about the attack, while the specific training details are more about understanding how deep learning works generally and implementing that in a straightforward form. So we begin with *run_attack.py*, which is largely influenced by the design of Shokri et al.'s paper and its released code (*https://oreil.ly/VSY0Y*).

We begin with a variety of imports. These are largely from PyTorch and focus on the methods needed. We also bring in some commonly used packages for reading command-line arguments, doing basic matrix manipulations, and reading from the file directories:

```
from classifier_methods import train, iterate_and_shuffle_numpy
from sklearn.metrics import classification_report, accuracy_score

from torch.utils.data.sampler import SubsetRandomSampler
import torchvision.transforms as transforms
import torchvision
import torch
torch.multiprocessing.set_sharing_strategy('file_system')

import numpy as np
import argparse
import os

np.random.seed(171717)
```

We also set some training parameters as constants:

```
#### CONSTANTS
TRAIN_SIZE = 10000
TEST_SIZE  = 500

TRAIN_EXAMPLES_AVAILABLE = 50000
TEST_EXAMPLES_AVAILABLE  = 10000
```

These were set based on the size of the data repository. In the original paper, Shokri et al. experiment with different training sizes for the data to see how the performance of the attack varied with the size of the data set, but here we are more interested in understanding how to implement the attack so we fully follow the logic.

In another bit of bookkeeping, we arrange directories to save our models and to save the data we generate as outputs of the shadow models, which in turn becomes the training data for the attack model:

```
MODEL_PATH = './attack_model/'
DATA_PATH = './data/'

if not os.path.exists(MODEL_PATH):
    os.makedirs(MODEL_PATH)
```

```
if not os.path.exists(DATA_PATH):
    os.makedirs(DATA_PATH)
```

We use two methods to manage our data:

```
def generate_data_indices(data_size, target_train_size):
"""Returns indices for data sizing and sampling
according to input parameters """
train_indices = np.arange(data_size)
target_data_indices = np.random.choice(train_indices, target_train_size,
replace = False)
shadow_indices = np.setdiff1d(train_indices, target_data_indices)
return target_data_indices, shadow_indices
### taken from
### https://github.com/csong27/membership-inference/blob/master/attack.py
def load_attack_data():
""" Loads training and testing datasets from presaved numpy files """
fname = MODEL_PATH + 'attack_train_data.npz'
with np.load(fname) as f:
train_x, train_y, train_classes = [f['arr_%d' % i]
                                   for i in range(len(f.files))]
fname = MODEL_PATH + 'attack_test_data.npz'
with np.load(fname) as f:
test_x, test_y, test_classes = [f['arr_%d' % i]
                                for i in range(len(f.files))]
return train_x.astype('float32'),
train_y.astype('int32'),
train_classes.astype('int32'),
test_x.astype('float32'),
test_y.astype('int32'),
test_classes.astype('int32')
```

The first method, generate_data_indices, takes parameters indicating the number of data points available and the number desired to be trained, and then generates nonoverlapping data points for the "real" model (since we train this rather than receiving it as a black-box model) and the shadow models. It's important that these not overlap since the whole point of this model is to show that without any access to the original model's training data, we can nonetheless make inferences about membership in that original training data set based on training on similar data.

The second method, load_attack_data, will take data from numpy files and reload them. This is useful, for example, if we want to train the target and shadow models only one time but then want to experiment with options for attack models, such as different architectures or training parameters. Remember, the training data for the attack model is the outputs of the shadow models, so the shadow models need to be trained only once even as you explore many potential attacks.

We also need other methods to build up to the global attack, namely train_tar get_model, train_shadow_models, and train_attack_model. To limit the length of this chapter and because this is not strictly conceptually necessary for the attack, we will not discuss `train_target_model`. This is simply a method implemented since we don't have a preexisting black-box model. However, in a real-world scenario, we would have such a black-box model—otherwise, there would be no point to the attack, so we won't spend time on this. Rather, we'll look at `train_shadow_models`.

This is a lengthy function reproduced in full here. If you are already versed in the mechanics of deep learning training, you can scan those parts of the code not highlighted with a code bullet and just focus on the code bits specific to this use case. If you are not already familiar with deep learning training code, you should read the code in full, including the comments in the code, which should help you understand the structure of deep learning training.

```
def train_shadow_models(train_indices, test_indices,
                        fc_dim_hidden=50, n_shadow=20, model='nn',
                        epochs=100, learning_rate=0.05, batch_size=10,
                        save=True):

    ## CIFAR image preparation ❶
    transform = transforms.Compose(
    [transforms.ToTensor(),
     transforms.Normalize((0.5, 0.5, 0.5), (0.5, 0.5, 0.5))])

    ## create a generator object to cycle through the data each epoch
    trainset = CIFAR10(root      = './data',
                       train     = True,
                       download  = True,
                       transform = transform)
    testset = CIFAR10(root = './data',
                      train     = False,
                      download  = True,
                      transform = transform)

    ## record shadow model output as x (input to attack model),
    ## train/test data set membership status of each data point
    ## (label for training the attack model,
    ## and class labels (e.g. is it a 4 or a 9?)
    ## so that we can train attack model aware of correct label
    attack_x, attack_y, classes = [], [], [] ❷
    ## train one shadow model at a time
    for i in range(n_shadow): ❸
        print('Training shadow model %d'%(i))
        trainloader = DataLoader(trainset,
                                 batch_size  = batch_size,
                                 num_workers = 2,
                                 sampler     = \
                                 SubsetRandomSampler(
                                     np.random.choice(train_indices,
                                     TRAIN_SIZE,
                                     replace = False)),
                                 drop_last = True)
```

```
testloader = DataLoader(testset,
                        batch_size = batch_size,
                        shuffle = False,
                        num_workers = 2,
                        sampler = \
                        SubsetRandomSampler(
                            np.random.choice(test_indices,
                            round(TRAIN_SIZE * 0.3),
                            replace = False)),
                        drop_last = True)

## This is where the training actually happens!
## The output layer represents the penultimate layer
## of a model, where the estimated probability per class
## is the output.
## The final layer would then narrow these down to the class with
## the maximum probability to solve classification problem
output_layer, _1, _2 = train(trainloader, testloader, ❹
                        fc_dim_hidden = fc_dim_hidden,
                        model         = model,
                        epochs        = epochs,
                        learning_rate = learning_rate,
                        batch_size    = batch_size)

## same quantities recorded globally
## on a per-model basis for shadow models
attack_i_x, attack_i_y, classes_i = [], [], []

## put the training/data onto a GPU if available
## otherwise use CPU
device = torch.device("cuda:0" if torch.cuda.is_available()
                                else "cpu")

## This is the inference stage
## (where the model has already been trained)
## We record the pairs of inputs and outputs
## resulting from performing inference with this trained model,
## recording pairs drawn from the training data but also from
## the test data. We need both pairs from the training and from
## the test data because whether the data is training or testing
## is its LABEL for the next phase of training the adversary
## So we forget about the original inputs, and the new "inputs"
## are the final layer values of the inferred model,
## while the label is the data origin (test or training).
with torch.no_grad(): ❺
    for data in trainloader:
        images, labels = data[0].to(device), data[1].to(device)
        outputs = output_layer(images)
        attack_i_x.append(outputs.cpu())
        # data used in training, label is 1
        attack_i_y.append(np.ones(batch_size))
        classes_i.append(labels)
```

```
        for data in testloader:
            images, labels = data[0].to(device), data[1].to(device)
            outputs = output_layer(images)
            attack_i_x.append(outputs.cpu())
            # data NOT used in training, label is 0
            attack_i_y.append(np.zeros(batch_size))
            classes_i.append(labels)

    attack_x += attack_i_x
    attack_y += attack_i_y
    classes  += classes_i

## Now we pass all the data from the training/testing
## data inference through the shadow model

## training data for attack model ❻
attack_x = np.vstack(attack_x)
attack_y = np.concatenate(attack_y)
classes  = np.concatenate([cl.cpu() for cl in classes])

attack_x = attack_x.astype('float32')
attack_y = attack_y.astype('int32'  )
classes  = classes.astype( 'int32'  )

## save this data so we can train many attack models without
## retraining shadow models
if save: ❼
    np.savez(MODEL_PATH + 'attack_train_data.npz',
             attack_x,
             attack_y,
             classes)

return attack_x, attack_y, classes
```

❶ We use utilities from `torch` to download and store the CIFAR data set if we haven't done so already. We pre-process the CIFAR images with standard normalization techniques that assist deep learning training for image-related tasks. For those who haven't worked on images with deep learning before, the pre-processing relates to bringing the pixel values within a set, small numerical range.

❷ We want to record three values for each data point that passes through the shadow model: (1) the outputs of the final layer of the shadow model, which will reflect a per-class estimated probability of membership in that case for the data point, (2) whether the data point was in the shadow model's training or test data set, and (3) the class label of the data point (i.e., was it a car or a frog). Knowing the correct class label of the data point simplifies the learning task for the attack model. We will train a different attack model for each class so that the attack model only needs to learn to recognize membership in the training data and not that *plus* what class. If we did not train one model per class, the attack model would have to simultaneously learn (a) class and (b) indicators of test versus training. This is possible but would complicate training and is not necessary since we have the class data.

❸ We repeat the training loop for as many shadow models as we desire.

❹ We train the *i*th shadow model with standard techniques, which can be seen by looking at the classifier_methods code, reviewed briefly later.

❺ Once the *i*th shadow model has been trained, we record its last layer output of the trained model (which is a vector length equal to the number of classes in the classification task) as well as the train/test status and correct class for each data point in the training and testing data sets. This is purely *inference* and does not involve any more model training.

❻ We combine all recorded data point outputs, their train/test status, and their class status.

❼ We save this combined data so that multiple attack models can be trained with this data set without the need to retrain the ensemble of shadow models.

Now that we have the ability to train a shadow model and save its outputs, we need to train the attack model. We do this with the following method:

```
def train_attack_model(data = None,
                       fc_dim_hidden = 50, model = 'fc',
                       learning_rate = 0.01, batch_size = 10, epochs = 3):
    ### either data is passed in to function or is loaded from files
    ### saved while training shadow models
    if data is None:
        data = load_attack_data()
    train_x, train_y, train_classes, test_x, test_y, test_classes = data ❶

    ## balance data sets
    ## training data may be over-represented compared to test data
    ## we use these functions to get a 50/50 balance of training and test data
    ## remember "training" and "test" data are lpredicted by the attack model.
    ## If we know the data sets are balanced, we can easily
    ## see how much better our attack model does than random guessing.
    train_x, train_y, train_classes = reduce_ones(train_x, train_y,
    train_classes) ❷
    test_x, test_y, test_classes = reduce_ones(test_x, test_y, test_classes)

    train_indices = np.arange(len(train_x))
    test_indices = np.arange(len(test_x))
    unique_classes = np.unique(train_classes)
    true_y = []
```

```
pred_y = []
## we train a model for each of the original classes in the data
## this is not conceptually necessary but makes it easier for the
## model to focus on learning the training/testing distinction
## without having to also learn the class
for c in unique_classes: ❸
    print('Training attack model for class %d...'%(c))
    c_train_indices = train_indices[train_classes == c]
    c_train_x, c_train_y = train_x[c_train_indices], train_y[c_train_indices]
    c_test_indices = test_indices[test_classes == c]
    c_test_x, c_test_y = test_x[c_test_indices], test_y[c_test_indices]
    print("training number is %d"%c_train_x.shape[0])
    print("testing number is %d"%c_test_x.shape[0])

    trainloader = iterate_and_shuffle_numpy(c_train_x, c_train_y,
                                            batch_size)
    testloader = iterate_and_shuffle_numpy(c_test_x,   c_test_y,
                                           batch_size)

    ## ❹
    _, c_pred_y, c_true_y = train(trainloader, testloader,
                        fc_dim_in = train_x.shape[1],
                        fc_dim_out = 2,
                        fc_dim_hidden = fc_dim_hidden, epochs = epochs,
                            learning_rate = learning_rate,
                        batch_size = batch_size, model = model)
    true_y.append(c_true_y)
    pred_y.append(c_pred_y)
    print("Accuracy score for class %d:"%c)
    print(accuracy_score(c_true_y, c_pred_y))

true_y = np.concatenate(true_y)
pred_y = np.concatenate(pred_y)
print('Final full: %0.2f'%(accuracy_score(true_y, pred_y))) ❺
print(classification_report(true_y, pred_y))
```

❶ We either receive the data directly in the function call or load it from saved numpy files.

❷ We balance the training data for the attack model so that it represents an equal mix of data labeled as training data and test data. This is not necessary but simplifies training and analysis of the attack model performance.

❸ We train one model for each of the classes in the original data set of the CIFAR images. As described earlier, this is purely to simplify the learning task and is not conceptually necessary.

❹ We use a fully connected architecture rather than a convolutional architecture, as this is not an image classification task and a simpler model seems justified.

❺ We print out performance metrics.

Incidentally, we balance the training and test data sets via the following function, which is called reduce_ones simply because the value 1 indicates that a data set was in the training data, and we will usually have a surfeit of training data relative to testing data. This is shown here:

```
def reduce_ones(x, y, classes):
    ## assumes more training than testing examples
    ## 1 as over-represented class is hardcoded in here
    idx_to_keep   = np.where(y == 0)[0]
    idx_to_reduce = np.where(y == 1)[0]
    num_to_reduce = (y.shape[0]-idx_to_reduce.shape[0]) * 2
    idx_sample    = np.random.choice(idx_to_reduce, num_to_reduce,
    replace = False)

    x       = x[    np.concatenate([idx_to_keep, idx_sample, idx_to_keep])]
    y       = y[    np.concatenate([idx_to_keep, idx_sample, idx_to_keep])]
    classes = classes[ np.concatenate([idx_to_keep, idx_sample, idx_to_keep])]

    return x, y, classes
```

With the preceding, we have the main components of running an experiment—that is, seeing how the proposed technique for a membership inference attack performs on the data. Let's take a look at how we put it all together with the following:

```
### divide up data set between target and shadow models
## training ❶
train_indices = list(range(TRAIN_EXAMPLES_AVAILABLE))
train_target_indices = np.random.choice(train_indices, TRAIN_SIZE,
replace=False)
train_shadow_indices = np.setdiff1d(train_indices, train_target_indices)
## testing
test_indices = list(range(TEST_EXAMPLES_AVAILABLE))
test_target_indices = np.random.choice(test_indices, TEST_SIZE,
replace=False)
test_shadow_indices = np.setdiff1d(test_indices, test_target_indices)

print("training target model...") ❷
attack_test_x, attack_test_y, test_classes = train_target_model(
    train_indices = train_target_indices,
    test_indices  = test_target_indices,
    epochs        = args.target_epochs,
    batch_size    = args.target_batch_size,
    learning_rate = args.target_learning_rate,
    model         = args.target_model,
    fc_dim_hidden  = args.target_fc_dim_hidden,
    save          = args.save_model)
print("done training target model")

print("training shadow models...") ❸
attack_train_x, attack_train_y, train_classes = train_shadow_models(
```

```
    train_indices = train_shadow_indices,
    test_indices  = test_shadow_indices,
    epochs        = args.target_epochs,
    batch_size    = args.target_batch_size,
    learning_rate = args.target_learning_rate,
    n_shadow      = args.n_shadow,
    fc_dim_hidden  = args.target_fc_dim_hidden,
    model         = args.target_model,
    save          = args.save_model)
print("done training shadow models")

print("training attack model...") ❹
data = (attack_train_x, attack_train_y, train_classes,\
        attack_test_x, attack_test_y, test_classes)
train_attack_model(
    data          = data,
    epochs        = args.attack_epochs,
    batch_size    = args.attack_batch_size,
    learning_rate = args.attack_learning_rate,
    fc_dim_hidden  = args.attack_fc_dim_hidden,
    model         = args.attack_model)
print("done training attack model")
```

This function is relatively short because we've already got all the main components. We proceed as follows:

❶ Break up the data we have into what we will use to train the target/black-box model and the shadow models. These indices should not overlap, as we ensured in our method.

❷ Train the target model. If a black-box model was provided, we would skip this step.

❸ Train the shadow models on similar but not identical data to that provided by the black-box model. In the earlier section we describe a variety of sources for such training data. Also, it's best if the architecture of the shadow model conforms as best as possible to whatever we know about the architecture of the black-box model.

❹ Train the attack model. This model receives the output layer of the shadow models for each data point along with information about whether that data point was in the training or test set for that shadow model. The attack model learns how the outputs of the shadow models systematically differ according to whether a data point was in the training or testing set.

The preceding code represents almost all the contents of the *run_attack.py* file, which is the bulk of the experimental logic. As you can see on GitHub (*https://github.com/ practicalfairness*), this file also contains other details, such as command-line parsing and an option to run only the training for the attack mode, assuming shadow model outputs have already been archived in a numpy model. For brevity, we won't discuss these, but they should be easy to recognize and read in the file.

I won't discuss the contents of the *classifier_methods.py*, *cnn_model.py*, and *fc_model.py* files, as these are fairly standard fare for anyone with familiarity with deep learning. I have left them heavily commented for those less familiar with deep learning generally or with PyTorch specifically.

Here are the outputs of this script when I run the full experiment:

```
{'save_model': 1, 'save_data': 0, 'test_ratio': 0.3,
  'num_shadow': 10, 'target_data_size': 10000, 'target_model': 'cnn',
  'target_learning_rate': 0.001, 'target_batch_size': 4,
  'target_dim_hidden': 50, 'target_epochs': 10, 'attack_model': 'fc',
  'attack_learning_rate': 0.001, 'attack_batch_size': 50,
  'attack_dim_hidden': 50, 'attack_epochs': 5} ❶

----------TRAIN TARGET---------- ❷
Files already downloaded and verified
Files already downloaded and verified
Epoch: 9 Accuracy of the network on the training set: 65 %
Epoch: 9 Accuracy of the network on the test set: 48 % ❸
done training target model

----------TRAIN SHADOW---------- ❹
Files already downloaded and verified
Files already downloaded and verified
Training shadow model 0
Epoch: 9 Accuracy of the network on the training set: 62 %
Epoch: 9 Accuracy of the network on the test set: 49 %
Training shadow model 1
Epoch: 9 Accuracy of the network on the training set: 64 %
Epoch: 9 Accuracy of the network on the test set: 50 %
Training shadow model 2
Epoch: 9 Accuracy of the network on the training set: 63 %
Epoch: 9 Accuracy of the network on the test set: 52 %
Training shadow model 3
Epoch: 9 Accuracy of the network on the training set: 65 %
Epoch: 9 Accuracy of the network on the test set: 52 %
Training shadow model 4
Epoch: 9 Accuracy of the network on the training set: 64 %
Epoch: 9 Accuracy of the network on the test set: 54 %
Training shadow model 5
Epoch: 9 Accuracy of the network on the training set: 62 %
Epoch: 9 Accuracy of the network on the test set: 50 %
Training shadow model 6
Epoch: 9 Accuracy of the network on the training set: 62 %
Epoch: 9 Accuracy of the network on the test set: 52 %
Training shadow model 7
Epoch: 9 Accuracy of the network on the training set: 64 %
Epoch: 9 Accuracy of the network on the test set: 51 %
```

```
Training shadow model 8
Epoch: 9 Accuracy of the network on the training set: 63 %
Epoch: 9 Accuracy of the network on the test set: 52 %
Training shadow model 9
Epoch: 9 Accuracy of the network on the training set: 65 %
Epoch: 9 Accuracy of the network on the test set: 51 %
done training shadow model


----------TRAIN ATTACK----------  ❺
Training attack model for class 0...
training number is 11987
testing number is 180
Epoch: 4 Accuracy of the network on the training set: 57 %
Epoch: 4 Accuracy of the network on the test set: 57 %
ACCURACY SCORE for class 0:
0.5722222222222222
Training attack model for class 1...
training number is 12037
testing number is 186
Epoch: 4 Accuracy of the network on the training set: 58 %
Epoch: 4 Accuracy of the network on the test set: 55 %
ACCURACY SCORE for class 1:
0.5591397849462365


...


Training attack model for class 8...
training number is 12025
testing number is 211
Epoch: 4 Accuracy of the network on the training set: 57 %
Epoch: 4 Accuracy of the network on the test set: 59 %
ACCURACY SCORE for class 8:
0.5971563981042654
Training attack model for class 9...
training number is 12096
testing number is 222
Epoch: 4 Accuracy of the network on the training set: 59 %
Epoch: 4 Accuracy of the network on the test set: 61 %
ACCURACY SCORE for class 9:
0.6126126126126126

----------FINAL EVALUATION----------  ❻
Testing Accuracy: 0.59
              precision    recall  f1-score   support

           0       0.60      0.54      0.57      1000
           1       0.58      0.65      0.61      1000

    accuracy                           0.59      2000
   macro avg       0.59      0.59      0.59      2000
weighted avg       0.59      0.59      0.59      2000
```

❶ Here are the hyperparameters chosen for training, printed for record keeping.

❷ If a black-box model is not provided, I train a model as a stand-in for the black-box model.

❸ The overall classification accuracy of the stand-in black-box model is reported for both training and testing. The model appears to be overfit based on the discrepancy between training and testing data. This is a common problem in real-world data and ML pipelines, and it's a problem that makes the membership inference attack more likely to succeed.

❹ I train 10 shadow models and report the final accuracy for training and test data sets for each of the models. Not surprisingly, these values are comparable to the original target model since we train with the same architecture and similar (but not overlapping) data.

❺ Now the attack model is trained, and its training data is the data produced and labeled by the shadow models.

❻ The final performance metrics are reported. This model identifies training as compared to test data with just under 60% accuracy, whereas a random guess would have produced around 50% accuracy. This may seem unimpressive, but it does constitute a privacy infringement based on a probabilistic assessment. What's more, we didn't try particularly hard, so it could be that the attack could become much stronger with more careful study of this particular data set or experimentation with hyperparameters.

Privacy is not binary most of the time. Certainly, when there is a data leak, a particular individual's data either has or has not been leaked. On the other hand, in a world increasingly featuring ML products embedded in digital products and open for attack, and where an individual either has or does not have privacy, something like this attack, which does give some probabilistic if imperfect indication, does indeed result in a breach of privacy.

Privacy Is Not Binary

Privacy is not binary. This is good news—it means you shouldn't give up just because you worry you can't have the perfect system. However, it also means that you should do your best to obscure information, such as from your training data, as much as possible when contemplating the release of an ML model into the world.

In a real-world scenario, if I could build a model that had better-than-chance odds of determining, from publicly accessible methods, whether a particular individual has a sensitive and costly health condition, this could be devastating to that individual. It could lead to social stigma or alternatively to health insurers finding pretexts to deny coverage to an individual (assuming a world without current legal requirements that insurers must take all individuals regardless of preexisting conditions). This could be catastrophic in the wrong environment.

Also, keep in mind that we didn't work very hard on this privacy attack. It was a proof of concept. But even with a simple proof of concept, we can compromise privacy by making probabilistic membership inferences as to the training data.

As I mentioned at the start of this section, a pre-programmed version of this technique is available via an open source project. Consider using that as well as you experiment with your own models to see how vulnerable they may be to a straightforward membership inference attack.

Other Privacy Problems and Attacks

Membership inference is not the only privacy issue presented by a machine learning model from the perspective of security.[4] Let's briefly discuss two other privacy-related considerations:

Data leaks

> In one case, given a model and some demographic information, attackers were able to predict a patient's genetic markers (*https://oreil.ly/adRif*). In another case, researchers could extract credit card information from a natural language model (*https://arxiv.org/pdf/1802.08232.pdf*). So this shows that specific elements of data can leak out from a model when that model is overfit, which can sometimes be hard to fully test. Detecting and defending against data leaks remains an open problem, but models that contain more parameters than are needed have more ability to memorize information and result in data leaks. This is often explored through the question of unintended memorization in a model (*https://arxiv.org/pdf/1802.08232.pdf*).

Model inversion

> In model inversion, some of the inputs of training data can be partially reconstructed based on attacks on the model; that is, given a model but not the original training data, a clever operator can extract some of that data. We can imagine that sensitive data may thus be extracted even though such data was only used with permission for model training and not with the anticipation that it, perhaps including private information, would be retrievable simply via access of the

---

4 That is, assuming that the model itself was built appropriately and in a fairness-aware manner, we now ask only whether others can still misuse it.

resulting model. This is clearly a complicated and difficult proceeding, but in cases where this is possible, we can see results as shown in Figure 9-3.

Figure 9-3. A model inversion: a photographic input is reconstructed to a high degree of precision—certainly enough to violate the privacy of the person in the photograph[5]

Model extraction

Model extraction results from attacks whereby an adverse party would seek to extract not bits of information from the training data but rather more about the underlying logic of the model. This could constitute a privacy violation in revealing general information about the training pool—information that really should remain private. Defending against model extraction remains an open problem, not only for privacy but also for the self-interested desire of the organization or engineer designing a model to protect the work and property value of that model.

Important Privacy Techniques

We've covered some specialized considerations of how model training and deployment could enable attacks that can extract data about or even from the underlying data set. This points to privacy concerns you should consider for model deployment.

You should also have concerns about how best to train your model or process a data set for release. Standard and well-known methodologies can address these issues—not out-of-the-box perfect solutions, but a series of conceptual tools and algorithmic implementations that allow you to incorporate such tools in your practice. However, a detailed and domain-specific analysis will be necessary to appropriately use these methods:

---

5 Frederikson, M., S. Jha, and T. Ristenpart. "Model Inversion Attacks that Exploit Confidence Information and Basic Countermeasures." *Proceedings of the 22nd ACM SIGSAC Conference on Computer and Communications Security*, (2015).

Differential privacy

I introduced differential privacy in Chapter 2, when discussing broadly how to define privacy. I didn't touch on then that models can be trained in a way that incorporates differential privacy—namely, by the use of specific algorithms that respect certain privacy settings involved in the definition of differential privacy. Additionally, these often come with a *privacy budget*, whereby different elements of a machine learning modeling process may successively "cost" privacy, but an engineer can ensure they don't go over the privacy budget. Some tools are already available to do this, and two worth investigating are IBM's differential privacy library (*https://oreil.ly/8ttDY*) and Facebook's experimental PyTorch implementation with differential privacy (*https://oreil.ly/4ytfB*). Both projects are under active development but already provide enough functionality to incorporate into standard industry use cases. Most important to understand is that differential privacy applies to *processes* performed with data. Differential privacy should be considered when you are thinking about how to report results about data or train models with data.

k-anonymity

I also discussed k-anonymity in Chapter 2. Now that we are further along in our discussion of privacy and fairness generally, the key notion to keep in mind here is that k-anonymity applies to *data sets* but not to processes. So k-anonymity and related techniques should be your go-to tool when you are thinking about how to make a data set itself secure, perhaps if you are going to publicly release a data set or even if you are simply going to open it more broadly within your organization.

Concluding Remarks

In the pre-ML era, concerns about preserving privacy in digital products was focused on topics in cryptography and systems security. Those remain serious concerns, but as ML products come into wider use, they create new routes for adversarial parties to attack products and compromise privacy. ML engineers have an obligation to test their models for vulnerability to privacy attacks and keep up-to-date on existing attacks and vulnerabilities implicated in the ML architectures or data sets they use.

You may be deeply concerned about antidiscrimination but not necessarily about privacy. It's a fuzzy topic related to external attackers rather than a concrete problem in an existing data set. Yet privacy is just as intrinsic to fairness in digital products and ML modeling as antidiscrimination is. Too often data scientists leave it to the systems security people at their organizations. While you should absolutely defer to security experts who specialize in systems security and cryptographic challenges, it's important to recognize the threats to privacy that emerge from the act of modeling, as is done in ML. Recognizing this threat and learning about best practices to address the most likely privacy attacks in ML will be essential to the ethical data scientist's toolkit.

CHAPTER 10
ML Models and Security

Security is not altogether separate from privacy, but in the context of this discussion, I approach security as a specific problem: when we release a model in which an adversary is able to make it behave in a way we did not anticipate. I speak broadly of adversarial attacks, for example, an adversary is able to engineer an incorrect classification with a specific incorrect target in mind.

In one example, merely rotating photographs of potentially cancerous lesions changed the results of a machine learning classification as to whether the image showed a cancerous lesion. As Beat Buesser pointed out at a PyCon UK presentation in 2018 (*https://oreil.ly/HF7HL*), rotating an image is hardly illegal, so this shows just how easily some machine learning algorithms can be gamed with legal and seemingly legitimate manipulations.

Importantly, this brief discussion of security aspects of machine learning in no way provides any sort of checklist for your own security considerations, for a number of reasons. First, security related to machine learning goes far beyond aspects of machine learning itself. For example, good data protection and cybersecurity measures are obviously a fundamental aspect of security for any machine learning product, and we make no discussion of these topics here. Secondly, these topics are quite complex and could themselves, even in the limited range of topics I discuss, easily turn into several books of material.

Security is also a more complex topic than concerns about discrimination. With discrimination, generally we have a metric we train to. We may discover that the metric is wrong for some reason we didn't understand about a specific data set, but the outcome can be transparent if we are looking for it, and we can incrementally improve toward the target we establish. In contrast, with security, our mantra is writ large: "be safe." But this is not easy to accomplish when an attack can come in any form and from any direction. This is why security is such a challenging and multifaceted topic and one for which there is no perfect solution.

Evasion Attacks

There are a variety of black-box evasion attacks. There are attacks in which specific data examples are crafted in response to an existing model to make a misclassification from the model quite likely, preferably in a way that is undetectable to an observer looking at the data. The most famous example is the first published one, "Explaining and Harnessing Adversarial Examples," shown in Figure 10-1.[1]

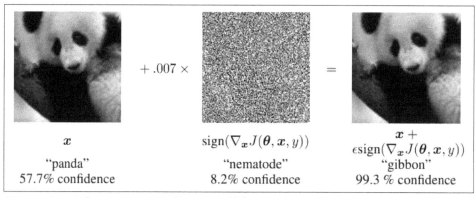

Figure 10-1. A famous example from Goodfellow et al., in which a panda was transformed into a gibbon even though the human eye still sees only a panda; the attacks fool the model and the human because it gives the wrong label, but the human doesn't know this will happen

Nor are evasion attacks limited to the digital world. In 2018, Eykholt et al.'s "Robust Physical-World Attacks on Deep Learning Visual Classification" developed a method to develop physical adversarial examples,[2] which resulted in the misclassification of stop signs in 100% of lab examples and field tests for one neural network architecture and more than 80% in the case of another architecture. In either case, these are terrifying examples because the researchers showed that simply by applying a carefully designed sticker to a stop sign, which looks to the human eye like a plausible example of graffiti or otherwise commonplace illicit but unsophisticated defacement of public property, they could manipulate the outputs of sophisticated image-analyzing neural

---

1 Goodfellow, Ian J., et al. "Explaining and Harnessing Adversarial Examples." Paper presented at ICLR 2015, San Diego, California, 2015. *https://arxiv.org/pdf/1412.6572.pdf*.

2 Eykholt, Kevin, et al. "Robust Physical-World Attacks on Deep Learning Visual Classification," Paper presented at the 2018 Conference on Computer Vision and Pattern Recognition, Salt Lake City, Utah, 2018. *https://arxiv.org/pdf/1707.08945.pdf*.

network architecture that might plausibly be integrated into self-driving cars. In Figure 10-2, you can see just how inoffensive the physical manipulation looked.

Figure 10-2. A famous example of a physical evasion attack that could lead to disastrous consequences from Eykholt et al.

Chen et al. helpfully discuss that quite a variety of adversarial evasion attacks occur on machine learning models and note that the variations can be classified according to three categories:[3]

- The similarity metric (for example, an L-2 norm or an L-infinity norm), for which the method optimizes examples

- Goal of the attack

  — A *targeted* attack seeks to push the classification toward a specific wrong answer. This might be used, for example, if bad actors wanted all stop signs to be classified as 65 MPH speed limit signs, resulting in a specific and quite bad outcome.

  — An *untargeted attack* seeks to push the classification toward an incorrect classification without any specific target. This might be used, for example, if a bad actor simply wanted to reduce the performance of a model generally. Perhaps a bad actor would push an image classification algorithm used by a self-driving car to be wrong in some way, which could result in life-threatening mayhem but could equally result in unduly cautious or inexplicable conduct

3 Chen, Jianbo, et al. "HopSkipJumpAttack: A Query-Efficient Decision-Based Attack." arXiv.org, April 28, 2020. *https://arxiv.org/pdf/1904.02144.pdf*.

(such as driving slower than is marked or stopping in the middle of the highway).

- The threat model
  — A *white-box model* allows the attacker to observe the model architecture and parameters
  — A *black-box model* allows the attacker to see only model inputs and outputs
    — A decision-based black-box model allows the attacker to see only the final output of the algorithm. So, for example, with an image classification algorithm, this would allow the attacker to see only the final label. Or for a binary decision-making algorithm, this would allow the attacker to see only the final decision. The attacker would not have a numerical score indicating the algorithm's relative confidence of the decision or classification.
    — A score-based black-box model is more open than a decision-based black-box model. In this case, the attacker can see the penultimate layer of the algorithm, which usually corresponds to estimates of the relative probabilities of the discretely enumerated list of possibilities.

Figure 10-3 depicts the various architectural components of a neural network model, with respect to what forms of attacks can access those components.

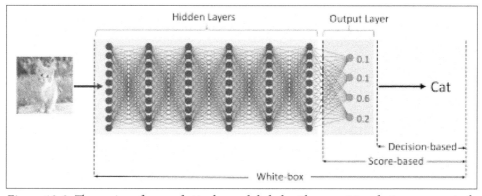

Figure 10-3. The various forms of attacks are labeled with respect to what component of the model they access

How It Works

We will use the HopSkipJumpAttack of Chen et al. While the mathematical details are a little heavy to cover in depth here, we will sketch out the overall approach before proceeding to the code demonstration. The particular advantage of the method proposed by Chen et al. is that it requires fewer queries to the black-box model, resulting in an attack that is more efficient from the attacker's perspective and less dependent on API calls. This is also notable because many black-box models may be rate- or volume-limited, in part to defend against such attacks. However, as black-box attacks are able to produce better attack examples with fewer API calls, this defense will be more limited.

The main insight Chen et al. have that allows them to improve on other attacks is the following. An earlier successful decision-based black-box targeted attack relied on beginning with a perturbed sample that was already in the target class (the wrong but desired label class). Then random perturbations were added to the target that would take it back to the original image (so as to minimize the obvious divergence from the class that would be expected). If the perturbations kept the sample in the target class, they were kept; but otherwise, they were thrown away. Chen et al.'s insight is that even if these perturbations do not keep the sample in the target class, they nonetheless provide information to estimate the gradient near the decision boundary. Figure 10-4 shows the steps by which HopSkipJump identifies promising perturbations for adversarial attacks against a black-box model.

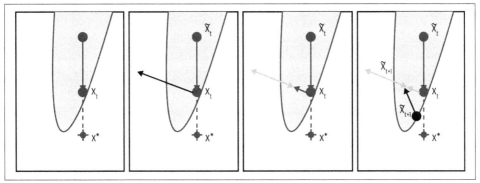

Figure 10-4. The four steps of the HopSkipJumpAttack algorithm[4]

4 Source: J. Chen, M.J Jordan, and M. Wainwright, "HopSkipJumpAttack: A Query-Efficient Decision-Based Attack," 2020, *https://arxiv.org/pdf/1904.02144.pdf*.

Chen et al. do quite a bit of mathematical work to show the validity and basis of their method. We won't go through that, but you can find those details in the original paper (*https://arxiv.org/pdf/1904.02144.pdf*). The core parts boil down to the three-step approach depicted in Figure 10-4, which includes the following necessary steps:

1. Perform a binary search from the current estimated point x_t to the target point on the other side of the decision boundary, X^*.

2. Estimate the gradient at the boundary point identified from the boundary search, and move back into the desired decision area away from the decision boundary.

3. Follow a geometric procession along the gradient and update $x_t \rightarrow \tilde{x}_{t+1}$.

4. Perform a binary search again to find the new binary point, beginning the cycle anew.

We need a Monte Carlo method to estimate the gradient at the decision boundary based on a number of independent and identically distributed (iid) draws at that boundary, as well as a mathematical expression that guarantees a limit on the bias of the estimate achieved with the Monte Carlo method. Because the Monte Carlo method for estimating the gradient direction is valid only near the decision boundary, however, the process needs to make the estimate for points near the boundary.

Chen et al. develop a method for conducting a binary search that begins with a decision point in the target class, which can determine a pairing with a point in the original class. Then a binary search can be conducted to arrive within a preset threshold distance of the decision boundary. This gradient direction can be used to find a place in the target class at an appropriate distance from the decision boundary, but also removed from the decision boundary along the gradient direction, to ensure a maximal difference in the decision-affecting parameters while keep a minimal distance to observers. The step size taken along this gradient direction must also be calculated.

What Is iid?

Iid is statistical shorthand for *independent and identically distributed*. This means we take many samples from the same underlying system (more formally, the same underlying probability distribution), and the value measured in one sample is independent of the value measured in the next sample.

If you learn nothing else from this book, the notion of iid is valuable for two reasons. First, from a fairness perspective, this can serve as a helpful reminder that each individual is a separate draw from an underlying probability distribution, so we should by default be wary of making inferences of one random variable based on another. (This comes with a lot of caveats, of course.) Second, from a bottom-line perspective, I find that in real-world applications, humans are very bad at remembering that iid samples truly are independent. Think about games of chance involving cards. I often hear people say, "What are the odds they would have the ace *again*," as though a previous game should matter. Statistically it shouldn't, and players who can remember that fact tend to prevail over those who think the universe has some kind of memory. In fact, many games and other questions in life are more like iid random variables.

From this we have the HopSkipJumpAttack:

Hop
    The binary search to get near the decision boundary, beginning with a sample generated to be in the target space

Skip
    Determining the direction of the gradient at the decision by Monte Carlo estimation

Jump
    Jumping away from the decision boundary with the appropriate size

Code Demonstration

We begin with standard imports, with the main ones coming from IBM's art module:

```
import numpy as np
import matplotlib.pyplot as plt

from sklearn.svm import SVC
from sklearn.pipeline import Pipeline
from sklearn.model_selection import GridSearchCV

from art.estimators.classification import SklearnClassifier
from art.attacks.evasion import HopSkipJump

import aif360
import pandas as pd
from sklearn.model_selection import train_test_split
```

We download data from the UCI Machine Learning Repository on detecting human occupancy in a room (*https://oreil.ly/78WfH*), and save this to a local file. We then read this in and inspect:

```
df = pd.read_csv("datatraining.txt")
df[10:20]
```

Figure 10-5 gives us a sense of what the data looks like.

	date	Temperature	Humidity	Light	CO2	HumidityRatio	Occupancy
11	2015-02-04 18:01:00	23.075	27.150000	419.0	690.25	0.004741	1
12	2015-02-04 18:02:00	23.100	27.100000	419.0	691.00	0.004739	1
13	2015-02-04 18:03:00	23.100	27.166667	419.0	683.50	0.004751	1
14	2015-02-04 18:04:00	23.050	27.150000	419.0	687.50	0.004734	1
15	2015-02-04 18:04:59	23.000	27.125000	419.0	686.00	0.004715	1
16	2015-02-04 18:06:00	23.000	27.125000	418.5	680.50	0.004715	1
17	2015-02-04 18:07:00	23.000	27.200000	0.0	681.50	0.004728	0
18	2015-02-04 18:08:00	22.945	27.290000	0.0	685.00	0.004728	0
19	2015-02-04 18:08:59	22.945	27.390000	0.0	685.00	0.004745	0
20	2015-02-04 18:10:00	22.890	27.390000	0.0	689.00	0.004730	0

Figure 10-5. Sample data we will work with from the UCI Machine Learning Repository's Occupancy Detection data set

We break the data into inputs and outputs and scale these:

```
X = df.iloc[:, 1:6]
y = df.iloc[:, 6]

## standardize
Xmin = np.min(X, axis = 0)
Xmax = np.max(X, axis = 0)

def scale(X_var):
    return (X_var–Xmin) / (Xmax–Xmin)

def unscale(X_var):
    return X_var * (Xmax–Xmin) + Xmin

X_scaled = scale(X)
```

We then break the data into training and testing data sets, as we have throughout:

```
X_train, X_test,
y_train, y_test = train_test_split(X_scaled,
                                   y,
                                   test_size   = 0.2,
                                   random_state = 18)
```

In this example we'll also take advantage of the `art` module's built-in support for `sklearn`. We will train a model using `sklearn`'s implementation of support vector classification (SVC), and what's more, we can put this inside an `sklearn` pipeline so you can also see how you could integrate an even more complicated pipeline:

```
svc = SVC(C=1.0, kernel='rbf')
pipeline = Pipeline(steps=[('svc', svc)])
```

We then conduct a grid parameter search:

```
param_grid = {'svc__C': np.logspace(-4, 4, 5)}
search = GridSearchCV(estimator  = pipeline,
                      param_grid = param_grid,
                      iid        = False,
                      cv         = 5)
search.fit(X_train, y_train)
print("Best parameter (CV score=%0.3f):" % search.best_score_)
print(search.best_params_)
```

This results in the following output:

```
Best parameter (CV score=0.992):
{'svc__C': 10000.0}
```

We can also inspect the model's performance to know what the baseline performance is on this simple model:

```
accuracy_test_benign = search.score(X_test, y_test)
print('Accuracy on benign test samples %0.2f' %
      (accuracy_test_benign * 100))
```

This produces the following output:

```
Accuracy on benign test samples 99.20.
```

That's good news—we can build a highly accurate model! Considering that determining room occupancy could be a fairly critical application (such as routing police officers to the rooms last known to be occupied during an emergency or allocating electricity only to occupied rooms), we can imagine that a model with poor performance could result in too many inconveniences or dangers to be allowed. That probably isn't the case here. However, we can fairly ask, what about attacking this model? That's what we'll do now.

First, we move our classifier into the `art` module's expected object. We also initialize the attack object, which requires the classifier object for its initialization:

```
classifier = SklearnClassifier(model=search.best_estimator_)
attack = HopSkipJump(classifier=classifier, targeted=False, norm=np.inf,
                     max_iter=100, max_eval=100, init_eval=100, init_size=100)
```

We then generate 50 adversarial examples. Be careful not to generate too many examples, as this will take some time (at least it did on my reasonably powerful laptop):

```
X_test_adv = attack.generate(X_test[:50])
```

The examples generated fully defeat the seemingly excellent classifier:

```
accuracy_test_adversarial = search.score(X_test_adv, y_test[:50])
print('Accuracy on adversarial test samples {}%:'.format(
    accuracy_test_adversarial * 100))
```

```
Accuracy on adversarial test samples 0.00
```

Finally, we can see whether these examples look putatively reasonable (not that we are experts on the physiology and physics of occupied versus unoccupied rooms, but let's see where the data leads us).

For this reason, we convert our adversarial outputs into a DataFrame and scale it back as well as scaling the original test data back to its normal values:

```
X_test_adv = unscale(pd.DataFrame(X_test_adv, columns = X_test.columns.values))
X_test_adv.head()

X_test = unscale(X_test)
```

We can then plot and compare the distributions to see whether anything jumps out, as is done in the following analysis, conducted via a series of visualizations.

If we plot a histogram of the temperature values for the first 50 test data points as compared to the adversarial evasion data points, we do see some difference in the distribution, although nothing that would necessarily raise suspicions to a casual observer.

We can compare the distributions of temperature for both the test data (Figure 10-6) and adversarial data generated from the test data (Figure 10-7).

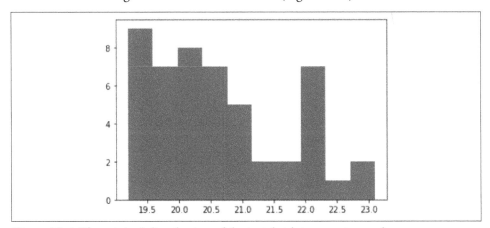

Figure 10-6. The original distribution of the test data's temperature values

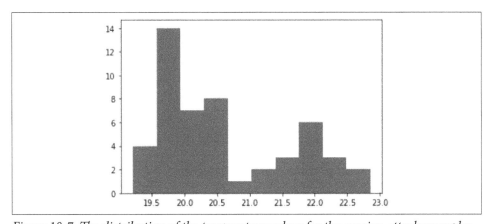

Figure 10-7. The distribution of the temperature values for the evasion attack examples

Likewise, we can see differences if we plot the original data points against their adversarial perturbations, as I do in Figure 10-8. The data points that don't fall along the $y = x$ line show how the adversarial data points are distorted from the original data points, with the y-axis showing the adversarial perturbation. Notably, none of these are particularly dramatic, as is consistent with the premise of most adversarial attacks, which keep the perturbations relatively small so as to elude notice of a human observer.

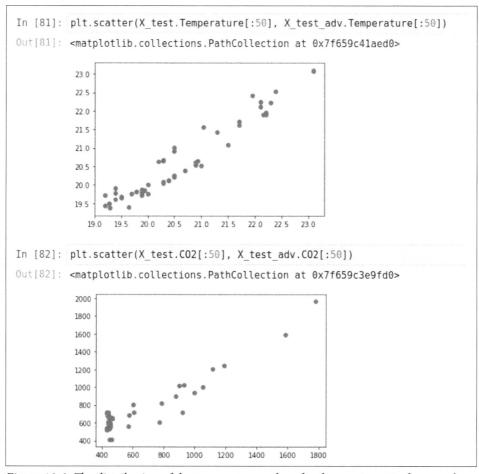

Figure 10-8. *The distribution of the temperature values for the evasion attack examples*

We can also consider whether the attack results in changes of the relationships of different variables within the original test data set as compared to the adversarial attack examples that result. We see these in Figure 10-9.

```
In [83]: plt.scatter(X_test_adv.Temperature[:50], X_test_adv.CO2[:50])
Out[83]: <matplotlib.collections.PathCollection at 0x7f659c392cd0>
```

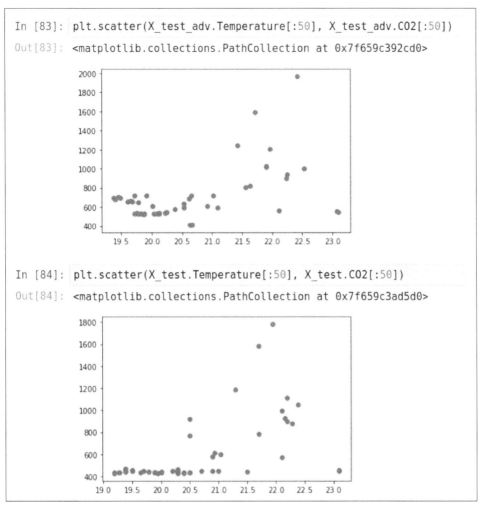

```
In [84]: plt.scatter(X_test.Temperature[:50], X_test.CO2[:50])
Out[84]: <matplotlib.collections.PathCollection at 0x7f659c3ad5d0>
```

Figure 10-9. Plotting two attributes of the test and adversarial test examples against one another to get an idea of how the adversarial attack affected the relationship between variables within the adversarial attack data set as compared to the original data set

Defending Against Adversarial Attacks

The preceding sections have discussed one recently developed method that can be used to attack black-box models to efficiently generate adversarial examples for performing an evasion attack. There are many proposed methods for black-box attacks and even more for white-box attacks. Hopefully, awareness of the ease of applying these attacks to models will enhance your caution as you develop models that might ultimately be rolled out in a way that provides an interface that would enable such attacks. However, we have yet to discuss potential solutions to this problem. Awareness of the problem is a good thing, but what can be done?

Researchers have identified the importance of developing robust machine learning models through showing that such attacks are more likely to succeed on models that are overfit, because these models tend to develop decision contours that are highly specific and difficult for individuals to understand but easy for such attacks to locate and manipulate.

One way to fight back against such attacks is with adversarial training. Specifically, you can use known attack methods to generate adversarial examples. Then you can add these adversarial examples to your training data with their correct labels rather than with the labels that an already trained model might provide. Some examples of this training are available in `art`'s set of examples (*https://oreil.ly/ZA67c*).

Such a basis for adversarial training is a start, but more important is the use of provably robust or near-r robust architectures or training methods that encourage robust models. A recently developed tutorial, "Adversarial Robustness—Theory and Practice" (*https://oreil.ly/jwu7J*), that was given at NeurIPS 2018 discusses these. In this tutorial the researchers present some helpful results with provably robust methods. They also point out that in addition to enhancing the defenses against known adversarial attacks, there are other benefits to robust or more robust models. One such result seems to be that the features emerging from complex neural networks are more semantically meaningful to human observers, likely because the models are generalizing more, resulting in fewer strange niches or kinks in the decision boundaries.

Not only is this a benefit in itself, but it can also result in some very cool effects. For example, the tutorial highlights the work of Brock, Donahue, and Simonyan,[5] who develop a GAN model with robustness-related training methodologies and show that these can also result in semantically interesting generative capabilities, as shown in Figure 10-10.

Figure 10-10. Impressive, seemingly natural transitions between a bird and a dog are produced by a GAN trained with robustness enhancing methods

---

5 Brock, A., J. Donahue, and K. Simonyan, "Large Scale GAN Training For High Fidelity Natural Image Synthesis," 2019, *https://arxiv.org/pdf/1809.11096.pdf*.

Some Evasion Attack Packages

Throughout this book we rely heavily on modules prepared by IBM. They have a variety of rubrics but share commonalities in the approach to their documentation and in the availability of IBM staff to maintain the open source modules and associated Slack channels. These projects were chosen in part because they are quite accessible to people new to these ideas and because they have a large and sophisticated technology company serving to quality control and implement much of the code.

However, for most of the problems we address and the techniques implemented to showcase them or defend against them, you can look to other projects and open source code bases. Here I'll describe briefly just a few such libraries, and you will no doubt find more as you develop experience in this area and look to what is available.

CleverHans

This library is maintained by Ian Goodfellow and Nicolas Papernot, two leading researchers in the field of developing adversarial evasion attacks. The organizational sponsors are Google AI, OpenAI, and Pennsylvania State University. The library supports adversarial testing of models developed with PyTorch, TensorFlow2, or JAX (another Google library that supports automated differentiation of native numpy or Python functions). CleverHans has numerous upsides in addition to its robust and star-studded list of contributors and organizations. These include the following:

- The example notebooks are relatively sparse but are continuously tested to guarantee that the example code still runs even as the API is upgraded.

- Convenient helper functions to load commonly used data sets and perform common basic model training in preparation to test adversarial examples.

- Easy options to perform adversarial training with easy interface design.

- Beautiful and easy-to-read code with standard formatting options strictly enforced.

- Coverage of cutting-edge adversarial evasion attacks, often contributed by the original developers of the methods.

Foolbox

This project is supported by the Bethge Lab, which has a focus on "perceiving neural networks," which common sense indicates would also include perceiving the faults exposed by adversarial evasion attacks. As with CleverHans, Foolbox works with PyTorch, TensorFlow2, and JAX models. Foolbox also works with models implemented in numpy. Advantages of Foolbox include the following:

- Very easy-to-use and accessible interface both for crafting evasion attacks and for useful evaluations, such as visualizations.

- Foolbox runs natively for all the APIs it supports because it is written in EagerPy, a framework with a wrapper around all these other APIs.

- A convenient `foolbox.zoo` option provides a way for any repository that implements the appropriate protocol to make pre-trained models appropriate for easy retrieval via the Foolbox API.

- Foolbox provides a wide range of cutting-edge, decision-based (black-box) and gradient-based (white-box) adversarial attacks implemented by academic researchers.

- Foolbox's API is so universal that it's easy to do relatively complex attacks, such as train and test attacks, either to ensemble them against a model or to see the relative strengths of different attacks.

Why Do Evasion Attacks Matter to You?

This chapter provided only a short overview of how one adversarial attack works as well as examples from potential real-world threats that occur. So far, there isn't a published example of an adversarial attack being used for crime or unfairness, but that doesn't mean such attacks are not being used and are not succeeding. Consider that, similar to other forms of digital compromise, businesses do not have an incentive to report these attacks unless they are legally obligated to do so.

One of the reasons that legislation requires companies to report data breaches to those affected is that, absent such a duty, a company would have no incentive to make public such an embarrassment (and potential lapse of good judgment and good practices). The public acknowledgment could open the company to bad public relations and perhaps even legal liability.

Likewise, we can imagine that companies may have experienced these attacks (almost certainly) and detected that they had been subject to such attacks (less likely but has probably happened). However, since companies do not have any obligation to report an evasion attack, successful or not, on their algorithmic systems, we likely wouldn't know about such attacks. Eventually we can expect that an example will become public, but we can assume in the meantime that this *is* happening.

We know that some very sophisticated attacks have been developed by just a few academics and trained on relatively accessible hardware, so we can imagine that small actors could perpetrate these attacks, but let's also think of some large-scale actors who could have the incentive to perpetrate such attacks.

Hostile governments attempting to integrate misinformation campaigns into their arsenal of attacks on adversary nations would have incentives to evade "fake news detectors" or other forms of speech classification. Online platforms, of course, may be seeking to cut back on divisive rhetoric, racist language, unsubstantiated but purportedly factual claims, and other forms of undesirable speech, either because of a legal duty or because of a desire to keep a platform of relatively high quality to retain users.

Large, sophisticated groups of cybercriminals may be seeking to take over credit card accounts and to maximize the amount of credit extended to these cards. By perpetrating evasion attacks, both to get a higher credit limit than would otherwise be available and to avoid any fraud-detection measures in place, the cybercriminals would no doubt reap a larger reward.

A tech company's competitor in the same sector might seek to make that company look bad by cleverly crafting evasion attacks that might become public, either through the competitor's publication (look how bad Company X's image classification service is) or because the company itself aggregates its results and in some way or other makes them public. Or a competitor might use an evasion attack to monopolize a company's resources, making it unable to respond to and identify real customers or real problems and forcing it to spend compute power on the evasion attacks.

As discussed, research into how to resist such evasion attacks is ongoing, and as with other challenges in machine learning, the no free lunch theorem applies—namely, we have no one-size-fits-all solution. However, we do know that research into provably robust machine learning models will be resistant to an adversarial attack no matter its form (even ones that have not been invented yet) and will have provable bounds on the degree of their vulnerability. When you are in a position to adapt such models, which are cutting-edge and not yet commonly used, you should do so with the knowledge that, depending on the application, you may have formidable adversaries who are keen to abuse either your employer or downstream users of your work product as they strategically manipulate inputs into any public APIs of a machine learning model.

Poisoning Attacks

Another important form of adversarial attack is a *poisoning attack*. A poisoning attack manipulates not data that will be used for inference (an evasion attack), but rather data that will be used for *training*. Importantly, poisoning attacks are a relatively old problem, but they are newly relevant as deep learning emerges as the dominant model for machine intelligence and as the emphasis on data, including data gathered in the wild, becomes only greater over time.

Poisoning attacks come in at least two forms: those intended to degrade model performance altogether (attacks on model integrity), and those intended to predictably misclassify specific instances or types of instances in a model (backdoor attacks).

As with adversarial evasion attacks, you can use many attack models when developing algorithms for poisoning attacks. Here are a few. Can the labels of the data be manipulated? Can the data itself be manipulated? What will the party know about/control about the training process?

We won't go through a code example of a poisoning attack, but poisoning attacks are available pre-implemented in the IBM adversarial robustness toolbox (`art`) as well as in a few other packages that are briefly discussed in the next section. We will also briefly cover a few separate poisoning attacks that have been developed in recent years.

How They Work

Poisoning attacks, like adversarial evasion attacks, are an ongoing and relatively new area of research. Such poisoning attacks come in a variety of flavors, with some requiring more information or having more far-reaching consequences than others. Here are a variety of ways to classify attacks and a variety of scopes of definition here for background information:

Availability attacks on specific models
> Availability attacks are designed to make a model completely unavailable, such as through poisoned training data that distorts the decision boundary so that the model is no longer useful and cannot determine an appropriate decision boundary at all. This is a very generic name for a class of attacks on models that can take many forms. Availability attacks on a laundry list of machine learning models have been developed for decades. For example, specific attacks were used to undermine the overall performance of support vector machines, or SVMs (*https://arxiv.org/abs/1206.6389*), and Bayesian networks (*https://oreil.ly/udQIQ*).

Poisoning attacks on pre-trained models
> A variety of attacks have been demonstrated in the case of pre-trained models, such as in a paper showing that such attacks are possible even with limited knowledge of the training methods and data used in the original model.[6] Poisoning attacks on pre-trained models are an important scenario because of the widespread existence of model zoos in machine learning, particularly in the deep learning field. In natural language processing and image classification tasks, using a fundamental model is quite common—often with subsequent fine tuning to suit a model for a particular purpose. The danger is that some methods can poison the pre-trained model in a way that is robust to fine tuning, such that

---

6 Biggio, Battista, et al. "Poisoning Attacks against Support Vector Machines." arXiv.org, March 25, 2013. *https://arxiv.org/pdf/1206.6389.pdf*.

models downloaded from a repository could already carry the makings of a backdoor attack that would remain available even after fine tuning.

Clean label attacks, generally

A clean label attack is a poisoning attack in which the poisoned data that introduces a back door into a model is likely to pass human inspection, hence the name, while nonetheless introducing a back door into a model for the attacker to control the model once it is in production. This attack is relatively new with respect to proof-of-concept, but it is particularly worrying and insidious. Even if a human inspected the poisoned data, they would be very unlikely to spot any potential threats. This form of attack was described by Shafahi et al. in a recent paper.[7] They describe an attack in which, rather than the label of the poisoned data being modified, a poisoned input is left available regardless of its label, which can result in creating a back door in a neural network. The purpose is to trick a model so that a poisoned data point will be labeled with an incorrect label at test time.

This list is far from comprehensive, but is meant to give you a sense of the scale and variety of poisoning attacks and to show just how influential a few poison data points could potentially be, particularly when models are trained in complete ignorance of this potential vulnerability and without any defensive measures or quality control.

Defenses Against Poisoning Attacks

As with evasion attacks, research into defenses against poisoning attacks are a current area of active research given the very real threats that they pose. Researchers have already determined that robust defenses with current methods cannot necessarily prevent data poisoning. For example, let's consider an important paper by Steinhardt et al.[8]

One interesting aspect of their work was to inspect data poisoning vulnerability as a function of a data set rather than simply as a function of a machine learning model or a training methodology. They also pointed out that while one method of assessing vulnerability would be to test a data set and model against a number of poisoning attacks (which is certainly better than nothing as some risk assessment), this could not prevent any mathematical information from empirical assessments, as this would not serve to define the space of possible attacks based on future developments and mathematical possibilities.

---

7 Shafahi, Ali, et al. "Poison Frogs! Targeted Clean-Label Poisoning Attacks on Neural Networks." Paper presented at the 32nd Conference on Neural Information Processing Systems, Montréal, Canada, 2018. *https:// papers.nips.cc/paper/7849-poison-frogs-targeted-clean-label-poisoning-attacks-on-neural-networks.pdf.*

8 Steinhardt, Jacob, et al. "Certified Defenses for Data Poisoning Attacks." arXiv.org, November 24, 2017. *https://arxiv.org/pdf/1706.03691.pdf.*

Steinhardt et al. make some simple assumptions about potential defenses; namely, that outlier removal will be undertaken and that supervised learning will be conducted—training a model to a specific loss metric. Under these fairly general assumptions, they then determine an upper bound on the efficacy of any data poisoning attack, a useful metric for any organization that needs to understand its vulnerability to such attacks. They then showed that the vulnerability to poisoning as far as the mathematical upper bound of poisoning efficacy depended on the qualities of the data set. Some data sets had little vulnerability, while others could have wide swings, such as the possibility of an attack increasing the error rate from 12% to 23%—with only a 3% poisoned data rate—on the IMDb sentiment corpus. Because of space constraints, we do not offer an overview of the mathematics in this model or the implementation, but the authors released code (*https://oreil.ly/FQR_N*) that enables you to replicate the results and to test your own data sets.

In addition to using a technique such as the one described by Steinhardt et al. to assess the vulnerability of a specific training data set and model, a range of *data sanitization* defenses can be used. Many of these are consistent with good data practices, such as integrating domain knowledge to formally limit what kinds of data and values of data are acceptable (e.g., in a clustering exercise, domain knowledge should point to location of clusters) and to remove data points that could obviously skew the data (outlier removal). There are also domain-specific examples, such as not allowing a natural language model to drift too far from a model established by a baseline corpus. Finally, there can be production time defenses, such as adding noise to any inputs to the model, partly to reduce the option of someone accessing the model to take advantage of any backdoor defenses that have slipped through security procedures.

Some Poisoning Attack Packages

Now let's briefly survey a few Python modules that implement poisoning attacks. These are not the only modules that do so, but these can be a good place to start if you are interested in learning more and testing your own models against their vulnerability to a variety of well-known poisoning attacks:

Adversarial Robustness Toolbox (ART)
We have used IBM's open source Python modules throughout this book, including the `art` module (for evasion attacks). This module implements a handful of data poisoning attacks, so this could be a good place to start when experimenting with poisoning attacks. The module includes example notebooks to show off the currently implemented poisoning attacks, including showing their performance with common models and data sets. The poisoning attacks offered by `art` include feature collision (a relatively new but surprisingly effective attack that works even on quite sophisticated models), an SVM-specific attack, and a backdoor attack that can be used in the case of a pre-trained model or an outsourced data set that includes pixel-specific manipulations to create a back door.

`secml`

The `secml` module is similar to `art` in offering a variety of evasion attacks and poisoning attacks. It is also similar to modules such as `Foolbox` because it offers its own model zoo for ease of use. `secml` currently implements model-specific poisoning attacks for linear regression, logistic regression, and SVM. `secml` is under active development, so more poisoning attacks might now be available.

Why Do Poisoning Attacks Matter to You?

If you've read the previous sections, you can see that poisoning could affect anyone collecting data of any kind from the internet to assemble a training data set. You could also use someone else's training data without having full knowledge of its assembly (e.g., if you use common data sets from machine learning repositories). Or, poisoning could happen if you are running an extremely large data repository and seeking to grow through additional user contributions.

As with evasion attacks, we can imagine obvious examples of this occurring:

- Many natural language models are built with publicly collected data. For example, many companies scrape Reddit and other online discussion forums for samples of natural language. But we also know that such forums, despite the best efforts of their moderators, are subject to use by hostile agents (both humans and bots) who would likely have the motivation and sophistication to plant poisoned data on these sites.

- Likewise, many image classification data repositories include examples scraped from the internet, including in proprietary data sets (such as those of Clearview AI), but even in the case of academic data sets people have been included without their knowledge or consent.[9] This shows the provenance must be web scraping, but also suggests that mischievous agents could easily add poison even to canonical data sets. Also important is that, unlike evasion attacks, it need not be the case that a poisoned data point is mislabeled, so that human review might not necessarily even detect such an attack.

- Finally, in any industry where we can imagine high-powered but competitive players (quantitative finance, Big Tech, different publishers), we can imagine each entity having the incentive to produce poisons for its competitor, which could degrade our digital environments. (This is reminiscent of the classic problem of misinformation being used by a hostile nation to harm another nation, but where

---

9 For an in-depth review of examples of even the academic community flouting research norms and collecting data without appropriate consent, I recommend Kate Crawford and Trevor Paglen's "Missing Persons" section of "Excavating AI," their history of data-driven AI (*https://www.excavating.ai*).

sometimes the hostile nation's own citizens or other agencies within a government themselves fall victim to the misinformation.)

So you can see many reasons that poisoning attacks might affect your machine learning models directly, without your knowledge, and how they could also be affecting machine learning models that you consume as a programmer using other people's products, as a customer, or as a citizen.

Relationship Between Evasion and Poisoning Attacks

As you have read this, you may have noticed that evasion attacks and poisoning attacks can look very similar. They are indeed similar. A poisoning attack aims to change the decision boundary through data, while an evasion attack aims to pull or push an example across a decision boundary based on determining information about that boundary.

In fact, these two attacks are conceptually linked through this mutual reliance on looking at the gradients at decision boundaries. These boundaries are the Achilles' heel but also the strength of machine learning, and so attacks will all tend to be related to the weakness or vulnerability of a method.

Concluding Remarks

To echo Chapter 9's discussion on privacy, you might not have been thinking of yourself as responsible for best practices related to privacy if you're a software engineer working on digital products, or a data scientist or ML engineer working on data-driven models. And yet, in 2020 so much is known about how to compromise ML models—to make them behave not as they should but as an attacker would want—that attacks are almost as reproducible and routine as the model-building process itself. Unfortunately, in many cases even sophisticated companies have failed to adapt to this new security reality, meaning that many digital products and mission-critical ML models remain alarmingly vulnerable to adversarial attacks.

As in the case of privacy, it is abundantly clear in 2020 (the time of writing) that security must now be taken into account in digital products, not just because of cybersecurity concerns but also security concerns created by the ML modeling process itself. A laundry list of common security problems exists, and we have some known results regarding how to make models that are less vulnerable to these attacks—namely, building more-robust and generalizable models with less-kinky and nuanced decision boundaries. Finally, with open source toolkits to easily test your models against common attacks, you have not just the ability but the obligation to test-drive any models you have that will be publicly available or that will be taking and responding to data from the public.

CHAPTER 11

Fair Product Design and Deployment

For the most part, this book has focused on the data analyst's and machine learning engineer's dilemma. What is fair data to use? What are fair questions to ask? How can models be trained more fairly?

But the reality is that such work will make its way downstream into a product. That product may be what the word most commonly denotes, an actual consumer good or interface of some kind. Maybe it's a game on which people will spend their time. Maybe it's a report that will be made available for management to make decisions about resource allocation. Maybe it's a SaaS that salespeople will go out and start selling to small government offices.

It is imperative that those upstream, producing code and models, think about how their work affects the products that are possible downstream. We have seen a trend of employees at large tech companies feeling deep concern and responsibility for the downstream uses of their work, as evinced by protests at Google, which have been successful (*https://oreil.ly/Pnpr-*), and Amazon, which have not been so succcesful (*https://oreil.ly/KVs3P*) when their employers have serviced contracts for controversial government uses of technology, such as immigration control or warfare.

It's important that the people directly responsible for "product," in whatever form that takes, develop a sense of responsibility and actionable guidelines for thinking about downstream uses of their product once they release it into the stream of commerce and consumption. Usually product managers are driven by and evaluated on KPIs just as technical personnel are, but the product managers' advantage lies in having a broader view of the ultimate uses of machine learning models.

The question of fairness is far broader in product design than in machine learning, in the sense that everything can be a product. So I'm not going to develop a philosophy defining *product* or *fairness* in that context, because that could fill an entire book.

Rather, I'll highlight some of the broad concerns evidenced in industry that are directly connected to upstream machine learning or data analytics work.

We'll treat the question of product deployment as another angle of the same discussion we have been having since Chapter 1. I'll continue with the same concerns we've had from a technical perspective but now think about them qualitatively as we see them manifested in the design or launch of a product built up from basic machine learning ingredients.

In our discussion, I'll work through basic guidelines that should be in place when considering the impact of deploying a model or releasing a product. Then we'll conclude the chapter with a general checklist that you and your team members can build out into a rollout checklist that makes sense for your organization, given the particular worries in your domain and vulnerabilities of your user base. Everything will need to be calibrated to a specific situation.

Reasonable Expectations

One way that product design needs to factor in fairness is to be sure that it complies with the reasonable expectations of end users. This requirement is seen in law from a variety of angles, from the notice and consent regimes that govern handling of personal data to the law of accidents (tort law) as applied to specific products. The general proposition is an intuitive one. If a product looks or acts like a duck, I expect it to continue behaving like a duck, and not, say, a grenade.

This same holds true for the design of digital products. If a product doesn't seem likely to record me while I use it (say, because it's a video game operated with buttons rather than an app that has anything to do with recording), then a reasonable expectation is that it will not be surreptitiously recording my every action. Alas, this may not be such a reasonable expectation given the conditions of the marketplace (*https://oreil.ly/c-vmY*). Notice that I am defining *reasonable* in terms of user expectations and norms rather than empirical realities in a marketplace rife with abuse and a lack of transparency or competition. Likewise, if an app sells itself as a "secure solution" to managing my IoT devices, a reasonable expectation is that the app was built with some knowledge of cybersecurity rather than merely basic undergraduate computer science know-how (which is a lot but unfortunately not enough).

One of the problems regulators struggle with in real-world digital products is exactly how to identify unfair or deceptive business practices. For the most part, we try to enforce rules and norms against inappropriate use of data—for example, with respect to privacy, via a notice and consent model. Essentially, within the limits of the law, businesses are free to do what they like as long as the consumers have a reasonable way of knowing what the business did. For example, for the time being, a website can collect just about any information from us, either directly by inviting us to share that information or indirectly by observing us and collecting metadata. So long as the terms of service make clear in legalese what will happen with data collection, that business can do just about anything it wants with the data, including selling it to our worst enemy (and likely all they'd need to say in their terms of service is "third party").

Yet, regulators and laypeople alike believe that baseline expectations of consumers, the people using a digital product, also matter for interpreting those terms of service. After all, if a practice is not common and might even be offensive, is that practice really included in what is allowed simply because it falls under the heading of fairly generic language? Probably not.

Expectations of Moving Targets

One problem to factor into responsible product design, in addition to reasonable expectations, is how those expectations might shift over time. It's not enough to meet the cybersecurity standards of many years ago. Rather, it's important that the product meet the cybersecurity standards that are relevant now.

Relatedly, it's not enough that the product use AI that was current several years ago. If you are claiming to offer state-of-the-art capabilities, you had better be sure that you are indeed offering them. Be sure to benchmark your performance against competitors and recognize where you might be falling short.

Finally, remember that lay descriptions of technologies tend to overpromise relative to the actual performance of those technologies, even in an era when we sometimes see superhuman capabilities. The press tends to emphasize the amazing aspects of a technology rather than some of its amazingly silly failures. For that reason, when you release products, people seem to expect them to be smarter and abler than they actually are. One example of a potential mismatch between consumer expectations and reality is voice-to-text transcription and artificial understanding of human languages. For example, users of Amazon Alexa and Google Assistant home devices were shocked to find out that people were listening to and transcribing their audio recordings (*https://oreil.ly/nEgSx*). While this may have reflected multiple failures, no doubt part of the misunderstanding arose from people having such high expectations of these devices that perhaps they didn't realize that the development of training data was still necessary.

Clear Communication

A major problem for companies, to ensure they are not guilty of deceptive business practices, is to manage expectations about their products. That partly relates to making sure they are clearly and actively communicating all relevant aspects of their product, and that they are telling the consumer everything the consumer would want to know about the development and operation of that product.

It's particularly essential for technical staff and product managers to be on the same page with respect to fairness. The product should be effectively labeled with respect to its performance. This labeling can be of two kinds, and whether one or both is most appropriate will depend on the situation. One form of labeling would include technical indicators of performance and would likely be most useful for regulators or technical reviewers of the product, perhaps in the case of downstream machine learning applications consuming outputs from some kind of pipeline.

On the other hand, a more intuitive and less jargon-filled explanation of the performance of a product would be needed in the case of laypeople as consumers. What this should look like is still very much a work in progress on the academic side, but it's clear that labeling of some kind is needed. Likely any form of labeling would be better than the current system of providing opaque product outputs without any inkling of what gears are turning behind the scenes.

Fiduciary Obligations

Some academics have argued that businesses collecting data about users and building models about those users might have fiduciary duties to those users. And by the way, let's call them people rather than users while we're at it.[1]

A fiduciary *duty* indicates that one party is obligated to act in the best interests of another party, even when it is at the disadvantage of the party with the obligation. There are different degrees of fiduciary *obligations*, but two examples are that parents generally have a fiduciary obligation to their minor children, and attorneys have a fiduciary obligation to their clients. I briefly mentioned the idea of "information fiduciaries" in Chapter 1.

These obligations come into play when we have a power imbalance. Why might a power imbalance arise in digital products? One purpose of machine learning is to develop superhuman performance, and often the most profitable models and interesting products come about by developing superhuman performance in spheres generally affecting humans, be it medical diagnosis or choosing fashionable outfits or determining someone's mental health status.

That last option should ring some warning bells. That sort of model begins to sound like a doctor and an entity with authority and superior knowledge, which could be dangerous to others. Products that look deep into our selves, diagnosing illnesses or in other ways identifying weaknesses or private information, should ask whether such knowledge imposes obligations. If so, it's important to make sure that products meet those obligations.

---

1 I am as guilty as anyone of "user"-ing people, and have probably repeatedly offended throughout this book. It's a difficult habit to break.

Respecting Traditional Spheres of Privacy and Private Life

Another striking aspect of products over time is the degree to which they have brought the marketplace into every aspect of human life. Goods and privileges that used to be first-come, first-served or acknowledged to belong to everyone are increasingly carved up in ways that help wealthier people save time and energy by avoiding search costs. For example, more than one app has been built to help people "trade" public parking spaces. The idea was that if you were pulling out of a parking space, you might as well let a specific person know and let that person pay you to save the spot for them. In most cities, this was a norm violation that had gone too far, and these apps were banned.

However, we need to probe the thoughts of the people building this product. Might they have asked themselves what would happen if they succeeded? The way I see it, the answer would have shown that they were taking an area of relative equality, at least between people who use public parking spaces, and introducing inequality by adding an economic component to something that is otherwise a matter of time and luck. What's more, we can ask whether this creates real value. Presumably, this app is useful only when parking spaces are scarce, but it doesn't actually create more parking spaces. It simply adds an economic variable to who gets those parking spaces. As a result, the once-neighborly gesture of letting someone know they could have a space would now become a market.

A more recent example is wealthy people using TaskRabbit and similar apps to pay others to wait on line for them for COVID testing (*https://oreil.ly/9iE8b*). This is a particularly problematic and corrosive behavior because, by enabling the wealthy to skip lines and opt out of the usual testing structure, these products remove the most empowered individuals from the political equation. Because wealthy people are able to buy their way out of lines, they are less likely to use political and democratic processes to make the testing process better for everyone. The marketplace in this case corrodes the usually equality-enhancing mechanisms that would otherwise assure a better system for all because wealthy people can buy their way out of a problem.

Likewise, consider the freemium models of products everywhere. They have pushed the marketplace into spheres of life that never used to be there. It used to be that when we called our parents or communicated with our family, we weren't bombarded with advertisements. But now, for example, we may communicate via a variety of forms of social media that embed ads in the screen. We are no longer alone in our private lives, inside our homes, talking to our friends and family, but rather we are constantly in the marketplace.

Part of the problem with the many products built on top of automation and machine learning now is that, because they are not powered at the moment by humans, they can always be available. They can reach out to and disturb us at times that are inappropriate. I've received bills in my email on Christmas, for example. Products that are designed to disturb humans or delve into their private lives without any care in how or when they do so are products that are impinging too far on the norms of everyday life and particularly private life, and that need to be rethought.

Value Creation

While we don't like to admit it, the truth is that some machine learning models probably shouldn't be developed and some products most certainly shouldn't be designed and launched on the basis of those models. That line may vary substantially depending on the part of the world you live in, the kind of background legal rules that are in place where you live, and the social dynamics of a particular place in time. You can't evaluate those social dynamics merely among your own circle either; you need to factor in the many kinds of users who may access your product.

However, the number of products and models that shouldn't exist at all is very, very small, and you can probably think of something sufficiently unfair off the top of your head, so I don't need to provide an example.

A distinct category of products should not be built at all due to their inevitable misuse and abuse: products that have little justification for the ends they are trying to achieve or the means that they use to achieve them. It can be tempting to try to digitize everything and to "apply AI" to "disrupt" and "solve" every problem. I notice the following general trends in such cases:

- Solving the problems of the upper classes because these are easy problems to solve
    - How can I get sushi at 4 a.m. in a booming cosmopolitan city?
    - How can I get someone to pick up my laundry and bring it back without having to talk to them?
- Solving a problem by cloaking the elements of a situation or transaction that make us feel uncomfortable or that seem particularly onerous
    - "Solving" problems digitally when really we are providing a platform to cover unpleasant elements when contracting for human labor. This seems to empower people to think less about the humans doing the work while receiving a traditional service that used to come with more of a social connection and a social contract.
- Redefining a problem as a simpler one so that we can call it solved
    - Upgrading the technical system of a small component of a major transit system to declare a victory, while not updating the major transit system.

Clever words can be used for some of these situations, but those words themselves are still very much within the culture of rewarding technical solutions for problems that pay, regardless of whether those problems really needed solving.

Some will argue that while capitalism may not be a great economic system, it's the least bad one that seems to work. From that perspective, inviting questions regarding value creation is akin to negating the system we have without a better proposal at hand. But such an objection ignores the number of products that are built on venture capital and expectations of gain rather than on actual gain. Increasingly, digital products proliferate for years without market discipline, thanks to venture capital investment bubbles.[2] So even for those who are supportive of the market determining value, we're not actually applying a market system and market discipline in the case of many digital startup products. So if you find yourself building a product that doesn't face market discipline, how might you determine whether the product is offering value?

First, ask yourself whether your product is solving a real problem, and a problem that can't otherwise be "solved." Will someone's life be better because the problem has been removed, or will your product simply create a new expense? Consider the ever-changing apps and accessories children need just to be minimally socially acceptable to their peers, even as in the pandemic-paralyzed world of 2020, millions are losing their jobs and struggling to cover basic expenses. Is your product contributing to that ecosystem of shifting but meaningless demand, or are you offering something genuinely new and useful?

Second, ask yourself whether your product creates value or merely offers cost-cutting or reallocation of existing value, perhaps shifting ever more wealth to the haves at the expense of the have-nots. If you are building an online learning platform, can you articulate why this supplements rather than replaces human teachers? If you are actually replacing human teachers, can you offer compelling evidence as to why this is a good thing?

Third, ask yourself whether your product merely helps users avoid uncomfortable or inconvenient truths. This truth obscuration function can happen with respect to both individual users of the product and institutional factors. At the individual level, an app may help people ignore uncomfortable truths about how little someone is paid to perform a time-consuming or laborious task. At the institutional level, the adaptation of new products rather than the announcement of new policies can bring about actual changes in policy or other law-like decision making that would be protested if passed by more traditional ways of rolling out policies.

---

2 See SoftBank's troubling influence on the startup market (*https://oreil.ly/Jf9yh*), for example.

Complex Systems

An important consideration for both product design and deployment is to try to understand how a product is likely to be received in the real world. Sometimes companies releasing a product show surprisingly little insight or foresight into this question. For example, a company released an electronic breathalyzer that was soon repurposed in a variety of ways, including by young people who turned it into a drinking game (*https://oreil.ly/9d644*). Critics wondered whether this product enabled drunk driving. After all, if you have to take a breathalyzer test to determine whether you can competently drive, that already seems to encourage behavior very near the line of what is legal.

With electronic products that can be developed quickly and for which the mantra is "move fast and break things," there is even less of a concern about misuse or consequences of product releases, or at least less time to consider and observe effects over time. Even before the effect of one version of a product can be fully measured and appreciated, the next big thing is being released. In fact, researchers trying to determine fundamentally important questions, such as whether our current digital environments impede our cognition, have even cited the very fast rollout and adaptation of these products as a difficulty in ever conducting the proper kinds of experiments that would give us an idea of their effects. While this has been true in the past, never have we had products that are so ingrained in our communities, our work, and our very sense of self, as we take them to formerly intimate places such as our beds when we sleep at night.

The Impact of the Product Life Cycle

When we think about iterative life cycles of a product, perhaps we need to slow this down so we can better understand how our product is being used and its effects on the community. Particularly with a product like the electronic breathalyzer I mentioned, perhaps a slower rollout would have shown some of the harm that could be done with such a product.

Hence, when products are being rolled out at a very fast turnover but are quite similar to one another, it bears asking whether every iteration really benefits either the product or the consumer. After all, if sufficient data cannot be accumulated in a transparent and reliable way to measure the performance of the product and allow laypeople to gain knowledge of the product, then we are slowing down the ability of people to learn whether a product works for them and which attributes they value most. It also means that we are cutting off the feedback loop, effectively turning consumers into just that, mere entities who consume rather than entities who can be engaged in an iterative and interactive cycle. People should be given time to evaluate products and see their effects over reasonable lengths of time before new versions are pushed forward merely for the sake of appearing innovative.

The Need for Record Keeping

The technical community has recognized this need (*https://oreil.ly/IEmAi*) to better understand and study how various digital products behave once they are released into the wild. Some consequences can be anticipated, but others can't.

Realistically, products need to do a better job of identifying their origins and explaining how to get information back to those origin points. Products built off of machine learning technologies are increasingly complex, as many APIs and data sources, training methods, and staff with different backgrounds are integrated into different components and modules. As a result, information from downstream will often fail to make it back up to the right person or group for correction, hence ensuring that downstream victims ultimately have no way to correct injustice through a technical or at least frictionless method.

How can we help correct this situation? We can take several independent and straightforward steps. In large part, they rely on treating fairness as an important metric, on par with business indicators. Provide clear documentation of how to get information back upstream about how the product is being used and could be improved with respect to fairness. Let people know downstream about potential fairness pitfalls you could envision given a product's design, or better yet, take steps to ensure the product is immune to those pitfalls or users of the product are unlikely to commit those errors. Make sure that the products you release are studied post-release, with infrastructure set up for downstream people to pass information back about how a product is affecting them, even if they are not direct customers. In general, make sure your fairness metrics are as well maintained and looked over as your business KPIs.

The Need for Experts

When time is of the essence, we have two other obvious ways to better anticipate downstream effects of products. One is to have a more diverse team with diverse perspectives. Another is to seek out the advice and interest of domain experts who know your target population well. Unfortunately, both options sound time-consuming and decidedly uncool in the sense of being old-school, institutionally important methods, but they are that for a reason. Think of many recent fairness failures, and it seems like basic domain expertise was not used, because if it had been, these would have been averted.

Clear Security Promises and Delineated Limitations

Any security expert will disclaim any 100% guarantee of security. Traditionally, indeed, the best way to improve the security of any product has been to hire people to try to break the product. Giving people an incentive, and plenty of time and exposure, usually does the trick to identify more problems and hopefully find a fix.

However, even acknowledging that products cannot be perfectly secure, digital products should come with clearer labeling than most currently do regarding what the company has contemplated but also where the company feels its expertise ends.

Reasonable Expectations of Security

The extent of intrusion into a person's life that a particular product enjoys should factor into both the reasonable expectations a consumer could have about the product and the obligations that a company has to ensure the security.

For example, a product such as a toy that features an IoT component will provide a direct channel to a vulnerable young child. For such products, it is particularly important that cybersecurity measures be of a high standard, or perhaps that the device not be online if the risks are not completely justified. While the upside of such a toy might be an added flavor of interactivity, this does not necessarily justify the risk if we factor into a risk-benefit analysis some of the nasty things hackers have done with young children's connected toys.

Consider recent examples in the media of baby monitors (*https://oreil.ly/J0XkJ*) and toys (*https://oreil.ly/O1fSI*) alike being hacked and used both to observe young children and to speak directly to and even scare them.

Possibility of Downstream Control and Verification

For the moment, those who release data sets, code to train a model, or trained model parameters have little or no control over how that information is used downstream. The control they do have largely relies on contractual agreements, which are not self-enforcing. However, we can imagine that all sorts of creative approaches could be taken to ensure that use of data sets and models could be controlled with technical guarantees rather than merely legal ones.

Verification Systems and Obligations

We won't review the possibilities that are currently offered or what is technically possible. That will always be a moving target and quite specific to the type of product. Instead, as digital products are put out into the online, digital, or IoT stream of commerce, we should think about whether companies will be able to keep adequately monitoring their product and whether feedback, complaints, or corrections will be able to make it back upstream to them.

Likewise, in the case of products that could be put to obvious, or less obvious, misuse, those who design and deploy these products should take steps to control them and ask whether those steps are sufficient. For those who say this is impossible or too difficult, we can look to the creative industries for one example of how, when adequate legal tools are available, such as the Digital Millennium Copyright Act, agents can be empowered to self-help. Just as those releasing artistic works in digital mediums were able to make use of a variety of self-help and enforcement mechanisms to protect their work product and livelihoods, we can imagine the same could be true for machine learning products.

For example, it could be that a data set cannot be fully accessed or downloaded by those who wish to train their data set. Instead, generators or an API would be provided to limit exposure of the data. This could be to ensure some control over how the data is used, perhaps by mandatory audits of downstream users known to have accessed the data, or perhaps by ensuring a licensing agreement whereby one could have the right to inspect products built with the data. How might this prove helpful?

Product Iteration Timelines

If you find that it's necessary to iterate on your product simply to preserve engagement, such as constantly A/B testing new flows to maintain interest, you might ask yourself whether your product is indeed offering value. If the only value of your product is novelty, it may be that you are fooling yourself regarding the technical sophistication of your methods.

Tracking Downstream Users

Perhaps every model should come with mandatory contact information provided, or every entity who downloads a data set should be registered so they can be informed if causal mechanisms are found that indicate exactly what form of discrimination needs to be accounted for. Such mechanisms are used, for example, in baby products as companies encourage end users of the product to mail back contact information should the product be recalled (because of their sensitive nature, baby products are recalled surprisingly often). If those developing digital products recognize a similar responsibility, the battle is already partly won.

Products That Work Better for Privileged People

One astonishing angle of some products is the way that they work blatantly for only some kinds of humans in a way that offends mainstream sensibilities about racial and gender discrimination. Consider, for example, that heart-rate monitors used in smart wearables likely work better for light-skinned people than for dark-skinned people (*https://oreil.ly/HSS9Y*).

This is because heart rate monitors rely on optical (light) measurements to determine heartbeats, and the frequency of light used is absorbed more by dark skin than by light skin. For a user with light skin, more information-carrying light will make it to the device, resulting in greater accuracy, as compared to a user with dark skin. Some might see this as an unfortunate fact of physics rather than a sociological data point, but consider whether the product would ever be brought to market if light-skinned users did not find the product had enough accuracy. Realistically, given the demographic background of IoT users right now, probably not. We can imagine in that case that a workaround of some kind would be found, so the question becomes whether the performance discrepancy rises to a level of unfairness resulting in a regulator stepping in.

In addition to a potential performance discrepancy, we also have an informational failing. Products that might be affected by this or other technical limitations that create disparate impact do not provide any information or guidance as to what kind of performance degradation users with certain physical characteristics might suffer as compared to others. So, for example, when someone with darker skin buys an IoT fitness device, they don't know the value they are getting for their money, as presumably the accuracy metrics are reported for the most favorable circumstances.

This isn't just for new technology, either. Consider that most safety devices and safety standards have typically been set with a prototypical human model of a white male. This has meant that women of all races have systematically not received the full benefit of various safety devices, while paying the same tax rates for government, presumably to fund regulations, and also while paying the same price (or more) for products.

But let's get back to modern tech, with a machine learning flavor. Voice recognition systems generally work better for men than they do for women (*https://oreil.ly/oUaP5*). As with the heart-rate monitoring devices, this is worrying because companies feel comfortable releasing a product even as it has clear deficiencies for an important and discriminated-against component of the population. It is also concerning from the point of view of thinking about consumer choice. In many cases, such as smartphones with voice recognition systems, the market is highly consolidated. Therefore, women (and likewise people with dark skin) don't particularly have a choice as to whether to buy or use a product they know works worse for them. For example, as a woman who wants to buy a new smartphone and faces a market that limits my choices to an Apple or an Android device, I have been disappointed to see reports that in both cases the voice recognition systems likely have a performance disparity. I will pay as much as a man for my smartphone, but a key functionality will work worse for me.

As many technological sectors are increasingly consolidated, as fewer and fewer large companies share a large portion of the economic pie, we have more reason to think that the companies themselves should be thinking about the disparate impact of their product. Perhaps it's less worrying if a product has a niche audience, where there is reason to believe other actors in the market can cater to ignored groups, hence empowering those groups. On the other hand, when a large company like Apple releases a voice recognition system that doesn't perform as well for women as for men, and when this disparity in performance goes on for years, this seems fundamentally unfair.

Part of this disparity likely could have been addressed upstream, using some of the interventions discussed previously. Perhaps the disparity stemmed from a data set problem, as too many men's samples were used in the training set relative to the number of women's samples. Or perhaps the engineers who tested the system were mostly men and tested the product on themselves in early stages when they were exploring different design opportunities.

However, if products are going to be managed and rolled out with all sorts of infrastructure, clearly there should be some room for assessing whether the product works equally, or at least reasonably, well for everyone. Particularly considering that many of these performance features are opaque to individual shoppers, it seems like a very unfair pricing mechanism to knowingly sell products to people who will systematically receive less benefit from these products than will others.

So at every stage of product design, you should be asking, "Are we excluding a particular kind of person?" If so, is that decision (be it an articulated or an unstated decision) based on an exclusion the person could identify before buying your product? If not, are there pricing concessions or disclosures you should offer in advance so that people are buying more in proportion to the benefit they receive? For example, perhaps you could adopt a pricing model wherein services were parceled out and priced so that people who wouldn't benefit from a service didn't have to purchase it.

Plenty of products cater to a particular audience, including a particular gender, ethnicity, or national origin. This is arguably good for a market economy to serve individual needs. The problem with some tech products that have different levels of performance and utility for people in different groups is that such qualities are not transparent. Unlike shampoo developed for certain types of hair, or clothing tailored for particular body shapes, it's not apparent to a purchaser whether a certain device or digital product will serve everyone. In such case, people are paying for products without being entirely sure they will get what is being advertised or rather just a subset of the full set of features, and of course it's particularly galling if this is a systematic problem across race or gender. Also, again, the market share of many of these products is so high that end users effectively lack a choice, because it is not possible for another company to get going to serve the underserved.

Dark Patterns

The computer science, policy, and legal communities have come to use the term "dark patterns" to refer to all sorts of undesirable and manipulative design elements commonly found in digital products, almost certainly to the detriment of the users of those products. Consider Luguri and Strahilevitz's characterization:

> Dark patterns are user interfaces whose designers knowingly confuse users, make it difficult for users to express their actual preferences, or manipulate users into taking certain actions. They typically exploit cognitive biases and prompt online consumers to purchase goods and services that they do not want, or to reveal personal information they would prefer not to disclose.[3]

The computer science research community has conducted empirical investigations to show that such dark patterns are, unsurprisingly, extraordinarily widespread.[4] Consider Mathur et al.'s work on this topic.[5] From an automated crawl of 11,000 websites, the researchers identified 1,818 dark patterns falling into 15 types, grouped into 7 broader categories.

I'll refer you to the paper for the full findings, but the categories delineated by the researchers are quite helpful. You may find this language can be good shorthand for describing fairness and for establishing a uniform language to talk to others about this. Most importantly, you may be able to use these seven categories as a checklist for ensuring the digital products you work on are not committing these practices:

Sneaking
> Examples of such dark patterns including hidden costs that are revealed only after shoppers are in the final stages of finalizing a purchase and a hidden subscription model that appears to users as a one-time fee or free trial.

Urgency
> Examples of such behavior include falsely claiming that a sale is a time-limited opportunity or even putting a timer on a sale to provide direct pressure to a buyer to complete the transaction in a hurried manner.

Misdirection
> One example of such behavior is visual design of an interface to deliberately steer users into the channel that the interface designer wants but likely not the one the

---

3 Luguri, Jamie and Lior Strahilevitz. "Shining a Light on Dark Patterns." Working paper 719, University of Chicago, Public Law, Chicago, 2019. *https://papers.ssrn.com/sol3/papers.cfm?abstract_id=3431205.*

4 An unofficial reviewer critiqued this book on the following basis: "It does not deal with the terrible yet utterly real fact that ethics in the software engineering industry seem to be at an all-time low." This is a representative impression from within the tech sector.

5 Mathur, Arunesh, et al. "Dark Patterns at Scale: Findings from a Crawl of 11K Shopping Websites." arXiv.org, September 20, 2019. *https://arxiv.org/pdf/1907.07032.pdf.*

user wants. Another example is using trick language to confuse users into making certain choices. My biggest personal gripe with many digital products falls into this domain: the use of the word "Cancel" when the appropriate word is "No." Many digital product designers are big fans of this method, seemingly having forgotten that "No" and not "Cancel" is the appropriate response to "Do you want to allow geolocation tracking?" or "Do you want to share your personal data with third-party vendors?" This reminds me of the language manipulation we might associate with the worst of extreme forms of communism or dystopian books like George Orwell's *1984*, where we can't even say what we mean.

Social proof

Examples of this include purported tickers of streaming information to demonstrate how other people are using the website (but of course, who knows whether such claims are true) or testimonials on product pages without full details as to origin (and which could potentially be untrue). I have found that in many tech startups, testimonials are technically true in the sense of being attributable to real persons, but often those persons are employees of the company in question, or their spouses. I have found this out more than once when looking at basic testimonials on up-and-coming tech company web pages. Practices like these can often make it feel like we are back in the days before we had rules and enforcement agencies precisely to prevent these sorts of dishonest and social-engineering-type business tactics.

Scarcity

Examples of this include "low stock" or "high demand" messages used to describe products. In this way, vendors are directly providing dishonest information about marketplace conditions, but it's quite difficult for ordinary people to determine the truth of these messages. If you are reading this book, you can probably write a web scraper to find out when a particular product really does seem to be scarce, but we should hardly require ordinary consumers to have that sophistication. Even for people who do have such technical sophistication, do we really want all buyers of products to have to independently verify such claims to have a sense of real market conditions? This is both unfair and strikingly inefficient from a social well-being viewpoint.

Obstruction

The most common example of this is making it difficult to cancel a service or transaction but very easy to start the service or transaction. It's hard to think of a digital product that *doesn't* do this. It seems to simply be considered good practice to make exit hard for consumers rather than respecting the obvious will of consumers. Businesses know that if they obstruct undesired actions, they will win, albeit quite unfairly.

Forced action

The most common example of this category is forced enrollment. For example, you may advertise a "free" service but then make it mandatory to create a user account. I have lost count of the services I have been asked to use, in both personal and professional contexts, in which I had to generate a username and password and often provide other information merely to participate. In many cases, I have been unable to opt out because of social pressures to comply and make things easy, but as a result I have unfairly had to surrender information to companies that did not have a fair basis for requesting such information in the first place. You've likely had that experience too.

Employing these practices can often be tempting (or even, stupidly, seem like "smart business") because they bring about the outcome that a product creator likely wants, but they aren't fair practices and they aren't consistent with traditional notions of fair business dealings. While the marketplace is not the intimate space of a friendship or a family, traditionally we do expect fair play and shared values even in the marketplace.

One consensus that emerges out of the dark patterns literature is that sophisticated parties are using behavioral science, combined with the opacity of digital platforms, to roll out scientifically anti-human industrial-scale trickery to ensure humans are in digital environments where the odds are stacked against them. I don't mean to paint all digital product developers as evil, but I am pointing out that when most competitors are racing to the bottom by implementing as many dark patterns as they can, the odds are really stacked against us as we simply try to lead normal lives.

Fair Products Checklist

We conclude with a fair product design and deployment checklist, grouped by the values that run through our discussion:

- Accountability
  - Does the product reckon with potential downstream effects, and have the designers actively sought out information about what this might look like?
  - Does the product have some form of self-documentation so that reports of problems can make their way back upstream, preferably automatically?
  - Does the product provide some form of labeling for those who would want to educate themselves before deciding whether to purchase or use the product?
- Autonomy
  - Does your product tend to enhance human autonomy or to increase human addiction to digital devices?

— Does your product use its superhuman knowledge and data mining to undermine human autonomy in targeted ways, such as identifying mental illness or other forms of vulnerability?

- Positive contribution

  — What would be the end result if the product succeeds? Is the world more of a place you want to live in?

  — Does your product face some form of market or user disciplines so that you know you will receive meaningful feedback in an automatic way that indicates people's actual choices in the world, assuming they have a choice?

- Real problem

  — What is the problem you are seeking to solve, and why is a digital solution appropriate?

  — Does your digital solution merely reallocate wealth from an existing industry to the new one you are seeking to create? If so, what's your justification for upsetting an existing market that may be relatively efficient already?

- Transparency

  — Are potential users of a product able to determine how well it will work and whether there is differential performance for different genders, races, etc.?

  — Are potential users of a product able to spot the dangers of that product with the usual level of sophistication you expect your users to have?

- Proof

  — What proof can you provide or seek out that your product actually does what you believe it does?

  — Are you allowing adequate time and testing to ensure that your product performs as expected and as desired?

Concluding Remarks

Fair product design is a very broad task, and a difficult one to define carefully. What I've tried to emphasize here is the diversity of ways fairness comes into play with respect to product design. It starts at the earliest stages of product design: why are you building a product, and does it have a fair purpose? And fair product design runs all the way through the product design pipeline, from whether a product should exist at all to how its design can best promote the well-being of the users of the product to refraining from tempting practices that tend to subvert the autonomy of others. Finally, fair product design doesn't end with the completion of the formal design process but also covers mechanisms to ensure the flow of information and accountability even after the product is released into the wild.

## CHAPTER 12

Laws for Machine Learning

I start with a provocation: law is the ultimate arbiter of what matters for fairness in machine learning, and that's a good thing.

We have had ample opportunity to see that fairness is not a problem that will be solved by pure market competition or reputational mechanisms. This is for a variety of reasons. Some important failings in waiting for economic or social pressures to enhance fairness in our digital environment are as follows:

- People make buying decisions for economic reasons, not fairness reasons.
- People don't have the information or technical training they would need to make fairness-aware decisions even if they wanted to.
- The people most affected by unfairness in digital products may not even be the people most influential in that particular market.
- Digital products make and influence markets and culture as much as they are, in turn, influenced by these forces.

I now elaborate on each of these factors in more detail.

First, people simply don't behave in the market as their ideological values would predict they should. Much behavioral research has shown that people may have core ideological values, but bottom-line economic factors tend to drive day-to-day decision making. One well-known example is the *privacy paradox*. People tend to state that they care deeply about privacy, but in lab or field experiments, they generally don't demonstrate a willingness to pay for their privacy when asked to spend even small amounts of money to enhance it. This doesn't mean that people are stupid or insincere in their belief that privacy is important. Rather, it shows that market mechanisms are often not a good way of measuring core values. This is where law can step in as a more effective and more reliable mechanism for operationalizing fairness in the marketplace, and specifically in the marketplace that applies to digital products.

Second, products are opaque with respect to their fairness implications, and what's more, fairness itself is a complicated matter. It's not realistic to expect an ordinary consumer to understand these questions and make product choices accordingly. They don't have the information or training to do so. Take this book as an example. This is a very limited introduction to fairness concepts and methods related to fairness, and yet it still runs to hundreds of pages and requires familiarity with statistics, probability, machine learning, user interface design, linear algebra, and calculus to read. We shouldn't expect or require an ordinary person to have exposure to these topics merely to have an opinion about and some protections from unfairness in the digital products that the entire population uses. This is again a reason why law is more effective and more desirable as a regulatory mechanism than the market. Laws will offer specific fairness guarantees and can connect the intuitions and desires of ordinary people, enacted via statute, into the technical constraints and information necessary to design a digital product, via regulatory rules.

Third, the people most affected by fairness in an ML product are often not those with an opportunity to influence that product. This is particularly the case when a minority of any kind (a numerical minority) is disadvantaged with respect to a product. By definition, that minority likely has a smaller market share. What's more, those affected by the fairness or unfairness of a product will not necessarily even be in the relevant marketplace. For example, the people who are described by search engine results that are discriminatory are not necessarily the people who are using a search engine. Likewise, the people who are targeted by biased policing algorithms purchased by police departments or the people who miss out on jobs because of discriminatory algorithms purchased by employers are not the people in the marketplace at all; they are third parties affected by the decisions of others. These *externalities*—that is, effects not priced into a deal—offer one explanation for why marketplaces will not solve ML fairness. Law can be effective at correcting inefficiencies and misallocations resulting from externalities, and this is yet another reason law should address ML fairness.

Finally, digital products make markets and they make culture. More than one generation has now come of age with new data-driven technologies, such as social media and targeted advertising, that characterize our lived digital experiences. For this generation and the next, the most fundamental and intimate experiences of growing up, developing friendships, even interacting with their family are closely tied to digital products, be they smartphones, social media, photo sharing, or news aggregation. We will increasingly have generations of human beings who are *users* of these products more than *consumers*, meaning they are more immersed in and influenced by these products.

We should also remember that, at present, many important digital markets lack elements of competition that would make consumer choice meaningful, which is one reason that antitrust investigations are underway into Big Tech design choices, including data use and interface design, which tend to concentrate the players in these valuable markets. It is not clear that small competitors, such as companies that might want to market a more ethical or fairer product, can gain a foothold when anticompetitive behaviors or structural realities in a marketplace make entry difficult. This again points to a lack of possibility for an economic or social campaign to result in meaningful changes in fairness.

These are just some of the reasons that a legal system backed up by a robust regulatory apparatus makes much more sense for ensuring our digital products align with the core values we support in democratic societies than do markets or other social mechanisms.

Notions of what is discriminatory and what is fair will change over time because of a variety of cultural changes, economic shifts, and social science discoveries. That's why laws change over time too, in the pursuit of fairness. But we expect that the law's notions of fairness will evolve more systematically than might changes in culture. We hope that if we have a well-designed legal system, the changes in definitions of fairness will lead to only greater fairness and justice for all. We hope to arrive at such a system with the principles enshrined in the rule of law, such as the requirements for justified, nonarbitrary decision making; fair outcomes; and equality before the law. These are nearly universal principles of rule that characterize what is described as "rule of law" when referring to legal systems of functional nation-states, driven by fairness principles that assure a robust and defensible system of legal decision making.

Law is not the sole or even highest arbiter for most people or organizations as to what is important. And that's as it should be. Law generates standards for *the bare minimum* required for legal conduct; that is, so long as conduct is legal, it will not trigger interventions from the government. That doesn't mean conduct is ideal or even morally acceptable. Some organizations will hold themselves to standards that they and their customers deem important, and in some cases these standards will exceed what is required by law. However, these can vary greatly from one organization to another and can also drift over time, sometimes for the better and sometimes for the worse. Law can anchor these behaviors to standards having the support of the larger society.

In general I support the idea of organizations going beyond the legal minimum, but I also recognize potential downsides to organizations, particularly powerful organizations, setting their own fairness standards. Such standards may implicitly or explicitly take authority away from the larger society, perhaps inappropriately.

I write from the perspective of late 2020, where antitrust investigations of Big Tech are underway and the techlash of 2019 and 2020 is continuing. Tech companies are awash in policies they attempt to use to show that they are exceeding legal standards, possibly in a bid to lessen the extent of regulatory action that may be taken now or soon in response to antitrust, consumer protection, or privacy concerns. While these policies may be a step in the right direction, they may undermine and diminish the extent of legal interventions in this domain and potentially set back efforts for fairness, relative to a movement for a universal legal standard and proper regulatory authority.

Consider Facebook's announcement of its "Supreme Court" of content moderation, the Oversight Board, which has 20 members who will make important decisions regarding content moderation. Facebook will fund the board with $130 million allocated for operations and appoint an initial roster that was international, glamorous, and high-profile. While this might seem like a great selection from a public relations perspective, it doesn't necessarily make sense with respect to democratic legitimacy. The process of selecting the members was not public, nor was much information given about how the members were selected. Even the fact that the process was international could seem like a good thing, or it could seem like an oppressively homogenizing force.

Was this fair? Was it appropriate? It depends on your perspective. Do you view Facebook as a privately run company, entitled to manage its affairs as it likes, with users free to come and go? Or do you view Facebook as an essential public forum, so useful to certain portions of society that they cannot afford not to belong to Facebook?

Law Is Not Always on the Right Side

Law is far from perfect as an agent of fairness. It's just another social institution with its own sets of failings that we have come to recognize over time. Law itself can suffer from strong biases that we later repudiate as a society.

One reason law has failed to deliver justice as we now view it is that what is and is not thought discriminatory will vary over time. For example, when the US Supreme Court upheld a law specifically limiting the work hours of women in *Muller v. Oregon*, 208 US 412 (1908), this was a victory for progressives of that era. Nowadays, however, such a decision would likely be viewed askance by progressives, who would seek to emphasize gender equality and find that fairness requires treating men and women equally rather than protecting the allegedly "weaker sex."

What's more, the alleged science and social science that drove the *Muller v. Oregon* decision, lending scientific credence to the idea of women as the weaker sex, has been called into question by more recent science. For example, women likely can and do outperform men in some physical endeavors, such as long-distance swimming

---

(*https://oreil.ly/knj66*), long-distance running (*https://oreil.ly/fV4-9*), and working in confined spaces (*https://oreil.ly/2jYQs*).[1]

Law has also failed to be consistent with our modern nations of fairness because of flat-out flawed morals. Shamefully, in 1926, the US Supreme Court upheld the legality of racial covenants, which were agreements white homeowners used to prevent the sale of property to black people by imposing a legal requirement that certain property not be sold to black people. Interestingly, such racial covenants had not been widely used until that terrible decision because their legality was in doubt given the post–Civil War constitutional amendments. The Supreme Court empowered a new and highly racist policy in 1926, and didn't reverse this decision until 1948. So the law can certainly serve as an institution that can introduce and reify *unfairness* by giving unfair practices institutional legitimacy and legal protection.

On the other hand, once legal actors recognize their errors, law can serve as a principal agent of change, even against an otherwise uphill battle. In the wake of the Civil Rights Movement of the 1960s, law served as a principal agent of change in restructuring the economy to reduce racial bias and ensuring that housing, education, employment, and healthcare could not be allotted on the basis of race, gender, or any number of other protected categories. These changes were made in response to a social movement but also *despite* enormous amounts of both grassroots and concerted efforts to slow the civil rights movement. Here I present a very simplified view of a very complicated event, but what can certainly be asserted is that law was used as an institution to force even resistant communities, where civil rights were not popular, to move toward a better model of fairness.

Content moderation is a famously controversial and difficult example in which various platforms, such as Facebook, Twitter, Reddit, and others, have had to develop their own policies. In some cases, such as Germany's NetzDG law, which requires online content platforms to moderate content and quickly remove hate speech, law has provided minimum standards. In other cases, such as banning users or particular forms of misinformation, the administration of these effectively public spaces for expression has been governed by the idiosyncratic decisions of a few executives, or possibly a lone CEO. That doesn't feel very fair. So while organizational initiatives may provide a way to reach an even higher quality of fairness than law, reasonable concerns and objections can arise when such power is wielded by exceptionally powerful organizations that can sometimes seem like they are their own countries.

Importantly, law can act as a stick and help to overcome institutional dysfunction or inertia to enforce minimum standards. This is what we saw in the wake of the GDPR

---

1 Perhaps the science I cite here will also come to be challenged. My argument is that many of these facts are hard to establish and perhaps show that the question of judging one gender against another, rather than focusing on individual merits, may not be particularly helpful in general.

coming into effect in 2018. Many of us were suddenly snowed under with a profusion of emails from companies not necessarily highlighting the GDPR but instead telling us how much they valued our privacy and what measures they were taking to protect it (see Figure 12-1). No doubt, most organizations had good intentions and genuinely did want to promote a culture that enhances privacy and protects personal rights to data. On the other hand, we can clearly agree that most organizations were not measuring up to the GDPR standards and had a lot of work to do to get into compliance in time. No wonder they all wanted credit for their magically enhanced cultures of promoting privacy.

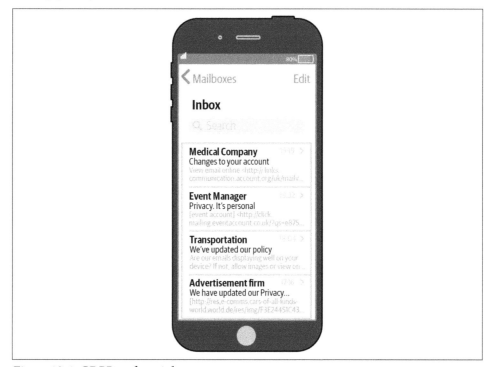

Figure 12-1. GDPR and my inbox

I do not say this to criticize companies. Businesses have many obligations and goals, and not all of these need to inure to customer or user benefit. What's more, entities can have the best of intentions but may not have a business justification or the logistical wherewithal to pursue all their values. The GDPR provided an impetus for many organizations to examine their organizational culture with respect to privacy, transparency, and accountability, and to bring their practices into compliance with a widespread standard backed by the rule of law.

So I give special attention to law rather than to ethical norms or cultural consensus because a big stick with actual enforcement power is what organizations will respond to, particularly when law gives clear definitions and expectations, allowing many entities in society to coordinate their actions and conform to the same standards. Without concrete definitions, ethics and fairness can seem a bit fuzzy and contested, and organizations may find many reasons not to knuckle down and implement fairness measures. Law takes the fuzziness out of the equation and provides an actionable standard.

Obviously, this chapter cannot offer exhaustive detail on law, nor can it even cover a single piece of legislation in enough detail to tell you how to conform to it. Rather, the goal here is to demarcate some major areas of lawmaking to be aware of and also some major legal principles likely to apply to machine learning when it affects fairness in digital products.

The following brief overview is designed to cover some interesting aspects of how the law might apply to algorithms even in unspecified domains. Because of both space limitations and the complexity of the topic, there is no way of also covering possible regulations even when focusing on just a narrow array of jurisdictions. I discuss some interesting aspects of how law regulates algorithms, with the heaviest focus on US law, but also some mentions of law from the EU and from some Asian jurisdictions. The coverage is itself necessarily quite biased but gives a flavor of what is out there.

Personal Data

Given the current dominant paradigm of *data-driven* machine intelligence, be it as "AI" or "ML" or "algorithms," one important source of law and regulations that will affect considerations of algorithmic and digital product fairness relates to personal data laws. Some major areas of personal data laws are covered next.

In recent years some landmark pieces of legislation on both sides of the Atlantic pose specific legal requirements expected of any business that would otherwise process personally identifiable information about consumers.

GDPR

The GDPR came into force in 2018 in the European Union. It defines what constitutes personal data quite extensively. As defined in Article 4(1), "Personal data are any information which are related to an identified or identifiable natural person." This means that obvious data, such as name and address, is personal data, but so are less obvious examples, such as a cookie identifier, data that has been pseudonymized or identified but could potentially be re-identified, and data relating to location or to one's smartphone, such as the smartphone's device identifier.

The GDPR provides numerous rights for the data subject (the person about whom data is recorded) and numerous responsibilities for entities that handle personal data. These rights can be easily gleaned even by looking at the titles of various GDPR

Articles, such as "Right of access by the data subject," which gives the data subject the right to know the nature of the information collected about them and the nature of the use. Other examples of rights conferred to data subjects by the GDPR include the following:

- Right to data portability
- Right to erasure (right to be forgotten)
- Right to correct personal data

These rights are the more concrete manifestations of a variety of general legal principles and privacy- and autonomy-enhancing principles that guide the GDPR, in general promoting the individual's right to agency in navigating digital data-driven products and right to understand how their information and the resulting outcomes are derived from the data. The GDPR empowers individuals through rights to information but also rights to affect how and whether entities can use their information.

The scope of application of GDPR is quite extensive. It applies to the processing of any personal data by a business "established" within the EU. Moreover, it applies to businesses outside the EU that serve or monitor the behavior of individuals in the EU. This second provision makes the GDPR quite global in scope, which explains why I received so many GDPR-relevant emails when not living in the EU or holding EU citizenship.

How far the GDPR can reach in practice is a matter to be determined over time. Initially, some industry and academic thinkers alike speculated that businesses might simply opt to comply with the GDPR globally to simplify operations and in expectations that other jurisdictions might impose similar requirements subsequently. This has, in fact, not occurred. There remains strong evidence that the experience, for example, of US internet users as compared to EU internet users is now quite different with respect to the level of notice and practices such as surveillance and tracking taking place. So the GDPR is a strong and very widely applicable law, but it has not achieved universal application or voluntary compliance beyond the reach of mandatory enforcement.

It is also interesting to note that the GDPR hasn't necessarily achieved as many fairness objectives as might be hoped. For example, one aspect of a digital environment conducive to fairness would likely be enough competition that new entrants can have a viable chance of making their businesses work. Evidence, however, reveals that the GDPR tended to consolidate (*https://oreil.ly/EXOFX*) the markets for internet advertising and tracking as businesses opted to trust only big players, thinking these big players would have the compliance aspects of the GDPR better implemented than smaller companies. Similarly, not all individuals have necessarily benefited from more privacy. Some preliminary evidence suggests that the GDPR led to some individuals opting out of tracking cookies, but this in turn led to more and better information (*https://oreil.ly/Boh6H*) about those who remained tracked by cookies.

This shows that the actual effects of legislation will often differ from what was presumptively desired. Nonetheless, there is a strong consensus that the GDPR sent an important signal to tech companies regarding the importance of privacy and fair data practices, as well as respecting principles consistent with a system that empowers data subjects and requires that data processors provide value from the data they process.

California Consumer Privacy Act

The CCPA came into force in 2020. This law has many similarities with the GDPR, particularly with respect to empowering consumers with control over their data, such as the right to opt out of their data being sold to third parties and the right to request information about what data is collected about them.

Given the preceding discussion of the GDPR, I discuss the CCPA in comparison to it to give an idea of differences. Importantly, the CCPA is much more narrowly applicable. The CCPA applies only to California residents; that is, the protections do not additionally apply to residents of other states who also do business with a California company.

Also, the GDPR is written to broadly cover just about all activities related to processing of personal data outside of specific entities, such as police departments. In contrast, in California the applicability is more narrowly drawn rather than governing all data processors. For example, for CCPA to apply, a company, in addition to doing business in California and being for-profit, has to be sufficiently large or be a data broker. CCPA does not cover the processing of some specific forms of data, such as health information or publicly available personal information.

The nature of the information itself is also more narrowly regulated under CCPA. GDPR applies to any data unless it is fully anonymized, while CCPA does not apply once information is de-identified or aggregated.

The CCPA also provides for a right of data deletion and additionally allows California residents to opt out of having their data sold. Likewise, the CCPA provides a right to be informed about the kind of data held and the purpose of the collected data. However, in a variety of details, the CCPA does not offer as broad a right as the GDPR does. For example, the right to see what information has been collected about oneself covers only information for the past 12 months under the CCPA, while it covers all data under the GDPR.

Finally, a major difference is that the damages provided by the CCPA are likely much smaller than the damages provided by the GDPR in the case of noncompliance. The GDPR in theory has a very high upper limit of fines, as it provides for a maximum penalty of 4% of the global annual turnover of a company or €20 million (whichever is higher), which can reach into billions of dollars, while the CCPA offers $2,500 for each violation or $7,500 for each intentional violation. It remains to be seen how narrowly or broadly a violation may be defined, but on the face of it, these fines don't appear to reach as deep into large company pockets as could GDPR.

CCPA has just been launched, and its status remains in flux. Industry lobbyists are already seeking revisions, and even consumer protection organizations say that CCPA needs clearer details regarding specific rules and enforcement. It's too soon predict the results on the structure of the digital marketplace or overall fairness, but what already seems clear is that, as with GDPR, most companies will comply with the law only for California and not for the entire US. In this case, it appears that we won't see a "California effect," a hypothesized effect whereby California, in setting applicable law in a very large jurisdiction within the US, could influence the US market generally. So the US is still very much in need of a comprehensive federal privacy and data processing law, but this is unlikely to happen soon given political deadlock in Washington, DC.

Data Broker Laws

Other US states have not moved toward such comprehensive personal data information regulation as California, but have started to take smaller steps to respond to consumer dissatisfaction with the online marketplace. For example, in 2018 Vermont passed a law to regulate data brokers, introducing requirements for them to register so that their very existence becomes more publicly available, whereas in the past consumers have not even been aware of the identity of such entities. What's more, Vermont imposed reporting requirements, such as that data brokers must indicate their general compliance with responsible cybersecurity and data storage practices.

Algorithmic Decision Making

These personal data statutes are one but not the only category of statutory action that applies to ML products and digital products. We now discuss examples of legislation that apply specifically to algorithmic decision making apart from rules specific to how data is to be handled.

GDPR

In addition to providing many legal standards regarding access to personal data and use of personal data, the GDPR provides some law that is specifically applicable to algorithmic decision making and ML pipelines. For example, it gives EU citizens the right not to be subject to a fully automated decision-making process for decisions that are legally significant or that have a similarly important effect in the life of the decision subject.[2]

Similarly, the GDPR requires that data processing have a lawful basis. This implies some limitations to a data processor's rights to build ML models, and particularly the need to make clear to the parties whose data is used what that data is being used for, including what kinds of modeling are practiced with a given data set.

Proposed US Laws for Algorithms

A number of proposed laws have been put forward in the US in recent years regarding algorithmic decision making. However, these have not been very ambitious or concrete, so if passed they would be quite unlikely to have the effect of GDPR. For example, the FUTURE of Artificial Intelligence Act of 2017 and the AI Jobs Act of 2018 proposed to make money available for retraining American workers to prepare for the impact of AI on the economy. Additionally, the FUTURE of Artificial Intelligence Act of 2017 proposed measures to understand and predict the impact of AI on the economy and to study best practices to protect privacy, promote investment, and ensure continued innovation. These were fluff pieces, designed to show action by specific lawmakers and the general interest of US lawmakers right now, with an emphasis on economic impacts, protecting jobs, and finding new jobs for American workers where possible.

A more targeted and practical approach to algorithmic decision making was put forward in the Algorithmic Accountability Act of 2019, which provided more specific and targeted guidelines, such as requiring larger companies to produce algorithmic impact assessments and giving the Federal Trade Commission a mandate to evaluate sensitive algorithms for bias, in response to privacy, discrimination, and general automation concerns related to algorithms.

Unfortunately, none of these proposals or any other proposed general measures related to AI, automation, or algorithms has gained much traction politically. At this point, it's much more likely that any federal legal reform in this sector will come out of a consumer protection regulator, such as the FTC, or as a result of the ongoing antitrust investigations of 2020. However, in either of these cases, these will likely be actions taken with respect to specific companies, as the FTC primarily enforces with specific consent agreements and enforcement actions, be they in the domain of antitrust or consumer protection. Likewise if the US Department of Justice pursues antitrust litigation, this too will be in the form of targeted litigation. So this sort of lawmaking is unlikely to result in the establishment of clear privacy, security, or

---

2 Interestingly, the GDPR was not the originator of this decision by any means. For example, a law was passed in the 1970s in France with a similar prohibition on subjecting humans to a decision that was purely algorithmic or computational in nature.

antidiscrimination measures that would apply industry-wide or even more broadly to algorithmic decision making generally.

Security

Physical security is a core expectation of government, but increasingly people look to government and law when ML algorithms, websites, or computing devices endanger them. For this reason, there are a variety of sources of law with respect to security and digital products. This section provides a few examples, but is far from a full depiction of the legal landscape with respect to digital security.

Cybsecurity is regulated by a variety of actors, although there is widespread agreement that the current regime (cutting across many different regulatory agencies, standard setting bodies, and areas of law) may be too heterogeneous. The following sections provide just a smattering of examples of laws that affect data and machine learning practices with respect to security.

HIPAA

The Health Insurance Portability and Accountability Act of 1996 introduced the first industry-wide standards for the storage of health information in the US, particularly with respect to electronic format. This was particularly important because the mid-1990s was the first time that medical care providers were moving significant amounts of health information into digital formats, and this legislation recognized the importance of mandating uniform standards to safeguard the privacy and security of that information. In contrast to the more general tort law regime also discussed in this section that governs some data breaches, health information is so sensitive and the prospective harm so great and irrevocable that HIPAA is an ex ante protection that mandates preventive steps rather than the ex post tort regime in which actual harms are compensated after the fact if a party has not been reasonable.

Importantly, by setting specific security standards, HIPAA does not serve only as a burden on technology in the healthcare domain. Rather HIPAA encourages healthcare providers to adapt to new information technologies by offering guidance on appropriate security. Additionally, the security guidance is flexible by design to allow organizations of different sizes, levels of sophistication, and sensitivity to adapt variation while meeting the rules. It also grants specific protections and rights to patients, also setting out a protocol that can make them aware of their legal entitlements under this framework. This domain-specific framework has succeeded in allowing technology to blossom by setting up a uniform standard, which has enabled medical technologies to have a shared basis for advertising their security provisions and competence to handle health information. HIPAA is an example of how law for security is enabling rather than merely burdensome.

FTC Guidance on Cybersecurity

Specialized sectors, such as banking and healthcare, are formally on notice that they face high expectations with respect to cybersecurity, not just as a business imperative but as a legal one. However, all businesses could also face legal action for law security practices through more general supervision under the FTC. In recent years, the FTC has become more active in encouraging good cybersecurity practices and in helping to establish those practices (*https://oreil.ly/8p4jG*). Additionally, if the FTC finds that businesses are making misleading statements about the security that their products provide, it can elect to prosecute, as it has done in past cases (*https://oreil.ly/HOr7Z*).

Tort Law

In the past, data breaches by a bad actor who breaks into an organization's data repository about its clients or members have been regarded as primarily punitive. This view was based on the bad publicity a firm suffered as well as any costs the firm might incur to right the wrongs, be that paying ransom (an insurable expense) or paying security consultants to undo the damage and improve the system.

However, recent decisions in US courts point toward the possibility that increasingly judges are asking whether lax cybersecurity means that a data breach represents a harm to consumers. For a specific example, imagine that all your highly sensitive financial information is stored with Bank A. Bank A is hacked, all your personal information is stolen, and later it turns out that the bank was not up to snuff regarding best practices for cybersecurity. In new cases with such circumstances, courts are open to the argument that you have suffered concrete harm from Bank A's failure to comply with obligations to you—specifically, that the increased probability of identity theft that you now face is a legal harm, and that Bank A failed in its duty to you. This need not apply only to industries with sensitive data, such as banking. If courts increasingly regulate a duty of data holders toward their data subjects, any business that is hacked and about whose customers sensitive information is released could face such tort liability.

Logical Processes

We have a collection of legal terms and rights that ultimately relate to the requirement that law and society strive toward logical processes. One of the merits of society is that we strive to create an environment that makes sense, where the right people are rewarded, or punished, for the right reasons. Hence, legal requirements and concepts apply directly to algorithms in some cases, or may come to apply to algorithms if they are deployed in certain use cases where a legal right applies, such as fundamental rights applicable when a government body uses an algorithm in carrying out its duties.

Right to an Explanation

The *right to an explanation* of a decision is, broadly, the right to know something of the process or logic that went into an outcome. The newest place we see this is in the GDPR. Debate continues as to whether the GDPR provides the right to an explanation and what that explanation might look like. This is because such a right is mainly discussed in a recital (that is, commentary on the regulation), rather than in the text of the law itself. Also, even if such a right to explanation does exist, it is limited to automated decision making with a legal impact or an impact of similar significance. So the right to an explanation would be unlikely to apply broadly. It should be noted that there is a right to explanation regulating credit decisions in the US, but we don't discuss this extensively given that this is a specialized and heavily regulated domain.

Freedom of Information Laws

Any company or developer looking to build products for government offices should be aware that their code or other work products might come under the rubric of freedom of information laws. Such laws are designed to ensure accountability of government to citizens. They are found in many countries and generally give people the right to see any government work product, absent compelling reasons the work product should not be released, such as national security or individual privacy. In recent years, as governments make decisions based on proprietary but privately developed software, increasingly people have tried to see the details of algorithmic implementations through freedom of information requests. For the most part, these requests have not been granted because of conflicts with intellectual property laws, but some governments in response have begun to develop policies of requiring acceptance of freedom of information requests as a condition to doing business with them. Future trends are not clear, but those who develop software privately and might ultimately end up in government use cases should plan for the possibility of code reviews resulting from freedom of information requests.

Due Process

Due process is a surprisingly large area of law, and often is the means for individuals to vindicate their rights against government and establish highly specific and important rights that conform to evolving cultural and ethical understandings. For example, it will seem uncontroversial that due process affects rights like freedom of religion and speech, but it also affects rights that have been implicated in algorithmic decision making lately, such as the right to keep one's public-school teaching job once one has tenure, or the property rights inherent in one's government entitlements, such as disability payments received from Medicaid.

In recent years, the US judiciary has decided cases on just these two forms of rights implicated by due process, in the case of an algorithm allocating disability benefits in Utah and an algorithm assessing teacher quality and leading to employment termination in Houston. In both cases courts found that the rights of the plaintiffs were constitutionally protected by the due process clause (not all rights are sufficiently important), and in both cases the government found that logic and transparency were missing in the decision-making process to such an extent that the plaintiffs' rights to due process—that is, to a reasonably logical outcome made for the right reasons—had been violated. Interestingly, and in contrast to the preceding discussion, in both cases the government had refused to release source code or provide implementation details citing proprietary source code. However, it is not clear such a defense will always succeed, as it provides a way for government to escape algorithmic accountability expectations simply by outsourcing the work of writing software. Bottom line: those who provide algorithmic software to government should be on notice that the software can be challenged in court and tested even if not inspected.

Due process and its manifestations in fundamental rights related to logical decision-making processes and logical outcomes (procedural and substantive due process respectively) primarily apply against governmental organizations. For example, US citizens have due process, rights against the federal government. Due process itself is a complicated idea with a variety of procedural steps to resolve questions. These are depicted in broad strokes in Figure 12-2.

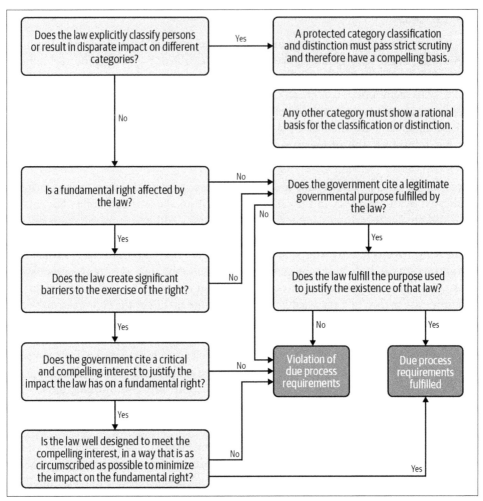

Figure 12-2. Due process questions

Some Application-Specific Laws

For the most part, laws that regulate algorithmic decision making in the US tend to do so in domain-specific ways. For example, the Fair Housing Act applies as much to the targeted advertising Facebook provided via "ethnic affinity" modeling as it does to traditional cases of housing discrimination against large landlords. The same goes for other heavily regulated domains, such as access to fair credit or academic admissions decisions.

On the other hand, novel domains specific to algorithmic use cases are also beginning to emerge as areas where domain-specific legislation is or may become important. These are discussed in the remainder of this section, and you should pay attention to these areas if you are seeking to develop related applications or even use related technologies.

Biometrics

At present, only four US states—California, Illinois, Texas, and Washington—expressly regulate the collection and use of biometric data. Of these, only California and Illinois provide for a *private right of action*—that is, the right for a specific aggrieved individual to go to court to enforce their statutory rights. Both states allow statutory damages: individuals need not prove a specific monetary value of their harm but can opt for the amount specified by statute.

Of course, with any new legislation questions remain regarding what is necessary to access the statutory damages, and in fact the American courts are only now in the process of working this out for the Illinois law, as many high-profile lawsuits have been brought in recent years, particularly against Facebook. In that litigation plaintiffs have argued that information stored for facial recognition constituted nonconsensual storage of biometric information, entitling Illinois residents who were users of Facebook to statutory damages. This represented a huge lawsuit because the statutory damages were set to $1,000 per violation, constituting an enormous source of liability. Facebook ultimately settled this lawsuit for $550 million.

The US as a whole does not regulate biometric information, so residents of states where regulation is not present have little protection other than through the Federal Trade Commission, which can enforce more general standards related to fair business practices. On the other hand, the EU has very strict laws against the collection and processing of biometric information,

Local Ordinances on Facial Recognition

Facial recognition has proven to be a particularly fraught and politically controversial form of technology. In addition to wildly disparate performance for different gender and racial combinations, this technology seemingly raises even more ethical concerns and populist anger when it does perform well as compared to when it doesn't.

Many localities in the US have now taken action regarding facial recognition technologies. Several cities around the country have banned the use of facial recognition software, including San Francisco and Springfield, Massachusetts. In some cases the ban has come in the form of a multiyear moratorium. In all such cases it is the governmental use of facial recognition technologies that has been banned. So far, no legislation prohibits use of facial recognition software in private hands, and this is unsurprising as it would seem to automatically implicate every smartphone in which users were opting for a facial recognition form of security rather than a passcode or fingerprint.

Chat Bots

California is the source of quite a few new tech laws in recent years.[3] This is not at all surprising, given the presence of Silicon Valley combined with some of the most progressive politics and sophisticated lawmakers in the country. One piece of legislation that hasn't gotten a huge amount of attention but has specific domain application is California's chat bot disclosure law, which came into effect in 2019. The purpose of the law is to make consumers aware of when they are not interacting with a human, even though it may not be obvious that they are interacting with a bot. The exact extent of what this means and what is covered remains to be determined. For example, some say that the language of the statute would appear to include even obviously automated emails, whereas others argue the disclosure should apply only in more dynamic environments, such as live chat with a bot.

In contrast to GDPR, there has not yet been a lot of affirmative evidence that companies are stringently complying with this regulation or that California is stringently enforcing it. Given the rapid progress of natural language processing models and AI to produce human language, on the other hand, there is every reason to think that the use of chat bots will only continue to grow. Figure 12-3 shows the relevant text of the California law requiring bots to self-disclose.

THE PEOPLE OF THE STATE OF CALIFORNIA DO ENACT AS FOLLOWS:

SECTION 1. Chapter 6 (commencing with Section 17940) is added to Part 3 of Division 7 of the Business and Professions Code, to read:

CHAPTER 6. Bots

17940. For purposes of this chapter:

(a) "Bot" means an automated online account where all or substantially all of the actions or posts of that account are not the result of a person.

(b) "Online" means appearing on any public-facing Internet Web site, Web application, or digital application, including a social network or publication.

(c) "Online platform" means any public-facing Internet Web site, Web application, or digital application, including a social network or publication, that has 10,000,000 or more unique monthly United States visitors or users for a majority of months during the preceding 12 months.

(d) "Person" means a natural person, corporation, limited liability company, partnership, joint venture, association, estate, trust, government, governmental subdivision or agency, or other legal entity or any combination thereof.

17941. (a) It shall be unlawful for any person to use a bot to communicate or interact with another person in California online, with the intent to mislead the other person about its artificial identity for the purpose of knowingly deceiving the person about the content of the communication in order to incentivize a purchase or sale of goods or services in a commercial transaction or to influence a vote in an election. A person using a bot shall not be liable under this section if the person discloses that it is a bot.

(b) The disclosure required by this section shall be clear, conspicuous, and reasonably designed to inform persons with whom the bot communicates or interacts that it is a bot.

Figure 12-3. Bot, identify yourself!

---

3 See, for example, CCPA, and California's chat bot law, California's new law outlawing the use of manipulated media of electoral candidates in the 60 days before the election, but also earlier incarnations of California's leading status as a tech-aware jurisdiction, such as its 2005 anti-phishing law.

Concluding Remarks

Law, and its relationship to ML applications specifically, and digital products more generally, will continue to evolve. We can expect some elements of fairness in the digital world to be resolved with traditional legal concepts and existing laws, as not all problems associated with fairness in technology are new or qualitatively unique problems.

On the other hand, sometimes lawmakers will judge that the best solution to a specific technical challenge is to target that technology or subset of fairness problems with specific interventions, be they regulatory rule making (that is, administrators imposing domain-specific standards) or new statutory regimes.

Clearly, we can expect law and technology to remain an area of active legal change and reevaluation as the big data and machine learning revolutions continue.

Index

black-box models
    justifications for using, 155
    post-processing and, 155
black-box threat model, 266
Bonchi, Francesco, 60
Brock, Andrew, 276
Buesser, Beat, 263

C

calibration, defined, 166
calibration-preserving equalized odds, 166-172
    code demonstration, 169-172
    mechanism of, 167-169
California Consumer Privacy Act (CCPA)
    GDPR compared to, 311
    personal data standards, 311-312
Calmon, Flavio, 125, 129
Castillo, Carlos, 60
chat bots, 320
Chen, Jianbo, 265
child labor, 4
Chouldechova, Alexandra, 43
Civil Rights Act (1964), 188
clean label attacks, 281
CleverHans library, 277
column generation subproblem, 205
community norms, 8
COMPAS
    bias in, 11
    ProPublica compilation of data from, 158-161
complementary fairness metric, 152
complex systems
    fundamental limits on data for, 86
    impact of product life cycle, 292
    need for experts, 293
    need for record keeping with, 293
    product design/deployment, 292-293
consent
    fair play and, 77-78
    reasonable expectations and, 79
consistency, 45
contextual integrity, 19
cost-benefit analysis, 38
counterfactuals, black-box auditing and, 183
Crenshaw, Kimberlé, 97
cybersecurity (see security)

D

dark patterns, in product design, 298-300
data broker laws, 312
data integrity
    data duplication and, 74
    ensuring, 69-74
    failures of external validity, 71
    proportionality and sampling technique, 73-74
    proxies and, 69-71
    true measurements, 69-72
    undescribed variation, 71
data leaks, 259
data sanitization, 282
data science pipeline, checklist for points of entry for fairness concerns, 61-65
data subjects, 16
data, fair, 67-98
    choosing appropriate data, 75-87
    choosing right question for data set/right data set for question, 87-89
    comprehensive data-acquisition checklist, 97
    ensuring data integrity, 69-74
    equity and, 75-80
    fundamental limits on data for complex systems, 86
    identifying potential discrimination, 89-95
    privacy and, 80-83
    relabeling, 102-103
    reweighting of data set, 115-121
    security concerns, 83-87
    timeline for fairness interventions, 95-97
data-driven explanation, 227-232
    code example, 228-231
    mechanism of, 228
debiasing, adversarial (see adversarial debiasing)
decisional interference, 18
deployment, fair (see product design/deployment)
design, fair (see product design/deployment)
Dhurandhar, Amit, 216
difference in mean outcomes, 42, 111
differential fairness, 44
differential privacy, 54, 261
discrimination
    data choice and, 75
    identifying potential discrimination, 89-95

disparate impact, 41, 43, 111
distributional concerns
    as domain of fairness, 30
    in-processing and, 151
documentation, complex systems and, 293
domain expertise, 293
Donahue, Jeff, 276
due process, 317
Dwork, Cynthia, 54

E
earthmover distance, 186
Eckhoff, David, 47
80% rule, 91-93
end users, reasonable expectations of, 286-288
    clear communication to manage expectations, 287
    shifting expectations over time, 287
ε-differential privacy, 54
ε-obscure data set, 185
Equal Credit Opportunity Act, 59
equality
    coding guidelines for, 30
    defined, 10, 33
    difficulties in attaining, 91
    equity versus, 10-13
    security and, 58
equality of odds, 43
equality of opportunity, 43, 161-165
equalized-odds-inspired post-processing, 161-165
    code demonstration, 165
    mechanism of, 163-164
equity
    antidiscrimination measures of, 40-45
    coding guidelines for, 30
    data choice and, 75-80
    defined, 10, 34
    equality versus, 10-13
    fair play and, 77-78
    measures of, 40-46
    privacy and, 58
    rationality measures of, 45
    reasonable expectations and, 79
European Union (see GDPR)
evasion attacks, 264-279
    CleverHans library, 277
    code demonstration, 269-274
    defending against, 275

Foolbox project, 277
    mechanism of, 267-269
    packages, 277-278
    poisoning attacks and, 284
    why they matter, 278
expectations, reasonable, 75
explainability methods, 201, 215-233
    attacks on explainable machine learning, 236
    checklist of considerations, 237
    data-driven explanation, 227-232
    LIME, 217-221
    limitations, 233-237
    metrics, 232
    SHAP, 221-225
explainability, as rationality measure of equity, 46
explanation
    defined, 202
    interpretation versus, 202-204
    right to, 316
external validity, failures of, 71
externalities, 8, 304
Eykholt, Kevin, 264

F
Facebook
    biometric data lawsuit, 319
    civil rights audit, 176
    ethnic affinity modeling, 318
    fines and lawsuits against, 26
    nonconsensual data collection, 77
    Oversight Board, 306
facial recognition software, 319
failure modes and effects analysis (FMEA), 179-181
failures of external validity, 71
Fair Housing Act, 26, 97, 318
fair play
    data choice and, 75
    equity and, 77-78
fairness in technology (generally), 1-32
    accuracy and, 42, 58
    assumptions and approaches, 22
    checklist for points of entry for fairness concerns, 61-65
    coding guidelines for, 30-32
    community norms, 8
    connected concepts, 57-60

Internet of Things (IoT), 59
Internet, data gathered from, 83
interpretable models, 201, 204-213
    code demonstration, 206-213
    GLRMs, 205
    interpretation versus explanation, 202-204
    limitations, 233-237
    mechanism of, 205
interpretation
    defined, 202
    explanation versus, 202-204
interrogation, as privacy violation, 15
intersectional theory, 44
intersectionality, 97
intrusion, 18
invasion of privacy, 18

J

Jha, Somesh, 260

K

k-anonymity, 50-54, 261
Kamishima, Toshihiro, 138, 140
Khosrowshahi, Dara, 5
knock-on effect, 9
Koh, Pang Wei, 281
Kranzberg, Melvin, 3

L

L-infinity norm, 272
labeling, incorrect, 170
laws for machine learning, 303-321
    algorithmic decision making statutes, 312
    application-specific laws, 318-320
    biometrics, 319
    CCPA, 311-312
    chat bots, 320
    data broker laws, 312
    due process and, 317
    facial recognition local ordinances, 319
    freedom of information laws, 316
    GDPR, 309
    law as imperfect agent of fairness, 306
    legal responses to fairness in technology, 20-22
    logical processes, 316-317
    personal data, 309-312
    right to an explanation, 316

security, 315
    tort law, 315
learned fair representations (LFR), 121-125
    code demonstration, 123-125
    mechanism of, 121-123
Lee, Su-In, 221-223
legal issues/legislation (see laws for machine learning)
legitimacy, as domain of fairness, 29
Liang, Percy, 281
life cycle, product, 292
LIME (local interpretable model-agnostic explanations), 217-221
    adversarial attacks on, 236
    code example, 218-221
    mechanism of, 218
local ordinances, 319
location data, 46
loss function, 134, 140, 150
Luguri, Jamie, 298
Lundberg, Scott M., 221-223

M

marketplace, as inadequate arbiter of fairness, 303-305
Mathur, Arunesh, 298
maximum mean discrepancy (MMD), 228
medical data
    for in-processing, 135-137
    privacy and, 46
membership attacks, 241-259
    code demonstration, 246-259
    mechanism of, 243-246
metadata
    defined, 82
    privacy and, 81
metrics
    AIF360 pipeline, 109
    defined, 35
    for equity, 40-46
    for explainability, 232
    for fairness, 36-57
    for privacy, 46-56
    for security, 56
minority rights
    as domain of fairness, 30
    in-processing and, 150
Mittelstadt, Brent, 234
MMD (maximum mean discrepancy), 228

About the Author

Aileen Nielsen is a software engineer who has analyzed data in a variety of settings, from a physics laboratory to a political campaign to a healthcare startup. She also has a law degree and splits her time between a deep learning startup and research as a fellow in law and technology at ETH Zurich. She has given talks around the world on fairness issues in data and modeling.

Colophon

The animals on the cover of *Practical Fairness* are klipspringers (*Oreotragus oreotragus*), rock-climbing dwarf antelopes native to East and Southern Africa. Klipspringers prefer rocky, sparsely vegetated habitats such as savannas, deserts, shrublands, and mountains at elevations up to 13,000 feet.

Klipspringers only grow about 2 feet tall and 2.5 to 4 feet long, and weigh only 20 to 40 pounds, but with their sturdy hindquarters, they can jump 10 to 12 feet high. Their dense coats of short, brittle hairs are varying shades of brown. The hairs are darker at the head and white under their bellies. Klipspringers can stand on the tiptoes of their hooves, which are each about the size of a dime.

Klipspringer pairs are monogamous, but rarely spend time close to each other. These territorial animals spend their days grazing on shrubs, grasses, flowers, and seeds, marking boundaries with their waste, and guarding that space by standing watch from prominent rock formations.

The IUCN Red List rates klipspringers as of Least Concern on their scale of threatened species. Many of the animals on O'Reilly covers are endangered; all of them are important to the world.

The cover illustration is by Karen Montgomery, based on a black-and-white engraving from Lydekker's *The Royal Natural History*. The cover fonts are Gilroy Semibold and Guardian Sans. The text font is Adobe Minion Pro; the heading font is Adobe Myriad Condensed; and the code font is Dalton Maag's Ubuntu Mono.

Milton Keynes UK
Ingram Content Group UK Ltd.
UKHW050558280923
429431UK00015B/324